OSHO RAJNEESH AND HIS DISCIPLES

SOME WESTERN PERCEPTIONS

Osho Rajneesh and His Disciples

SOME WESTERN PERCEPTIONS

Edited by
HARRY AVELING

MOTILAL BANARSIDASS PUBLISHERS
PRIVATE LIMITED • DELHI

First Edition: Delhi, 1999

ISBN: 81-208-1598-x (Cloth)
ISBN: 81-208-1599-8 (Paper)

MOTILAL BANARSIDASS
41 U.A. Bungalow Road, Jawahar Nagar, Delhi 110 007
8 Mahalaxmi Chamber, Warden Road, Mumbai 400 026
120 Royapettah High Road, Mylapore, Chennai 600 004
Sanas Plaza, 1302, Baji Rao Road, Pune 411 002
16 St. Mark's Road, Bangalore 560 001
8 Camac Street, Calcutta 700 017
Ashok Rajpath, Patna 800 004
Chowk, Varanasi 221 001

PRINTED IN INDIA
BY JAINENDRA PRAKASH JAIN AT SHRI JAINENDRA PRESS,
A-45 NARAINA INDUSTRIAL AREA, PHASE I, NEW DELHI 110 028
AND PUBLISHED BY NARENDRA PRAKASH JAIN FOR
MOTILAL BANARSIDASS PUBLISHERS PRIVATE LIMITED,
BUNGALOW ROAD, DELHI 110 007

Dedicated to the memory

of the late Roy Wallis

who saw that in the path of Osho

Religion could be Fun

Preface

This volume addresses itself to two questions: Who was Osho Rajneesh? What has it meant to be his disciple?

The book is intended, on the one hand, to be a work of scholarship. I have sought to gather here the best short pieces available in English on Osho and his Sannyasins. The authors include professional writers, sociologists, psychologists, therapists, a philosopher, and a dentist. They represent a range of viewpoints. All write with intelligence and insight.

It is also a work of love. At the end of the book *Tantra: The Supreme Understanding* (1975: 253), Osho says:

> So if you are really authentically, sincerely a seeker
> then find someone with whom you can move
> in deep commitment,
> with whom you can take the plunge into the Unknown.
> Without it you have wandered for many lives and you will wander.
> Without it the supreme accomplishment is not possible.
> Take courage and take the jump.

The questions of the book are the questions of my

own life. I bow at Osho's feet in gratitude for all that he has given me and all that he has taken away.

HARRY AVELING
(Yogacharya Swami Anand Haridas)

Contents

IV. Conflict and Renewal

V. Postscript

[illegible]

[illegible] A Social Psychological
Analysis of the [illegible]
[illegible]

[illegible] and [illegible]: A Study of the [illegible]
Leadership of [illegible]
[illegible]

[illegible] after the [illegible]
[illegible] Members
[illegible] and AIDS [illegible]

[illegible]
[illegible] Norman D. [illegible]
Richard A. [illegible]
and Richard A. [illegible]

[illegible]

[illegible] International [illegible]
[illegible]

[illegible]

Introduction

"Osho. Never born never died. Only visited this Planet Earth between Dec. 11, 1931—Jan. 19, 1990." These are the words engraved on the memorial stone placed to commemorate the late Osho Rajneesh (variously known as Chandra Mohan Jain, Acharya Rajneesh, Bhagwan Shree Rajneesh and during the last years of his life simply as Osho) at his Ashram in Poona. They emphasise the very paradoxical image which Rajneesh strove to present to the world. He was an individual who denied being an individual. In response to the question: "Who are you?", he replied:

> The person is non-existent, a non-entity. In fact, there is no person, or there is only one person. Only God can be said to have a personality, because only God can have a centre. We have no centres at all.
>
> (Rajneesh 1977a: 1)

He was a Guru who denied being a Guru. "There should be disciples", he states in the First Chapter of this collection, "there must be disciples—but no Gurus!" Similarly, he asserted on this same principle, that although there was a great need for the disciple to be open and vulnerable to the work of the Master, once the disciple realised that he or she was merely participating in a game, the game of Master and disciple, and that neither of them really existed, the game was over, for "that will be the day of your enlightenment" (Rajneesh 1979a: 341, cited in Chapter Five below). He was, therefore, a Master with thousands of disciples worldwide, who had no disciples.

From this perspective, there is no way of answering the two questions: Who was Rajneesh? And who were his disciples (themselves variously known as Sannyasins, neo-Sannyasins, Rajneeshees and even the Rajneesh)?

Nevertheless, a wide range of books have attempted to answer these questions in a variety of ways. Some of these have been celebratory, some deprecatory, some apparently inquisitive, and some studiously academic. In the most general terms, the celebratory books include all of Rajneesh's public addresses and intimate discussions with disciples, published by the Jeevan Jagriti Kendra, Motilal Banarsidass, the Rajneesh Foundation in India and America, and the Rebel Publishing House in Germany. More specifically, they include Ṃa Satya Bharati's exploration of discipleship *The Ultimate Risk* (1980); Vasant Joshi's authorised biography *The Awakened One: The Life and Work of Bhagwan Shree Rajneesh* (1982); and the historical and apologetic works published in the late eighties by some of Rajneesh's closest disciples—Sue Appleton *Bhagwan Shree Rajneesh: The Most Dangerous Man Since Jesus Christ* and *Was Bhagwan Shree Rajneesh Poisoned by Ronald Reagan's America*; Juliet Forman's *Bhagwan: The Buddha for the Future, Bhagwan: One Man Against the Whole Ugly Past of Humanity* and *Bhagwan: Twelve Days that Shook the World;* the work of his doctor, George Meredith *Bhagwan: The Most Godless Yet the Most Godly Man* and *The Choice is Ours*; and that of his washer-woman Ma Prem Shunyo *Diamond Days with Osho: The New Diamond Sūtra.*

The deprecatory books are at their most bitter when written by former disciples, such as Hugh Milne

Bhagwan: The God that Failed (the title which presumably provoked the celebratory "Bhagwan" books); and Kate Strelley *The Ultimate Game: The Rise and Fall of Bhagwan Rajneesh* (1987). More balanced, but sadder and wiser, books by former disciples include Charles Wright *Oranges and Lemmings* (1985); Sally Belfrage *Flowers of Emptiness* (1981); and Satya Bharati Franklin's later book *The Promise of Paradise: A Woman's Intimate Story of the Perils of Life with Rajneesh* (1992).

The more neutral seekers' books feature some of the fascination of the celebratory books and some of the despair of the deprecatory books at the prospect of a radically innovative spiritual experiment which had apparently come to naught. The most interesting of these is James S. Gordon's *The Golden Guru: The Strange Journey of Bhagwan Shree Rajneesh* (1988). The academic books tend to be less racy and more objective, and heavily reliant on the methods of the social sciences, particularly sociology and psychology. The first of these was Bob Mullan's *Life as Laughter: Following Bhagwan Shree Rajneesh* (1983). This was followed by Judith Thompson and Paul Heelas *The Way of the Heart: The Rajneesh Movement* (1986); W. E. Mann *The Quest for Total Bliss: A Psycho-Sociological Perspective on the Rajneesh Movement* (1991); Lewis F. Carter's magisterial *Charisma and Control in Rajneeshpuram: The Role of Shared Values in the Creation of a Community* (1990); and my own *The Laughing Swamis: Australian Sannyasin Disciples of Swami Satyananda Saraswati and Osho Rajneesh* (1994). Latkin (1987: 74, Chapter Nine below) has noted that almost all of the written material on Rajneesh and the neo-Sannyas movement tends to be either "anecdotal and frequently polemical, historical", or, on the other hand, "analytical and textual, the latter especially by those interested in the religious and philosophical nature of Bhagwan's thoughts". The academic authors attempt to add a more empirical strand to the historical and textual approaches and are often heavily reliant on the close observation of one or a few small communities.

This present volume aims to bring together some of the best of the shorter pieces of writing on Osho and the neo-Sannyasin movement. In some ways it may be seen as a sequel to Susan J. Palmer and Arvind Sharma *The Rajneesh Papers* (1993). That book, however, stemmed from a single-day Symposium on the Rajneesh Movement, held on May 29, 1989, at the Faculty of Religious Studies of McGill University, Montreal. The papers presented here derive from a number of smaller academic journals, most not readily available to a wider general audience. I have also added two chapters from books (Brent and Menen respectively), which provide a picture of the earlier Acharya, prior to the establishment of the Rajneesh Foundation. The first chapter was published in 1973, the last in 1996. Overall, they focus on the period from approximately 1970 to 1994. For convenience, the volume is divided into four parts: on Osho, Community, Meditation and Therapy, Decline and Renewal. There is, of course, a fair bit of overlap between the various parts of the collection. As with the longer books, some of these pieces are celebratory, some less impressed, some inquisitive, and some doggedly academic. All are interesting and together they give a rounded picture of a complex man and a vibrant religious movement.

Osho

The basic external facts about Rajneesh's life are simple and are to be found in a number of the papers printed here (usually with a footnote to Joshi's biography, 1982). Rajneesh Chandra Mohan was born into a Jain family near Jabalpur in Central India in 1931. He claimed to have experienced full enlightenment in March 1953. After graduating with the degree of Master of Arts in Philosophy in 1957, Rajneesh taught at Raipur Sanskrit College that same year and then at the University of Jabalpur until his resignation in 1966. He had already begun holding regular meditation camps in 1964, and the Jeevan Jagriti Kendra was founded in 1965 to organise his extensive preaching tours throughout India, the camps, and to publish his books and a monthly magazine in Hindi. In 1970 Rajneesh initiated his first Sannyasin disciples, including some westerners. The following year he dropped the use of the title "Acharya" (Teacher) and became instead "Bhagwan" (The Blessed One). By 1970, too, he had settled into a flat in Bombay and was conducting regular, public meditations there.

Brent (Chapter One) shows us Acharya Rajneesh, "a teacher, a travelling preacher, a man who numbers hundreds and even thousands when he speaks on Bombay maidan or in the other centres at which he pauses to spread his ideas on God and Man". There are three facets to this presentation. The first relates to the Acharya's ideas on the relationship between the Guru and the disciple, which we have already touched on: "the very concept of a Guru is basically irreligious and unspiritual . . .". The second relates to Rajneesh's physical appearance:

> He sits cross-legged, his plump and hairy stomach slightly creased as his shoulders droop forward. He holds a blue towel across his lap; from the waist down he is wrapped in a fine white robe. His hair has receded, leaving a smooth, pale brown skull, now gleaming with sandalwood oil, and a fringe of long, grey hair which hangs down behind his ears to his shoulders. His beard is long, its black, oiled ringlets almost dividing so that it looks forked. As I settle myself, he fixes me with a rolling, slightly goatish, light brown eye.

In the next paragraph, Brent refers to the Acharya's fluent "high youthful voice", and his habit of emphasising his points "with elegant, long-fingered gestures resembling those which Indians have codified in their dances". (The essay also provides a fine description of its setting, "the house of one of his richer supporters", in all its fading imperial splendour.) The third facet is Brent's acknowledgement of the Acharya's intellectual ability, entirely befitting one who used to be "a good lecturer at the university where he once taught":

> He seems to have been delighted by the very act of speaking, taking pleasure in the play of his mind, so that sometimes he has made the same point in several different ways for the sheer gratification the turning, interlocking wheels of his intelligence give him.

After his address is done, Rajneesh moves among his audience, "like a champion mildly elated after some minor skirmish, an exhibition".

Aubrey Menen (Chapter Ten) is, like Peter Brent, a professional writer. He, too, is impressed by the power of Rajneesh's mind, noting that "Rajneesh's own thinking is firmly based on the austere principles of the original sages" of the Upaniṣads. But what captures his attention is the "simpler way" which the Swami (as Menen insists on calling him) has invented for "at least getting a glimpse of what the original sages were talking about". The method is dynamic meditation, a "mass meditation", which Menen found "interesting, practical, and spectacular". (The description of the meditation in Menen's *The New Mystics,* is set in "the garden of some institution unconnected with Rajneesh"; the accompanying photographs are from a setting beside the harbour of Bombay.) Menen comments on Rajneesh's relaxed qualities, his lack of rhetoric, the "gentle, almost feminine invitation" of his unpraised hands, as well as "his tranquil expression" and "the controlled beauty of his expression". Like Brent, Menen too is drawn to the metaphor of the performer:

> Whether the audience really meditates or not I cannot say. I can confirm that after the drumming and the frenzy there is that sort of silence which only a great solo musician can command. Even he could not produce that utter stillness: no coughing, no fidgeting. Like the soloist, Rajneesh is there on the platform, gyrating in his chair. But a large number of those in an enviable state of calm relaxation were not even looking at him.

This last point serves to confirm an earlier remark that "there was no magnetism" about Rajneesh's performance: "As for me, I thought of a play by Sophocles performed in classic style, where the actors spoke lines filled with passion from behind immobile masks."

In March 1974, Rajneesh left Bombay and moved to Poona. The Rajneesh Foundation was established in 1975, while the Jeevan Jagriti Kendra was wound down. Swami Prem Amitabh's article (Chapter Five) is a wonderfully intense, yet delighted and light account of life in the Ashram at that time. Later, in March 1981, Rajneesh entered into what was expected to be "a new and ultimate stage of his work . . . silence" (Joshi, 1982: 157). By July of 1981, the Rajneesh Foundation had purchased the "Big Muddy Ranch" in Oregon, in the north-west of America, and Rajneesh and his work had moved to the New World. Carter (Chapter Eight), Drennan (Chapter Eleven) and Latkin (Chapters Nine and Fourteen) all provide pictures of the Ranch and of its residents at that time.

While Rajneesh was in silence in Oregon, the visible

organisation of the movement passed from the three persons he had appointed to represent him in India (Ma Yoga Laxmi, Swami Anand Teertha and Swami Satya Vedant) into the hands of Ma Anand Sheela. Sheela's style was bold and confrontationist; this exacerbated, rather than diminished, the hostility which was steadily building within Oregon and beyond to the Rajneesh movement. The movement itself became more hierarchical and more authoritarian, and less willing to compromise with the outside world. (The psychodynamics of this conflict are analysed in two deeply insightful essays by Carl Latkin, Chapters Fourteen and Fifteen below.)

In 1984, Rajneesh was refused permanent residence in America, partly because a number of immigration and taxation problems within the movement were currently under investigation by the United States Government, and partly because he was not teaching. (Not everyone appreciates the paradox of a teacher who does not teach.) Rajneesh began speaking to small groups in October 1984 and the size of these groups was increased after July 1985. He spoke on true religion, freedom, the possibility of the disease AIDS killing a large portion of humanity before the end of the century, and he also seemed to be trying to take back some of the power which he had ceded to Sheela. On September 14, 1985, Sheela, and then some fifteen to twenty other senior members of the Commune, left Rajneeshpuram. Rajneesh called a major press conference two days later and denounced Sheela and her 'fascist gang' for a series of crimes which included "three poisoning attempts, salmonella food poisoning in the Dalles, wiretapping, bugging rooms, and financial abuse which left the commune $55,000,000 in debt" (Palmer, Chapter Sixteen below). Ten days later, September 26, sannyasins were told to stop wearing red clothes and the *mālā*, which was the symbol of their initiation. Their alacrity to do so led to an angry outburst on Rajneesh's part on the eighth of October (cited in Prem Shunyo n.d.: 69-70):

> You have been clapping because I have dropped red clothes, *mālā*. And when you clap, you don't know how it hurts me. That means you have been a hypocrite! Why have you been wearing red clothes if dropping them brings you so much joy? Why have you been wearing the *mālā*? The moment I say 'Drop', you rejoice. And people rushed to the boutique to change their clothes, they have dropped their *mālās*. But you don't know how much you have wounded me by your clapping and by your changing.
>
> But now I say to you one thing more and I would like to see whether you have guts to clap or not: that is, now there is no Buddhafield. So if you want enlightenment, you have to work for it individually, the Buddhafield exists no more. You cannot depend on the energy of the Buddhafield to become enlightened. Now clap as loudly as you can Clap!...

And he concluded:

> But I don't want you to do anything against your will. Now I don't even want to help you towards your enlightenment against your will. You are absolutely free and responsible for yourself.

On October 27, Rajneesh himself left the Ranch with a few senior disciples and was arrested when his plane landed at Charlotte, North Carolina. He was tried in a court of law on the 14th November, 1985 on some thirty-four charges, most relating to "sham marriages" arranged among his disciples in order to circumvent American immigration laws and entered a technical plea of guilty with relation to only two of the charges. After paying a fine of $400,000 and being ordered to leave America within the next five days, he left on the following day.

He did not remain long in India. After settling briefly in India, Rajneesh spent the period from January to July 1986 travelling the world, searching for a new place to settle and re-establish the commune. During this period, he was deported from or denied entry to more than twenty-one countries (see Appleton, 1987). Eventually he resettled at the site of the old Ashram in Poona, dropping the title "Bhagwan" on January 7th, 1989, and the name "Rajneesh" in September of the same year. He assumed the uncommon Japanese Buddhist title of "Osho" in February 1989. On the 19th January, 1990, the body, weakened by what his disciples claim was radiation poisoning administered while he was in prison in America, ceased to live. The visit to planet earth was over and he was cremated on the same day.

There are many ways of making sense of another person's life. The essays here show some of the ways in which their writers have tried to assess the significance of Rajneesh's life.

Brent and Menen, as we have seen, grouped Rajneesh with other "godmen of India". Gussner, in his wonderfully informed essay on Rajneesh's teachings on *karma* and rebirth (Chapter Three) does the same, to some extent (it must be stressed). Gussner comments that: "Indians who oppose Rajneesh, and those who don't, tend to agree that he is traditional in what he teaches, but untraditional in his methods and disciplines," adding "he is not entirely traditional in his teachings, yet is substantially so". Gussner shows, based on his reading of Rajneesh's comments on Patañjali's *Yoga Sūtras*, that Rajneesh accepted most of the essentials of the classical theory of *karma* (the law of repetition, the types of *karma*, and the power of *karma*, or habit, to enslave the individual), yet he rejected the aspects which served to link *karma* to society and morality in a repressive and authoritarian manner. For Gussner, the central element in Rajneesh's thought is the insistence that "the basic polarity in regard to any subject whatsoever is between awareness and unawareness (*avidyā* and *vidyā*)". Awareness means both "alert mindfulness. . . noting what is going on in your mind, in your movements and in your surroundings", and "cognizance of your own subjective presence as a crystallized witness, which arises as a shadow-reflex of mindfulness practice carried on without slack or strain, and which has a quality of deep silence in it". Gussner's essay is the more valuable because to date very little work has been done on placing Rajneesh's thought in the context of the richness of Indian thought, whether as a professor of philosophy or, more demandingly, "a Jain with Buddhist sympathies" (the phrase is again Gussner's).

Devageet (Chapter Two) and Amitabh (Chapter Five) see Rajneesh within the tradition of Indian teachers and yet as a remarkable spiritual figure who not only stands out from what has gone before him but also completely supercedes it. For Devageet, Rajneesh is "an elightened master", who has:

> . . . devoted his entire life to the task of bringing modern man into an experiential, harmonious relationship with existence. His influence in the world of religion, philosophy and psychology is immense, and his words and ideas are so powerfully resonant that they shake the very foundations of established power structures; political, scientific, ideological, theological or cosmological.

Rajneesh is a Master of the same status as Jesus,

Buddha, Lao Tzu and Pythagoras: his task is to herald in the next stage of human evolution, "beyond the barbaric, biological endgame in which civilisation finds itself today". For Amitabh, too, Rajneesh offered not just "a glimpse, a taste of a transcendent state", a state beyond the pain of personal conditioning, "but the whole eternal banquet", such as is offered by other "Transcended Masters", like Buddha, Lao Tzu, Muhammad and Zarathustra, "who seem to have come from the other side of some great divide". These Masters offered "a simplicity and clarity of perception, a strange indifference to the pulls and pushes of the world we know, a oneness and harmony with nature, and a non-resistant orientation to impending danger". The difference, however, was that Rajneesh was alive, free of "dependence on commandment, dogma, or method", and available for a direct personal relationship with the disciple. Further:

> He is a man of our time . . . the targets he aims at are those he sees at the root of the modern person's dilemma: sexual and aggressive repression, being controlled and controlling, convention, living for the future, attachments to physical and psychological survival.

Gussner, towards the end of his paper, presents Rajneesh's comments on his own birth as having "something new to say" about the "rebirth choices of *bodhisattvas* and those who attain enlightenment in this life".

Drennan (Chapter Eleven) describes himself as "open to all possibilities, accepting nothing without the cold objective appraisal reflected by my middle name—'doubting' Thomas" (and, frankly, as "a typical booze-and-meat-hound psychologist"). As a psychologist, he was fascinated by Rajneesh's brilliance, humour and frankness, but, prior to visiting Rajneeshpuram, decided that Rajneesh was "either one of the biggest egotists in the world or a person transcendent to all false humility and probably enlightened". Clarke's essay (Chapter Four) argues for the first side of Drennan's two possibilities. He begins with the essential features of the narcissistic personality disorder as outlined in the *Diagnostic and Statistical Manual* of the American Psychiatric Association:

> A gradiose sense of self-importance or uniqueness; preoccupations with fantasies of unlimited success; exhibitionistic need for constant attention and admiration; characteristic responses to threats to self-esteem; and characteristic disturbances in interpersonal relationships, such as feelings of entitlement, interpersonal exploitiveness, relationships that alternate between extremes of overidealisation and devaluation, and lack of empathy.

Clarke tests these propositions, one by one, against various claims made about himself by Rajneesh in his various books, and by some of his more disenchanted disciples, and concludes that Rajneesh's vision of "creating a new archetypal human" failed because of: "His inordinate self-grandiosity, insatiable need for adulation, lack of sensitivity towards others, exploitiveness, unwillingness to compromise, deceitfulness, recklessness, lack of respect for the law, contempt for social order and convention, and lack of political awareness—and, perhaps above all, a lack of any sense of his own limitations . . .". Clarke's style is shrewd, sardonic, and prepared to let the subject speak for himself, especially when it is not in his own interest to do so. Some readers will be deeply annoyed by the essay, others no doubt delighted, depending on their personal perspectives. It stands, nevertheless, as one of the very few studies committed to the use of "the empirical and conceptual tools of contemporary psychiatry and clinical psychology" to provide intelligibility into "this self-avowed holy man's otherwise enigmatic and bizarre behaviour". Those who see Rajneesh differently may use these same tools to create a difference image.

Susan Palmer (Chapter Sixteen) uses the tools of the sociologist, and especially the concept of "charisma" as propounded by Weber and reformulated by Wallis. Palmer sees Rajneesh as the exemplary leader, whose preaching says "nothing about a divine mission or an ethical duty, but rather directs itself to the self-interest of those who crave salvation, recommending to them the same path as he himself traversed" (citing Eisenstadt); or, in her own words: "(Rajneesh's) charismatic authority is based on his claim to be the 'Enlightened One' who returns throughout the millenia to awaken spiritually an elite group of seekers."

Palmer's concern is with the process of institution building around the charismatic leader, which simultaneously serves to extend his (or her) charisma to a wider audience, but also to contain, distort and eventually disperse it altogether. She notes that there is no clear boundary between charisma and institutionalisation, and the relationship between them is a subtle one: "for charisma cannot exist without institutions, and the process of institutionalisation is fed by charisma". Rajneesh both tended to encourage the routinisation of his charisma and to discourage it, when it seemed not to his liking.

He encouraged it during the early phase of the movement, when he was willing and able to direct the movement, set policies and handle administrative decisions; give counsel to his followers; resolve conflict;

and deal effectively with the wider society. Here Palmer distinguishes between three stages: (1) the claiming of charisma, expressed in 1970 with the beginning of the conferral of Sannyasa; (2) the building of charisma, from 1971 to 1974, with the assumption of the title "Bhagwan"; and, (3) the encouragement of charisma, after 1974, with the foundation of Shree Rajneesh Ashram in Poona and the establishment of a core group of "institution builders to run the Ashram with maximum efficiency."

With Rajneesh's declining health after 1979, he was less well-placed to deal with all aspects of life in the Ashram. In Palmer's opinion, "the institutional charisma of the *saṅgha*, or community, now equalled the personal charisma of the master, and . . . due to his physical inaccessibility Bhagwan was in danger of being reduced to a symbol, or (in Durkheimian terms) a totem of his community". With the move to Oregon, and the rise of Sheela to power, Rajneesh entered the next stage, (4) of acquiescence, "in which the charismatic leader, finding himself trammelled and constrained, acquiesces to the situation with more or less good grace" (citing Wallis). In coming out of silence in October 1984, Rajneesh exhibited traits of both (5) prophecy and resistance: he claimed an increase in his own charisma, due to his experiences while in silence, and asserted his resistance to the "religion" of Rajneeshism created by Sheela. In so doing, he began to block Sheela's attempted displacement of him and instead moved to protect his own charisma. (Palmer calls this sixth stage "Phase VI—Sheela's Betrayal: Attempted Displacement"; exactly who was attempting to displace whom is open to argument.) The move, however, also laid him open to "the charge of irresponsibility and weak leadership in remaining ignorant of her abuses".

The final phase discussed in Palmer's article is that of (7) abdication: The actions of abdication included the rejection of the colour red and the *mālā*, the abolition of the "gacchami" ritual, Rajneeshism and the Rajneesh Foundation International (in favour of the Friends of Rajneesh International). Abdication allowed him to "renounce the responsible role of pastor, while retaining the role of performer"; helped him "salvage his reputation and protect his personal charisma" by distancing himself from the more unfortunate actions of Sheela and Rajneeshism; and it enabled him to "change shape", to "a mysterious, unattached, and elusive 'teacher' who communicates his vision through verbal performances and cryptic behaviour rather than through the creation of coherent belief systems or the building and governing of a utopian society" (Palmer's last sentence, modified). The process of shape-changing, we may suggest, was to intensify until his death. Today, his charisma is contained within the community.

The Community

Palmer's discussion of the leader and his institutional bond with his followers leads us to another paradox. Rajneesh was a distant, mysterious figure, whose biography emphasised his own autonomy and independence of mind, and in whose presence one could ask the most personal questions about oneself but nothing about him. His Sannyasins, on the other hand, led a communal lifestyle, often living in experimental 'intentional communities', and emphasised the personal development techniques of the Human Awareness Movement, in such a way as to encourage "gregarious behaviour and physical and emotional intimacy".

Gussner, again, sees the community in traditional Indian religious terms. He argues that Rajneesh's basic concern was to create the *saṅgha* "as a transformative example outside of an official Dhārmic social order". The classical renunciant withdrew from his conventional roles and duties and managed his spiritual development in his own way; the religious community did not seek to assimilate society to itself nor did it wish to prevent society from continuing to enjoin the doing of good deeds upon its members. As Gussner suggests, "Society and *saṅgha* ran in two parallel lines, intermixed to some extent, to be sure." Rajneesh, however, presents "an offensive from the side of the *saṅgha* against the social tyrrany of 'the good'", as conceived of in terms of a rigid and authoritarian morality. Times have changed. Society is more repressive; it cripples spiritual growth by creating "suffering" through the "sealed-in repression of anger, sadness, loneliness", and the "distancing" of the individual from his or her "real feelings". But the individual is "more mature as a separate ego. Being a mature ego, the individual, although less spiritual than the giants of the past, is ready to assume responsibility for his spiritual growth basically free of the domination of the super-ego. The super-ego may have been appropriate in the past, but modern man finds it toxic now".

Gussner's use of the term *saṅgha,* and that of Palmer above, is highly unusual. It may derive from the ritual chanting of the "*gacchamis*" which was practised between 1981 and 1985:

> *Buddhaṃ śaraṇaṃ gacchāmi*
> *saṅghaṃ śaraṇaṃ gacchāmi*
> *dharmaṃ śaraṇaṃ gacchāmi*

These were translated as "I go to the feet of the Enlightened One. I go to the feet of the community of the Enlightened One. I go to the feet of the Ultimate Truth of the Enlightened One." In this formulation, the *saṅgha* receives pre-eminence over the *dharma,* unlike the original formulation of *Buddha-dharma-saṅgha*. To the best of my knowledge, Rajneesh seldom used the term.

Instead, he spoke of the "Buddhafield" (an energy field in which the Master can work to bring his disciples to enlightenment), and, very simply, "my people". These terms were in accordance with his understanding of Sannyas as an individual bond between the disciple and the Master. As he stated (see Amitabh, Chapter Five):

> My effort here is not to create a following, not to create believers, but to create individuals, lovers, meditators, who can stand on their own, and each one can become a light. The night is going to become darker and darker everyday—we will need millions of lights around the world, millions of people who are capable of love, unconditionally, without asking anything in return and who are so silent, and who are so blissful, that wherever they are they will be able to dissipate darkness.

The number of "millions" was never reached: Amitabh (below) estimates that in 1979 there were about 100,000 Sannyasins worldwide. Mullan (1983: 23) further suggests that: "At any one time there were about six thousand Rajneeshees in Poona, some visiting for weeks or months to do groups or meditations, with about two thousand working and living on a permanent basis in or around the Ashram." Carter (below) gives the same figure of about two thousand for those living at Rajneeshpuram at its height.

Who were these "individuals, lovers and meditators"? The answers in statistical terms are reasonably clear. One of the first surveys was done by Swami Krishna Deva at the Poona Ashram in 1980 (cited by Wallis). Krishna Deva polled three hundred American Sannyasins. He found them to have an average age of just over thirty. Sixty per cent had been Sannyasins for less than two years and most still lived in America (half were from California). They were 97% white; 81% were from middle class and upper middle class homes. Nearly two-thirds had university degrees and "regarded themselves as successful in worldly terms". Three quarters "had been involved in some therapy". More than half had previously experimented with some other spiritual group; 25% were Jewish.

Latkin's survey of August to September 1983 (Chapter Eight), found that 54% of his respondents were female, with an average age of 33.9 years; and that 46% were male, with an average age of 34.7 years. A surprisingly high proportion of the residents, 74%, reported that they were married; 14% were single, 10% divorced, and only 2% widowed or separated. Only 25% of the respondents reported having children and less than half of these had children actually living at Rajneeshpuram. Ninety-one per cent of the respondents had a "white" ethnic background. Ninety-five per cent had graduated from high school, 65% from a university. About half had been Sannyasins for over five years and almost two-thirds, 63%, were living in a neo-Sannyas commune before coming to Oregon. Almost half had grown up in cities of over 100,000 people; about two-thirds considered their political background to range from "very liberal" to "radical".

In a later survey in 1986, Latkin (Chapter Seventeen) found that women now made up 60% of the residents of the ranch, and that their average age had fallen to thirty; while the men, 40%, were even younger, with an average age of only 28. The number of those who had attended college remained very high. The number of those who now reported themselves as married fell to 29.7%, separated 21.8%, divorced 33.6%, widowed 0.4%, and never married 14.4%. These figures concur with Krishna Deva's figures of 1980 that 45% of the Sannyasins he surveyed had never married, 36% were divorced, and only 19% were currently married. Mullan (1983: 50-51), based on his own research, suggests that: "the 'average' Rajneeshee is 'middle class'; well-educated, professionally qualified, has been divorced at least once, has suffered a 'personal crisis', has been through mysticism, drugs, politics, feminism, and is 'thirtyish'—in short, the counter-culturist brought up to date".

Wallis' analysis of the "typical follower of Rajneesh" (Chapter Six) is not based on empirical research but on a sensitive reading of one "darshan diary", *Don't Look Before You Leap,* which records the evening meetings between Rajneesh and some of his disciples held in Poona during May 1977. On the basis of the occupations listed there, Wallis notes that Sannyasins tended to come from liberal or autonomous professions or a craft background, and not from those occupations which are routine and highly bureaucratic. Their backgrounds had provided them with "a certain amount of choice as to the future", and they had opted to pursue "a course more concerned with creativity and the imagination, with human contact and with more spiritual values". They sought, on the one hand:

> Freedom from the constraints imposed by social roles weighing heavily upon those who had passed through rigorous education and demanding parental expectations, delaying gratification to achieve knowledge or abilities required in later skilled occupations.

On the other hand, they also shared:

> A desire for greater expressivity in themselves and in those with whom they interacted; openness, spontaneity and intimacy less restricted by role playing and social conventions; and enthusiasm and joy in life, less burdened by inhibitions, by a past history of rejection or failure, or their anticipation in the future.

Their comparative youth, occupational independence, and freedom from family ties allowed them the opportunity "to take time out" to travel to the Ashram in India and remain there for some time, before returning to the West again.

Meditation and Therapy

If the Sannyasins surveyed in these studies were united by a more or less common background, outlook, and set of opportunities, they certainly did not share a set of common religious beliefs. Krishna Deva noted that 25% of his American respondents were of Jewish background. Latkin's first study, 1983, found that 14% of his respondents had no religious background; 27% Roman Catholic; 20% Jewish; 30% Protestant; Hindu or Buddhist 4%; other 4%. In 1985, the figure for no background remained at 14.2%; Catholic 30.2%; significantly higher than before; Protestant 36.4%; Jewish, 8.2%; significantly lower; and other 10.6%. Clearly few Sannyasins were in a position to appreciate the subtleties of Rajneesh's approach to the philosophies and religions of South Asia.

In fact it proved hard for the researchers to establish exactly what Sannyasins believed in. Palmer (Chapter Sixteen) notes that Rajneesh's leadership constantly fluctuated in its style and its authoritative claims, and that the history of his movement is "remarkable for its abrupt change in policy, and the varied and contradictory demands made upon its members". Carter (Chapter Eight) noted that:

> The analytic task is complicated by the changing and inconsistent nature of the Rajneesh movement which makes no claim to consistency of ideology. Further, beliefs, practices and goals are extremely changeable, though a few enduring patterns may be established.

Carter concluded:

> The Rajneesh movement appears to be totally 'manufactured' in the sense that beliefs, practices, corporate identities, and physical location may be changed quickly to suit necessities and convenience of the moment. Just as Sannyasins are urged to live in the 'here and now', their social systems and legal identities are very impermanent.

There were two solutions to this problem. One was to take one, or a few, of Rajneesh's books and assume that, because he taught this, they believed it. The other and more productive solution was to look away from what was said and focus on what was done.

Palmer and Bird (Chapter Twelve) note that: "More than most new or old religions, the Rajneesh movement . . . has incorporated therapies into its programme as a vital, if not essential, part of its spiritual life." They point to the importance of therapy groups both in Poona and at Rajneeshpuram; to the high proportion of Sannyasins with degrees in humanistic psychology; and quote Frances Fitzgerald's comment that Rajneeshpuram "was awash in the human potential movement". In their paper, they suggest that therapy functioned as "a form of social control", which served to promote "identity change by means of the ritual breaking of taboos, through educating members in a new system of ethics and new patterns of self-other relating, and through initiating members into the charismatic community" by identifying and expressing their own personal powers. The various styles of therapy are explored in the vital and detailed chapters by Amitabh (Chapter Five) and Veereshwar (Chapter Thirteen). Drennan, too, notes that: "One of the major reasons for my initial interest in Rajneesh . . . was the indirect knowledge that a great deal of eclectic psychotherapy and growth interventions were taking place in Poona, India, where (Rajneesh) resided before coming to America."

Hummel and Harding (Chapter Seven) note that Rajneesh had a great familiarity with the ideas of humanistic psychology in the early 1970s and "no hesitation over enlisting in his service western therapists . . . and thus turning his Ashram in Poona into 'the greatest human growth centre of the world' as it liked to describe itself". Like Palmer and Bird, Hummel and Harding first see the Rajneesh movement as "a psycho-religious movement" and they are able to show how Rajneesh's monistic interpretation of the world and his emphasis on the need to transcend the mind were translated by those familiar with humanistic psychology, and new age spirituality in general, to fit their own immediate problems and desire for personal change.

Again, both Hummel and Harding, and Palmer and Bird, link the prominence of therapy to the veneration for Rajneesh as a Guru. Hummel and Harding's second description of the Rajneesh movement is that it is a "syncretistic Guru-cult". In their article they draw attention to "certain ritual elements of honouring the Guru"; Rajneesh's passivity and unambiguous "presentation of himself as a screen for people to project their ideas on to"; the trust he continually demanded; and his claim that he is an 'enlightened master', saying the same thing as every enlightened master before him. (Hummel and Harding's third dimension of the Rajneesh movement is that it is "an esoteric school of mysteries".) Palmer and Bird suggest that the "ultimate transference" of the therapeutic process is seen as transference onto the Master, who simultaneously acts as a model of the "real self" and as a justification for distancing oneself "from the authoritative claims of parents, teachers, priests, and for dismissing the judgement of others".

Conflict and Renewal

Carter describes Rajneeshpuram as "an exclusive (almost reclusive) total society with restricted outsider contact, limited to catering for the spiritual and therapeutic needs of well-to-do 'seekers'." It is hard to know how accurately that description fits the present Ashram or the earlier one, especially when so many Sannyasins lived "in or around" Koregaon Park.

Latkin's essays (Chapters Fourteen and Fifteen) show how some of the attitudes and beliefs linked with therapy and the counter culture worked against the best interests of the community as a whole. As Latkin notes, the first arrivals in Oregon made peaceful overtures to the surrounding communities; within one year they were engaged in serious disagreements with their neighbours, and this "quickly escalated into bitter hostility. The Rajneeshees took an aggressive stance, became exceedingly litigious, and sued dozens of groups and individuals".

Theoretically one might have expected the community to work to minimise conflict. The vast majority of Sannyasins were from middle and upper-middle class backgrounds and might have been expected to "place a premium on conflict resolution, discuss their grievances rationally, and settle disputes diplomatically". Their respect for high interpersonal sensitivity, reinforced by the experience of psychotherapy, might have been expected to encourage empathy and a respect for others. The belief in individuality ought to have strengthened Sannyasins not to act as a group. Having been discriminated against, they might have been expected to be more sensitive to prejudice and discrimination.

Unfortunately, these expectations remained unfulfilled in Oregon. The situation was new and ambiguous; it was hard to know what standards applied to their leaders' and their own behaviour, which was "beyond good and evil" and subject to constant change and redefinition. By reason of their education and professional training, many Sannyasins felt superior to those in the local community which sought to degrade them as "cult members, freaks and deviants" and responded aggressively and frankly, as they had been trained to do. The strangeness of the situation, and veneration for Rajneesh and those he had apparently appointed to lead the new community, allowed the top leadership to make up their own rules and enforce them firmly, without fear of question or even disagreement. The leaders were able to use the threat of expulsion, their own grip over the flow of information, and the concepts of "personal growth" and "surrender to the Master" as controlling devices. "It is plausible," Latkin writes, "that the leadership of Rajneeshpuram was hostile to outsiders, whereas most Rajneeshees were not . . . however, our data suggests that the leadership's antagonistic rhetoric was consistent with members' attitudes."

The last paper, again by Latkin (Chapter Seventeen), indicates that the majority of his respondents "after the fall" still felt a "high positive regard for Rajneesh" and felt love and gratitude to him as their teacher or Master. These feelings diminished a little over the next year but, in general, Sannyasins continued to "fulfil affective needs and provide special support" for each other. The events of Sheela and her 'gang' had become another learning device, for their personal growth, and they were "the wiser for the experience".

That there are no papers here on the period after the collapse of Rajneeshpuram does not mean that the Rajneesh movement came to an end in 1986, or even in 1990 after the death of the living Master. On the contrary. The teachings of Osho are distributed in India, and abroad, on a scale never before possible. There have been few new studies of Osho and His disciples: E. Puttick "Sexuality, Gender and the Abuse of Power in the Master-Disciple Relationship: The Case of the Rajneesh Movement", *Journal of Contemporary Religion*, 10:1, 1995, 29-40; Hugh B. Urban "Zorba the Buddha: Capitalism, Charisma and the Cult of Bhagwan Shree Rajneesh", *Religion*, 26, 1996, 161-182; and a chapter in Anthony Storr's *Feet of Clay: A Study of Gurus*, HarperCollins 1996. Roger Housden's reflections on what is often called "Poona II", however, serve to provide a fitting postscript, one which is both contemporary and open, to our journey.

Osho (1983b: 253) has suggested that:

> The myth of the phoenix is not just a myth: it is the story of man, the story of spiritual rebirth.
>
> Each disciple has to be a phoenix. He has to be consumed by the fire the Master is. And out of that, out of the ashes, a new being is born . . . the resurrection. And that is your eternal life.
>
> The false has to be taken away for the real to be; the false has to cease, it has to make space for the real to come in.

The myth of the phoenix may encourage one to see a positive future for neo-Sannyasa: "One has to die—only then can God be," Rajneesh concluded these remarks. To recognise and let go of the past is to find the present.

HARRY AVELING

(Yogacharya Swami Anand Haridas)

Acknowledgements

The papers published here originally appeared in the sources listed below and are produced with appropriate permissions. The articles by Amitabh, Drennan and Veereshwar are reprinted by permission of Sage Publications, Inc.

Peter Brent, 1973: "Acharya Rajneesh", *Godmen of India*, Penguin, 150-157. Reproduced by permission of Penguin Books Ltd.

Charles Newman, 1987: "Bhagwan Shree Rajneesh: A New Man for all Seasons", *Self and Society*, 15:5, Sept./Oct., 221-227.

Robert. E. Gussner, 1986: "Teachings on Karma and Rebirth: Social and Spiritual Role in the Rajneesh Neo-Sannyasin Movement", in *Karma and Rebirth*, (ed.) R. W. Neufeldt, SUNY, Albany, 301-324.

Ronald O. Clark, 1988: "The Narcissistic Guru: A Profile of Bhagwan Shree Rajneesh", *Free Inquiry*, Spring, 33-35, 38-45.

Swami Prem Amitabh, 1982: "Shree Rajneesh Ashram: A Provocative Community", *Journal of Humanistic Psychology*, 22: 1, Winter, 19-42.

Reinhart Hummel and Bert Hardin, 1983: "Asiatic Religions in Europe", *Concilium*, 161, Jan., 23-28.

Roy Wallis, 1986: "Religion as Fun? The Rajneesh Movement", *Sociological Theory, Religion and Collective Action*, Queen's University, Belfast, 191-224.

Lewis F. Carter, 1987: "The 'New Renunciates' of the Bhagwan Shree Rajneesh: Observations and

Identification of Problems of Interpreting New Religious Movements", *Journal for the Scientific Study of Religion*, 28:2, 149-172.

Carl A. Latkin *et al.*, 1987: "Who Lives in Utopia? A Brief Report on the Rajneeshpuram Research Project", *Sociological Analysis*, 48:1, 73-81.

Aubrey Menen, 1974: *The New Mystics*, Thames and Hudson, London.

William T. Drennan, 1983: "Rajneeshpuram: Hound Dogs with the Scent", *Journal of Humanistic Psychology*, 23:3, Summer, 82-100.

Susan J. Palmer and Frederick Bird, 1992: "Therapy, Charisma and Social Control in the Rajneesh Movement", *Sociological Analysis*, 53-S, S71-S85.

Swami Anand Veereshwar, 1983: "Jealousy and the Abyss", *Journal of Humanistic Psychology*, 23:2, Spring, 70-84.

Carl Latkin, 1991: "From Device to Vice: Social Control and Intergroup Conflict at Rajneeshpuram", *Sociological Analysis*, 52:4, 363-378.

Carl Latkin, 1992: "Seeing Red: A Social-Psychological Analysis of the Rajneeshpuram Conflict", *Sociological Analysis*, 53:3, 257-271.

Susan J. Palmer, 1988: "Charisma and Abdication: A Study of the Leadership of Bhagwan Shree Rajneesh", *Sociological Analysis*, 49:2, 119-135.

Carl A. Latkin *et al.*, 1994: "Feelings After the Fall: Former Rajneeshpuram Commune Members' Perceptions of and Affiliation with the Rajneeshee Movement", *Sociology of Religion*, 55:1, 65-73.

Roger Housden, 1996: *Travels through Sacred India*, Thorsons (HarperCollins), London, 206-209.

Sarva dharmān parityajya
māmekaṃ śaraṇaṃ vraja.

BHAGAVADGĪTĀ 18:66

I

BHAGWAN SHREE RAJNEESH–OSHO

Chapter One

Acharya Rajneesh

PETER BRENT

We sit in a long room, I on a black plastic-covered couch; three doorways lead to a wide, balustraded terrace, their blue hangings flapping as the fan overhead stirs the heavy air. In the house of one of his richer supporters we are waiting to speak with Acharya Rajneesh, a teacher, a travelling preacher, a man who numbers hundreds and even thousands in his audiences when he speaks on Bombay *maidan* or in the other centres at which he pauses to spread his ideas on God and Man. A mirror surrounded by a deep, carved framework stands against one wall of the room so that ghostly figures—we ourselves gathered here in ones and twos to see the *acharya*—stare strangely out; it is as if we were separated from our reflections by a trellised arbour. Beside the mirror hangs an overcoloured picture of Mahatma Gandhi; a little lower down hangs a certificate from the Imperial Society of Knights Bachelor. On it, in fading copperplate, the name of some member of the family once of service to the King-Emperor. Against the opposite wall stands a glass cabinet filled with tarnished silver: on one shelf lies the insignia of that Imperial approval, now as much a part of history as the Moghul ascendancy or the Aryan invasion.

Later, shoeless, I am led past a pale blue, patterned curtain to where, beyond it, Acharya Rajneeshji sits on a bed, caught in light as if for a performance. I approach, others crowding behind me. The Acharya, haloed by the scent of sandalwood, taps the foot of the bed and smiles. At his nod I sit down. The rest press closer, stand beside him, sit on the floor about my feet, lean in over the end of the bed. They look expectant—a stranger has come to interrogate their sage.

He sits cross-legged, his plump and hairy stomach slightly creased as his shoulders droop forward. He holds a blue towel across his lap; from the waist down he is wrapped in a fine white robe. His hair has receded, leaving a smooth, pale brown skull, now gleaming with sandalwood oil, and a fringe of long, grey hair which hangs down behind his ears to his shoulders. His beard is long, its black, oiled ringlets almost dividing so that it looks forked. Half-hidden in this is his small and smiling mouth. As I settle myself, he fixes me with a rolling, slightly goatish, light brown eye.

When he speaks, it is fluently in a high, youthful voice; one can believe that he was a good lecturer at the university where he once taught. He does not falter, even when the microphones of the faithful tumble, or quarrelling voices shout under the window, or, beyond them, someone lets off a late *Diwali* fire cracker. As he speaks, he emphasizes his points with elegant, long fingered gestures resembling those which Indians have codified in their dances. He watches me with great intensity as he answers my questions, his eyes fixed on mine. I look into them, then past him through the small window at the dark trees, and at the high lights of an apartment block sending out their interrupted beams like signals as the breeze pumps the branches to and fro.

'As far as I am concerned, that type of relationship which has been in existence between Guru and Śiṣya—to me it all seems immature. In a spiritual relationship, nothing like this can exist. There is no possibility of it. But it has been in existence and that has been the rock on which the whole of Indian spirituality has been based. It has been the foundation stone—but the wrong foundation stone. Because of it we seem to be spiritual and we are not. There should be disciples, there must be disciples—but no Gurus. But in this life there are Gurus and no disciples; there is no attitude of learning. Because that attitude demands an attitude of ignorance. A person who thinks, "I do not know" can become a disciple, but in this day no one thinks like that: everyone knows only. So there are Gurus; a Guru means a person who says, "I have known" and to me this very assertion is absurd. Because life is not such a thing that you can say, "I have known." There never comes a moment when you have reached and nothing remains further to travel. It is always travelling, it is always a reaching but never a reached point. The very concept of a Guru is basically irreligious and unspiritual.

'Whosoever claims to have reached the end of that road, the very claim negates them. The claim comes not from knowing but from ignorance. The Guru also comes not from knowledge but from ignorance. Because to be in a situation of knowing, one is bound to know simultaneously that life is endless; there is a beginning but there is no end. The same people who claim to have known, claim too that God is in everything, that God is in you. They say, too, that God cannot be defined. They say, too, that the truth is infinite. If the truth is infinite then you can never be a knower as they claim—you cannot be. A religious man is a man who is not claiming knowledge but is claiming on the contrary the mysteriousness of life. If you claim knowledge then life becomes not a mystery but an open secret; then even God is not a mystery.

'A person can be aware of the mysterious, of the *mysterium*, one can be one with it, one can live with and love it, until he himself becomes mysterious; his very presence becomes something mysterious. And in his presence, something can happen, but that is something like infection not teaching. His presence can become infectious and something may happen within one in his presence; his presence may work but that is not teaching. And if he begins to teach directly, then that happening will be hindered, that happening then becomes impossible. When I become a teacher, then your mind is not concerned with my presence, then you are concerned with my teachings. . . . If one is to become infectious it is better to be silent and live with somebody; it may happen at any moment, no one can predict it—it may happen! And there is more possibility of its happening if the person is silent. When the person is not silent then there is a direct effort to teach; the mind of the teacher becomes tense and the mind of the pupil too becomes tense; then there is only a verbal communication. But we need a deeper mingling; no deeper participation than that participation is possible.

'When one effort comes to failure then you begin another effort; when one Guru fails then you go to another; when one method fails then another and another and another. . . . And this can go on for lives together. But when you come to the point when everything has become a failure and you know that no Guru can help you, no method can become a process, then you have come to the absolute failure—only then is the "I" dissolved because there is no question of its being in existence: it has gone. It lives in the hope of achievement in the future and it gathers its strength from its hope in the future. Sometimes nothing can be achieved, just as it happened to Buddha when he was in total failure and he left everything; *sādhana, yoga*, the practice, everything, the meditation . . . everything was left and he was in a total vacuum about what to do. Because everything had proved nonsense and he had come to a point of no return; there was no question of going to another method again. There was no possibility of any dream now—not only of worldly dreams, but the spiritual dream too had failed. And in that total vacuum, in that night, the happening took place and he was not present any more. So Buddha could say, "It is not that I have achieved it, I could not achieve it. When I became a total failure, this came. I have not brought it, it has come to me."

'So you cannot prepare for it although the mind longs for preparation, it longs for method, technique, and that is why the mind can be prepared for everything. In a scientific experiment there must be preparation; in our worldly living there must be preparation. But the unknown cannot come to your prepared mind; it must be an effortless achievement.

'But in another way it can be meaningful: the relationship of a disciple with a Guru from the standpoint of the disciple can be meaningful; but not from the standpoint of the Guru. For the disciple, if he feels reverence towards somebody. . . . Another thing—a Guru expects reverence and says that a Guru must be respected and reverenced; but to me, when you feel reverence towards someone, that is the relationship. Not that the Guru is to be revered but when you feel reverence towards anyone then you may feel the relationship of a disciple towards the Guru. But that is totally the standpoint of the disciple; there is no Guru as far as the Guru is concerned. He feels reverence—well, he can feel it, but it must not be demanded. And if it comes without any demand, then it has got meaning because to feel reverence towards somebody is to become open to their selves. When someone demands love then the mind towards which the demand is made becomes closed. Whenever the mind feels insecurity it becomes closed, and whenever there is a demand it feels insecurity.

'And one thing more; when the Guru becomes the centre the relationship becomes one to one and the Guru demands that, "This reverence that you pay to me must not be paid to any others." When a wife demands, "This love must be towards me and not anyone else," she feels that when it is overflowing towards everybody she is cheated; and the Guru, too, feels he is cheated if this reverence goes to anybody and everybody. So there is also the second demand: "It must be only towards me— I am the Guru and no one else can be your Guru." This too becomes binding and closing. When the disciple is at the centre there is no question of this closing; then there is simply an attitude of learning. He comes to you and learns and feels reverence, then he goes to someone else and learns and feels reverence, then he goes on and goes on. . . . Then the whole life becomes the teacher, the whole life becomes the Guru. Then God, the very divine, becomes the Guru. And the moment comes when there is nothing which cannot be revered, when everything becomes a point of reverence. This must be; and this can only be when the disciple is at the centre and not the Guru. When the Guru has been at the centre the Guru has failed the disciple; he has not helped him.

'I am reminded of a story: a certain monk was celebrating a particular festival, a festival known as the Day of the Teacher. But no one in his village knew that he had a teacher so everybody asked, "Who is your Teacher? Why are you celebrating this day, a day sacred to one's Teacher, living or dead? Who is your Teacher?" The monk laughed and said, "There was one man who refused to be my Teacher. And because he refused, I learned. And now I am paying my respects to him."

'In the Indian tradition the Guru has been in the centre, and that is why there has come to be a rich tradition but not one rich in spirituality; a long tradition but not one rich in spirituality. And once it is understood that verbal communication is teaching, then the scriptures too can be felt as Gurus; the Sikhs call their scripture *Guru Grantha*—the book as teacher. When the verbal communication is teaching there is no need of a living person; verbal teaching can be taught by scripture, through a computer or through any mechanical device. Once verbal teaching is taken to *be* teaching then a dead tradition is bound to develop. The written tradition can be relevant in everything but religious experience, because the happening cannot be recorded; it is impossible to record it. There is a record of what Kṛṣṇa said but there is no record of how Kṛṣṇa became Kṛṣṇa. And that is the essential point, not what he said.

'There is a very lovely incident in the Buddha's life: one day he comes to teach a gathering; so many people have come, he sits on the dais. . . and sits and sits and sits. After sometime there are whisperings, "What is going on? We must begin now." But he is silent; half-an-hour, then one hour passes. And everyone is asking, "What is going on? He must talk to us, he must say something to us." Then Buddha says, "I have said that which could be said; now I was saying that which could not be said. Have you heard?" But no one had heard. It happened that one man, who had never spoken anything, for the first time laughed, laughed uproariously. Buddha was holding a flower in his hand; he called the man and gave him the flower and said to the gathering, "That which could be said, I have said to you; and that which could not be said, I have given to him." So there has grown up a tradition of two thousand years; monks have asked what was transferred to this man, what was said to him? But nothing was said—not said, but heard! Something was heard in that total silence, someone felt what it is and became aware of some unknown happenings.

'I arrived at these thoughts, not over a long period of thinking, but over a long period of searching. And every search failed. I knocked on every door and every door was a failure. A moment came when I left everything and I was doing nothing for a year—for a whole year, almost nothing, just sitting, just standing, just thinking. Then it came. There was no preparation—then it came. This year was rather a negative process of preparation. Any unconscious effort that may have been made dissolved. Then there was no beginning and there was no going and no reaching and no effort. Then it came.'

Tiny beads of sweat sit for a while on his smooth, young-looking brow, then disappear. Now and then a current of air passes through the crowded room, an intermittent mercy. After fifty minutes or so he leans back; the audience is over. He seems to have been delighted by the very act of speaking, taking pleasure in the play of his own mind, so that sometimes he has made the same point in several different ways for the sheer gratification the turning, interlocking wheels of his intelligence give him.

Now he stands, leaning over the side of the bed, relaxing. He takes my raised hand between his; his palms are warm and dry. He smiles, he is happy, he moves to and fro on the bed like a champion mildly elated after some minor skirmish, an exhibition match. He speaks to favourites, laving them with his enjoyment.

I go away, pick up my shoes, walk with them in my hand to the long room where I first waited. I have a pain in my left temple. I feel very tired.

(1973)

Chapter Two

Bhagwan Shree Rajneesh: A New Man for all Seasons

CHARLES NEWMAN (SWAMI DEVAGEET)

Religion is a neglected phenomenon for most people today. Our experience of the organised religions show them to be political organisations using theological language, and as such, to be hollow shams, riddled with lies and hypocrisy. Their terrible emptiness has so conditioned us that to even mention words like God, Truth, and Grace, is enough to make us yawn and turn to the other channel. If we are really pushed, then we will defend the beliefs of our parents, calling them 'our religion', but knowing them to be an embarassing collection of superstitious nonsense utterly out of place in any modern society.

Religion has faded from our lives because it is all talk and no action: it doesn't deliver the goods, and hasn't been able to for a very long time. Organised religions have robbed us of our spiritual dimension by having debased and devalued it with their worthless slogans, centred around fear-of-hell and greed-for-heaven, for many centuries. Nietzsche told us long ago that "God is dead!" and science finally nailed His coffin shut. Bhagwan Shree Rajneesh goes even further, he tells us that, "God was never alive. He is the greatest fiction that never lived."

Who is Bhagwan Shree Rajneesh? He is an enlightened master, at present living in Poona, India. He attained enlightenment on 21 March, 1953 and since then has devoted his entire life to the task of bringing modern man into an experimental, harmonious relationship with existence. His influence in the world of religion, philosophy and psychology is immense, and his words and ideas are so powerfully resonant that they shake the very foundations of established power structures; political, scientific, ideological, theological or cosmological.

Bhagwan Shree Rajneesh has been described by Tom Robbins as "The most dangerous man since Jesus." Tom Robbins is a famous author from the U.S.A. and the man he is talking about is perhaps the most controversial, religious genius in the world today.

We have been conditioned to believe that all great religious innovators belong to the past; scriptures must be ancient, and leaders must be dead. We prefer our spiritual geniuses to be dead, the longer the better; that way they are much less threatening. A living enlightened master is a tremendously potent catalyst for change, both in ourselves and in our society, and the powers which rule us, those entrenched guardians of the *status quo*, can feel his presence, and they tremble.

It is my opinion that Bhagwan Shree Rajneesh is a master of the same status as Buddha, Jesus, Lao Tzu or Pythagoras. His vision is to raise the consciousness of mankind beyond the barbaric, biological endgame in which civilisation finds itself today, into the next stage of human evolution; from *Homo Sapiens* to *Homo Novus*...the New Man.

He is the living embodiment of his vision; seeing him, being in his presence, one experiences some of the vast possibilities available to those who can bring their consciousness to the same peak. He has the courage and vision from which great changes stem. He has the mysterious quality, the charisma, which total individualisation brings. It is these qualities which attract many sincere seekers to him, and attract the opposition of the powerful. He is indeed a dangerous man; he can waken ordinary men and women to their inner richness, to immense inner resources of intelligence, clarity, and freedom, as he has done himself. The New Man is awakened man; awakened from his own unconsciousness which prevents him from seeing the depths to which our cultures have sunk.

Humankind is at a critical stage. We are facing destruction from many sides—all self-inflicted: overpopulation and starvation; ecological breakdown in the atmosphere, the soil, and the oceans; AIDS, a plague which is only now gathering its deadly momentum; nuclear stock-piles which can kill each man, woman and child seven times over! If ever there was a time when humanity needed to change dramatically, it is surely now.

The old ways of thinking have brought us to the brink of the abyss. *Homo Sapiens* is looking with horror into his future. He has come to the end of the road. We have crushed and poisoned our beautiful planet with our greed and blind groping for power. Now is the time to wake up to ourselves, for a new consciousness to arise; for a new man to be born. And the man who has been showing us where we are headed and how we can change the direction is Bhagwan Shree Rajneesh.

All the great masters from the past were seen to be a threat to the society into which they chose to be born; Moses was a revolutionary who gave the Jewish people their freedom from slavery in Egypt; Buddha scoured the ancient traditions of Hinduism of all the superstitions and magical practices, bringing a whole new way of consciousness to the East; Jesus came to cleanse Judaic religion from the politics and power-seeking that went on in the name of God. These masters worked to save their culture and their society. Now the problem is much greater; Mankind itself is facing a global suicide, and old methods, and old solutions cannot help. There is a need for a global change otherwise we will perish. It is shatteringly clear that unless we wake up now, there may well be no tomorrow.

Bhagwan's ways to awaken us are based on the premise that each human being is born with the innate capacity to attain to his own inner godliness, his enlightenment. He works in multi-dimensional ways to bring us in touch with our conditioning, to de-automatise us. Using a variety of meditation techniques, some traditional, some entirely orchestrated for our modern minds, he sharpens our awareness to the state wherein we can see our own barriers to understanding.

He has attracted the ablest therapists from the Human Potential movement and using their methods, with unique variations of his own, he encourages his followers to explore their inner world, to experience the incredible treasures simply waiting for the asking. Through these techniques, he gives us the experience of a whole new way of being, a new way of being alive; joyful, juicy, and loving.

Each day he gives daily discourses morning and evening, spontaneously dealing with both personal questions and world problems. He always supports and reinforces the essential while clearly outlining the inessential in our search. His way is that of the rebel, the individual, the intelligent enquirer who refuses to accept other people's answers, and who pursues his own enquiry until his personal experience shows him the irrefutable truth.

Speaking personally, Bhagwan has shown me that the quality of religiousness has nothing to do with the established pathways known as "religions". He has shown me that the process of self-discovery can be delicious, filled with laughter and delight. For Bhagwan, seriousness is a disease which can so easily put out the tiny spark of awakening which barely penetrates the darkness of our unknowing. He has no time for life-negative attitudes and the long faces that accompany them. His is the way of reverence-for-life, an enjoyment of all that life has to offer, with gratitude to existence for the sheer joy that it brings. That is a hint of Bhagwan's religiousness. And that joy is not a false or forced thing, it bubbles up spontaneously when life becomes full to overflowing. Perhaps that is another reason why traditional religions oppose him; Bhagwan has made the "vale of tears" approach seem neurotically unnecessary. Who needs the guilt of centuries laid on your back for an original sin which doesn't seem such a big deal anyway? His whole message is to dissolve your guilt; it is only a priest's device to stoke up your repressions while feeding your greed for those white-hot temptations which will be satiated beyond your wildest dreams in some after-life.

Bhagwan Shree Rajneesh is an enlightened master; his whole being is his message. Simply being in his presence can evoke another, higher level of consciousness in you if you are available to him. He has done it for many. He has done it for me. But he does not, indeed cannot, do anything against your will. He is the well; if your thirst is enough, then you will drink.

There are many, who for reasons of their own, want to destroy or minimise Bhagwan's work; some are disaffected followers, disappointed that their expectations were not met; some are world-weary cynics who believe that the wastelands they have created of their own lives are a tribute to their intelligence; others are the anonymous, but powerful, vested interests who recognise Bhagwan's work as a threat to their ambition and manipulation. All of these add up to an organised attempt to promote endarkenment rather than enlightenment. As if our world was not dark enough already!

Hugh Milne is an example of the classic disaffected follower. He has written a bitter and dishonest book. He is an ex-disciple clearly floundering and lost, peddling his salacious stories to the highest bidder. Using his book as a standpoint to try and understand the phenomenon we know as Bhagwan Shree Rajneesh is like trying to gather information about Great Britain using the revelations of Kim Philby, or Burgess and Maclean. That Milne has an axe to grind is obvious, but how far he is willing to bend the truth and distort matters of public record in order to justify his view, needs careful consideration before taking what he says as anything more than petulant gossip.

When Bhagwan was in America, his secretary, Ma Anand Sheela and a small number of her friends, misused the trust placed in them by Bhagwan and became involved in criminal activity. It is a matter of record that when Bhagwan came to know of Sheela's criminal acts, he denounced her and invited in the police agencies, telling all Sannyasins to cooperate fully. He knew well that the governmental agencies wanted to destroy the commune—it was apparent to everyone through their pattern of continual bureaucratic harassment and delaying tactics. (See, Dell Murphy's book, *The Rajneesh Story*, Linwood Press.)

Each day, Bhagwan held a press conference open to any journalist who wanted to come, and they came from all over the world. This is scarcely the action of a man with something to hide. The government agencies did use the opportunity to break up the commune. After they repeatedly refused to interview Bhagwan for his evidence, it became clear that their actions were politically motivated. This was confirmed at the time of Sheela's trial in a statement given by U.S. assistant attorney Turner in answer to a question by journalists as to why Bhagwan was not put in jail in place of Sheela.

Turner gave three objectives behind the actions of the governmental agencies, and the order he gave them is as revealing as their substance; he stated that:

1. The main objective was to destroy the commune at Rajneeshpuram, which would be best achieved by removing Bhagwan from America.
2. The second objective was to avoid making Bhagwan a martyr.
3. There was no evidence (!) found against the Bhagwan despite exhaustive enquiries by police agencies on the two continents where he had lived, namely India and America.

These words simply mean that Bhagwan is innocent of any crimes. Despite Sheela giving evidence, and her close associates corroborating her story, even though she had secretly taped her conversations with Bhagwan and made them all available to the police as part of her plea bargaining, there was still no evidence that Bhagwan had any part in their crimes.

Despite the overwhelming fact of Bhagwan's innocence, there seems to be an ugly, undercover attempt to denigrate his tremendous reputation throughout the world. The method is largely through the circulation of untrue and distorted facts about him and his work. Many disaffected followers speak of being approached by secret agents to help smear Bhagwan with lurid tales of their lives as Sannyasins. Most have not stooped so low, but for reasons best known to himself, Milne lent himself and his "first-hand" experiences to this twentieth-century equivalent of the crucifixion.

Bhagwan left America after his lawyers advised him that his life was at risk if he stayed to face the charges ranged against him by the immigration department. Just one hour before being finally released, after a 12-day ordeal in prisons and chains, a bomb was discovered in the Portland maximum security jail where he was being kept. Everybody was evacuated, except Bhagwan, who was kept inside.

Even after he left America, the same politicians who wanted him removed, presumably threatened various governments to prevent Bhagwan from being allowed to stay in their countries. He was arrested and thrown out of Crete in February 86, after Greek Orthodox archbishops threatened to dynamite the house where he was staying. In Switzerland, his 7-day visa was cancelled on arrival, having been declared "*persona non grata* because of immigration offences in the U.S.A.". In Sweden, he was met by armed police and told that he "is a threat to national security". In England, Bhagwan was not even allowed to stay overnight in the first-class lounge while the pilots of his jet rested. Instead, he and his companions were locked up overnight in a dirty cell crowded with African and Asian refugees. They flew to Ireland where they were allowed to stay for a few days before police came and asked them to leave the country. Canada refused permission even for Bhagwan's plane to be refuelled on its flight to Antigua.

Meanwhile Antigua withdrew its permission for him to go there. Holland refused to allow him even a tourist visa. Germany had already passed a "preventative decree" not allow Bhagwan to enter their country. In Italy, his application for a tourist visa was kept on file for one year before they refused on the grounds that his application was out of date and needed to be renewed. Uruguay invited him with an offer of possible permanent residence. But pressure was applied in the form of telexes containing "secret diplomatic information" from "anonymous sources" mentioning "rumours of drug smuggling and prostitution". The same misinformation had preceded Bhagwan in all the countries he had named as his destination.

On May 14, 1986, the government of Uruguay wanted to announce at a press conference that Bhagwan had been granted permanent residence there. That night, Sanguinetti, the President of Uruguay, received a call from Washington D.C. telling that current U.S. loans of $6 billion will be called in, and no future loans given if the offer or residence was made. Bhagwan had to leave Uruguay on June 18. The very next day, Sanguinetti and Ronald Reagan announced from Washington, a new loan to Uruguay of $150 million. Bhagwan flew to Jamaica on a 10-day visa; while his plane was still on the landing strip, a U.S. military jet landed and two civilians were seen to emerge carrying diplomatic bags. The next morning, the visas of the people in Bhagwan's party were cancelled. Bhagwan is now at Poona, India, after having amply demonstrated the rights of the individual to travel freely.

A modern Nostradamus scholar, John Hogue, has an intriguing reference to Bhagwan in his fast-selling book. (*Nostradamus and the Millenium,* published by Doubleday, U.S.A.). After accurately predicting the current trend to annihilation, Nostradamus has predicted that a new religious consciousness would arise and flower before the end of this century, which, if it leads to a change of world consciousness, would bring one thousand years of peace in this planet. He called it "The Age of Truth", where science and religion would merge into a higher consciousness.

The leader of this new religiousness, according to Nostradamus, would be a "Man from Asia who would also be at home in Europe". "A teacher who will travel widely in his desire to infuriate." A man who will shake up the established order and be outlawed. He would be charged with destroying the established religions, using ornate speeches. And all other religions would unite against him and his 'red ones'. Finally, his name will be associated with the moon, and his religion associated with birds.

Hogue discusses ten candidates for this role of new religious leader: Swami Paramahansa Yogananda, Meher Baba, Swami Prabhupada, L. Ron Hubbard, J. Krishnamurti, Swami Satya Sai Baba, Rev. Sun Myung Moon, Bhagwan Shree Rajneesh, Da Free John, and Swami Maharishi Mahesh Yogi. Of them all, he notes, only "Rajneesh seems to match all the clues". He draws a chart to simplify the case:

> Rajneesh was born and raised in India, where he is currently living. He has travelled extensively in the West where most of his followers, who wear red, live. The symbol of his religiousness is two flying birds and his name means 'full moon'.
>
> He certainly seems to have the desire to infuriate, how else to describe his admittedly ornate speeches which vehemently attack not only the established religions, but all vested interests. He has been outlawed, literally, from twenty-two countries in the Western world, and is frequently spoken against by other religious leaders (Shankaracharya Swaroopanand Saraswati's recent press statement that 'Rajneesh posed a kind of danger to society that was unprecedented in India's history').

Dell Murphy summarises in this way, "people all over the world are trying to silence the Bhagwan, but if they silence him, what will they gain? You can destroy a man more easily than destroy an idea. And you can deny the truth, or hide it, or turn your back on it, but you cannot destroy it".

Speaking personally, I have found Bhagwan to be a lighthouse in a world full of storms and darkness. It is easy to follow the fleet, but for some of us, there is a need to know who we are, where we are going, and whether this vast human flotilla is not just sailing on a voyage of futility. Being with Bhagwan, I have felt my soul take flight on the journey it has been seeking for eternity. I can only give him my gratitude for showing me a new life full of laughter, delight and overflowing juiciness.

(1987)

Chapter Three

Teachings on Karma and Rebirth: Their Social and Spiritual Role in the Rajneesh Neo-Sannyasin Movement

ROBERT E. GUSSNER (SWAMI ANAND JINA)

Because it is scarely a dozen years old, the Rajneesh movement represents the most recent post-classical development concerning teachings on *karma* and rebirth. In this movement we find a trend to prune traditional doctrines on *karma* and rebirth of aspects (1) that legitimate the present social order east or west, (2) that recommend ways to manage *karma* tending to leave power in the hands of priests, parents or others with official system-roles in the society, (3) that teach ways to repress yourself, or, (4) that instil fear of punishment in the next life or in the interval between lives.

We shall also see that in the Rajneesh movement the connection between unawareness and *karma* is strong, and the connection between unawareness and rebirth is strong, but that any link between *karma* and rebirth is remarkably muted. Or put another way, one post-classical development at work in the Rajneesh movement is to insist that the basic polarity in regard to any subject whatsoever is between awareness and unawareness (*avidyā* and *vidyā*). Thus, of the root afflictions (*kleśas*) in *Pātañjala Yoga*, *avidyā* alone is emphasised; of all the links (*nidānas*) in the chain of conditioned co-production (*pratityasamutpāda*), *avidyā* is stressed in preference to *saṃskāras* (subliminal-activators, or *karmic* substratum-deposits). In part, this severing of *karma* from rebirth and society may be due to Rajneesh's upbringing in the Jain community and to his Buddhist leanings, but even more so it is due to two other factors: his view that societal repression of the individual has rendered him so inauthentic that he cannot progress in the spiritual life unless he becomes real, and that this requires an approach of allowing emotional, sexual and inter-personal genuineness as the prerequisite to healing the mind-body split in modern man. This is preliminary to any spiritual life because only the united energies of mind and body are powerful enough to carry you beyond into the spiritual. Thus, Rajneesh's teachings on *karma* and rebirth are largely determined by his views on the spiritual path—an illustration of the way in which Indian philosophy is "path philosophy," according to Karl Potter. His particular path requires authenticity and cathartic release of repressions at the outset, and a de-focal expressive mode of meditation further on. Beyond this, Rajneesh's teachings also seem to presuppose a kind of "second coming of age" in man's evolution—a new maturity that frees him from the need of society's moral tutelage even more radically than did man's first coming of age in humanism and secularism. Of this, more in my conclusions. Throughout the paper I trace how

Rajneesh's teachings on *karma* and rebirth are fashioned in such a way that if you are aware (to be defined later) you can be real, even apparently immoral, and not fear that you are incurring bad *karma* thereby, or an unfortunate birth in another life.

Karma Theory: Awareness vs. Cultivation of Good Karma

The most substantial and systematic references to *karma* in Rajneesh's works are to be found in his ten-volume commentary on the *Yoga Sūtras* of Pātañjali, entitled *Yoga: The Alpha and the Omega.* In those *sūtras, karma* as a word occurs on five occasions (I.24, II.12, III.22, IV.7 and IV.30). Rajneesh accepts without qualification the existence of the three traditional types of *karma—sañcita, prārabdha,* and *kriyāman* (Rajneesh, 1977e: 10). *Sañcita karma* is the total accumulated *karma* from all of your past lives. *Prārabdha karma* is that portion of the total that you have to work out, or fulfill in this life—what you will act out, realise, suffer, and pass through. *Kriyāman karma* is the even smaller day-to-day portion of the *prārabdha karma*. Each moment one is presented with a chance to do something in reaction or not to do something. The correct way to work out *karma,* according to Rajneesh, is not to attempt a good reaction rather than a bad one, but rather not to react at all. One can *observe* the reaction within the mind to an insult and allow it to be, but unexpressed. Expressed, more *kriyāman karma* again falls into the *sañcita karma,* accumulated for future lives. If you don't react to an insult by a person (whom you may have insulted previously) then the account is closed and a past *karma* is fulfilled (Rajneesh, 1977e: 11). An aware person wil be able to detect a subtle inner freeing and he will be happy (Rajneesh, 1977e: 11).

Rajneesh identifies *kriyāman karma* with the conscious domain of the mind; in psychological terms the *prārabdha* domain is the subconscious. Below that is the even deeper area of the *sañcita*, which he calls the unconscious (Rajneesh, 1977e: 20). His strategy for working with *kạrma* is to bring awareness to the surface realm first, and then, progressively, to the two deeper layers. One starts by becoming aware of day-to-day activities like eating or walking, remaining focused on the activity, instead of mentally wandering here and there like a zombie (Rajneesh, 1978c: 70). And whatever you are saying can be said with full alertness. This he equates with the modern ideal of being here-now (Rajneesh, 1977e: 21). After practice of this first step, you can move to the subconscious, and you will not only become aware when you have become angry, you will be immediately aware when you have been insulted that a very small, subtle wave has begun to move in your subconscious. Awareness of subtle nuances and shades of emotions is awareness of *prārabdha karma*. The more you grow in this ability to sense, the more you can grow in awareness of the *sañcita karma*. When you completely bring the light of consciousness into the deepest core of your being, and nothing is dark, you become a Buddha (Rajneesh, 1977e: 21).

In the above views, the centrality of the notions of awareness and unawareness is already apparent. In one sense awareness means alert mindfulness in the Theravadin sense of *satipatthana*, noting what is going on in your mind, in your movements and in your surroundings. In a second and deeper sense, it means cognizance of your own subjective presence as a crystallized witness, which arises as a shadow-reflex of mindfulness practice carried on without slack or strain, and which has a quality of deep slence in it. For those who are familiar with Gurdjieff/Ouspensky terminology, this second sense of the word awareness is equivalent to self-remembering with its double-arrowed consciousness and peculiar sense of "I am here." Rajneesh also uses the word awareness (or consciousness) to mean fully enlightened and liberated consciousness. In what follows, the context will usually suggest which sense is intended.

The notion of awareness, even in its first and minimal sense, is central to Rajneesh's concept of what an act is and what *karma* is. He holds that "whatever you do in unawareness (identification) becomes a *karma*" (Rajneesh, 1977e: 11). A simple mechanical reaction is the usual example, and this is contrasted with a response which is total, spontaneous, and centred. A response is not an action, for Rajneesh, and leaves no trace (*saṃskāra*) on the mind-stuff. Any such action is complete in itself, and this is not an action. Thus, the crucial differentia of a *karma* which leaves a subliminal-activator deposit is its incompleteness. That defines the category of action for Rajneesh (Rajneesh, 1977e: 11). In terms of *Yoga Sūtra* I.3, Rajneesh seems to hold that every thought and every act leaves a mark only so long as you are in a state of being identified (*sārūpyam*) with the mental fluctuation (*vṛtti*), but not when there is a standing, witness-like, in your own nature (*svarūpine'vasthānam*). He says this can happen momentarily whenever the observing-self briefly cognises the object-self.

As an aside, I might note that mindful responses, not being acts, tend to complete two types of *karma* without adding *karma*. Thus, such responses are *nivṛtti*, not in the sense that a response is not motivated by desire and need (it is, as are all doings prior to enlightenment), and not in the sense that one need be outside of householder social structures to perform the act, but in the simple sense that it is a turning in, a turning down, into awareness of mind and of *kriyāman* and *prārabdha karma* in the sense discussed above. As such, it is the opposite of *pravṛtti*, mind-fluctuations going outward in unconscious reactions with a mechanical identification with the *vṛtti* (mind fluctuation) and the production of *karma*. *Pravṛtti* is outward going in the sense that it takes you further away from the last observing act that will finish off your last residue of *sañcita karma*, and *nivṛtti* is inward turning in the sense that it is homeward bound, is a return into your nature and ground as enlightened. The concepts seem essentially directional in nature.

Elsewhere, in commentary on *Yoga Sūtra* II.10-14, central concepts in Rajneesh's presentation of *karma* theory are developed differently. They are repetition, the self-energising action of habit, the ego's rationalisation of its freedom, and ultimate slavery to *karma*. These form four stages in an ontological descent into skid row. The way out of *kārmic* entrapment lies in (1) realising your rationalisation; (2) seeing deeply into the fact that you alone are absolutely responsible for all your misery and dissatisfaction; and (3) most importantly, undertaking the process of *pratiprasava*, or flowing back to the cause.

The first point to note is that Rajneesh is not saying that whatever you repeat becomes a habit. Rather, he says, "Whatsoever you do creates its own repetition" (Rajneesh, 1977d: 163). This, says Rajneesh, is the heart of the theory of *karma*. "Each action has its own way of persisting. If you were angry the day before yesterday, you created a certain potentiality to be angry yesterday" (Rajneesh, 1977d: 163). The act creates a channel into your being and the energy coming from the First Principle will run into readily available channels. The channel being there it will deepen itself. This view of *karma* articulates with Raymond Panikkar's characterisation of *karma* as "the act that acts," (1972: 32) but here in a double sense.

The way the habit grows is that this channel "starts absorbing energy from your being, from you" (Rajneesh, 1977d: 163). According to Rajneesh this absorbing may be subconscious; moreover it can occur after the anger has gone away and you think that you are not angry any longer. When the mood of anger has gone, nothing basic has happened, the wheel of the mind has only moved and the spoke that was up has gone down (Rajneesh, 1977d: 163). If, on the other hand, you should still be conscious of lingering anger and attempt to suppress it, the anger will suffuse throughout your being. The indirect attention of avoidance also feeds the channel. So the persistence and deepening of the channel is not something for which the ego need give itself credit. The channel automatically and mechanically deepens itself, by and large. As the channel gathers energy it will sooner or later achieve the status of a habit, it will become second nature. In fact, says Rajneesh, it becomes your first nature; your real nature as pure, free consciousness becomes an appendix, a footnote in the book, and habit (character) becomes the main body of the book (Rajneesh, 1977d: 163). Eventually you end up in the grip of the habit; you live through the habit, or rather the habit lives through you. It finally takes enough energy so that it becomes the master and you become just the servant, a kind of shadow in the situation. The habit will give the order and you will be the obedient servant coming and going from the background somewhere.

At this point the third step in the descent occurs the ego must rationalise the habit. You must befool yourself that you are doing it. The ego goes on thinking that you are still the boss. It may say, "I had to be angry, otherwise the children would go astray, or the office would go into chaos, or the wife would get out of place" (Rajneesh, 1977d: 163). This is a deception because, says Rajneesh, the anger was only apparently forced by outer circumstances, but, fundamentally, the reaction or the mood boiled up from within. True, something may have pushed your button, as it were, but consider well. If you had been in an all-wants-supplied isolation chamber, in perfect conditions and completely apart from human stimulation, you would still move through all the moods that you have in relationships—euphoria, sadness, anger. Basically something comes from within and you hang it on someone else. It surfaces mechanically as a response to stimulus, but it comes from within. If you do not realise this, you lock yourself behind the double door of the twofold rationalisation: I am really the boss, and something did it to me. Then one is blind to the mechanism of imprisonment and to the fact of imprisonment; consequently, one has no reason to seek release, or even to suspect that escape is necessary. Here one may live on and on.

This brings us to the nadir of the *karmic* situation, and the beginning of the way out. Escape happens in three deep insights: (1) seeing that reactions come from within; (2) realising that you (as higher self and also as witnessing lower self) are absolutely responsible for whatsoever happens to you; and (3) reliving the root cause of the reaction in the clear light of consciousness and healing the wound or impressions. This is the step of *pratiprasava* (return to the original state).

The point about responsibility is probably the most problematic, so I shall begin there and end with a word on *pratiprasava* as rebirthing.

As I understand Rajneesh, there are at least three senses in which one is responsible. First, you allowed the channel formation in the first place by being unaware and so engaging in identified action. Secondly, you are responsible because you make your experience what it is by how you construe and interpret it. Finally, in your nature as witness (*dṛṣṭi*) you can respond in such a way as to eliminate the pattern. If the root cause is some initial wound, you can heal that wound with the light of awareness in *pratiprasava*.

Let us consider this process as it is promulgated in the Rajneesh movement, for it is the basis of primal scream work, encounter groups, and so on. Says Rajneesh, notice, for example, when you wife is nasty to you. Perhaps you are reading the paper and she calls you insensitive, ugly, unsuccessful, unfaithful, etc. You alone are responsible for your experience of being hurt. The wound that was touched is in you; how you construe the exchange—as an insult or whatever—is also your doing.

If you actually achieve the insight that this is so, you may be depressed and frustrated at first. You are helpless and debarred from doing the things you usually do in this situation—reasoning or trying to change the other (the most unfulfilled wish in human life, according to Rajneesh). To change another is to try to change their marks and the turning of their wheel, and they are largely unconscious about this. So we usually try to get a sleepy person to wake up. It seldom happens.

Instead, you can see that your wife, in the last analysis, is nasty because of her own inner mechanism and channels. The habit of complaining, with its energy, is coming up as the wheel turns for her. In a sense, she is not nasty with you in any very specific way; if you were not there she would have been grumpy with the child, irritated with the plates or impatient with the radio. She had to do something. You were available at the wrong moment. She is responsible for her being and her behaviour.

But so are you. Probably you have to react in anger. But once this happens you can go back from this effect to the cause, a wound perhaps from a previous life. By trying to go back within yourself, you take the first step, to stop throwing the responsibility outward. You stop trying to find out why your wife is nasty. Instead, you find out why you are hurt by the nastiness.

The method of *pratiprasava* is to relax, then penetrate

into the anger until you feel it intensely inside. Then let this aroused energy help move you back toward the past, closer to the basic wounds in your memory. The wound may be one big one, or several small ones. Whatever the case, the point is to unroll the spool of film backwards to the root cause. Consciously feeling the wound, not in remembering, which is an impotent process, but in an intense reliving, where you become the child again, heals the wound.

The real secret of this healing, according to Rajneesh, is that consciousness is the healing force, "just the light of consciousness heals" (Rajneesh, 1977d: 169). But the observing must be done without judgement or condemnation, otherwise the mind will close the wound and the ego will hide it. Then the mind becomes divided; you create a basement of the mind, and the disastrous modern dissociation begins.

Successfully done, witnessing keeps the mind in a oneness, deeply heals the *karmic* mark (anything you can complete, you are free from), and releases the mind from the past, making it available for a present-centred mode of experiencing. If there are dated emotions, or unfinished business from the past, says Rajneesh, then the present moment in your life will be just a fleeting passage from the past to the future. You will miss going deeply into the now-moment concealed in the vanishing present, and hence miss the vertical dimension which the now-moment is. Notice that for Rajneesh, the degree of solid contact with the now-moment is the exact measure of the degree of freedom operating *vis-à-vis karmic* bondage. It is the test of how much freedom you have. Solid contact, of course, is synonymous with awareness in its first sense.

By daily practice of the art of going backwards, re-experiencing the events of the day every evening, you will become proficient at *pratiprasava* and be able to open many deep and remote *karmic* wounds rapidly. You need only see them. No overt doing is required. This daily practice will also largely prevent burdening the mind with new *karma,* since anything re-experienced with sufficient intensity eliminates the impression on the mind. As we have seen, for Rajneesh this is a very fundamental law:

> Any experience that is complete, you are finished with it. It leaves no trace—not even footprints. It simply disappears, evaporates. It leaves no *karma,* it creates no *karma.* This can happen in primal scream therapy (Rajneesh, 1981b: 201-2).

Here I should remark parenthetically, since this is a discussion of a post-classical development in *karma*-theory, that the use of Western growth groups such as Primal Scream workshops surely represents a development in the processing of *karma,* if not in its theory.

Let us now assess what Rajneesh accepts and what he rejects in classical *karma* theory. Clearly he accepts most of its essentials—the law of repetition, the three types of *karma,* its near-terrifying power to enslave. For him, only power of awareness, the mysterious expression of one's very self, is stronger. Only this saves man from a complete psychological subjugation and Rajneesh's position from philosophical determinism.

But what does he reject? Most popular applications of *karma* theory to social life, the effort to build good *karma* (in the form of good habits and good character), and, finally, the linking of *karma* to *jāti* (rebirth-species) and to *āyus* (length of future life). He does not, however, refuse to link *karma* to *bhoga* (experiences of life that you will meet). Let us consider this briefly.

Rajneesh's acceptance of a *karma/bhoga* link and his rejection of a *karma/jāti* link and a *karma/āyus* link occur in his commentary on *Yoga Sūtra* II.13. Pointedly ignoring the *jāti/āyus* portion of the total *sūtra*, which reads, "When root *karma* exists, it will ripen in species of birth, length of life, and types of experiences," he speaks only of types of experiences. Seeds, he says, that are unfinished will be fulfilled in millions of ways as you see situations and opportunities to complete them. The main result of *karma* seems to be the creation of character, or disposition, which finds situations attractive, challenging or baffling. This seems to be the sense of this commentary on *Sūtra* II.13:

> In this life you may be rich, but you are a miser and live the life of a poor man. That is *karma*. You have riches but you cannot live those riches, thinking perhaps that it is not religious . . . . On the other hand you may be a beggar and yet live like a rich man and worry about nothing. You have nothing to lose and enjoy yourself. This man carries the seeds of a rich life from his past and will find situations and opportunities to enjoy himself. Wherever you are it will not make much difference. You will have to live through your past (Rajneesh, 1977d: 182).

Rajneesh seems to side with those Indians who say that *karma* is not so much what happens to you (e.g., getting hit by a truck), as your reaction to what happens to you (being cheerful, having a nervous breakdown, etc.). In any event, he is silent about any nexus between caste, *karma* and *guṇa* or the like, such as we find Kṛṣṇa expressing in the *Bhagavadgītā*.

Let us turn to those aspects of popular *karma* doctrine that Rajneesh surely rejects. In one passage he says, "This is one of my most fundamental ideas that you have to understand: I am against the whole idea of *karma*." (Rajneesh, 1982a). Here he means its popular and priestly applications. His indictment is lengthy. *Karma* theory is a strategy of the mind to throw responsibility for misery on an unchangeable past; it makes people feel like helpless victims and needlessly ruins their lives. Again, it is an invention of the priests to keep people in poverty, yet content and causing no trouble for the *status quo.* It has prevented revolution through all of Indian history, has created a conformist mind about accepting whatsoever is, and this mind led to the disappearance of Buddhism from India. It gives the feeling that to take money or land from the rich is a sin that goes against God, and a horrible thing to do, like breaking the walls of a prison and letting the prisoners escape (Rajneesh, 1982a). He ridicules *karma* as the theory which says, "Put your hand in the fire now, and you will get burned in the next life" (Rajneesh, 1982a). Clearly the result of an act is not some future event for Rajneesh, but the wound-mark in the mind which life always gives immediately (Rajneesh, 1982a).

More basic is his rejection of attempts to balance bad *karma* with good acts. He distinguishes two general attitudes in India toward what should be done with the *karmic* burden—one is that of Patañjali and the other is that of Mahāvīra, the last *tīrthaṅkara* of the Jain community. "Mahāvīra says, if you have done wrong you have to right it, otherwise you will suffer. Do good to the world" (Rajneesh, 1977d: 185). This standpoint is concerned with actions, morality, "shoulds and shouldnots" (Rajneesh, 1977d: 185). It addresses what to do, not how to be. Patañjali, on the other hand, stresses bringing the energy of awareness to your past; it is consciousness-oriented, not action-oriented. Not surprisingly, Rajneesh says, "I am all in favour of Patañjali" (Rajneesh, 1977d: 185).

This approach negates the whole Brāhmaṇical panoply of procedures for accumulating good *karma* through doing your duty in the social order called the *varṇāśramadharma* system, as well as merit accumulation through study, penance, austerities and the like. More, it is an expression of an underlying repudiation of the cultivation of good habits, and, in fact, of all cultivation, as such. Consideration of the topics "habit" and "cultivation" will reveal what actuates Rajneesh's rejection of selected aspects of *karmic* teachings. His is an opting for the needs of the individual to throw off repression as a first step toward God-realisation rather than opting for the needs of society for good individuals. Let me document this briefly from Rajneesh's discussion of *karma* in connection with *Yoga Sūtra* IV.7, where he interprets the aphorism, "The yogi's *karmas* are neither pure nor impure because they come out of original mind."

His discussion here centres on habits. The basic problem is that habits cannot be dropped in any simple sense because of the overriding power of *karma*. There are only two ways to deal with them (Rajneesh, 1978c: 169). One is to substitute another habit for the one you have. This is cutting another channel for the water of your being to flow into. It is changing one problem for another. Even if I develop a habit of helping others and doing saintly acts, then desires will arise to do more good, and if all my associates are away, I will feel restless to find someone to help. All habits are bad from the standpoint of God-realisation, though not from society's standpoint. If the habit to do good becomes second nature, then when you want to drop it, that will not be easy. "Never," Rajneesh says, "try to change a bad habit into a good one". The temptation is great, of course, because of social pressure. If you begin going to church everyday instead of the pub, you become moral, and once you are moral society is not bothered with you. It is finished with you except to cheer you and garland you with respect. You are a very good man. "But," says Rajneesh, "you yourself have yet long to go. The journey is not complete yet" (Rajneesh, 1978c: 69). Habit as such is against your original nature (Rajneesh, 1978c: 69).

Here we see Rajneesh's basic concern to create a *saṅgha* as a transformative example outside of an official *dharmic* social order. We might explain this as due only to his being a Jain with Buddhist sympathies, and because he is overwhelmingly concerned with enlightenment, not life in Hindu society. But from the general emphasis of his works as a whole, the decisive motivation seems to be compassion for modern man everywhere, whom he sees as suffering from sealed-in repression of anger, sadness, loneliness, distancing from his real feelings.

This is reflected in his advice to deal with habits by awareness. Awareness "is the fire that burns the past" (Rajneesh 1977d: 185). Don't worry about dropping the habit, he counsels. "Whenever you repeat the habit, become aware." Repeat it, but with a witnessing, an alertness, an awareness. That makes you separate from the habit and the energy that was going in the habit channel and cutting the groove deeper doesn't go there any more. The energy you were giving the habit unknowingly doesn't go anywhere, doesn't make a new groove. It accumulates in your being against the day of a final explosion in realisation. And by and by the habit will shrink.

This brings us very close to the heart of Rajneesh's stance on *karma*, namely that he rejects any view of *karma* and any application of *karma* theory to cultivate character. In fact, for him, *to cultivate anything is to become "pseudo"* (Rajneesh, 1981b: 339). It means "you are creating something around you which you are not" (Rajneesh, 1981b: 339). It means creating a split between your organismic reality/flow and your facade. "Then you live in a camouflage" (Rajneesh, 1981b: 339). Cultivation creates holier-than-thou attitudes, gives the ego satisfaction; it does not create true morality (which comes from contacting being within and is an overflow of love), it creates only ugly puritans (Rajneesh, 1981b: 339). His opposition to cultivation is many-sided and poly-dimensional. It puts you in a prison when you cultivate because, deep down, you create its opposite. What you suppress suffuses your being, and you have to fight its emergence and can never really relax. And you will feel one thing and show another, you will say one thing and do another. It will make you diplomatic (one of the most pejorative buzz words within the Rajneesh movement) and infect you with the most basic of diseases, the disease of seriousness, another buzz word in the movement used in contrast to sincerity (being what you are at the moment). Cultivation cripples, divides energy, results in mankind dragging at low levels of vitality, creates deadness, and prevents morality. Real morality, he holds, is not to be cultivated, but comes as a shadow of being aware, consciousness. The way to this state is to begin by being aware of your neutral habits—walking eating, talking, feeling the wind, the coolness of the sheets in your bed at night, etc. One should be conscious of doing one's good habits and finally try and move to awareness of one's bad habits as they are being done. "Once you have become aware of your whole habitual pattern, that habitual pattern is your mind. Any day the shift will happen. Suddenly you will be in no-mind" (Rajneesh, 1978c: 71).

We can now summarise the decisive role of awareness in Rajneesh's *karma* theory. An act is an act only if done with identification and unawareness. Only this kind of act creates a channel. If a channel is made, it will have to be completed. If a channel exists in the mind you will meet situations that activate that channel, and it will be self-active too. So, on one side of his theory are the elements unawareness-act-channel-incompleteness, and, on the other side, the elements awareness, a non-act, no channel creation, and a completeness of that unit of experience. So completeness can be obtained either by never creating the mark in the mind in the first instance, or by living it through in balancing of accounts through many lives and innumerable experiences (Mahāvīra), or by awareness of habits that shrink and silt-up the channel (Patañjali as interpreted by Rajneesh). This summary of his position on *karma* should clarify what I said at the beginning about it being pruned of elements that connect it to society and morality, and it being decisively shaped by Rajneesh's espousal of the awareness path in spiritual life and his general sense that modern man need no longer be a ward of society. We shall see the same position operating in his presentation of death, the *bardo* state, and rebirth.

REBIRTH

Rajneesh accepts the fact of transmigration in Buddhist terms: there is transmigration but no transmigrants. The idea behind the device of teaching many lives, and the significance of the original message, was this:

> Remember that you have been living in the same rotten way over and over again. Can't you see it? You are moving in a wheel, going in circles. Are you not bored yet? Can't you see the futility of desiring the same thing; succeeding and failing and dying every time? Can't you see that something more is needed? This world won't do; you have to transcend it (Rajneesh, 1980c).

What really happened was something totally different, just the opposite. The unconscious mind interpreted the whole purport of the message to be, "There is no hurry, we will think of God in old age or in the next life" (Rajneesh, 1980c). The devices created by conscious minds harm, not help. Nectar from the Buddhas becomes poison by the time it reaches you.

Similarly, in the West the idea behind teaching only one life on the part of Moses and others, who knew better, according to Rajneesh, was this:

> Time is short, so don't waste it on non-essential things, material things, trivial things, accumulating money and gadgets. Think of the essential, not the accidental and superficial (Rajneesh, 1980c).

But people turned it completely upside down so that they became interested in the non-essential. They began to say:

> There is not much time, so eat, drink and be merry. You are not coming again—who knows about God, heaven and the other world—so enjoy this life as much as you can; squeeze every moment to your heart's content (Rajneesh, 1980c).

This is the conclusion that prevailed in the West. The hurry of having only one life, he says, begets a pressure and an ability to do everything quickly and skilfully. The mind is well-developed. There is not a lot of thought about where you are going, but the speed with which you go and do is nearly perfected. In India, on the other hand, everything from the government to the mind to technology became 'lousy' because time to improve was endless. The general ability to do declined and speed was less than ideal. The conclusion Rajneesh draws from all of this is that a new universal mind is needed. This mind will not think in terms of one life, or many lives, but only in terms of consciousness (Rajneesh, 1980). All thought of hemispheres East and West, all thought of tradition as a basic category, all thought of race, blood and nationality must go, and only the familiar emphasis upon the difference between awareness and sleep is stressed.

Although *bardo* states (between life intervals) and

rebirth are secondary topics for Rajneesh, he teaches them as a fact on the authority of his own conscious death, *bardo* state, and rebirth. And there is much lore in the movement about the past lives of present disciples, and a strong sense that they work together recurringly down through the centuries.

In this discussions on rebirth, Rajneesh discusses four principal subjects: the importance of remembering past lives, vegetarianism, the nature of the interval state between bodies, and the free rebirth of conscious souls, and in each case the discussion is dominated by the theme of awareness.

Remembering past lives is important for Rajneesh because it saves time and energy in the practical matter of progress in the spiritual life. As animals don't evolve because of lack of communication, and each monkey must start his learning all over at the level that his father began, so a soul may merely repeat the building of the foundation of his house over and over again. By searching out your past lives you will start from where you left off, and not be only a repetition. The knowledge can produce a spiritual revolution in you (Rajneesh, 1975b: 58).

In remembering past lives, techniques of regression are the least difficult thing. Harder is the courage to remain undisturbed and centred in the midst of difficult memories which come to you, not in instalments, but in their painful entirety. The lightness of mind and fluid ability to receive imagery is also hard to come by. And the key to this is vegetarianism, says Rajneesh. It is no coincidence that all the vegetarian religions (Hinduism, Jainism, Buddhism) believe in transmigration, and Western ones do not:

> When a person is utterly vegetarian he can easily remember his past lives. His clarity is such that he

> can look into his past lives. He is not gross, his energy is not blocked, his energy moves easily. His river of consciousness can penetrate to the ancientmost times; he can go backwards as much as he wants. The consciousness of the non-vegetarian is blocked, he has been absorbing gross matter in himself. That gross matter functions as a barrier. That's why all three religions that were born outside of India, and have remained non-vegetarian could not come to the idea of reincarnation. They could not experience it (Rajneesh, 1981b: 194-5).

Disagreeing on many other things, Indian religions could not disagree on rebirth because of their experience of past lives. This comes out of deeper meditation, which, in turn is aided by vegetarianism. Eating meat and meditating, says Rajneesh, is like climbing a mountain carrying big rocks—it can be done, but it is more difficult. Vegetarianism is advocated as an aesthetic and spiritual matter, not a moral and religious one.

Let us now take up the complex, and for Rajneesh, relatively unimportant subject of the nature of the state between bodies, the interval state. Here we find a tremendous potpourri of points to sort out. I shall present them as a series of questions, or issues:

(a) *The issue of the nature of Bardo experience.* Whatever experiences can be had in the interval will be such as can be had without a body (Rajneesh, 1975b: 127): a few can meditate, a few can explore by psychic capacitites, most are in a dream-like state. As dreams are experiences from seeds in memory, so interval experiences are, too. As in a dream there is little doubt about the reality of those experiences, so here, too. As in a dream impossible transformations don't appear impossible, so here, too. In the interval things can seem even more vividly real than in a body, because while awake in a body there is room for doubt about the "realisticalness" of happenings

(Rajneesh, 1975b: 127). Demons seem absolutely real, as do heavenly damsels.

(b) *The issue of heaven and hell.* Heaven and hell are just deep dream lives. A dream might be only of heaven, or only of hell, or mixed. Descriptions of heaven and hell differ, as the persons with faint memories of the dream have different mental states (Rajneesh, 1975b: 109). Newborns generally remember the dream for six months, very sensitive people a little longer, up to five years (Rajneesh, 1975b: 111).

(c) *The issue of finding a new womb.* There are three types of souls. A minority are *pretas*. They are evil and for them it is difficult to find another birth because the wombs with which they fit are a microscopic minority. Existence is like a bell-curve in this regard. Similarly some are *devas*, serene calm beings, who also find wombs scarce. We shall consider the rebirth prospects of the would be *Bodhisattva* separately when discussing Rajneesh's rebirth experience. The third type of soul, the average majority, have some differences of character and so of interval-experiences, but are all essentially of the same type. Some can be psychic and aware in the interval, but most go into a coma and are reborn immediately or within a few years (Rajneesh, 1975b: 189). They may even be dying and entering the womb of a couple having intercourse simultaneously (Rajneesh, 1981c: 196).

(d) *The issue of time-sense.* The length of time passed between lives is not clearly measured in the memory of the disembodied. As a dream may seem like eight hours and be only five minutes, so when dead you would not know if your dream night had been lengthened to eight years. During the interval there is no clear awareness of the duration of time (Rajneesh, 1975b: 110).

(e) *The issue of movement.* The question as to whether the dead are stationary or in a movement condition does not apply. These depend upon a body and its sense of time and space, but these are absent. The boundaries of time and space, within which movement or non-movement is observed by the person, do not exist during that interval (Rajneesh, 1975b: 123-5).

(f) *The issue of space.* The dead are right here, so to speak. As in this room space is filled by different things that do not conflict, so with souls. This space can have an aroma of incense, it can have air waves of sound, it can have radio waves, and they do not interfere with each other; so the subtle matter of the mind can be right here (Rajneesh, 1975b: 129-30).

(g) *The issue of spirit-possession.* Since there is no movement on the part of disembodied souls, it is not right to say that souls will enter a body. This is a linguistic fallacy. It is better to say that somebody may behave in such a way that it will cause a soul to enter. Two types of living persons are in a state of deep receptivity to souls: those in great fear, and those in a deeply prayerful moment. In both, the soul contracts and vacates parts of bodily space. Souls that are in misery and agony enter empty bodily space within the fearful, who are like ditches that catch downward moving things. In the same way, higher souls enter the prayerful, induced by the many techniques of invocation and invitation existing in all religions (Rajneesh, 1975b: 129-30).

(h) *The issue of communication.* Communication is not possible for souls with each other in their dream state. It is like a roomful of sleeping people. It is only possible to communicate if a soul can enter someone's body. Then communication is possible between the entering soul and the soul existing in the body. So the Vedas were communicated to the *ṛṣis* via auditory experiences. Two souls can communicate with each other if they both take bodies. Ordinarily, communication requires body and brain. But people who have developed ESP and can communicate without the brain routing, may succeed, while bodiless, in establishing relationships with *preta* and *deva* spirits. Few have that capacity; however, information about the spiritual world has been given to us only by such souls (Rajneesh, 1975b: 139). It is like twenty drunks in a room. One, by practice, can stay conscious a bit longer and can tell us about the experiences of being drunk. The others could not tell because they become unconscious before knowing anything (Rajneesh, 1975b: 139). Those dying with no ESP capabilities cannot recognise, communicate with others, nor possess a living person's body. They die in a coma, deeply unconscious, awaiting a new birth. A kind of natural anaesthesia happens.

(i) *The issue of development*. These is no development of any type whatsoever during the interval state, even if it is a hundred years. You begin your new birth right from where you left off. All development is blocked; even the gods can't reach liberation while in heaven (Rajneesh, 1982c: 209). However, in the moments-of-death, when the body might be technically dead, but not subtly so, when one is semi-deceased in Tibetan terms, some development is possible. One can recognise all the high levels of one's being, and Tibetan *bardo* work is actually a training to create a dream sequence in this semi-deceased state, where one still has a body in a certain sense. Once past this state, when actual death comes, there is a gap until one begins re-entry into the world and into a body. In that gap ninety-nine per cent are simply unconscious (Rajneesh, 1977e: 9).

(j) *The issue of knowing your approaching death.* The hour before you fall asleep and the hour just after you awaken have a certain quality of "dream-smoke". This time is traditionally called the *sandhyākāla,* the twilight time. It is not necessarily at the junction of day and night. It is the hour before you go to sleep and the hour after you awaken, which might or might not coincide with the dawn and dusk. If you utilise that hour properly in meditation and prayer you can know exactly your time of death six months before your death because that quality which was previously coming for only one hour will remain continuous and steady through those last six months (Rajneesh, 1975b: 113). Also six months before death the eyes become "loose" and begin to roll up; one will not be able to see the tip of one's nose any longer. Nine months before death, Rajneesh also asserts, a sensitive person can feel a click in the abdominal region, in the *hara*. Further, a person able to make a *saṃyama*, an act of absorption, will be able to look at his *prārabdha karma*-room and see that only a little is left in one corner, so that this life cannot last much longer (Rajneesh, 1977e: 18).

To make the point about the absence of connection in Rajneesh's presentations between *karma* and the circumstances of rebirth, I shall quote one typical answer to a question that illustrates, at the same time, the inevitable connection in his thought between consciousness/awareness and rebirth.

A Sannyasin asked, "In my pre-sannyas period, my life with my family was unhappy. Why did I choose an unhappy family to be born into?" Probably the questioner had in mind some penalty for being evil in a past life implying a theory of *karma* of punishment for being naughty and the whole image of an infantile humanity implied in that.

The answer, however, ignores that and comes swiftly to an even more devastating point: "You didn't choose; if you could have you wouldn't have chosen this family. You moved into the womb robotlike" (Rajneesh, 1980c). This is saying, on the basis of our preceding classification of souls, that the questioner is in the average majority.

The answer continues:

> You died unconsciously and entered the womb unconsciously. Death is the condensed moment of life. If you have been unconscious in life, the moment of death will be a tremendously condensed unconsciousness. Millions of people are making love all over the world. Many wombs are ready. They are unconscious as you are unconscious. They don't know what is happening. They are making love out of unawareness, not out of awareness. If a couple who has exactly the same kind of unawareness that you have is making love, then immediately you will enter into that womb. That fits with you. You did not choose to be born into an unhappy family; you could not have done otherwise. You have done it many times, and beware or you will do it again. You can choose only when you are aware (Rajneesh, 1980c).

It should be clear, I think, that compared to this overwhelming emphasis on the connection between consciousness and rebirth, that Rajneesh's infrequent and unelaborated connections between *karma* and rebirth can only be said to be unimportant. This, surely, is a striking shift of emphasis from anything we find in classical times.

We should turn now to what may be a post-classical development about the rebirth of *bodhisattvas*. Rajneesh teaches about this in relation to his own present incarnation, and has something new to say, I think.

Rajneesh was not completely enlightened in his last life, he says, and came only with "near-about" full knowledge, that is, twelve of the fourteen steps *(guṇasthānas)* in the Jain reckoning completed. He had not skipped over any steps; he had intact the *tīrthaṅkara bandha*, or desire to be a teacher. Situated at step twelve there is only a curtain between you and reality, and you can lift it. Lifting it is the thirteenth step and going completely beyond is the fourteenth. After the twelve steps, he says, the last steps can be stretched out from one to three births. Here we have a Jain version of the Buddhist *bodhisattva* teaching being unfolded. If, however, you go beyond the curtain, at most one more birth is possible (Rajneesh, 1975b: 71).

If you stay on this side of the curtain, where no walls separate you from seeing reality, you have the possibility to set aside the last two steps. This certainly is the *Bodhisattva's* turning back.

Buddha and Mahāvīra did not use the opportunity to stop at stage twelve because their circumstances were different. They had many advanced students and one life was enough to teach them, and to entrust to special ones the left over work with the circle of disciples in question. And, says Rajneesh, in Mahāvīra's time, eight fully realised people were at work in the state of Bihar alone (Rajneesh, 1975b: 72). There were many "near-about" people to whom the work of finishing could be entrusted.

Now, however, in Rajneesh's case the situation is completely different. As always, full knowledge can be taught only to very advanced students, but now developed *sādhakas* are practically nil (Rajneesh, 1975b: 73). So it is very hard to find a birth to take. Suitable parents are a problem. Rajneesh says he was previously born about 700 years ago, reckoned by seeing in this life that one of his disciples with whom he was working in his last life had taken ten births. During the interval that a high level person has to wait to take births, which is getting to be a thousand years nowadays (Rajneesh, 1975b: 73), the persons with whom he was working get ten layers of new problems in ten lives (Rajneesh, 1975b: 73). There are more impediments needing cutting through. So future teachers will have to work for many births to complete the work. To make matters worse, the deteriorating times leave the would-be teacher bereft of adepts able to finish his work. So, before taking a birth, an illumined soul, or a *bodhisattva*, has two considerations to weigh: the fear that his labour may go to waste, and the fear that he may actually harm you. This last seems strange, but Rajneesh's argument goes like this: in one birth it is not possible to do much; a compassionate person needs to take something away from you and then give you something in replacement; you need to be able to receive what he gives in replacement for stability, otherwise you will be destabilised and disoriented. You will be in danger, not able to see what you could see before (Rajneesh, 1975b: 73). The *bodhisattva* will feel that taking away alone is not good, unless you are able to show something as well. This is just how a compassionate person is (Rajneesh, 1975b: 73). In this situation, Rajneesh feels it is good that he did not attain enlightenment (being stabbed three days before his fast was to end in enlightenment) because now he can still take yet another birth. "Whether I take another birth," he says, "depends on whether I feel it will be useful" (Rajneesh, 1975b: 73).

We hear much about the degenerate age of the *dharma* in Buddhist literature. Here, I think, we have the novel glimpse of a discussion of that as it affects the rebirth choices of *bodhisattvas* and those who attain enlightenment in this life. It is something new in the tradition and worth further investigation by scholars.

Conclusion

Indians who oppose Rajneesh, and those who don't, tend to agree that he is traditional in what he teaches, but untraditional in his methods and disciplines. As we have seen, he is not entirely traditional in his teachings, yet is substantially so. It may be well to try to specify more exactly where he is traditional and not.

On *karma*, Rajneesh's exposition is similar to tradition at many points: channel theory echoes much about *praṇāla* and *śrota* noted by J. Bruce Long (1980: 58) in the *Mahābhārata*. It also echoes Jain doctrine, where "*karma* is not in any sense considered to *impel* the soul; it functions, rather, to direct the motive force which is already present" (Jaini, 1980: 230). And Rajneesh certainly selects for emphasis a point found in the *Caraka Saṃhitā*, namely, that the root ill (*dosa*) in all deeds comes from their being done *prajñā-parādha*, that is, lacking in the wisdom and concentration associated with centred awareness (Weiss, 1980: 115). Finally, the heart of what Rajneesh has to say about *karma* management articulates with the Theravadin recognition, mentioned by James McDermott (1980: 180-1), that there is a class of deeds which leads to neither dark, light or mixed results, but which, rather, consumes past *karma*, because it is non-purposive action, choicelessness, or selflessness. These are the principal elements played up in his discussion of *karma*, always stressing that it can be mastered by awareness, and always downplaying any mastering of it by the gradual paths of duty, conformity to codes, and so on. If we ask what is common to emphasising consciousness and de-emphasising morality, the answer is consistency with the *sādhana* of mindfulness and awareness, what Rajneesh call the *via negativa*. Of this, more later.

On rebirth, we hear echoes of the Jain view of *samaya*, that the soul moves into another body in a single instant after death, as discussed by Padmanabh S. Jaini (1980: 221). On the other hand, he also accepts an interval-state of a being (*antarābhava*) similar to the *Vaibāṣika* theory of the *gandharva/gandhabba* studied by both McDermott and Jaini (McDermott, 1980: 171). Apparently, Rajneesh tries to reconcile these two seemingly contradictory positions by saying that between embodiments the time-sense is unclear and so people with any memory of the interval will give conflicting recollections of it, and by saying that some persons do, in fact, go into immediate rebirth and others not, depending upon variables of ability to stay aware. This ability harkens back, I think, to the Jain teaching on *upayoga*, or scale of awareness doctrine, noted by P.S. Jaini (1980: 233).

Throughout this essay I have been arguing that it is Rajneesh's choice of spiritual path more than his Jain background that determines his doctrine. Now it may be the time to contrast the two paths that he sees in order to make this point clear. Rajneesh contrasts a *via positiva* with a *via negativa* and endorses the latter. The awareness path is the *via negativa*, and some may call it non-traditional merely because it is non-Hindu. It is not non-Indian except in its expressive, cathartic preamble.

The awareness path is also called the path of surrender, and the path of the let-go. It is expressive, and contrasts with the path of striving, of the warrior, of concentration, of control, of holding on, of struggle and fighting to advance. It is de-focal (takes no one object of meditation in order to focus on it) and flowing. It has no preferences. But, the warrior path is the *via affirmativa* because it says yes to society, family, morality, cultivation of character. It is a training, a "yang" path; you have much to do in the way of exercises, *ascesis*. You advance gradually. There is a technology and clearly defined steps and stages of progress. It is technique-centered and so requires time to prepare, learn, improve. It is a path that can be explained, and is quite orderly and scientific. It begins with morality and moves to awareness. It respects scriptures as authorities, legitimates system-roles and gives them a spiritual direction; its saints tend to be advisors to the religious and political powers-that-be. Usually it is a path of prayer, devotion, God. It is the way of mainstream Christianity, Hinduism, Judaism, Islam. It affirms positive values in society, affirms doing, rising step by step, effort (Rajneesh, 1979f: 231-6). It articulates with creating good *karma*.

The *via negativa*, of course, is the opposite at every point. This is what Rajneesh mostly teaches and this determines what he says about *karma* and rebirth, and what he omits or de-emphasises, too. This path is the path of the rebels like Lao Tzu, Bodhidharma, Nāgārjuna, Buddha, Krishnamurti, and so on. It simply witnesses the body and mind, without particular effort to change things. It is waiting, not seeking. It is "yin" receptivity, watching. "It is where you have exactly nothing to do" (Rajneesh, 1979f: 232). So it is a mysterious path, no technology, no steps, no clear stages and explanations. It doesn't care much for the opinions of society, of ordinary ego-mind, scriptures, traditions, social leaders. It is the way of the Tantric adept, of the Baul mystic, of the Taoists; meditation not action (Rajneesh, 1979f: 232).

And, of course, *karma* theory has to do with action and the effects of action and the use of action to improve. To the path of choicelessness, the idea of improving implies preference, and hence, is the antithesis of choicelessness. It is along these lines, I think, that we must look if we want to interpret why he skips over developing good *karma* and good habits so lightly. But, even here, Rajneesh's mode of discourse is not without precedent in India.

In yet other ways, Rajneesh seems traditionally Indian. For example, J. Bruce Long (1980: 60) in his study of the *Mokṣadharmaparvan* portion of the *Mahābhārata* notes that the work "puts the spotlight on the nature of the path to enlightenment." And aspects of the doctrines of *karma* and rebirth are developed "rather curiously" (Long, 1980: 60). They function only as a springboard to the more elaborate articulation of the nature of liberation and ways of achieving it. In particular it deals with the cancelling and creating of *karmic* debts "until the embodied self achieves a true knowledge of the duties required by that contemplation which leads to liberation" (Long, 1980: 60). Rajneesh obviously shares the text's concern for enlightenment. And the text seems to view doing good (building good habits) only as a means for coming to the real understanding that is needed on how to manage *karma,* namely what one comes to know in and through contemplation. Rajneesh's presentation differs from that of the *Mahābhārata* only by telling you that the preliminaries of good work are just that, and that the preliminaries are not really needed. He moves directly in his discussion to the essential subject of contemplation. Again, this may be non-Hindu, but it is not on that account non-Indian.

Let me try to summarise and position Rajneesh in the larger history of *karma* and rebirth thought. In classical times, tribal ideas of a routine rebirth were changed. They were linked to the performance of good deeds as socially defined by the great tradition that was replacing, or supplementing, the little traditions. Individual ethics began to supersede tribal *mores* and the calculations of omens, divination, and augury as guides to the correct actions that would please the spirits. Better actions resulted in a better birth in the social system, and improving your *karma* and your rebirth was linked to doing your duties in the social structure. Then, with the rise of the Buddhist *saṅgha, karma*-attenuation by contemplation apart from roles and duties in the society appeared. The individual withdrew from society; he managed his reconstruction his way, while society continued to enjoin the doing of good deeds upon its members. The *saṅgha* drew apart, but did not seek to assimilate the society to itself, nor to abolish society's strategem. Society and *saṅgha* ran in two parallel lines, inter-mixed to some extent, to be sure. With Rajneesh we see, I think, an offensive from the side of the *saṅgha* against the social tyranny of "the good", as seen in his position on cultivation of character. It is as if times have changed in two ways: society is more repressive to the point of crippling spiritual growth; and the individual is more mature as a separate ego. Being a mature ego, the individual, although less spiritual than the giants of the past, is ready to assume responsibility for his spiritual growth basically free of the domination of the super-ego. The super-ego may have been appropriate in the past, but modern man finds it toxic now. Whether this is in fact true or not, I shall not argue. Rather, my point is that interpreting the significance of Rajneesh's position on *karma* and rebirth seems to require the conclusion that he thinks it is true.

(1986)

Chapter Four

The Narcissistic Guru: A Profile of Bhagwan Shree Rajneesh

RONALD O. CLARKE

Bhagwan Shree Rajneesh, the flamboyant and controversial Indian Guru who was deported from the United States in late 1985 immediately upon conviction on two counts of immigration fraud, claims that writing a biography about him—or, for that matter, a psychological profile—is impossible. The reason, he says, is that "he" is no longer there. He alleges that he (the pronoun is inescapable in linguistic communication) is an enlightened spiritual master, a "living Buddha", one who has permanently dissolved the ego with all its worldly desires and attachments. He now dwells, he says, in a state of continuous and undefiled awareness, bliss, freedom, and compassion; but this "he" is not a "self", not an individual person, but a presence, an emptiness, inextricably one with the whole of things (Rajneesh, 1977a: 13; Rajneesh, 1980b: 120). There are no empirical or conceptual mechanisms for grasping or describing such a state of being, he insists. Hence, any attempt to do an "ego-biography" or psychological profile of him is bound to be superficial (Rajneesh, 1985a: 499).

The present study is undeterred by Rajneesh's disclaimer. In it I shall indicate how the empirical and conceptual tools of contemporary psychiatry and clinical psychology provide a diagnostic framework that lends intelligibility to this self-avowed holy man's otherwise enigmatic and bizarre behaviour. Specifically, I endeavour to demonstrate that Rajneesh's claim that he has permanently dissolved the ego and all worldly desires and attachments is the product of a delusional system associated with a narcissistic personality disorder.

The American Psychiatric Association's *Diagnostic and Statistical Manual of Mental Disorders* (hereafter referred to as *DSM*) describes the essential features of the narcissistic personality disorder as:

> a grandiose sense of self-importance or uniqueness; preoccupation with fantasies of unlimited success; exhibitionistic need for constant attention and admiration; characteristic responses to threats to self-esteem; and characteristic disturbances in interpersonal relationships, such as feelings of entitlement, interpersonal exploitiveness, relationships that alternate between extremes of overidealisation and devaluation, and lack of empathy (*DSM*, 351).

A descriptive analysis illustrating how these criteria apply to Rajneesh should prove helpful not only in understanding this particular Guru; it may also provide clues that are useful in deciphering the personality and behaviour of other charismatic religious leaders of both the East and West who are currently competing in the spiritual supermarket. To what extent, for example, are such features also found in a Jim Bakker, Mahareshi Mahesh Yogi, Jimmy Swaggart, J. Z. Knight, Pat Roberston, Sun Myung Moon, or, for that matter, in the local pastor of St. John's-by-the-Gas-Station? Perhaps most of all, this essay will offer a graphic example of how the role of the spiritual Guru can provide both a refuge and a vehicle for certain narcissists who combine mystical proclivities with cleverness and imagination, boldness, and a flair for showmanship.

Grandiose Sense of Self-importance or Uniqueness

DSM indicates that one who suffers from a narcissistic personality disorder possesses an exaggerated sense of self-importance that tends to be expressed in terms of extreme self-centredness and self-absorption complemented by an unrealistic overestimate of one's abilities and achievements (*DSM,* 315). Theodore Millon stresses that the "narcissistic" label connotes more than mere egocentricity, which all humans possess to a degree. "Narcissism signifies, more particularly, that the individual overvalues his personal worth, directs his affections toward himself, rather than others, and expects that they will recognise and cater to the high esteem in which he holds himself.... His self-image is that of a superior person, someone 'extra-special', entitled to unusual rights and privileges....Anyone who fails to respect him is viewed with contempt and scorn" (Millon, 1969: 261f).

Bhagwan Shree Rajneesh's sense of self-importance and uniqueness seems to possess no limits. Historians of religion inform us that, in many cases, the honorific titles associated with several of the founders of world religions ("Buddha", "Mahāvīra", "Christ", etc.) were assigned to them by their zealous devotees, often after their death. This is not true for Rajneesh. He has deliberately assumed the title "Bhagwan," meaning "the blessed one"—one who is fortunate enough to recognise his own divine being, one who is fully enlightened, who has no unfulfilled desire or longing, and who resides in a state of ultimate and permanent biss (Rajneesh, 1980b: 119f). In his earlier discourses in Bombay and Poona, he explicitly aligned himself with all the "Buddhas" (enlightened masters) of previous religious traditions (Gautama, Mahāvîra, Lao Tzu, Bodhidharma, Kabir, Jesus, Muhammad, etc.). More recently, however, mere alignment with these spiritual virtuosos of the past has ceased to satisfy his escalating desire for personal grandeur and uniqueness. He now proclaims his superiority to all previous Buddhas and holy men. For example, he asserts: "Jesus can be found again very easily... . But to find a man like me—who has travelled thousands of ways, in thousands of lives, and has gathered the fragrance of millions of flowers like a honeybee—is difficult" (Rajneesh, 1985a: 45). Also, in referring to his alleged enlightenment during one phase of his career as a Guru, he claimed: "I myself have come to where you cannot go any higher... a moment of spiritual growth which is untranscendable" (Rajneesh, 1985a: 197). But, in a 1986 discourse, he asserts that he has progressed *beyond* enlightenment, that he has transcended the "untranscendable", a self-discovery that, he claims, makes him "a milestone in the history of man's growth and consciousness" (*Rajneesh: The Newspaper* 1986, 1:7, 10).

Rajneesh's latest claim to spiritual pre-eminence has occurred in connection with a vision allegedly experienced by a Bombay disciple, Swami Govind Siddharth. In Siddharth's vision, Lord Maitreya, the great Coming-Buddha, whose incarnation to inaugurate a new age is awaited by millions of Theravadan and Mahāyāna Buddhists, appears and announces that he is merging his "third body" with Rajneesh's energy, "without disturbing His (Rajneesh's) individuality". Referring to Rajneesh, Maitreya purportedly affirms: "In Him all enlightenments—past, present and future have become alive and active; a unique event that has not happened before nor will happen again....From my third body, I address him as 'Bhagwan,' but from now onwards He will not be only 'Bhagwan Rajneesh' but He will be 'Bhagwan Rajneesh, the Buddha, Lord Maitreya..." (*Rajneesh: The Newspaper* 1986, 1:7, 1). Rajneesh's response to Siddharth's vision is most revealing: he acknowledged the vision's content to be "absolute reality" and declared that the merging of souls would not affect his own individuality, nor keep him from "criticising 'the old Buddha' [presumably Gautama] whenever his teachings are not right for the present and the future". It hardly comes as a surprise to learn that a few days later, Rajneesh declared that Siddharth had become "enlightened" (*Rajneesh: The Newspaper* 1986, 1:7, 1).

On the basis of his immediate mystical experience, Rajneesh claims possession of absolute and total spiritual truth. "Truth, to me," he says, "has not been a fragment... . Truth has revealed itself to me as a total organic unity" (Rajneesh, 1986b, 696). Believing this, he feels that he has nothing to learn from other spiritual leaders, of whom he is largely contemptuous. Here, for example, is how he refused one invitation by a group of religious leaders to engage in a dialogue: "What dialogue can they have with me? If they know, there is no need to come here. If they do not know, then it is going to be a monologue. I will speak and they will have to listen. A dialogue is not possible... . I say I know. So with me there is only one possibility—a monologue" (Rajneesh, 1985b: 480).

Fantasies of Unlimited Success

According to *DSM*, the narcissistic disorder involves proneness toward fantasies involving "unrealistic goals that may include achieving unlimited ability, power, wealth, brilliance, beauty, or ideal love" (*DSM*, 315). Millon refers to this narcissistic trait as "cognitive expansiveness". He explains: "Narcissistic individuals... place few limits upon their fantasies and rationalisations; their imagination runs free of the constraints of reality or the views of others. They exaggerate their powers, freely transform failures into successes, construct lengthy and intricate rationalisations to inflate their self-worth, justify what they feel is their due and depreciate those who refuse to accept or enhance their self-image" (Millon, 1969: 262).

Rajneesh's reliance on imagination and fantasy to serve his inflated ego-needs encompasses the past as well as the present and future. For example, he claims to have spent a previous incarnation in the Himālayas seven hundred years ago as a spiritual master of a mystic school of disciples representing many religious traditions. Rajneesh's biographer and devotee, Vasant Joshi, provides the following details:

> The Master lived to be one hundred six years old. Prior to his death he entered into a twenty-one day fast that would have brought him to enlightenment when finished. But he had the option of taking one more birth before finally disappearing in the eternal. He looked at his family of disciples; there were many who were still on their way, needing help. He also saw the great potential for bringing synthesis between East and West, body and soul, materialism and spiritualism. He saw the possibility of creating a new man—a man of the future totally discontinuous with the past. He, who had come so

> close to the ultimate achievement (i.e., enlightenment) for which he had worked so hard for so many lives, decided to come back again into a human body. Out of pure love and compassion he promised his disciples that he would return and share his truth with them and bring their consciousness to a state of awakening (Joshi, 1982: 15).

Aside from the questionable belief in reincarnation that is presupposed in this "reminiscence", and the fact that the tale bears the familiar stamp of the *Bodhisattva* ideal of Mahāyāna Buddhism, its veracity is suspect on at least two additional grounds. First, it is highly implausible—and curiously anachronistic—that issues such as an East-West synthesis and a creation of a new man "totally discontinuous with the past" would have entered the minds of members of a remote mystic school, say in Nepal or Tibet, seven hundred years ago. And second, the idea of a yet-to-be-enlightened individual serving as master of a mystic school is incongruous with Rajneesh's own standard that a "true master" is one who is already enlightened.

Turning to his present life, Rajneesh clearly considers himself to be a man of world-historical significance. He has conceived his spiritual mission to be one of world transformation. His role, he has declared repeatedly, is that of a "midwife" assisting in the birth of a "New Man" on the planet (Rajneesh, 1984: 192). He regards his disciples ("sannyasins") as "the first rays" of the "New Man" (Rajneesh, 1981b: 48), and his experimental commune in Central Oregon was to have served as a "Buddhafield" (energy field) wherein the "New Man" would be born (Rajneesh, 1984: 192). The Guru frequently impressed upon his followers the world-historical significance of his mission in words like the following: "...you are participating in something of eternal value—a great experiment upon which the whole future of humanity depends" (Rajneesh, 1980b: 292). Such a declaration was often accompanied by an apocalyptic prediction that failure to achieve a world transformation of consciousness (to create a "New Man") within the next two or three decades would inevitably result in a nuclear holocaust ("World War III").

The collapse of his Oregon communal experiment and his conviction of immigration fraud and subsequent deportation have failed to dampen his sense of world-historical significance. During a "world tour" in 1986, wherein he was denied access to various European and Latin American nations, Rajneesh relied on fantasy to recast the frustrating situation in the most favourable light: "...it has never happened in history that the whole world should be against a single man" (*Rajneesh: The Newspaper* 1986, 1:7, 1). Or again: "It seems that no government will allow me in any country. It is a good sign. It means that they have started to recognise me... . So this is something to rejoice about, that I may be the first man in the whole of history who is being persecuted around the world. But this is not bad news, it is good news. It means I have threatened all the powers of the world—religious, political, social. A single man single-handedly has been able to prove the impotency and poverty of all great powers, of great theologians, of great organised religions. What more reward can I receive?" (*Rajneesh: The Newspaper* 1986, 1:1, 9). And in Bombay, in August 1986, Rajneesh sounds a similar note of self-grandeur, this time in conjunction with the publication of a new volume of his discourses: "It is not only the birth of a new book, it is also the declaration of a new phase. Today, this moment: 7 p.m., Saturday, the 16th of August of the year 1986—one day this moment will be remembered as a historical moment" (*Rajneesh: The Newspaper* 1986, 1:10, 1).

In addition to indicating Rajneesh's impermeable sense of world-historical importance, these quotes also reveal his narcissistic penchant for transforming failures into successes via the mechanisms of fantasy, repression, rationalisation, and projection (Millon, 1969; 262, 264). Several additional examples are worth citing. One of Rajneesh's Sannyasins reports the following incident immediately after the Guru's deportation from the United States: "Upon arrival at New Delhi Airport, Bhagwan recounted the story of His abuse and torture in American jails and said it had not affected Him in the least: 'I was simply a witness to all this idiotic fascist strategy... . I have come a winner. This proves that a single man of innocence is more powerful than any nuclear power'" (*Rajneesh: The Newspaper* 1986, 1:1, 3). Later in the same report, the Sannyasin says that Rajneesh "told his Sannyasins that with the destruction of Rajneeshpuram (the Oregon commune) the commune has become indestructible and has spread all over the world."

In yet a different context, the Guru justifies the commune's failures by resorting to a "necessary-phase" mode of rationalisation. In what surely was a moment of supreme and total narcissistic self-absorption, he stated: "We had to pass through that phase. And we have passed through it without any damage, because *unless I am damaged, nothing is damaged*" (*Rajneesh: The newspaper* 1986, 1:1, 16—emphasis added). Several thousand Sannyasins, who were deeply traumatised and psychologically wounded by the commune's sudden collapse, and many of whom lost all their worldly possessions in the process, must have found this remark by their "compassionate buddha" difficult to digest.

Finally, the following, uttered shortly after his expulsion from Crete during his "world tour", illustrates not only his reliance on empty braggadocio, but also his customary tendency to view himself as dualistically pitted in a contest against regnant powers of evil, powers that he is perennially on the threshold of subduing in his subjective world of fantasy: "I am ready for a public contest with Reagan. I will be back with a commune in the U.S.A. in five years, but it won't be in a desert. It will be in Washington, D.C." (*Rajneesh: The Newspaper* 1986, 1:1, 11). A more extreme example is found in his response to a reporter during a news conference held during the time when the Oregon commune was beginning to disintegrate. Referring to government officials who were investigating the allegations of criminal activity in the commune, Rajneesh remarked:

> They cannot do any harm to this commune. My people are around the earth and everywhere there will be protests if any harm is being done. No American embassy all over the world will be left intact. I know also how to deal with these idiots. Our people can also hijack American planes if worst comes to worst. Then no American agency in any country can function. I have enough Sannyasins everywhere. So don't be worried about power. No need to be worried. (*The Rajneesh Times* 1985, 4.5, A5).

Having, no doubt, been advised subsequently of the potential grave consequences of this impetuous outburst, he quickly attempted to make amends by declaring that it was "just a joke" (*The Rajneesh Times* 1985, 4:6, B1), an escape mechanism frequently employed by Rajneesh when he has backed himself into a corner.

Such narcissistic coping mechanisms, however, do not afford total shelter from the harsh reality of failure with its attendant feelings of rage and frustration, not even for one so imaginatively versatile as Rajneesh. Witness the narcissistic rage and arrogant presumption only thinly veiled in the following pronouncement, issued after repeated dismissals from various nations during his "world tour": "I have called you simply to say that I am utterly disappointed, disillusioned... I will (henceforth) live only for those people who are individually interested in evolving; as a humanity there is no hope.... All hope that some day man will become human seems to be a faraway utopia..... I have been against the Third World War, but with great pain, I have to tell you that perhaps the Third World War is needed. This humanity is so rotten that it should be destroyed; at least, the world should be cleansed of ugly human beings. My effort from today will be just to work for those few individuals who want to grow into meditation, into peace, into silence. And I drop all hope for this humanity and all hope for this planet. It is in ugly hands, and it is impossible to change because they have all the powers" (*Rajneesh: The Newspaper* 1986, 1:7, 12). The latent frustration (and envy) surfaced publicly a second time when he verbally attacked several of his leading therapist Sannyasins during a May 1, 1986, discourse delivered in Uruguay. He accused these therapists, who had been so singularly devoted to him, and who had played such a vital role in attracting Westerners to his movement of betraying him. They "had no spirituality"; they had "failed in the West", having joined the movement merely "to gain clients", he charged. His inability to find a place in the world to establish a mystery school provided his therapists an opportunity "to exploit the situation", he said. They "started feeling they had become kind of Gurus.... They are not even mentioning my name", he lamented (*Rajneesh: The Newspaper* 1986, 1:3, 3). This totally unexpected attack on those who had served Rajneesh so faithfully sent shock waves through his constituency around the world; and it provoked a flood of rebuttals, not only from the therapists themselves, but also from many rank-and-file Sannyasins. Some typical rejoinders: "Rajneesh's lies have hurt people"; "Your statement felt to me like the words of an old lover who wants to stay in control"; "Whenever Bhagwan hits he has never had much respect for the facts. He just hits... ", (*Rajneesh: The Newspaper* 1986, 1:4, 3f.).

Need for Constant Attention and Admiration

Referring to narcissism, *DSM* states: "Individuals with this disorder are constantly seeking admiration and attention, and are more concerned with appearances than with substance" (*DSM*, 316). British writer Sally Belfrage has perhaps most poignantly summarised Rajneesh's insatiable need for attention and adulation. Here is her reaction based upon attending several of his discourses at the Poona Ashram:

> He is on a chair on a platform; we are on the floor. We never stand when he stands; we do not even know how tall he is ... . He is indulged in every way. Being the object of the passionate love of many imaginative people, the quality of indulgence is amazing. He is capable of accepting that love; that is his supreme difference. Most people can't handle unqualified adoration, even from only one other person, believing themselves unworthy of it. *He believes himself worthy of it* (Belfrage, 1981: 222—emphasis in original).

My own impression, resulting from several visits to the Oregon commune, echoes Belfrage's. Rajneesh thoroughly delights in being the sole focus of attention of his thousands of adoring devotees. Being surrounded by a horde of singing, chanting, dancing disciples celebrating one's very presence must be enormously intoxicating to the ego. And Rajneesh obviously thrives on it. Furthermore, nothing must be allowed to stand in the way of total attention to the Guru. He will tolerate no distractions. For example, people were not even allowed to cough during discourses in Poona and Rajneeshpuram.

A powerful mechanism employed by Rajneesh to guarantee that he remained the constant centre of attention among his devotees was the ubiquitious-photo technique. Until the time of the Oregon commune's dissolution, his disciples were required to wear his picture in the locket attached to their *mālās*—the 108-bead necklace they wore around their necks. Moreover, his portrait dominates virtually everything associated with the movement. Every volume of his published discourses displays his picture on the cover. His portrait is prominently featured on virtually every page of every edition of Rajneesh newspapers. And often such newspapers have included multi-page special sections that were exclusively photographs of the Guru. Finally, his picture was displayed everywhere throughout the Oregon commune. Once while shopping at the commune bookstore for postcards depicting the people and physical environment of Rajneeshpuram, I discovered that all but two cards out of an ample assortment were portraits of the Guru. These observations lend plausibility to Hugh Milne's contention that Rajneesh once stipulated at Poona that only pictures of himself were to be used on the covers of the movement's publications, and that "the only full page photographs that were to appear were those of Rajneesh himself. No ordinary disciple could take up more than a third of a page" (Milne, 1986: 122).

Milne, a former personal bodyguard of Rajneesh and now a defector from the movement, and others, have noted the Guru's addiction to publicity (Milne, 1986: 120, 164f). Much of his bizarre behaviour, including his outrageous verbal attacks on others, appears to be motivated to a large extent by his desire to attract media attention (Callister, Long, and Zeitz, 1985: 4, 6). Whether publicity proved favourable or unfavourable was not of great concern to Rajneesh. Milne quotes him on this point as follows:

> Now it does not matter whether I am famous or notorious. I do not care whether people see me as Buddha or as Rasputin. Few people will think of me as Buddha, and the majority will probably regard me as Rasputin. That's beautiful. One thing I am certainly interested in is that everybody should think *something* about me (Milne, 1986: 164—emphasis in original).

Rajneesh has admitted openly that the purchase of ninety-odd Rolls Royces by the commune was, in part, a device to acquire media attention. Milne plausibly contends that the Guru needed them also as reassurance of his disciples' adulation (Milne, 1986: 232). One curious incident clearly demonstrates how ultrasensitive Rajneesh has been about the retention of his followers' devotion. On September 26, 1985, shortly after Ma Anand Sheela's abrupt departure from the Oregon commune, Rajneesh issued a "surprise announcement" that his disciples no longer were required to dress in "sunrise colours" or wear the *mālā* with his portrait. Apparently his disciples responded to the announcement with excessive alacrity, for, during a discourse a few days later, he told them that they had hurt him by being so enthusiastic about abandoning their red clothes and *mālās*. "You have been clapping because I have dropped red clothes, *mālās*, and when you clap you don't know how much it hurts me" (*The Rajneesh Times*, 1985, 4:7, A-1). (The reader will recall that, by Rajneesh's own definition, an enlightened master supposedly has transcended all mundane feelings and attachments.) The

Guru proceeded to suggest that those who had eagerly abandoned their red clothes were hypocrites. Apparently unable to resist indulging in an intimidating reprisal, he then announced the withdrawal of his "Buddhafield" (a spiritual energy allegedly radiating from the Guru's being that enhances his disciples' spiritual growth). From that moment on, he stated, if his disciples wished to become enlightened, they were on their own. They could no longer depend on his spiritual energy for support. "Now clap as loudly as you can. Clap!" he spitefully concluded (*The Rajneesh Times,* 1985, 4:7, A1). During the following day's discourse, however, Rajneesh reassured his sannyasins that he could not withdraw the Buddhafield "because he loved them so much." "I just said it to shock you," he confessed.

Disturbances in Interpersonal Relationships

Those who suffer from a narcissistic personality disorder invariably experience disturbances in interpersonal relationships such as: entitlement ("expectations of special favours without assuming reciprocal responsibilities"); lack of empathy; interpersonal exploitiveness; and lack of sustained, positive regard in relations with other (*DSM,* 316).

Entitlement: The narcissist usually considers himself "exempt from the responsibilities that govern and give order to societal living. Others are expected to submerge their desires in favour of the narcissist's comfort and welfare; he operates on the fantastic assumption that *his* mere desire is justification enough for possessing whatever he seeks. Thus his lofty disdainfulness is matched by his exploitiveness, his assumption that he is entitled to be served and to have his wishes to take precedence over others, without expending a shred of genuine effort to merit such favour. In short, he possesses illusions of an inherent superior self-worth, and moves through life with the belief that it is his inalienable right to receive special considerations" (Millon, 1969, 261—emphasis in original).

Implicit at the core of Rajneesh's self-concept is his assumption that *his very presence on Earth*—the result of his decision to accept a final earthly embodiment—constitutes a great gift of existence to the human species. The mere fact of his being here is, in itself, sufficient justification for humans to rejoice and bestow upon him all the amenities, comforts, and loving devotion imaginable. This "rich man's guru" makes no apology for the extravagant luxuries and wealth heaped upon him by his disciples. Rather, he often boasts about living off the largesse of others: "Neither has anybody else been this way, with this style: having nothing and living as if you own the whole universe" (Rajneesh, 1985a: 685).

Millon says that the narcissist's mere desire "is justification enough for possessing whatever he seeks" (Millon, 1969: 261). Rajneesh expresses a similar attitude: "I have never asked anybody whether I am right or wrong. Wrong or right, if I want to do it, I want to do it and I will make it right.... I have never allowed anyone to interfere with me" (Rajneesh, 1985a: 156). "Right and wrong have never been my consideration. What I happen to like is right...". Rajneesh seems to lack any genuine sense of social reciprocity. As he has put it, "You will have to cope with me, there is no other way. I never coped with anybody, so I don't know how to..." (Rajneesh, 1985a: 359). He likens social compromise—the *sine qua non* of social coexistence—as "poison" (Rajneesh, 1975b: 229). "I am not here to compromise—" he exclaims, "not an iota of compromise" (Rajneesh, 1985a: 622).

Rajneesh's grandiose sense of entitlement is perhaps most dramatically revealed through his role as social critic and iconoclast. His persistent attacks on all external authority (politicians, priests, "the Polack Pope," etc.) are caricature-laden, intemperate, and, as Frances Fitzgerald has said, "mean-spirited" (Fitzgerald, 1986: 302). It has been his common practice, both in word and deed, to provoke hostility and opposition deliberately. "I know the art of how to make enemies," he candidly has admitted (Rajneesh, 1985a: 567). His wholesale assaults on the beliefs, values, and character of all "outsiders" appear designed to nourish an "us-them" syndrome and paranoia among his followers, and thereby to strengthen the solidarity of his movement. Despite such expressions of alienation and hostility toward the outside world, Rajneesh and his followers have self-righteously assumed that they are fully entitled to be treated as a socially legitimate and credible movement. Any individual or group who responds otherwise Rajneesh has maligned as "fascist" or "bigoted". In short, he believes that he is entitled to all the rights and privileges afforded by the larger body politic, but can remain exempt from its attendant responsibilities and obligations. Evidence that has emerged in conjunction with his 1985 conviction of immigration fraud clearly suggests that Rajneesh considers himself to be above and beyond the law, entitled to its protection and other benefits but free to bend or violate it whenever it becomes an inconvenience or a hindrance to his purposes.

Interpersonal exploitiveness: Narcissists commonly seek to take advantage of others in order to indulge their desires for self-aggrandisement. Such attempts are carried out with disregard for the personal integrity and rights of others (*DSM*, 316). Whether Bhagwan Shree Rajneesh is truly an enlightened spiritual master is open to dispute. But it is beyond question that he is a "master" at manipulating and exploiting other people. A pattern of exploitation of others for self-aggrandisement persists throughout his life history. The evidence is legion. Here I shall cite only a few typical examples.

I have already referred to the exploitive episode wherein Rajneesh traumatised his Sannyasins during the closing days of the communal experiment by theatening to withdraw his "Buddhafield." According to Kate Strelley, a former Sannyasin who served as personal secretary to Ma Anand Sheela in the Poona Ashram, Rajneesh resorted to a similar form of "emotional blackmail" on several earlier occasions by threatening to "leave his body" if his disciples failed to love him enough (Strelley, 1987: 296, 332).

During a morning discourse that I attended while visiting the Oregon commune in July 1985, Rajneesh made a startling confession of a form of manipulation in which he had been engaged through the years in Bombay and Poona. During that period, he had delivered hundreds of discourses celebrating and interpreting the teachings and spiritual contributions of the world's great mystics (Gautama, Lao-Tzu, Bodhidharma, Kabir, Mahāvīra, Patañjali, the Upanisadic writers, Jesus, Muhammad, Pythagoras, etc.). Although he criticised them mildly on occasion, he basically honoured them and stressed the congruence between their work and his own. However, in the discourse I attended in 1985, Rajneesh attacked many of these mystics in the most deprecating terms. He then confessed that his earlier favourable interpretations were simply "a device to hook people" into becoming his followers. Here is how he rationalised such manipulation in a discourse prior to my visit:

> To speak on Mahāvīra was necessary because without that it was impossible to get any Jainas to hear me. And with Mahāvīra I do not agree on all points. In fact my disagreement is on more points than my agreement. So I had to do a strange job. I

> had to choose those points on which I can agree; and not talk at all about those points which I will be absolutely against. And even on the points on which I have a certain agreement, I had to manage another thing: that was to give new meanings to their meaning... . If this whole crowd of Jesus, Mahāvīra, Buddha, Lao Tzu, Chuang Tzu somewhere meets me they will all be mad at me because I have made them say things they would never have dreamed of. They could not. Sometimes I have even put meanings into their words which go basically against them (Rajneesh, 1985b, 1.8).

Another manipulative technique that Rajneesh employs is the "double message". On the one hand, he has said repeatedly that his disciples' "surrender" to him does not mean that they must imitate him or simply become his robots. Surrendering to him is only a device to conquer the ego, he has maintained. On the other hand, he has also instructed his disciples to *surrender totally* (Rajneesh, 1975a: 47, 75, 284 f.), and he has indicated his willingness to accept responsibility for their well-being and spiritual growth (Rajneesh, 1977a: 134). And, at least on one occasion, he referred to an almost classic case of masochistic surrender on the part of one of his disciples as "beautiful" (Rajneesh, 1985a: 397-400). Furthermore, whatever the nature of Rajneesh's rhetoric regarding surrender, the therapy groups and life-as-a-whole at Poona, says Strelley, were, in fact, geared toward developing absolute trust in Rajneesh and total obedience and surrender to his authority (Strelley, 1987, 82). The message shifted again during the period preceding the collapse of the Oregon commune. In the discourses I attended in July 1985, the Guru stressed several times that he was not responsible for his disciples' fate. And, as the commune began rapidly to unravel a couple of months later, he sounded the same theme in an interview with *Newsweek* reporter Pam Abrahamson: "I don't feel any responsibility about anybody." Referring to his Sannyasins, who, by this time, were thoroughly traumatised by what was occurring at "the Ranch," he stated: "They are all mature people and they have their own responsibility. They are not dependent on me" (*The Rajneesh Times*, 1985, 4:7, A4).

Rajneesh attempts to justify the more blatant manipulations of his disciples by claiming that such practices are simply "devices" to awaken them from their spiritual slumber and thereby enhance their development of consciousness. In resorting to such techniques, he says, he is following a precedent established by George Gurdjieff, a Russian-born, early twentieth-century shamanic leader noted for his despotic and exploitive spiritual growth techniques. (It is worth noting here in passing that Rajneesh uses the concept "device" not only to justify his manipulative behaviour *vis-à-vis* his followers but also as a rationalisation for whatever suffering the latter are forced to endure as a result of his errant leadership. The catastrophic collapse of the Oregon commune, for example, was one such "device". Here it becomes readily apparent that Rajneesh's reliance upon this rationalisation is in itself another technique of manipulation.)

Lack of empathy and sensitivity toward others: Rajneesh's lack of empathy and concern for the feelings of others has already been sufficiently documented in the preceding section as well as earlier. (Where, for example, could one find a more glaring illustration of insensitivity than his aforementioned remark "Unless I am damaged, nothing is damaged"?) Additional evidence will be cited in later portions of this paper.

As previously indicated, Rajneesh appears to take delight in generating anger, confusion, and fear in others by deliberately provoking controversy. His contempt for all efforts to ameliorate the plight of the world's poor and oppressed is widely recognised. Furthermore, the condemnation and consignment of the "whole-of-humanity" to nuclear destruction because it rejects his message does not appear to be an act of a compassionate man. In short, his claim to possess universal and unconditional love and compassion for others is incongruent with his attitudes and behaviour. Whatever compassion for others he is capable of experiencing appears to be restricted to those who serve his purposes and affirm his sense of superior worth.

Lack of sustained, positive regard for others: One of the most striking characteristics of Rajneesh's life is that it has been singularly devoid of intimate friendship and interpersonal attachments. Rajneesh is a "loner", a man of near-total aloofness and aloneness. His refusal to become emotionally involved with others apparently stems from his traumatic experience at the age of seven, when his maternal grandfather died. He frequently refers to this sudden and painful loss as a pivotal event in his life, one that has, he says, "determined my whole course of life" (Rajneesh, 1985a: 161f.). Here is Rajneesh's description of the effect the experience had upon him: "Aloneness became my nature. His death freed me forever from all relationships. His death became for me the death of all attachments. Thereafter I could not establish a bond of relationship with anyone. *Whenever my relationship with anyone began to become intimate, that death stared at me"* (Joshi, 1982: 24—emphasis added). Rajneesh's biographer also remarks that the growing sense of aloneness that followed in the wake of the experience "was, in fact, a state of becoming centred in his own self; it was a state in which he no longer felt dependent on the other. It was actually this freedom from dependence that made him permanently happy".

Joshi elaborates: "In experiencing his aloneness, Rajneesh became more of an 'outsider', a 'stranger'. He became rooted in a state of detachment in which even in the midst of activities and people, he remained unidentified, an outsider. 'I became a universe unto myself,' says Bhagwan" (Joshi, 1982: 48).

Grooming and Lying

Several additional characteristics are frequently associated with the Narcissistic Personality Disorder. Two are particularly worth mentioning in this profile of Rajneesh: preoccupation with grooming and resorting to prevarication or "outright lying" (*DSM*, 316).

In virtually all of Rajneesh's portraits and public appearances, he seems strikingly well-groomed. Not a strand of hair is out of place. His nails are perfectly manicured. And never a wrinkle or flaw is to be detected in his regal garments. His bejewelled robes have been carefully tailored to give him the appearance of maximum height. Clearly, Rajneesh qualifies as the world's best-dressed Guru. Additional evidence of a preoccupation with grooming is contained in a revealing set of photographs taken of him in his private quarters at the Poona Ashram that appear in *Glimpses of a Golden Childhood*. Two of the photos show the Guru very attentively and meticulously grooming himself before the mirror. To me, these photographs suggest a sense of personal vanity in the man that seems incongruous for one who purports to have permanently dissolved his personal ego.

In light of such evidence, Milne's contention that Rajneesh always insisted on carefully posed photographs and scrutinised and edited all photographs seems quite credible (Milne, 1986: 121, 146). Equally plausible is the former Sannyasin's report that after a "World Festival" at Rajneeshpuram, Rajneesh noticed in a videotape replay of one of his discourses that his socks did not perfectly match his robes. Milne recounts the incident as follows:

> First he castigated his three seamstresses and his tailor, then the video team was broadsided. A full week before the next celebration a few months later, the tailoring team and the video crew assembled at exactly the right time of day to take footage of the Bhagwan's new robes, together with his socks and hat, hanging over a chair. The results were scrutinised carefully, and a copy of the film then sent to Lao Tzu House for Bhagwan's seal of approval (Milne, 1986: 259f).

Prevarication and "outright lying" constitute another feature often associated with narcissism that applies to Rajneesh. Deception and falsehood form a pattern running throughout the Guru's life. His penchant for rationalisation has already been referred to in this essay. His addiction to exaggeration is commonly recognised among his own followers. His public discourses are notoriously laden with caricature, stereotypical thinking, factual error, and paraphrasing without attribution. Rajneesh's rhetorical methods warrant a thorough critical analysis in themselves. Here, however, I shall restrict my focus to an enumeration of a series of discrete, deliberate acts of deception or falsehood that are indicative of a lifelong behaviour pattern.

The pattern apparently was established during childhood. Rajneesh's mother has reported that her son sometimes invented stories to avoid attending school, which he detested. Joshi cites one such incident:

> Once he came home crying and said he would not go back to school because his teacher had given him physical punishment. His mother became upset and asked Rajneesh's youngest uncle, Shikharchand, to

go and straighten out the teacher immediately. The uncle took young Rajneesh with him and headed for school. On the way, however, Rajneesh admitted to his uncle that he was pretending and that the teacher had not punished him (Joshi, 1982: 25).

In a reminiscence in his *Glimpses of a Golden Childhood*, Rajneesh confesses that he frequently practised truancy from school, and, to hide the fact from his father, he entered into collusion with school officials—who were relieved to have the young troublemaker absent from class—to falsify his attendance record (Rajneesh, 1985a: 687). Elsewhere in *Glimpses*, Rajneesh says that whenever he did attend school he would deceive his teachers "by just scribbling", pretending that he was rapidly taking notes. He adds: "I used to laugh when they were deceived. But it is impossible to deceive me..." (Rajneesh, 1985a: 389).

The pattern persisted, it appears, through his college career. For example, he tells how on one occasion he pretended to be an ardent devotee of the black goddess Kālī as a means of ingratiating himself with the principal of a college to gain admission to the institution. After Rajneesh had succeeded in being admitted, the principal soon discovered that he had been duped. The principal then confronted him and accused him of being a rascal. Rajneesh's rejoinder is instructive: "I said 'You should have understood, even on that day. You are not a saint either, but I wanted admission. What else to do?' " (Rajneesh, 1985b, 2:838). On yet another occasion, as a graduate student at Saugar University, Rajneesh managed to avoid two years of compulsory military training at the institution by persuading a vice-chancellor to "take care of it", meaning to secretly doctor the records (Rajneesh, 1985b, 1:737).

Rajneesh also admits to having resorted to deception to veil his prolonged and excessive absences from the classroom during the years he was employed as a philosophy professor at Jabalpur University. He says, "I would come back after three days for a few hours, just to show myself in the university, that I was there—because they could not give me that much leave nor could I take that much leave; otherwise from where could I get money?" (Rajneesh, 1985b, 2:144). Another tactic he employed to disguise his inordinate absence from teaching duties indicates how elaborate and calculating his deceptive schemes sometimes have been:

> So this was the arrangement: one of my students used to take my car and park it in the same place where I would normally park it. The car was always parked there; that was a symbol that I was in the university. I told him, "So park the car there at two o'clock and at four o'clock—take it away—just two hours. Everbody should know it is there because that is the rush hour, when everybody is there, and everybody knows that I never come before two… . So there is no problem" (Rajneesh, 1985, 2:144 f).

That some of his acts of dishonesty were in violation of law does not seem to have deterred Rajneesh. For example, he once persuaded an acquaintance to backdate an announcement of intent to marry which, according to Indian law, must be posted on a court bulletin board one month prior to the marriage: "Do one thing. Post it, backdate it one month tonight. Who will prove that it was not there a month?… . You *have* to do it. It is not a question of law, it is a question of love. You *have* to do it!" he urged (Rajneesh, 1985b, 3:659—emphasis in original). A short time later, he denied that he knew anything about the arrangements for the marriage—an outright falsehood (Rajneesh, 1985b, 3:660). In light of this incident it is significant to note that arranging fraudulent marriages was included in the thirty-five count indictment brought against Rajneesh by United States immigration officials on November 14, 1985. Shortly after he pleaded guilty to two counts of the indictment, and was convicted, sentenced, and immediately deported from the United States, he is reported to have said that he had lied—"for the first time in his life"—when he pleaded guilty (*On the Road Again*, 1985).

The Guru's attitude toward honesty and truthfulness can perhaps best be summarised in his own words:

> I believe in Gautama Buddha's definition that "Truth is that which works." Now, this is a strange definition because sometimes a lie can work, and I know that many times truth does not work at all; the lie works. But I agree with Buddha. Of course he would not agree with me, but I am more generous than Gautama Buddha himself. If something works, brings the right results, what does it matter whether it was a lie in the beginning, or a truth? What matters is the end, the ultimate outcome (Rajneesh, 1985a: 444).

In reviewing this litany of prevarication and deception, perhaps the reader is impressed, as I have been, by the candour of Rajneesh's disclosures concerning his dishonest behaviour. Virtually all the evidence cited above comes from the Guru himself. Why would he be so forthright, even casual, about disclosing so unseemly an aspect of his character? The answer may be provided in a comment by Millon concerning the narcissistic personality: "Since he cares little for the opinions of others, his defensive maneuvers are transparent, a poor camouflage to a discerning eye. This *failure to bother dissembling* more thoroughly accounts in part for his overt immodesty and obvious arrogance" (Millon, 1969: 262—emphasis added). Millon's point perhaps clarifies, in psychological terms, a strange and obfuscatory statement by Rajneesh concerning his truthfulness: "I am always speaking the Truth—sometimes in a way that looks like a joke, sometimes in a way that it looks like a contradiction, sometimes in a way that it looks like a lie—but I am always saying the truth, and truth alone" (*The Rajneesh Times*, 1985, 4:8, A-4).

WHAT CAUSES NARCISSISM?

A considerable amount of uncertainty exists concerning the etiology of the Narcissistic Personality Disorder. Since no distinguishable biological factors have been identified, those who do venture an etiological explanation concentrate on psychological factors.

Millon, for example, traces the roots of narcissism to parental overvaluation and indulgence, to conditions wherein parents "pamper", indulge, and fawn over the youngster in such ways as to teach him that his every wish is a command to others, that he can receive without giving and that he deserves prominence without effort (Millon, 1969: 263). In short order, says Millon, "the child learns to expect subservience from others... . On the other hand, however, he fails to learn to cooperate and share or to think of the desires and interests of others; he acquires no sense of interpersonal responsibility, no skills for the give-and-take of social life. The world revolves around him":

> Exposed repeatedly to acquiescent and indulgent parents, he expects comparable treatment from others, and learns to employ the presumptuous and demanding strategies which effected favoured reactions in the past. Should desire be frustrated, he can act only in one way—to demand and exploit...
> (He) learns also to view others as weak and subservient. By their obsequious and demeaning

> behaviour, the parents of the narcissistic child have provided him with an image of others as manipulable, docile, yielding and spineless (Millon, 1969: 263).

This child-rearing scenario fits Rajneesh's early life to a striking degree. Rajneesh was born in the home of his maternal grandparents in Kuchwada, India, on December 11, 1931. According to Joshi, the newborn infant was endowed with such "grace and beauty" that the grandfather, Nānā, became convinced that he had been a monarch in some previous life. So, he spontaneously named the infant "Raja," meaning "the King" (Joshi, 1982: 14). Nānā apparently was so enamored by his infant grandson that he refused to allow him to return to the village of Timani, where Rajneesh's father was employed as a struggling cloth merchant (Joshi, 1982: 14). Rajneesh was reared by these doting maternal grandparents for the first several years of his life.

During these formative years, he developed such a deep attachment to his grandparents that, to this day, he regards them as his "real parents". Although both grandparents left their imprint on him, apparently it was his grandmother, Nānī, who influenced him more than anyone else. "For my first years I knew Nānī as my mother; those are the years when one grows… . My own mother came after that; I was already grown up, already made in a certain style, and my grandmother helped me immensely." "I never saw a more beautiful woman than my Nānī. I myself was in love with her, and loved her throughout her whole life… . All that is beautiful in vision somehow comes through her. She helped me in every way to be the way I am." "Perhaps I am her vehicle; perhaps she has poured herself into me. She loved me so deeply that I never considered my real mother to be my real mother" (Rajneesh, 1985a: 22, 83f., 109).

According to Rajneesh, Nānī was born in Khajuraho, a city famous for its many temples containing countless erotic sculptures and to which Rajneesh referred as "the ancient-most citadel of the Tantrikas" (Rajneesh, 1985a: 4). He has further speculated that Nānī may have been born into a Tantric family (Rajneesh, 1985a: 62). Whether or not this was the case, Nānī's outlook appears to have been decidedly Tantric, especially as evidenced in her child-rearing practices. According to Rajneesh, Nānī was totally indulgent and permissive. He reports that she "helped me to dare everything—I mean *everything*... . Whatsoever I wanted she arranged... . I don't remember her ever saying no to me" (Rajneesh, 1985a: 53, 56f.—emphasis in original). Nānā, it appears, was equally indulgent. Neither grandparent ever punished the young child for his frequent acts of mischief. Referring to these mischievous acts, Rajneesh reminisces, "That was my way during those first years when I lived with my grandfather, and yet I was absolutely protected from punishment. He never said 'do this' or 'don't do that'.... That was enough to allow me to do whatsoever I wanted" (Rajneesh, 1985a: 58-60). Again, he relates, "my grandfather not only loved me but loved everything I did. And I did everything that you could call a nuisance. I was a continuous nuisance. The whole day he had to listen to complaints about me, and he always rejoiced in them... . He never punished me. .... He simply allowed, absolutely allowed me to be myself" (Rajneesh, 1985a: 36 f.). Rajneesh recounts an incident that graphically reveals the extent to which his grandmother was willing to go to satisfy his every whim as a child:

> I used to carry a small suitcase, just like the doctors'. Once I had seen a doctor passing through the village, and I said to my Nānī, "Unless I get that suitcase I will not eat!"... . You know what she did?

> That's why I still love her—she told Bhoora (the family servant), "Take your gun and run after that doctor and snatch his bag. Even if you have to shoot the man, get his bag. Don't worry, we will take care of you in court" (Rajneesh, 1985a: 248).

In addition to demonstrating extreme "parental" overindulgence, this anecdote is noteworthy in two other respects. First, it indicates that the young child already had developed a habit of resorting to intimidation ("Unless I get that suitcase I will not eat!") to get whatever he wanted, a pattern that he has also applied to his disciples in later years ("If you don't love me enough, I'll leave my body") (Strelley, 1987: 296). Second, it also suggests—as do other of Rajneesh's reminiscences concerning his grandmother—that Nānī may well have fit Otto Kernberg's description of narcissistic parenting: "Chronically cold parental figures with covert but intense aggression are a frequent feature of the background of (narcissistic) patients" (Kernberg, 1986: 22).

Following the traumatic experience of grandfather Nānā's death when Rajneesh was seven, Rajneesh moved to Gadarwara, where his biological parents were then living. He reports that he did not relish living with his parents, because of the number of relatives who stayed with them. "This is not a family," he remarked at one point, " It's a bazaar" (Rajneesh, 1985a: 260). The solution to this problem soon came when Nānī also moved to Gadarwara and settled in a separate bungalow. In effect, he spent some of his daylight hours with his parents, but his nights were usually spent with Nānī (Rajneesh, 1985a: 55, 718f.). Nānī apparently continued to indulge her grandson by granting him permission to do whatever he liked. Of the six rooms in her bungalow, she kept only one for herself and turned the other five over to

Rajneesh, allowing him to use them as he wished, even consenting to his insistence that no one—not even she—be allowed to enter one particular room, his "sacred place of learning", where he allegedly mastered "all kinds of magical tricks" (Rajneesh, 1985a: 713 f.). Nānī's continuing pattern of total permissiveness, as well as her aggression and hostility toward others, is disclosed in her response to one of his pranks: leading unsuspecting persons toward an unprotected well in the dark of night. One individual, the town sweetmaker, when led to the well, actually fell in. When Rajneesh later confessed the incident to Nānī, her reply was "Great! Good! That man deserved it. Did he really fall into the well just as you said?" Rajneesh's recollection of her reaction continues:

> I can still hear her laughter. She laughed herself to tears. She said, "That's very good, but is he alive or not?" I said, "He is perfectly okay." "Then," she said, "there is no problem. Don't be worried; that man deserved it... ." I asked her, "Don't you want to say anything about it?" She said, "No, because I have watched you from your very childhood. Even if you do something wrong, you do it so rightly, and at exactly the right moment, so that even a wrong becomes a right." It was she who told me, for the first time, that right in the hands of the wrong man becomes a wrong; and wrong in the hands of a right man becomes a right (Rajneesh, 1985a: 110f.).

Rajneesh's parents apparently exhibited greater concern for their son's unruly and uncooperative behaviour. But their attempts to control him were halting and ineffectual. In their confrontations with the headstrong youth determined to have his own way, they invariably acquiesced, and eventually they abandoned all attempts to discipline him. His mother, Saraswati, for example, prevailed on him once or twice to fetch vegetables from the town market. When Rajneesh adamantly refused, she "dropped the idea forever" (Rajneesh, 1985a: 362). On a couple of occasions, his father, Dadda, did attempt to punish him for misbehaviour; but, when Rajneesh accepted the assigned punishment with overt relish, he, too, quit trying from then on. The following incident clearly reveals both the pattern of parental acquiescence and Rajneesh's stubborn defiance of parental authority. Dadda once remonstrated with his son for allowing his hair to grow long and for wearing a Punjabi garment that resembled a skirt. Embarrassed by townspeople taking Rajneesh for a girl, Dadda issued an ultimatum to his son: "Cut your hair; otherwise I will cut it for you!" Rajneesh's defiant response so angered Dadda that he forcibly cut a lock from his son's hair. But the son was not to be outdone in this power struggle with his father. He promptly went to the barber and had his head completely shaved, a customary Indian gesture whenever a child's father had died. In a reminiscence of the incident, Rajneesh describes the final outcome of the confrontation:

> ...my father had learned a lesson. He said to me, "I have repented enough. I will not do such a thing again." And he never did. He kept his word. That was his first and last punishment to me. It is even unbelievable to me, because I did so many troublesome things. But he listened patiently to all complaints, and he never said anything to me. In fact, he tried his best to protect me (Rajneesh, 1985a: 464).

What Next?

The evidence contained in this essay runs counter to Rajneesh's claim that he is an enlightened master—if the latter is taken to refer to one who has permanently dissolved the ego and transcended all worldly desires and attachments. It does not challenge his contention that he had a profound mystical experience in a public garden in Jabalpur, India, at age twenty-one. Nor does it rule out the possibility that this experience may have involved a vivid sense of ego-loss. What I have questioned is Rajneesh's grandiose self-interpretation that, he insists, stemmed from and was confirmed by that experience. Rajneesh's self-avowed Buddha-status is instead part of a delusional system associated with a severe narcissistic personality disorder. In other words, his condition is one of ego-inflation rather than egolessness.

According to Joshi, Rajneesh's enlightenment occurred in the wake of a year-long spiritual crisis marked by intense feelings of doubt, insecurity, and emptiness. "He almost went mad," Joshi reports. Rajneesh has described his condition at that time as "one of utter darkness":

> It was as if I had fallen into a deep dark well. In those days I had many times dreamt that I was falling and falling and going deeper into a bottomless well. And many times I... awakened from a dream full of perspiration, sweating profusely, because the falling was endless without any ground or place anywhere to rest my feet... . It was all darkness—aimless and ambiguous. My condition was full of tension, insecurity and danger (Joshi, 1982: 51).

He also reports that his emotional state was accompanied by physical symptoms such as appetite-loss, severe headaches, and lack of a sense of the existence of his body. Referring to the latter, Rajneesh says: "The body was so non-existential that I had to hurt myself to feel that I was still in the body. I had to knock my head against the wall to feel whether my head was still there or not. Only when it hurt would I be a little in the body" (Joshi, 1982: 52). Heinz Kohut and Ernest S. Wolf refer to the latter phenomenon as "fragmentation", a symptom severely experienced in narcissistic patients whose self-esteem has been taxed for prolonged periods (Kohut and Wolf, 1986: 185).

From a depth-psychological perspective, therefore, it is plausible to argue that Rajneesh's crisis was triggered by a failure of his narcissistic coping mechanisms to counter threats to his sense of grandiosity and self-esteem. If so, then his "enlightenment" may be viewed as an experience involving, at the psychological level, the formation of a new grandiose delusional system aimed at resolving his crisis of threatened grandiosity and self-esteem. Such an interpretation is supported by the self-grandeur that is evident in his subsequent account of his enlightenment experience. Rajneesh relies on a customary metaphor to describe his experience of ego-dissolution: "For the first time I was not alone, for the first time I was no more an individual, for the first time the drop has come and fallen into the ocean." His ensuing statement, however, subtly shifts the metaphor's traditional meaning in a decidedly narcissistic direction: "Now the whole ocean was *mine*, I was the ocean. *There was no limitation.* A tremendous power arose as if *I could do anything whatsoever*" (Rajneesh, 1984: 459—emphasis added). Rather than egolessness, we find here an intoxicating sense of unlimited power and possessiveness—a hallmark of pathological narcissism.

It is conceivable that under more favourable circumstances Rajneesh's communal experiment might have enjoyed a happier denouement. Under a different style of leadership, the commune might have succeeded in disarming its outside opposition and endured as an alternative society. Though it is unlikely to have succeeded in fulfilling Rajneesh's grandiose vision of creating a new archetypal human that would eventually transform the world, its celebrative lifestyle, productivity, and ecological orientation might have earned widespread admiration and respect. But Rajneesh's own narcissistic and anti-social behaviour proved the major obstacle to such an eventuality. His inordinate self-grandiosity, insatiable need for adulation, lack of sensitivity toward others, exploitiveness, unwillingness to compromise, deceitfulness, recklessness, lack of respect for the law, contempt for social order and convention, and lack of political awareness—and, perhaps above all, a lack of any sense of his own limitations—these are the myriad ingredients that contributed to the failure of his experiment. It may sound trite, but it's correct to conclude that "he was his own worst enemy".

Rajneesh has cut his losses (and rationalised them away) and is currenlty attempting a comeback once more in Poona. It is probably only a matter of time until he suffers another setback.

(1988)

[illegible] centrality [illegible]

[illegible] widespread admiration and support [illegible]

[illegible] around the [illegible] such an [illegible]

lack of sensitivity toward others, extravagance, [illegible]

[illegible] enemy.

[illegible]

II

COMMUNITY

Chapter Five

Shree Rajneesh Ashram Poona

A Provocative Community

SWAMI PREM AMITABH

The humanistic psychology movement over the past 30 years has created a new context for people to move past merely resolving inner conflicts into actualising their potential, attaining "peak experiences" and living more fully in the here and now. Emphasis has shifted from struggling with the negative to affirming the positive. People saw that they could view their "cups" as either half empty or half full, and began to experience that they had choices about how to live their lives.

One outreach of the movement was a glimpse, a taste, of a transcendent state—a state where, though one still had one's conditioned tapes and personal dramas to contend with, one could function, even momentarily, from a different space where these dramas had no hold. Perls, Rogers, Assagioli, Maslow, Lowen, Erhard—each created a context for persons to transform the energy attached to their conditioned behaviour so that they could experience enlightenment. And some people who did catch a glimpse did "lighten up" and began living lives more simply, expansively, and less indulgently. I remember once as a graduate student taking a course with Carl Rogers. He read a letter from a client of his, a passage of which I never forgot: "It isn't that I understand better any of the problems I came to see you about, but the trees are greener, the sky is bluer, and people are more beautiful."

Some teachers, throughout time, have offered not just a taste but the whole eternal banquet. Buddha, Jesus, Lao Tzu, Mohammed, Zarthustra—various Transcended Masters—seem to have come from the other side of some great divide. Their message has carried the same essence: a simplicity and clarity of perception, a strange indifference to the pulls and pushes of the external world we know, a oneness and harmony with nature, and a non-resistant orientation to impinging danger. They seem to have lived at, and sent their messages from, that transcendent place touched upon by those gifted humanists mentioned above.

To his disciples, Bhagwan Shree Rajneesh offers what the Masters before him offered. The potent difference is that he is a alive, so rather than a dependence on commandment, dogma, or method, we are able to have a personal experience, a communion, a love interconnection, and in so doing, directly touch the transcendent space within.

Further, he is a man of our time. Thus, the targets he aims at are those he sees are at the root of the modern person's dilemma: sexual and aggressive repression, being controlled and controlling, convention, living for the future, attachments to physical and psychological survival. In fact, any position at all, even being caught in the choice between a meditative and worldly life, comes under scrutiny as just one more subtle form of entrapment.

This article, written in 1980, covers my experience with Bhagwan at his Ashram in India during the previous six years, and affords some glimpses of the way Bhagwan works with his disciples:

> My effort here is not to create a following, not to create believers, but to create individuals, lovers, meditators, who can stand on their own, and each one can become a light. The night is going to become darker and darker everyday—we will need millions of lights around the world, millions of people who are capable of love, unconditionally, without asking anything in return...and who are so silent, and who are so blissful, that wherever they are they will be able to dissipate darkness (Rajneesh, forthcoming).

Shree Rajneesh Ashram, 1980

I am currently in the midst of some rapid changes both as a person and as a therapist. I don't appear to be making an effort to change; the changes just seem to be happening. I came to the realisation some six years ago that my life wasn't that much more joyful and alive than those persons I was seeing professionally in my private practice, and I found that no matter what new growth method appeared on the horizon, the ceiling for actualising oneself seemed so low that neither my clients nor I were standing fully erect. Thus, I began to search around for alternatives. What follows is a description of a context whose ceiling I have not yet been able to see.

A unique, experiential laboratory in consciousness unfolded at Shree Rajneesh Ashram in Poona, India. A center for transcendental psychology emerged, bringing together Eastern esoteric teachings and meditative practices with Western therapeutic and humanistic growth methods. The person responsible for creating this melding of ancient Eastern with current Western practices was Bhagwan Shree Rajneesh.

In the manner of a magician, Bhagwan created this from apparent nothingness. In the span of a few short years he presented the world with a stage upon which a new level of human actualisation is possible. Five years ago, when I first came to India and sat before Bhagwan, he had perhaps 100 followers, mostly Indian. He said then that in a few short years all the Western therapies would come here. When combined with Eastern meditation practices, they would synthesise into a unitive psychology, a Third Psychology called the Psychology of the Buddhas, the psychology of transcendence:

> We are trying to present a new synthesis between East and West. The Eastern methods are more individualistic, more inwardgoing, and more concerned with solitude, aloneness, and the person. They are meditative methods, more concerned with the person and his integrity. They are not group methods.
>
> The Western methods are mainly group methods, and are outgoing, more concerned with communication and relationships, with the group and integrity in relationships, not in aloneness. So, they can be reduced to: the western methods are more concerned with love, the eastern methods more with meditation.
>
> These are the two polarities of human consciousness—love and meditation. Meditation means to be alone, as if you alone exist. And love means that you are not, the other is; as if you exist only in relation to the other, and there is no other existence. These are the two polarities, and taken separately they both become extremes, and both are dangerous.

> The East has tried the first extreme—of meditation. It became life-negating and escapist—hence the poverty, the ugliness. There has been no scientific progress in the east, because nobody has paid any attention to society. All those who were interested in any search always escaped to the forest and the mountains.
>
> In the West, the society has progressed. There is a better standard of living, more affluence and comfort, more convenience, more health, and more life. But they have moved to the other extreme and the individual has by and by disappeared.
>
> The whole emphasis here is that there are no opposites, there are only complementaries. Meditation and love are not opposites, they are complementaries... .
>
> So we are trying to create a synthesis...not as an ideology, but in the beings of the people who come here. A world psychology has to be given birth to.... Now there should be a unitive psychology, global, in which there is no East and no West, but the polarities meet and dissolve (Rajneesh, 1976a: 19).

By the fall of 1979 there were over 100,000 Neo-Sannyasins (the name given Bhagwan's disciples) throughout the world. Two to three thousand Sannyasins and visitors sat before him each morning listening to his daily discourse; 1,000 Sannyasin-workers carried out the work on the six-acre commune grounds; over 80 different therapy and meditative groups happened each month, ranging in duration from three days to two weeks, providing 2,000 spaces monthly for group participants. An additional 3,000 to 4,000 spaces were available for individual body and therapy sessions. Nearly all groups except those that could handle large numbers of people were full from one to two months in advance. In short, the most broad-based therapeutic community and growth centre in the world was flourishing in Poona, India.

Personally, my attraction to Bhagwan was much like to one that drew me to Carl Rogers, Eric Berne, Fritz Perls: the urge to grow personally and professionally. Feeling somewhat deadened and agitated, I attended an Association for Humanistic Psychology conference in San Diego, California, in the spring of 1974. The second day there I felt restless and took a walk rather than join friends for lunch. I was drawn to a door, which I entered, and was amused to find myself in an empty room (so much for my uncanny, intuitive sense, I thought). Then I noticed another door at the far end of the room and upon opening it entered a huge, high-ceilinged room where I saw about 100 people lying on their backs, some deeply still, some jerking awkwardly, some crying, some wailing. In the centre of this mass, a man in an orange robe stood with arms raised and eyes closed.

The shock I felt was profound. I dropped to sitting cross-legged, closed my eyes, wept softly, and sank effortlessly into peacefulness. The journey to San Diego opened a door I needed. Three months later, I found myself in Poona, India, at the Ashram of Bhagwan Shree Rajneesh.

THE EASTERN INFLUENCE

The Disciple-Master Relationship

One unique feature of this melding ancient Eastern with current Western teachings and practices is that it is interwoven with the fabric of the master-disciple relationship. For the Westerner, this relationship brings up more resistance and negative judgement than any other aspect of spiritual seeking. Surrender to another human being? Sit at the feet of a Master? Sell out one's sense of individuality, separateness? By inference, demean the psychological profession by admitting its gross limitations in confronting the basic challenges of our times? Such practices and decisions are anathemas to the ego.

In fact, discipleship exposes one inexorably. It is a precision barometer for determining where one is existentially and at what level of functioning one is currently stuck. Once I became a disciple it was as if a new level of awareness immediately presented itself. At a basic level, I was given the opportunity of seeing my attached positions regarding trust, distrust, autonomy, dependence, freedom, love. In each case, I could see how the position I held was either nourishing to or destructive of my well-being.

The essence of the master-disciple relationship is personal: of the heart, not of the mind; an intimacy rather than a contractual agreement; an admission of one's life not working and an openness to something new; an acknowledgement that aliveness and freedom are our birthright, not something we need to achieve.

> That which you don't have and think you have has to be surrendered to me. You don't have it, so you will not be really surrendering something to me, just an illusion... . You are living a kind of illusion that you are separate from existence.
>
> Your reality, I want to give it back to you, you have forgotten about it. And your unreality, I want to take away from you.
>
> I don't gain anything because of your surrender. So don't be miserly...just your dream is lost. But you gain much out of the surrender. You get reality, you get your authenticity back (Rajneesh, 1979a: 220).

The taking of Sannyas (becoming a disciple) was an

unexpected experience for me. Two days after my wife and I arrived at the Ashram we were given a *darśana* appointment. "Darśana" means "sitting in the presence of an Enlightened Being." With Bhagwan, in addition to taking Sannyas, it was a chance for several seekers at a time to speak with him, ask him questions, be blessed.

The day before my *darśana* appointment, I ruminated over whether or not to take Sannyas and came to the "heady" conclusion that I would not. I was experiencing too much ambivalence, and I didn't want to give up "my independence". My wife also expressed reservation:

> Then there are those who are skeptical: who are not yet finished with their egos; who still hope that something is going to happen through their egos; who still hope that their mind is going to deliver some paradise, some happiness, some bliss to them; who still think that through logic, reason, they will arrive at knowing what truth is (Rajneesh 1978b: 206).

There were about ten of us for *darśana*. As we entered the marble porch and approached the chair where Bhagwan was sitting with several close disciples about him, he seemed to lean to one side, look "through" our approaching group, and reach to my wife and me with his eyes. He chuckled several times, and, gesturing, said, "Come here, both of you. I have been waiting for you for a long time. First you take Sannyas, then we talk. I have your new names already."

Adrenaline poured through me. My knees weakened. I doubted whether my legs would take me the rest of the way to his feet. My wife began laughing out loud. We were being swept up like the underbelly of a wave, to crash down into something new. I felt loved, wedded, honeymooned...and a little shanghaied. I laughed at his playing with us: all that thinking, weighing, considering—all for nothing. My wife became Ma Prem Anupama; I became Swami Prem Amitabh.

Disciplehood, Bhagwan-style, is different from its historical antecedents. It retains some of the traditional: the wearing of ochre or orange, a new name, and a *mālā* around the neck made up of 108 beads. The similarity ends there. The old version of Sannyas was one of renunciation, deprivation of the senses, escape from the marketplace, spartan discipline. To Bhagwan,

> Sannyas is rejoicing. Rejoice in life, in love, in meditation, in the beauties of the world, in the ecstasy of existence—rejoice in everything.
>
> My Sannyas is to accept challenge. To live dangerously... . The more dangerously you live, the more risks you take, the more you grow, the more you become integrated, crystallised...*Live life totally, love life totally, get involved with your life! Don't hold back.*
>
> I want to bring a totally new concept of Sannyas to the world: a Sannyas that loves, a Sannyas that knows how to become committed, a Sannyas that goes to the deepest core of life.
>
> But nobody else can decide it for you.... I can give you a map, but you have to go, you have to journey. You are so unique that nobody else's map can be your map. Yes, by understanding my map you will become aware of many things about yourself, but you are not to follow it blindly, otherwise you will become a pseudo human being (Rajneesh, 1981).

Although I was given Sannyas on 9th August, 1974, I didn't truly "take" Sannyas until several days later as a result of an extraordinary happening. In the days following the 9th, I became more and more agitated. The meditation camp began on the 11th (different meditations all day long for ten intensive days, from 6.00

a.m. to 8.00 p.m. daily). As I went into each meditation, a host of psychological hang-ups from my past began erupting. Especially, I felt paralytic fears of abandonment, loss of identity and self-importance, and low self-esteem. At the same time, I saw that there was no support for these notions. They were erupting without cause, as if an electrode had penetrated my brain, and I was conditionally reacting like an automaton. Anupama was devotedly loving and, as my mood darkened, she suggested I go see Bhagwan. I remember saying angrily, "What the hell can he do? I've had these hang-ups all my life. Psychotherapy hasn't resolved them, what is he going to do? Say a few magic words, touch my head, and make it all go away?"

A day later, as I withdrew into myself even more, I realised I had no other option and made an appointment to see Bhagwan the following evening.

For the next day and a half, I kept busy rehearsing my psychodynamic drama: unpreferred child; frightening, intimidating father; seductive distant, though loving mother. If he was going to help me, I wanted to be as clear and brief as possible.

There were some 12 to 15 people in *darśana* that night. One after the other, Bhagwan called upon each person to come forward. The fourth person told him of her sexual frigidity and he showed her a meditation that included lying on her back nude with her feet in the air while rubbing a towel in one direction over her lower belly. He looked at me sharply and said, "Amitabh, this would be good for some of your patients in the West!"

I was taken aback by his piercing expression, flattered that he singled me out, and wasn't too keen on his suggestion, considering the plethora of malpractice suits happening in California at the time. Perhaps this was his way of telling me, "Amitabh, I know you are here!"

When he had addressed about half the people, a sense

of apprehension arose in me which crystallised into the thought: He isn't going to call me. I immediately dismissed this notion as coming from my ego-need to be special ("the uncalled one"). However, as he completed being with three-fourths of the people, the message was clear and unequivocal: *He was not going to call me and that was the assistance I was being given.* I closed my eyes, opened to the experience, and in a moment saw clearly. A surge of energy swept through me. What was happening to me over the past three or four days was perfect: My madnesses, my distortions, my unfinished past were erupting automatically. Age-old resentments were coming up like those fast-motion, old-time, comic silent movies. The work was being done. I need only allow, watch them come, let them go, see their habitual, chronic, mechanical nature.

To talk about them would be to split myself, dissipate the energy, and come from the position, "Dear Doctor Bhagwan, help me get rid of the negative parts of myself, help me change into something better," a chant familiar to the ears of every practising psychotherapist in the West. My job wasn't to reject these apparitional monsters, but to allow them their expression. Just be silent, go into these experiences deeply, be courageous, don't be afraid. It was so simple. I was filled with love, gratitude, awe. Was I actually receiving something on a non-verbal level or was this mere coincidence?

The *darśana* ended. I was the only one not called. I beamed, radiated, felt about to burst. I sensed I was with someone the likes of whom I had never experienced before. My doubts regarding taking Sannyas diminished. I wanted to experience life in this energy field...and he wasn't finished yet.

We went to leave. Halfway to where we had placed our shoes I heard, "Amitabh?" It was Bhagwan's voice. I turned and saw him still sitting in his chair.

"Yes, Bhagwan?"

Smiling, with head tilted, he said, "You have something to say to me?"

I laughed and said, "I did, Bhagwan, but I don't anymore. You gave me more than I ever could have dreamed. Thank you."

"Good! Now come back!"

I returned, shaking and weak, and sat at his feet. We were alone. He said:

> I am working very hard on you. When you came here, you had a harmony about you, but it is not deep enough. It is a man-made harmony, made by you. Now you must find a deeper harmony, one not made by you. To reach this harmony, you must allow yourself to go into disharmony.
>
> So, you go into this disharmony, into these feelings. Go totally into these feelings. Be the watcher. Look at them deeply, and one day, they will be gone, totally, only the watcher will remain, and a deep harmony will come—one not made by you. Good, Amitabh, everything goes well.

I left his presence stoned. I couldn't assimilate what had happened. My mind was being exploded. I was obviously in a world beyond the mind being given a glimpse of something new:

> Your being a disciple and my being a Master is a drama. Play it as beautifully as possible... . From your side it is a great reality, from my side it is a game. One day you will also understand that it is a game. That day will be the day of your enlightenment (Rajneesh, 1979a: 341).

After three weeks in India, Robert M. Birnbaum, Ph.D., clinical psychologist, returned to his private practice in the middle-class, suburban Californian city of Walnut

Creek as Swami Prem Amitabh, dressed in orange, wearing *mālā* beads and a locket around his neck

I was totally unprepared for what followed. I entered full time psychotherapy, Bhagwan-style. What before had remained underground and subliminal, burst forth into my awareness full force. I was graphically shown my self-protective facades of new-wave psychotherapist, independent, "together," male, open-minded seeker. I was self-conscious and embarrassed over my dress. My other-directedness regarding my image became painfully transparent to me. I was as hung up on my image as the troubled people who came to me for professional help.

There was no exit. Over and over, I was confronted with the energy that was kept in reserve to maintain these postures. It wasn't that any image was bad or wrong, it was just artificial, an excess weight. The orange clothes, the *mālā,* the Hindu name, kept these quick-change costumes reeling before my eyes. The within grew stronger. I was on a roller coaster of awareness:

> That is why I insist on a certain dress, a *mālā.* It has nothing to do with spirituality. It has something to do with you as you are. It is just . . . so you can remain in a continuity. Moving in ochre in the west will create trouble. People will look at you. You will look strange, odd, and that will make you alert and aware. You can use that situation (Rajneesh, 1978b: 21).

This was Sannyas for me—nothing esoteric—just the heightening of awareness of my games: a simple, immediate shift from unawareness to awareness with accompanying release and lightness. I was beautifully in over my head, drowning, and more alive that I could remember ever having been before:

> I call Sannyas the last game: on the periphery it may look serious but at the center it is a deep laughter....

> Beyond it the whole world of games disappears. Then there is reality... . Delight in it, dance in it, let it be a deep singing, a rejoicing (Rajneesh, 1976g: 311).

After a year in the west as Sannyasins, Anupama and I returned to the Ashram. Our lifestyle from then until mid-1980 turned out to be living in India during the temperate months between October and March and returning to the West the remaining months. My body would wilt and become ill during the intense heat and monsoon season, necessitating a return for recuperation.

Bhagwan Shree Rajneesh

Creative Source

Bhagwan's approach to transformation is experiential, existential. He created an environment where a wide spectrum of human existence could be experienced. From natural childbirth to the burning of the dead; from groups experiencing freedom in sex and anger to austere, Eastern meditations like ten days sitting in silence focused on breathing; from individual sessions in rolfing, postural integration, or patterning to sensory deprivation in one of the *samādhi* tanks; from serving in the kitchen washing dishes to building a new bamboo hut; from typing, editing, publishing books, to cleaning toilet bowls—all were immediately available for direct, personal experience.

Bhagwan eschews analysis and mental insights as vehicles for change. He constantly creates situations that cause people to become aware of and confront directly their deeply conditioned resistances to change. One's attachment to the repetitive dictates of the mind—the ego mechanisms—those processes that separate and compartmentalise to fit belief systems which, in effect, control, cope, arrest spontaneity, are seen by Bhagwan as the agents for conformity and mediocrity, the chains that fetter and prevent freedom. His effort is not in curing the mind, but in transcending the grip the mind holds on consciousness. Mind itself is the disease.

> Mind is a disease. This is a basic truth the East has discovered. The West says that mind can become ill, can be healthy. Western psychology depends on this. But the East says that mind as such is the disease, it cannot be healthy. No psychiatry can help. At the most, you can make it normally ill (Rajneesh, 199c: 98).

What he refers to as "the mind's disease" is its essential duality: the pervasive attitudes for or against, the ego's selective attentiveness, the arbitrary compartmentalising of existence.

Bhagwan's alternative to dependence upon the mind: choiceless awareness, consciousness:

> The nature of consciousness is to be a mirror. The mirror has no choice of its own: whatever comes in front of it is reflected. The mirror does not prefer, does not judge. When interpretation enters, when consciousness is divided, it becomes the mind. It loses its mirror-likeness.
>
> At the root, mind is consciousness. If you stop making dual divisions—choosing this against that, liking this, disliking that—if you drop out of these divisions, the mind again becomes a mirror, a pure consciousness. The whole effort for a seeker is how to drop opinion, philosophy, preference, judgement, choice.
>
> Understand the basic problem, otherwise you can make this, too, a choice: "I will not choose, I will remain choiceless...now I am for choiceless awareness." This has become the same thing again—you have chosen. Now you are against choice and for choicelessness. You have missed.

> So what is to be done? Simple understanding is needed, nothing is to be done. The ultimate is not achieved through effort but through understanding... . You cannot *do* anything—you have to simply be alert to the whole situation. If you are alert, in a sudden illumination...(identification with) the mind falls. Suddenly you are one with the mirror-like consciousness (Rajneesh, 1975e: 75).

Meditations

> Meditation is a jump into the unknown... . It can bring you out of the imprisonment that is the mind. And when you have come out, you will laugh. It was so easy...only one step was needed...but we go on in a circle and the one step is missed... .
>
> Somewhere the continuity must be broken. If the continuity is broken, if you become discontinuous with your past, then that very moment is the explosion. In that very moment you are centred in your being. And then you know all that has always been yours, all that has just been awaiting you (Rajneesh, 1977b: XIX).

The revolutionary nature of Bhagwan's work is no clearer revealed than in the nature of the meditations he has devised for the twentieth-century person. The body of the modern person is armored through centuries of fear, distortion, and repression. Some breakdown of established defensive patterns is needed before something fresh and new can be experienced. Each of Bhagwan's hour-long meditations begins with body activity and release, moves through more subtle layers of resistance, works through to softer energies, ends in silence.

The Dynamic Meditation, familiarly called "The

Chaotic", is the meditation designed to tap the most basic emotions:

> My emphasis is first to dissolve your inner division, your neurosis, to make you one—a unity. Unless you are one, nothing can be done. So the first thing is: how to dissolve your neurosis?
>
> My technique of Dynamic Meditation accepts your neurosis as it is and tries to release it.... Whatever is hidden must be released. You must not go on repressing. Rather, choose expression as the path. Do not condemn yourself. Accept what you are... . The moment you accept, you go beyond, because acceptance creates a unity, and when you are unified within, you have the energy to go beyond... .
>
> Release your insanity! Inside it will become poisonous. Throw it out, remove it from your system totally (Rajneesh, 1977b: 28).

The Chaotic is done blind-folded, on an empty stomach, with loose-fitting or no clothes. The first 10-minute stage consists of deep, rapid, vigorous breathing without any rhythm while letting the body open up. The accompanying, cacophonous, recorded sounds further the totality of the effort:

> This breathing is to create a chaos within your repressed system. Your fears have created a shallow breathing. What you have made of yourself this chaotic breathing is to destroy... . (Rajneesh, 1977b: 29).
>
> If you can destroy the settled patterns of breathing, then all the patterns in all your bodies (e.g., physical, psychic, spiritual) will be loosened (Rajneesh, 1977c: 103).

The first stage ends abruptly with a "bong" and the

second 10-minute stage begins with an immediate catharsis of whatever comes up for you. Be mad, scream, cry, jump, rage, laugh, be soft, go crazy, fall apart, allow everything out totally, hold nothing back:

> Be *consciously* insane! Whatever comes to your mind—whatever—allow it to express itself; cooperate with it. No resistance, just a flow of emotions (Rajneesh, 1971a: 31).
>
> We are working to bring out all the suppressed emotions...your anger, your hate, your sexuality...it will follow automatically... . It is just like a dirty river falling into the ocean: the ocean will purify it (Rajneesh, 1977b: 105).
>
> This unburdening is basic...without it there can be no meditation... . With this second step—when things are thrown out—you become vacant... . In this emptiness something can be done. Transformation can happen; meditation can happen (Rajneesh, 1977b: 32).

The third 10-minute stage consists of jumping vigorously up and down with arms raised, shouting "Hoo! Hoo! Hoo!" repeatedly so that the sound hammers deeply into the sex centre. The meditators are encouraged to go all out, to exhaust themselves in reaching a crescendo:

> Sufis invented the sound "Hoo"... it goes directly to the sex center... . This age is so sexual that you need a hammering on the sex center. The heart is no more there. If you are going to try "Aum", you are knocking at a door which is vacant... . "Aum" is very non-violent... . "Hoo" is the sound for this age (Rajneesh, 1978b; 35).
>
> I use this stage as vehicle to bring your energy upward. These three steps are cathartic. They are

> not meditation, just the preparation for it (Rajneesh, 1978b; 35).

This third stage ends in a sudden "stop". During the fourth, 15-minute stage there is a sudden cessation of all movements: perfect stillness regardless of the position you are in. In stillness, witness the energy that comes up:

> The energy simply moves upward, and you are not to do anything...anything can be a diversion and you will miss the point. Anything, just a cough or sneeze, and you miss the whole thing—because the mind has become diverted... . When the energy moves upward you become more and more silent (Rajneesh, 1977c: 108).

Soft, lyrical music introduces the final stage. This 15-minute period is one of celebration. Dance, sing, rejoice in whatever has arisen in you. Celebrate life.

Each of the other hour-long meditations Bhagwan has created releases some trapped energy within us, whether sexual, aggressive, or more subtle. Gradually, through stages, each meditation brings the potential for opening into these contracted areas, allows for some movement within the opened space, and concludes in simple, meditative silence.

Bhagwan called his morning discourses "the menu" and one's own meditation "the food". Much was happening here in this active, pulsating, creative community, but when you parted the leaves (the therapy groups, Bhagwan's discourses, the community, the playing, the work), the seeds and formative shoots within us came essentially from meditating.

From the 11th to the 20th of each month, a 10-day intensive meditation camp took place which included five hour-long meditations and a two-hour discourse by Bhagwan daily. Newcomers were urged to go totally into these camps, to go past their resistances, their fatigue, their mind's reservations. The intensity of these camps worked much like a weekend sleepless marathon, only of 10 days' duration. Defenses tumbled; new awarenesses came and went. There was not enough time for the mind to assimilate, compartmentalise, understand. Trust and acceptance were given room to blossom; a deep cleansing became possible.

The Western Influence

Groups

The therapy groups at the Ashram took place from the 21st of each month to the 10th of the following month. Trained Western professionals, all Sannyasins, led the Western therapies and the Eastern methods: from primal, encounter, gestalt, bioenergetics, neo-Reichian, rebirthing, and enlightenment intensive to zazen, Vipassana, and tantra. Over 80 such groups took place each month, accommodating 200 participants.

Bhagwan is a master gestaltist. His existential dictum: To try to change, to be involved in "getting better", is to do the same old, stupid, senseless, endless thing you have always been doing, whereas to bring your energy to the present moment, without judgement or evaluation, accepting whatever comes up for you, *allows change to happen.*

The therapies in the West emphasise working on what I call the "second lie", namely, "I can improve," "I can get better," "I can change these negative images I have about myself." This breeds the therapy of adjustment, what Bhagwan calls "the therapy of the normally ill"!

Bhagwan's alternative: experience the "first lie" directly and the energy for the second lie abates—a moment of transformation is possible. The first lie is, "I am not alright as I am," "There is something wrong with me the way I am." Re-experience those moments when you needed to internalise that lie; explore the motives, the benefits to you in taking that position of "not-all-rightness". Usually, its root is in the need to keep your parents alright in the face of their volatile, punitive actions against you. Consider, for a moment, the child aged one or two who takes the *accurate* position with respect to the parents: "You continue to be harsh and unloving with me, aggressive in your demands. You continue to make me feel there is something wrong with me. Your repeated messages are harmful to my growth and development. I must reject you as harmful." Then the child packs his or her bags and toddles off down the street. I suspect that some individuals, labelled psychotics, figuratively speaking did just that, and unfortunately the remaining environment was not sufficiently supportive of their courageous position.

The more survival-oriented position expediently taken by most of us is to internalise the parent's negativity toward us (make it our own view of ourselves), for then we are not helpless, but rather, in control. We can try to change (the second lie begins: change is possible through our will). If we smile more, cry less, demand less, share more, don't shit in our pants, then Paradise will be regained (we will not be unloved or treated harshly anymore). The main difficulty with this is that we will spend the rest of our lives and part of our psychotherapists' lives failing once more to achieve the desired end.

An option: become aware that your solution of not being alright previously worked for you, but you don't need to carry it around with you anymore. It has become a cancer eating your energy. If you can simply accept that you have a space within you where you feel acceptable to yourself, that in certain circumstances it becomes activated and you become the effect of it, then simply acknowledge it when it arises, watch it, observe it, see if you can witness its beginning. The moment you can see when you introjected this identity, you open the space to see the moment before, the moment when you were perfect within yourself, when the "not alright" message was still outside yourself. Then a hard part comes: the willingness to live in the space of loving yourself and loving whatever comes up for you, not living in misery.

Over 30,000 persons travelled to Poona each year from all over the world, with a potpourri of ethnic backgrounds and social strata—European aristocrats, American middle class, Japanese Buddhists, the well-educated and the not-so-well-educated, old and young—all came together in these groups to let go of their false fronts, their illusions and their games:

> I give these group processes just as a learning. The ultimate is to go with me. If you can allow the group process and you can go with it, slowly, slowly, you will know the secret of going totally into things. And the danger in a group process is not big, so you can afford it. The danger with me is great… .
>
> So in each group you have to remember one thing: to go as deeply as possible… . And, slowly, slowly, the more you allow, the more you will feel blissful. Then you can allow more. And the ultimate is to allow me! (Yatri, 1980: 354).

People were first placed in introductory groups whose task was to assist in awakening self-awareness: *centring,* a seven-day, structured, playful group emphasising processes dealing with attentiveness, and learning how to tune in to one's self space; *enlightenment intensive,* a three-day, 18-hour per day, residential group, focusing intensively on the question, "Who am I?"

After the introductory groups there were the following group experiences:

• *Body-oriented groups:* groups using neo-Reichian methods such as those developed by Charles Kelley at Radix: bioenergetics; body awareness; massage; dance; relaxation therapy.

• *Opening, releasing, expanding groups:* gestalt; encounter; psychodrama; improvisation and spontaneity; and tantra, a popular three-day group exploring one's sexual inhibitions and taboos.

• *Early life re-exploration groups:* the fourteen-day intensive; residential primal therapy group; rebirthing.

• *Groups tapping the subconscious:* hypotherapy; energy; direct awareness; healing; creativity; love.

• *Eastern-oriented groups:* groups exploring intensive meditation techniques such as kyo, Vipassana, mysterium, zazen.

Individual sessions were offered in such diverse approaches as acupuncture, Alexander, massage, neo-Reichian, gestalt, polarity balancing, postural integration, rebirthing, reflexology, foot massage, patterning, rolfing, shiatsu, and *samādhi* tank.

No matter what its particular orientation, each group was designed to be a vehicle for the person to live more effortlessly, in harmony with existence, in a state of no-mind. Group leaders knew these people had travelled far, were submitting themselves to physical hardships just living in India, had come because they were discontented with themselves and disillusioned with Western attitudes and explanations, and were available to experience alternatives directly. Thus, there existed a built-in powerful motivation for change.

Swami Ananda Teertha, the leader of the encounter group, used to say to the participants:

> Don't think you've got to do it all by yourself. You can't. You've just got to do *all* that *you* can do. It's not that the way you are now is bad, it's just that

> it's not working. You're not living in bliss—and bliss is possible... .

Later, talking about his role as leader, he goes on:

> Most of the things that go on in the group, I don't understand with my mind at all. They feel absolutely right, absolutely harmonious but I'm not in touch with them on an intellectual level. They just happen through me.
>
> The function of a group leader in this Ashram is not to be there; is to be out of the way; is to just say or do whatever comes through.

I remember once when four days into a lively seven-day tao group I was leading, several women members brought in an Ashramite (one who lives and works in the Ashram) who wasn't officially in the group.

"Amitabh, Prabha needs to be here. She's in hell!"

So we opened the space for Prabha. She was a young, attractive, Rubenesque lady working as a supervisor in the kitchen. She was in remorse over her gradual weight gain over the preceding months, an episodic pattern since childhood. We assisted her in looking at what was coming up for her regarding her body. She anguished, beat pillows in self-hate, berated her mother for being overcontrolling and undernourishing. Although she was able to release energy and target well, she kept coming up unfinished, with something missing. The group was showing signs of agitation, indicating that the energy was being sucked up, rather than released. She remained stuck. It was draining.

Before giving up, I closed my eyes, cleared away all images that came before me, allowed Bhagwan's presence to fill the space in whatever way that would happen, and made the conscious choice to accept and go with whatever came through me at that moment.

The word "fat" came across my internal, audiovisual screen three times: "Fat! Fat! Fat!" Okay, Bhagwan, let's see what happens. I said out loud, "Fat! Fat! Fat!" Once said, energy coursed through me, and I continued, "Prabha, you are fat, dear. Fat, fat, fat." My tone was matter-of-fact, not judgmental. "You aren't overweight, you don't have a problem of obesity, or a weight problem, or a problem in overeating, either. You are just fat, Prabha, and I want you to get it. That's right, Prabha, I want you to start getting it."

By this time, I'm pacing the room hardly able to keep up with the energy pouring through me. Everything and everyone is sparkling. I ask, "Will someone please go and get a full-length mirror and a hand-mirror." When they arrive, I ask Prabha to remove all her clothes (the removal of clothes in the Ashram groups is no unusual occurrence, and Prabha has been through several groups) and stand in front of the mirror. I begin pointing out the different fatty areas on her body: her thighs, belly, upper arms, lightly shaking the areas to accentuate the bodily experience and visual impact. "Look, Prabha, that is fat, just fat." Then, handing her the hand-mirror, and asking her to turn around and look at her back, I graphically point out the chubbiness of her rear. Then I ask her to move while continuing to look at herself.

Finally, I said, "Okay, Prabha, this is it! This is as far as I go. There's something here for you to get and I don't know what it is. Somewhere you do know and I want you to find it. So what is it, Prabha? What's really going on?"

She looked at herself quietly in the mirror for some moments, turning slowly, then smiled and said, "I like it. I like the way I look." The room burst with laughter and applause. "I like the way I look," she repeated. " I'm beautiful." Much love and aliveness permeated the room. She began swaying and dancing. She took up some

Indian shawls and began a sensuous, spontaneous dance. Her loving energy flooded the room. Everyone joined her.

That was it! Once she found a way of dropping her mind's notions learned from childhood about how she *should* look, and discovered that she actually liked her body heavier, she became beautiful. For weeks afterwards, I would see Prabha walking about the Ashram, clearly valuing herself, loving herself, moving with sensuous grace.

I acknowledged to myself then and countless times afterwards that when I gave myself permission during moments of confusion to trust totally in the moment, in existence, in the emptiness of Bhagwan, that I was working with a most unique, revolutionary co-therapist.

I'd like to end this section with an amusing, heretic notion: the notion that Bhagwan created the space for nearly all the leading psychotherapeutic and growth methods to happen, not because they all, more or less, equally work, but because they *don't.* I sometimes play with the idea that rather than have his disciples, discouraged in their quest for the elusive butterfly of *nirvāṇa*, take years hopping from group to group, weekend to weekend, est to Fisher-Hoffman to bio-energetics to primal therapy, he gave them all what they would find in the West in a six-month, intensive pot-pourri so they could discover that if you keep mucking about in the mud, you don't become a lotus, you just get a dirty face. You find that there is no way to get "there"—that the world of struggling, of striving for betterment, is no different whether you are seeking a pay raise, enlightenment, or to exorcise a part of yourself you don't like. To see your journey in an old, time-oriented way as having a beginning, a middle, and an end, is to set out on an endless journey that only creates more of *itself*—further struggling and striving.

With total immersion in this trying-to-change-for-the-better orientation, the dawn may come when it isn't *what* you're struggling to overcome that is at issue, but that you have grown accustomed to *struggling* as a way of life. You may "get" that you are simply over-conditioned to climb one more aspirational mountain, or to slay one more inner dragon as a main pastime that keeps you in a familiar, over-identified, problem-oriented perennially becoming state:

> Within fifty years, for the first time psychology will be really born. Freudian psychology is very primitive; it is like an aboriginal religion compared to Buddha. After a hundred years it will look simply silly. And all these people who are working in Encounter, Psychodrama, Bio-energetics, Gestalt and others—they are all going to contribute. All these groups will disappear; they are not going to stay for long. Their work is to contribute, to pool, all that is possible from every direction, and once the real psychology will start taking shape, they will disappear. They are tributaries: once the river is there, they will not be there (Yatri, 1980b: 360).

Meanwhile, you meditated, morning and evening, and more intensively during meditation camps. And meditation is just a long word for a short, timeless, state: the experience of being. After the crazy breathing and let-go of the Dynamic Meditation, or the vigorous shaking and dancing of the Kuṇḍalini Meditation, one often reaches a state of stillness, of no-mind, of effortless presence, of being in the here and now.

Thus, "being", as an alternative, presents itself simply and directly. It was always there alongside "becoming", and as one just gives up trying, it seems to enter through a back door, only, in truth, it is the front door—you were just facing in the wrong direction.

Gradually it comes : There is nowhere to go, nothing to do; just relax and allow whatever is to be:

> Sitting silently,
> Doing nothing,
> Spring comes,
> And the grass grows by itself.
>
> (Rajneesh, 1976g)

Coming Together

Discourse

Every morning, 365 days a year, after Dynamic Meditation from 6.00 a.m. to 7.00 a.m., a bath, and a cup of *cāya* (Indian tea), Bhagwan's disciples, along with visitors, congregated in an open-air auditorium to listen to Bhagwan deliver a spontaneous two-hour discourse clarifying and revitalising, from his inner experience, the words of the Enlightened Ones who had come before—the sayings of Buddha and of Jesus, the *Yoga Sūtras* of Patañjali, the songs of the Vedas and of the Upanisads, the poems of the Baul mystics, of Meera and Kabir, the keys of the Taoist, Zen, Sufi, and Hassidic Masters. Or he might talk on the aphorisms of Werner Erhard, or on the tonal purity of the message of Krishnamurti:

> My whole effort here is to make you fall in love with Lao-Tzu, Chuang-Tzu, Lieh-Tzu, Buddha, Kṛṣṇa, Christ, Krishnamurti, Raman, Ramakrishna—a thousand and one. I am not jealous (Rajneesh, 1980a).

An inspiring, melodious speaker with the touch of a George Jessel for delivering a joke ("I would like you to laugh your way to God"), he spoke for one month in English and the following month in Hindi. He urged his listeners to become more and more aware of the silences between his words, to relax the mind, allow the sounds of the birds to enter awareness, let in the train whistles in the distance, feel the fresh, morning air on the skin, listen to the sounds of the wind and rain—and then to the silence within. Soon something of an altered, meditative state of consciousness would arrive where his emptiness was obvious, where his words were experienced as coming from nothing, and we could have a taste of presence, vastness, and enlightenment.

On alternate days, Bhagwan responded to questions submitted to him by disciples, seekers, and guests. This allowed him to focus upon issues of immediate concern to his audience, such as sex, love, relationships, religion, on becoming a Sannyasin, politics, masculinity-femininity, surrender versus self-will. It also gave him the opportunity to touch his loving Zen stick to his disciples, which sometimes felt like a sledgehammer, sometimes like a kiss:

> I am not here as a person but only as a vehicle... . I am not doing anything at all. Things are happening, but they are not being done. I am as much a spectator as anybody else. I am also surprised, just like you. When you expect a sledgehammer, I also expect one. And when I see the kiss happening I say, "Gosh! What is He up to?"...
>
> When so many times you expect something and just the opposite happens, slowly, slowly you learn a great secret: that expectation is not the way to be with the Divine; it is the barrier, not the bridge. Expect and you will be frustrated. Don't expect and simply wait, then whatever happens has tremendous beauty.
>
> What I do here with my disciples is not my doing; I simply allow something to happen. I don't know what is going to happen. I don't know what I am going to say, I don't know what is going on: why

> you are here, why I am here. But something mysterious is happening. I *am* here, you *are* here, and between the Master and the disciple something transpires which belongs neither to the disciple nor to the Master.
>
> It is a mad, mad game in which a third party is involved who is invisible. Yes, I call this disciple-Master game a *mad* game: M stands for Master, A for and, D for disciple (Rajneesh, 1980a).

None who have been with him even for a short time have any doubts regarding his pinpoint accuracy as bombardier in targeting in on our spiritual and emotional con games.

Each 30-day series of lectures, whether in Hindi or in English, was transcribed, edited, and published. By 1980, approximately 130 English books and nearly 200 Hindi books had been published, and approximately 85 English and 35 Hindi books were in some stage of being published.

Bhagwan's daily lectures seemed to me like the entrance into the womb of the Ashram: the day's beginning, the inviting and nourishing temperate weather of early morning, sitting silently with other Sannyasins, doing nothing, feeling the love simply, effortlessly, allowing in the presence of Bhagwan, experiencing his absence, and then coming home to a reality within myself that just is.

Many times in his discourses Bhagwan intimated that his words were only toys to keep us entertained while we learned to sit and be with his inner silence:

> I would like you to get ready as soon as possible so that we can simply sit in silence...listening to the birds and their songs, or listening just to your own heartbeat. Just being here, doing nothing.
>
> Get ready as soon as possible, because I may stop

> speaking any day...those who want to understand me through words, they should come soon, because I may leave speaking *any* day (Rajneesh, 1980a).

Finally, in March 1981, he did just that. He began *satsaṅga,* or silent discourse, wherein he sat with his Sannyasins for an hour each morning while musicians played meditative music interspersed with silent periods. The time was ripe, and their communion with the Master deepened.

THE COMMUNE: A COMMUNITY TO PROVOKE HUMANKIND

Bhagwan's commune as it was in Poona, and as it is today in hundreds of Rajneesh Sannyas Ashrams all over the world, is variously a space, a quality of consciousness, a provocation, a call. He envisions a clear pool where the consciousness of many may merge to create a new, heightened energy field:

> We pool our consciousness into one space and then each affects the other. Then great energy is released. Alone, you cannot go very high. Alone, you have all kinds of limitations. When you are with many, infinite energy is available, and many things will start happening which cannot happen alone.
>
> You are pooling your energies with me... (Yatri, 1980b: 254).

This field of energy Bhagwan calls "The Buddhafield":

> I am creating a Buddhafield...away from the world, far away, so that a totally different kind of energy can be made available to you (Rajneesh, 1979a: 350).

One day, while I was sitting at my desk I was so moved by the impact of what was happening in the moment that I just let my hands write exactly what was coming through me. The following is what came:

I write this article somewhere in the centre of the

Ashram in an open-air, roofed, bamboo hut amidst countless typewriters, much gaiety and laughter, each person sending out clearly the message, "I love being here," monsoon rains teeming five feet away. Ten yards from my desk, across a garden path, is Buddha Hall, from where throughout the day one programme after the other takes place. Beginning with Dynamic Meditation at 6.00 a.m., through Bhagwan's discourse, ending with 7.00 p.m. meditation or Music Group, a kaleidoscope of sounds and energies float by all days long:

> Buddhafield means a situation where your sleeping Buddha can be awakened. Buddhafield means an energy field where you can start growing, maturing, where your sleep can be broken, where you can be shocked to awareness; an electric field where you will not be able to fall asleep, where you will have to be awake, because shocks will be coming all the time (Rajneesh, 1979a: 350).

Sufi Dance, the 10.30 a.m. 'till noon meditation, now happens. Hundreds are lying on their backs resting, meditating, after an exhilarating blues-jazz, mad, dancing-singing, "I'm a Buddha as I am, oh yeah" Sufi celebration, Bhagwan-style, created by Aneeta, the Sufi leader, and her friends. Now, as all rest, Aneeta and others sing and play together, their harmony penetrating me; typing stops, eyes close, feelings of contentment and joy enter. I'm glad to be here at this moment, simply appreciative of everything and everyone.

> The new commune is going to be a great experiment in Buddhahood. Energies have to be made available to you, possibilities have to be made clear to you. You have to be made aware of your potential, and you have to be given a safe place from where you can work; a place where you are not distracted by the world...a place where

> ordinary things, taboos, inhibitions, are put aside; where only one thing is significant—to become a Buddha—where everything else simply disappears from your mind—money, power, prestige—when all else becomes what exactly it is: a shadow world—and you are no more lost into the apparent (Rajneesh, 1979a: 351).

At noon Mallika leads Tai Chi with a breathy, deep, sensuous voice inviting those attending to go inside, to open. The music is Eastern, slow, haunting, centuries-old; people moving infinitely slowly together, alone, in secret synchronicity:

> In the silence of a commune, in the uninhibited, untabooed atmosphere of a commune, the Master and the disciple can enact the drama totally (Rajneesh, 1979a: 351).

Now from Buddha Hall, healing happens. Scores of people sit silently, cross-legged, Buddha-fashion, in the center of a large circle. Scores more are running about the periphery frenetically, leaping, gesticulating, faces twisted into grotesque leers. In the midst, one Indian man, Swami Bodhisattva, stands upon a table emanating energies as if coming from the very bowels of Hades, bringing to mind images of gargoyles and goblins, goading the demons of illness to rise from their inner chambers to be dispelled into the Universe. The music builds in tempo—those in the middle begin to shudder and quake. Some fall over in paroxysms of vibrant energy. The encircling ones go frantic and lose control. Then all suddenly stops. A feverish pulse remains and remains and remains; it is a deafening quiet! Then with infinite softness, over the loudspeaker comes: "Aum, shanti, shanti, aum, shanti, shanti," ending the healing. Back to the typewriter for me, a bit shook up by it all.

How will the end of this article even remotely be like the beginning. Oh, Well!

> And the more people are there, the bigger Buddhafield will be there and the more powerful it will be. The possibility is that we can create one of the greatest and the most powerful Buddhafields ever created in the world, because never before was there such a search, because never before was man in such a crisis.
>
> We are on the threshold of something new that is going to happen to humanity. Either humanity will die and disappear, or we will take a jump, a leap, and a new being will be formed… . By the end of this century, either man will die in a third world war or man will take the jump and will become a new man. Before that happens, a great Buddhafield is needed—a field where we can create the future (Rajneesh, 1979a: 354).

And all of this happening about me was the periphery, the outside, the obvious manifestation, some of the forms and colours used by the artist. There was so much more even in the manifest: Bhagwan's diminutive juggernaut, his right hand in the world, Ma Yoga Laxmi; the proposed Rajneesh International Meditation University; the counsellor training programmes; the training programmes in body work; the celebrative evening, dancing, singing, Music Group; the electrifying energy *darśanas*; the crafts, pottery, weaving, carpentry, dress, and boutique shops; the all-day, everyday, life groups of the office, cleaning, guarding, gardening, and kitchen departments—all blending and jarring, melting and erupting, each contributing to the gestalt—creating a delicate airy space and a down-to-earth marketplace.

And always slowly, slowly, the manifest would somehow recede and the subtle emerge on a different plane, whose boundaries weren't reachable, weren't knowable, where there was no path, no direction, no guideline—a presence that seemed to be as much an absence—like what remains after a lone, white cloud passes beyond the limits of sight.

Bhagwan, meanwhile would sit in his room, coming out twice daily, once for morning discourse, and once for evening *darśana*. Otherwise, never leaving his room from one year to the next—allowing all, preventing nothing, being unselective, undifferentiating, being a source to each moment—without a guide, without antecedent, without precedent—he created with profound commitment in the moment, out of nothing, into nothing, as he does to this day.

I thrived and quaked in Poona. There was no external support system available to nourish the pervasive attitude of "protective isolation" I used to call my independence; nor was there any support for my mental mountain-climbing towards betterment that gave me a sense of self-worth. Yes, there was a "marketplace" where I could express my desires and resist growth, but there was a mirror at each corner for me to take an on-the-spot look at the game being played. Ambition, greed, lust, the quest, for specialness, and especially fear, all continued to rear their ancestral heads, but once seen for what they were their grip on me lessened.

And there was a support system there for seeing there is no way out—only a way in. Within this milieu, there was and there still is, the option, if I'm willing to take it, of seeing myself as I am, of leaving myself alone when newness and change frighten me, and of giving myself the space to discover what the next moment will bring.

One day, in discourse, Bhagwan put it succinctly:

> To be with me,
> You have to risk
> Finding yourself.

(1982)

Chapter Six

Religion as Fun? The Rajneesh Movement

ROY WALLIS[1]

"I teach rejoicing, not renouncing."

(Bhagwan Shree Rajneesh)

INTRODUCTION

This chapter explores in detail one movement which absorbed many of the leading figures in the Human Potential Movement, and displays many continuities with it, namely Rajneeshism, the Neo-Sannyas Movement of Bhagwan Shree Rajneesh. Rajneesh Chandra Mohan, an Indian of Jain parentage is said to have attained Enlightenment in 1953, at the age of 21. After completing his university education, he became a teacher of philosophy at Raiput Sanskrit College and later the University of Jabalpur. In the early 1960s he began giving lectures throughout India on spiritual and philosophical themes. In 1966, he gave up his university post and under the title of Acharya (Teacher) Shree Rajneesh, devoted himself to delivering public lectures; to personal contact with enquirers and an emerging group of Indian disciples; and to the organisation of regular meditation camps utilising an eclectic range of meditational techniques, later to issue in his own technique of "dynamic meditation". At these camps he would also deliver daily discourses on themes from various sacred literature and in response to questions.

Rajneesh displayed an extraordinary facility as a speaker. His recorded discourses have been transcribed into literally dozens of published volumes, which, while they exhibit considerable redundancy, also show familiarity with a very wide range of source material both Western and Eastern. His early following was overwhelmingly Indian, but inevitably in India in the late 1960s, Rajneesh came to the attention of a few travelling hippies and spiritual seekers from Europe and North America. (Joshi, 1982: 175, refers to "hippies", "flower children" and "drop-outs" as constituting this first group of Western followers.)

For many of these, Rajneesh was but one among a variety of Gurus and teachers on the occult circuit around India. Not all by any means were to make this their final port of call, but a number of Westerners did find what Rajneesh had to offer particularly compelling. Dynamic meditation was a technique involving catharsis and relaxation rather than contemplation or concentration, and despite the otherwise conventional Indian character of the early movement, Rajneesh's philosophy and spiritual message had substantial elements which were to appeal to a particular Western clientele of a distinctive kind.

Rajneesh's world-view derived most explicitly from Tantrism, a philosophy and practice which adopted a non-moralistic conception of enlightenment as surrender to union with the universe. Existence, the universe, is also the divine, and thus such surrender and union represent the realisation of the divine within each individual. The greatest barrier to merging with the universe is the ego:

> The whole of religion is nothing but that: dropping

> the ego, disappearing as your own master... . Then life becomes such a grace; because all tension arises out of ego...all anxiety, anguish, despair, frustration. All illness of the mind is because we have taken this wrong attitude... . Dissolve yourself as a separate entity. Become part of the cosmic whole (Rajneesh, 1983a: 87).

The ego comprises the inheritance of social conditioning and constraint to which the individual has been subjected since birth, and the patterns of belief and expectation which he has developed on the basis of them. Society inculcates false needs in conflict with the real self. The individual becomes dependent upon the roles he plays, the possessions he has acquired, the people with whom he associates. He experiences conflicts between his feelings and the beliefs which he has come to hold through socialisation. These lead to dissatisfactions with himself and the world around him, and to activity aimed to try to remedy these dissatisfactions through the pursuit of new roles, more possessions, other people to love and be loved by. However, since these attempts to change the world and his circumstances are predicated upon unreal beliefs and expectations, upon desire and non-acceptance, they cannot for long still the conflict or resolve the tensions.

Enlightenment, harmony with the universe, bliss, cannot come from the pursuit of satisfaction of the ego, from attempting to change oneself or one's circumstances. The ego is the principle barrier to Enlightenment, and attempting to change the world or oneself arises from false expectations and attachments. Enlightenment can come only from living entirely in terms of one's true identity experienced through the feelings. The ego must be "dropped", the past which it entails and the future which it predicates have likewise to be abandoned, in order to live entirely in the present moment:

> If while eating you can just eat, if while sitting you can just sit—not doing anything else, if you can remain with the moment with no future, no past, if this moment now is the only Existence, then you are a Buddha... (Rajneesh, 1976b: 165-6).

By total awareness of the present moment, by non-judgemental acceptance of oneself, one's feelings and one's circumstances, the individual will awaken from sleep, from mechanically responding to stimuli and his beliefs and expectations about them. "The immediate is to be used as a door to the Ultimate. The Ultimate happens if you enter the immediate" (Rajneesh, 1975a: 347). Through acceptance and through surrender of the ego, the individual begins acting in harmony with the universe, from the divine centre within.[2]

In summary, Rajneesh puts it as follows:

> Tantrism says take this world as your fate and do not be worried about it. Once you take it as your...fate, you accept it, and whatsoever it is. You are not worried about changing it, about making it different, about making it according to your desire. Once you accept it as it is and you are not bothered about it, your total energy is relieved, and then this energy can penetrate inwards (Rajneesh, 1975a: 302).

Acceptance is a far-reaching notion, entailing not merely not trying to change life and its circumstances, but also recognition of all aspects of oneself, abandoning the attempt to suppress those characteristics which the world regards as sinful or unworthy. Rajneesh avers that:

> A man needs to be natural, spontaneous, accepting all his aspects. The dark side has also to be

> accepted—it is a side of you—and when all is accepted, great transformation happens through that acceptance (1983a: 354).

Everything is to be accepted and the individual must become aware of those things which he has repressed since, until they are brought into consciousness, while the individual still struggles with them, they will continue to affect him, to form part of his conditioning, and thus a barrier to surrender. In addition, acceptance entails trust in what occurs, and more particularly in the suggestions of the Enlightened Master who has attained a state of egolessness, and can see both the fundamental principles on which the universe operates, and also precisely what each person requires to advance towards Enlightenment.

The Following

This philosophical view accounts for a great deal about the attraction of the movement during its earlier years and the form which it took. Rajneesh stood out from among the holy men and Gurus available to Western seekers in the late 1960s and early 1970s. He was far more sophisticated than many, having a considerable familiarity with other religious traditions and with contemporary Western writing in psychology and philosophy. He did not resort to the magical conjuring tricks of Sai Baba which often appear crude to Western eyes, nor did he demand a life of renunciation. Dropping the ego did not entail dropping sexuality, shaving the head, or the rigorous practice of any demanding ritual routine. Indeed, the philosophy he propounded suggested rather that nothing should be suppressed. Sexuality was a means of fostering surrender, and of bringing into awareness things long repressed which—while hidden from view—continued to control thought and behaviour. A life of enjoyment and comfort was not in any way incompatible with the path to Enlightenment.

Thus, in this respect, the price of accepting Rajneesh as a spiritual Master was not high. The potential disciple need not abandon the pleasures of conventional life. He was encouraged to accept his sexuality, to act out desire rather than repress it, since only by accepting and being aware of it could he transcend it. Followers could indulge their impulses without guilt and, as long as they did so with full attention and awareness, they could feel that this was a way of eliminating the hold of the past, of enhancing the ability to surrender, and of gaining a foretaste of union with the cosmos.

Prior to the establishment of the Neo-Sannyas Movement, moreover, the spiritual seekers and hippies who came to Rajneesh were not even expected to maintain an exclusive commitment to him. One Sannyasin reported continuing for sometime to wear the *mālā* of another Guru. Even when Rajneesh began to formalise his following in 1970 with the formation of the Neo-Sannyas Movement, the person whom he initiated as a Sannyasin was one who did not "renounce the family, the society, or possessions, instead, he gives up his ego-attachment to them, he drops his passion for and possessiveness of them" (Joshi, 1982: 4). He undertook only to wear orange clothing (or related shades symbolising the sunrise), which could be of the most fashionable cut and quality; to wear a *mālā* or necklace of beads bearing a picture of Rajneesh; to take a new name chosen by Rajneesh; and to practise a daily meditation.

Not only were followers given a justification to indulge in normally repressed or restricted sexual behaviour, they were also given the opportunity to do so in an increasingly large community of the like-minded who were often youthful and physically appealing. They were encouraged to focus attention solely upon themselves (and the Master), ignoring the less attractive features of the world around them—in India a world of poverty, disease and squalor—to pursue their own path to Enlightenment. "Be selfish", Rajneesh enjoins his followers, "only then can you be altruistic" (1976: 30), and "Just look for the beautiful; forget the ugly" (1976: 60). They were provided with an opportunity for cathartic expression of frustrations, guilt and pent-up emotion, and relieved of their responsibilities for others, their commitments—particularly those which had begun to show signs of strain.

The costs of commitment were low except in terms of a radical change in attitude. What was more demanding, of course, was the intention, and the practice concomitant upon that intention, of abandoning the ego: "When you join me as a Sannyasin, you are dropping yourself, disappearing. When you join the commune then you have to utterly efface yourself" (Joshi, 1982: 46).

As Rajneesh's Western following grew, reports of him filtered back to the West, sparking an interest in a wider range of potential disciples. These reports tended to travel through networks of people engaged in spiritual pursuits or in marginal therapeutic exercises. Particularly influential were to be a group of individuals involved in the Human Potential Movement. By the mid 1970s, a number of such people who had been leaders in the movement had come to feel that although it had proven effective in releasing much of the hold of the past, there was further to go, and Human Potential activities were insufficient to take them there.

Rajneesh's ideas and activities were to have a peculiar attraction for them because they displayed a clear continuity with those of the Growth Movement. This too had provided occasions for the cathartic abreaction of repressed emotion—as did Rajneesh's dynamic meditation. As Rajneesh has said:

> The whole society is ill! That is why I so much insist on chaotic meditation. Relieve yourself, act out whatsoever society has forced on you… . Act them *(sic)* out, relieve yourself of them, go through a catharsis (1975a: 292).

The Human Potential Movement had offered opportunities and resources for confronting the inhibition and constraints implanted by past conditioning; for exploring feelings and acknowledging the emotions; it had encouraged the participant to see himself as he was—to be aware of his characteristics, even those he might wish to ignore, and to accept them. It had stressed the importance of focusing on the present, rather than dwelling in the past or future, to be aware of what was happening now rather than bemoaning what was past or aspiring to what might very well never come. Rajneesh's tantrism overlapped extensively with the principal ideological elements of the Human Potential Movement, but offered something far more, a path to Enlightenment.

Humanistic therapists and Human Potential group leaders began to come in substantial numbers, first to Rajneesh's apartment in Bombay and then to the Ashram which he established in Poona. It was entirely compatible, therefore, that from 1975 a wide range of Human Potential groups began to be offered to the increasing numbers of Westerners who found their way to him.

If hippies and spiritual seekers were the first group of Westerners to find him, and leaders in the Growth Movement were the second important group, it was inevitable that their clients should be the next. Many Growth Movement leaders travelled back and forth between India and the West, carrying their new commitment to their clients and encouraging them in turn to make the journey. Rajneesh centres were established in Europe, America and Australia, providing a major base for the continuation of Growth Movement activity in the West as other independent centres folded. Although not a zealously proselytising movement, Rajneesh's Sannyasins inevitably conveyed their commitment and enthusiasm to friends and acquaintances, but the broader third group of those who came to Rajneesh were far from being a random cross-section of the population.

In part, of course, this followed from the largely word of mouth transmission through networks of friendship and acquaintances. People are normally disproportionately acquainted with people like themselves. But more than this, Rajneesh's philosophy of life had a peculiar affinity with the circumstances and aspirations of certain kinds of 1970s and 1980s Westerners. Thus many followers were also attracted by Rajneesh's prolific writings as these became more available in the West in the 1970s.[3] There are some clues as to the distinctive character or Rajneesh's Western following.

A study of 300 American Sannyasins at the Poona Ashram conducted by Swami Krishna Deva in 1980 found them to have an average age just over 30. Sixty per cent had been Sannyasins less than two years and most were living in America, making periodic trips to Poona. Half were from California; they were 97% white and 25% Jewish. 81% were from middle class and upper middle class homes. Nearly two thirds had degrees and "They regarded themselves as successful in worldly terms" (*Rajneesh Foundation Newsletter,* 1 June, 1981: 5). Three quarters "had been involved in some therapy" and "more than half had tried belonging to some other spiritual group".

The impression of a relatively successful group in worldly terms of above-average educated people constituting the main body of Rajneesh's followers today is borne out by the occupations listed for disciples who received initiation into Sannyas from, or were spoken to at *darśana* by, him in May 1977, as reported in the volume of transcribed talks which he gave at each *darśana*. Occupations were not reported in every case, and it is possible that this reflects a systematic bias in reporting, but there is no good reason to believe that this is so. Below we list all occupations given, the sex and, where available, nationality of the Sannyasin or enquirer.

Sex, occupation and national origin of sannyasins and enquirers recieving *darśana* from Rajneesh in May 1977

Sex	*Occupation*	*National Origin*
F	Student	England
M	Photographer	—
F	Student	France
M	Karate Instructor	—
M	Assoc. Prof. of Psychology	—
F	Economist with U.N.	United States
M	Dentist	England
M	Prof. of Comparative Religion	United States
F	Clerical/Administrative	United States
F	Musician	Israel
M	Student	—
M	Social Worker	Holland
F	Fischer-Hoffman Therapist	United States
M	Musician	—
F	Student	Holland
M	Potter	England
M	Rock Musician	England
M	Sculptor	United States
M	Film Producer	India
F	Prostitute	Australia
F	Psychoanalyst	England
M	Pilot	United States
M	Doctor	India
M	Patent Examiner	Germany
F	Student Teacher	Scotland
F	Therapist	—
M	Painter	Germany
F	Writer/Poet	—

Sex	*Occupation*	*National Origin*
F	Yoga Teacher	United States
F	Creative Dance Teacher	Australia
M	Architect	United States
M & F	Journalists	Germany
M	Lawyer	Germany
M	Cameraman	United States
F	Go-Go Dancer	Denmark
M	Alexander Therapist	—
M	Record Producer	United States
F	Novelist	England
M	Ex-politician	India

Only those cases in which an occupation was given have been listed.
Source: Rajneesh, 1979g.

Occupations have not always been listed so carefully as in this book, but a later volume of talks gives only the following additional occupations for Western Sannyasins:

Restaurateur
Farmer
Actor
Social Researcher
Pediatrician
Psychiatrist
Clinical Psychologist
Child Psychotherapist
Air Hostess
Former Nun (Rajneesh, 1983a)

These lists, although certainly not exhaustive of the occupational backgrounds of Rajneesh's following, would seem to be reasonably typical of a large number. They are striking not merely for their overwhelmingly middle class character, but also for their tendency to consist of occupations of a professional, semi-professional and craft nature. They are overwhelmingly occupations either of a creative kind, or in which their main role is service to others, particularly of a human developmental kind. What are noticeably absent from these lists are occupations—even middle class occupations—in which the main tasks are routine and highly bureaucratic, and few of them imply working within a corporate framework. The typical follower of Rajneesh is from a liberal or autonomous profession or semi-profession or a craft occupation. There are certainly former business people, accountants and civil servants in the Neo-Sannyas Movement, but they are a minority and do not by any means set the tone. The typical follower is drawn from the *comfortable* margins of the modern corporate industrial world. He or she came from a social and educational background which gave a certain amount of choice as to the future, and the typical follower chose specifically not to be located in the industrial, commercial or bureaucratic core of the modern world. Rajneeshees, by and large and *before* they had become Sannyasins, had already rejected the routine predictability of corporate life, its impersonality and rationalisation, to pursue a course more concerned with creativity and the imagination, with human contact and with more spiritual values.

Those drawn to Rajneesh, whether from the initial itinerant hippies in India, the Human Potential leaders and the later mass following of middle class professionals, artists, craftsmen, therapists and those who aspired to such roles, all identified themselves with the pursuit of the *expressive* life. Although many of them were wealthy and materially comfortable, often by their own efforts, this did not constitute their primary definition of the ideal human condition.

Rejecting, or relieved of the necessity to focus entirely upon, the pursuit of improved income or occupational advancement in a bureaucratic or corporate career, it was precisely this group in Western societies who could concentrate their attention upon the pursuit of the ideal self. What constituted the ideal self may have differed greatly in detail between particular individuals. However, such conceptions contained certain clear common themes. First, was freedom from the constraints imposed by social roles weighing heavily upon those who had passed through rigorous educations and demanding parental expectations, delaying gratification to achieve knowledge or abilities required in later skilled occupations. This may go some way towards explaining the over-representation of Sannyasins from Jewish backgrounds. Second was a desire for greater expressivity in themselves and in those with whom they interacted; openness, spontaneity and intimacy less restricted by role playing and social conventions; and enthusiasm and joy in life, less burdened by inhibitions, by a past history of rejection or failure, or their anticipation in the future. Those who had been less successful occupationally or educationally, or who had eschewed the prerequisites of such success, sought recognition of their intrinsic, inner worth, unmediated by universalistic assessment of their worldly accomplishments. They sought acceptance of the inner self often hidden in conventional interaction, freedom from guilt, and access to human contact often restricted in its availability in the urban industrial setting. Ma Prem Pankaja, in the "Introduction" to *Rajneesh* (1976b, xi), touches on this when she refers to the relief Rajneesh's message was for her:

> To a Westerner, so used to jumping through hoops of guilt, and ought and ought not, it is a staggering relief to be allowed just to be.

Moreover, since they probably shared many of these aspirations with some occupants of corporate bureaucratic roles, the other significant factor leading them to Rajneesh was the fact that such occupations as those listed above (or even the lack of any occupation at all) provided the *opportunity* to take the time out to spend at the Ashram in India. Those drawn to Rajneesh were peculiarly free to follow their inclinations. They were not part of continuous bureaucratic careers which would be disrupted by prolonged absence. A few Rajneeshees who came from commercial occupations were self-employed. Others were in senior positions with enlightened employers willing once or twice to permit leave of absence before causing difficulties. But in other cases, association with Rajneesh in India was possible only at the cost of the individual's job. When returning disciples established Rajneesh Centres in Europe, America and elsewhere, this difficulty was alleviated to some extent. A Sannyasin could be initiated by mail, or by Rajneesh's local representative, and visit the centre during vacations or at weekends. But yet the number in conventional commercial, industrial or bureaucratic occupations does not seem to have been great even then. The attitude and orientation of Rajneeshism was not one that would readily have accommodated to the regulation, materialism, instrumentalism, emotional repression and restricted openness and sincerity required for successful accomplishment of such occupations. Outside California, even the wearing of a *mālā*, and being obliged to attend work in clothing between the shades of orange, russet, pink, purple and the like, could be difficult. Respondents report that even sympathetic employers might keep the Sannyasin out of official sight on occasion.

Even in the face of these difficulties some Sannyasins have found it possible to retain conventional occupations with the aid of coping strategies such as a sober maroon or reddish brown tweed business suit and wearing their *mālās* underneath a jersey or shirt; and women, with more flexibility in business wear, were less disadvantaged in this respect than men. But the therapist, artist or *yoga* teacher would clearly face fewer problems in this area, and could leave off and take up work again with a less significant loss in continuity or less inconvenience to others. The pilot or university teacher, while employed by a large corporation possessed considerable freedom, flexibility and an ample leave entitlement.

The followers of Rajneesh were thus a group who had largely pursued particular careers because of expressive and creative interests and a desire for autonomy and freedom from the restrictions of commercial and bureaucratic employment. Such careers often exhibited a preoccupation with the same values as those to which Rajneesh offered access. Moreover, they provided resources and opportunities to pursue those values in a distant location such as Bombay, Poona or Oregon.

They were available in other respects also. Of the sample of American Sannyasins surveyed by Swami Krishana Deva in Poona in 1980, 45% had never been married and 36% were divorced. Only 19%, therefore, were currently married. Moreover, more than two thirds had no children (*Rajneesh Foundation Newsletter*, 1st June, 1981: 5). They were thus predominantly free also in respect of commitments to spouses and children.

Developments in Rajneeshism

From an overwhelmingly Indian following during his years of travelling lectures and up to settlement in Bombay in 1970, the composition was to shift progressively to an overwhelmingly European and American following.

In Bombay and the coast down to Goa, more Westerners were to be found, and Bombay was often a first port of call for visitors from the West. There Rajneesh began giving regular daily discourses to followers and inquirers, and introduced the dynamic meditation as a regular practice. There too he introduced the concept of Neo-Sannyas (to distinguish it from traditional Sannyas), and founded the Neo-Sannyas International Movement, by initiating six disciples, "to create a spiritual awakening all over the world" (Joshi, 1982: 95).

> The old concept of Sannyas... was to give you a rigid discipline, to give you a character, to give you a certain form, a pattern, a lifestyle. My Sannyas is not like that at all—it is a radical change. I don't give you any character, because to me the man of character is a dead man. I would like to take all character from you so you are left in a creative chaos...so each moment one has to respond to life, not out of a certain pattern.
>
> To respond in the moment without any pattern, just out of spontaneity—whatever the feel of the moment decides to act just like that *(sic)*—is what I call "creative chaos"—a characterless consciousness, a present without past, a freedom unhindered by any discipline (Rajneesh quoted in Joshi, 1982: 96).

Foundation of the neo-Sannyas Movement led to a certain rudimentary organisation. Rajneesh appointed two secretaries who began increasingly to mediate between him and the wider following. Some of his writings became available in English, and returning Sannyasins were encouraged to set up centres in the West where his writing and tape-recordings of his discourses would be available and the meditational techniques could be practised.

In 1971, Acharya Rajneesh changed his title to Bhagwan (Blessed One) Shree (an honorific) Rajneesh. Although "Bhagwan" can be translated as "God", Rajneesh is a universalist in this respect, since all beings are divine and indeed all creation is divine. "God", he says, "is not a person but another name for the totality of all" (Rajneesh, 1983: 189). (Although, as Belfrage (1971) points out, in practice some people in the movement appear to be considered more Godlike than others.)

Early Western followers were sometimes sent out with Indian disciples in Kīrtana Maṇḍalī, small groups travelling to Indian villages to sing devotional songs, conduct meditations and play taped discourses (Joshi, 1982: 120, asserts that only Indian followers were sent, but Western respondents have said they also participated). Westerners were also sent "to live in a work-farm commune away from Bombay" (Joshi, 1982: 118), to undertake field and building work in imitation of Gurdjieff's work as a technique to create awareness and promote surrender.

As numbers of followers increased, a new, more spacious site was required and in 1974, Rajneesh moved south to Poona. There in 1975, an extensive range of encounter and therapy groups was introduced. New arrivals were encouraged to participate in these groups which were sometimes conducted in a more unconstrained fashion than in the West. Indeed they became notorious in the local community and the mass media when the acting out of aggression led to broken bones, and when the release of sexual inhibition led not only to sexual encounters—a frequent occurrence—but also to accusations of rape in the groups. The Poona Ashram became a Human Potential supermarket, and these groups therefore became a major source of finance. In the Western centres, Sannyasin therapists were to be the major remaining suppliers of Growth group activities in the late 1970s and early 1980s.

Sannyasins were encouraged to remain as long as possible at the Ashram. Some were granted the privilege of working in the Ashram without pay, although they might receive food and accommodation. Many even had to pay for this privilege of living in the Ashram by way of a substantial donation to building costs. As numbers grew larger, so Rajneesh began to withdraw from close contact with his followers, only being seen at *darśana*, to which he was driven daily in a large car (later he was to become a mass media celebrity in part because of the number of Rolls Royces donated to him—reputed to be over 70 at latest reports), and at the daily discourse. In March 1981, Rajneesh entered a phase of public silence, and appeared only for silent *darśana*, and in Oregon, he was only seen by most followers in his daily drive-past in one of the Rolls Royces.

A coterie of close followers was given authority to organise the day-to-day affairs of the commune. Rules were introduced controlling access such as the requirement that anyone attending *darśana* be smelled by gate guards to ensure that they carried no offensive odour (including shampoo and soap) which might upset Rajneesh's delicate metabolism.

As the numbers of Sannyasins in Poona grew, relationships with the local inhabitants and authorities deteriorated. The Western Sannyasins often flaunted their new-found freedom from convention in a manner deeply offensive to conservative local people. A few, in order to finance their stay, turned to drug smuggling and also—it was said—to prostitution (see, for example, Floether, 1983: 7). The leadership too began to behave in a high-handed manner, claiming persecution as their justification. Reporters and photographers were allegedly manhandled, and a number of complaints of sexual assault and molestation were made, sometimes against people, such as the Ashram's landlord, with whom there had been some dispute. Certain of these were said to "have...been written-off by the police as false complaints. 'These were simple cases of entrapment,' said a senior police official. 'Whenever they found anybody stepping out of line in his dealings with them they would set him up and trap him in a molestation case'" (*India Today*, 15th June, 1982: 137). The Ashram was experiencing other difficulties with the authorities such as a substantial assessment for tax arrears, and refusal to permit the development of a new, larger Ashram on an agriculturally zoned site.

Late in May 1981, a warehouse used to store books and another building belonging to the Ashram were set alight by petrol bombs. Ashram officials blamed their landlord once again, and declared the loss to be some thirty times the amount later set on the damage by a police valuer. A report in *India Today* (15th June, 1982: 137) alleged that, "A year later both police and CID officials in Pune (Poona) are unanimous in their charge that the incidents were rigged by Rajneesh followers."

In the face of mounting tension, criticism and possible punitive action by the authorities in relation to some of these disputes, Rajneesh departed for America, allegedly for treatment of certain health problems. There, in the vast, thinly inhabited expanse of central Oregon, he was able to establish a commune on a site large enough for his needs. Sixty square miles of land were bought and leased, on which to found Rajneeshpuram, a Sannyasin city.

An immense investment and development programme was instituted. Funds were solicited as donations or interest free and low interest loans from Sannyasins. Some who came to live in the Oregon commune donated all their resources, or all income from their investments. Ashram dwellers were housed, clothed and fed, but received no pay. During the summer months, additional workers were imported from other centres or from among the independent Sannyasins to work on the development of Rajneeshpuram, and in preparation for an Annual Festival, which all Sannyasins were encouraged to attend. Living in tents of 3-4 persons at a cost of $500 per person, the 15,000 participants at the 1984 Annual World Celebration would have proven a major source of Ashram finance.

When Poona was abandoned, returning Sannyasins were encouraged to establish local communes in Europe and elsewhere. These too were funded largely by loans, gifts and debentures, but money was also raised through group and therapy programmes, activities for weekend Sannyasin visitors paying a fee and accommodation costs, and by establishing commercial businesses including restaurants, discos, printing and design, computer programming and building, utilising the skills and labour power of residents to fund the running costs of the commune, and the additional cost of sending all residents to the Annual Celebration at Rajneeshpuram. A number of Sannyasins were, therefore, to find themselves engaged in precisely the routine commercial activity they had long sought to escape or avoid. However, they could do it for a cause, they could do it "wearing Orange" and with Sannyasin workmates, and they could legitimate it with the thought that they brought more "love" and creative imagination to the task than their non-Sannyasin competitors. They also had a further ideological buttress in that those who worked in and for the commune were believed to be sufficiently advanced on the spiritual path not to need to continue the usual meditation required of Sannyasins. Work was said to be their meditation, or—as they increasingly donned the trappings of religion in Oregon, perhaps to avail themselves more readily of constitutional protections and privileges—work was their "worship".

The shift from Poona to Oregon was not to end the tension and conflict with the surrounding environment, however. The small neighbouring town of Antelope, near Rajneeshpuram felt swamped by the Rajneeshees, who soon outnumbered locals and took over the Town

Government, leading to outcry and counterattack by the commune. Libel suits were initiated against vocal local critics, and lengthy litigation undertaken to permit the incorporation of Rajneeshpuram as a city, to enable Rajneesh to remain in the United States beyond the expiry of his entry visa, and to secure permission to hold the Annual Festival. Opponents fought back with political pressure, petitions, legal action, and even on one occasion detonated a bomb in a Portland hotel recently purchased by the Rajneeshees.

In America, Rajneeshism was formally declared to be a religion, with a priestly hierarchy.

Interpretation of Developments

How are these developments to be interpreted? Elsewhere, Wallis (1984) has argued that the new religions in the West can be understood as falling into three analytical types. The world-affirming movement accepts much of what the modern world has to offer, but advances alternative, spiritual means of achieving the valued features of the world, whether improved human relations, greater prosperity, relief from psychological disability, better health, increased power and status, or some combination of these. The world-rejecting movement on the other hand construes the modern world as irremediably depraved. Only complete transformation can save it from final destruction. Rather than seeking to enjoy the benefits of conventional society, believers in a world-rejecting new religion separate themselves from it in a communion of the elect, preserving themselves unspotted by the world until the cataclysm or the millennium. The world-accommodating movement is the most "denominational" in character, offering essentially a more zealous and enthusiastic form of religion for people who feel that the conventional forms of religious expression have become cold and lacking in experiential spirituality.

Atthough one can readily enough identify examples of each of these types, it must be remembered that empirical examples will only be approximations, often containing elements of more than one type. Indeed, there may be distinctive advantages in such a synthesis. The predominantly world-rejecting new religion risks the complete alienation of its social environment through the hostility it displays towards it, and its indifference to or rejection of normal convention. It may, therefore, generate intolerable levels of social control. This is clearly what occurred to Manson's Family, perhaps the Peoples's Temple, Synanon and to a lesser extent the Children of God. Intense rejection of the world also risks the loss of new recruits who find the distance between the world they inhabit and the movement too great to cross. Finally, it risks the loss of any viable economic support base, as new recruits are not drawn in, bringing wealth and income, and as sympathisers and other supporters are frightened off, becoming less willing to make donations or even to do business with such a group.

The predominantly world-affirming movement, with its highly permeable boundaries, risks the loss of any distinctive character for its salvational commodity as its ideas are taken out into the wider culture or other organisations. Its distinctive character may also suffer from the low level of social control which can be exercised over members who may be inclined to proliferate new ideas and practices of their own, or synthesise one movement's ideas and practices with those of quite different movements. The loss of a distinctive salvational commodity may entail the loss of members or clientele who can find more or less the same thing elsewhere and possibly at lower cost. The world-rejecting movement is tempted to set the barriers around itself too high, while the world-affirming movement is often poorly placed to raise them high enough for its own survival. World-accommodating movements risk the classic consequence of denominationalisation, the gradual attenuation of their distinctively enthusiastic character and a resulting loss of support as they become less distinguishable from competing established purveyors of salvation.

An organisation that can sustain elements of all three may hope to attract three types of members or clients while also maintaining its distinctive character. What form would such a movement take? We shall identify these characteristics and argue that the Rajneesh Movement succeeded in embodying them.

Such a movement would possess an inner elite or cadre who would fulfill the major organisational tasks, carry out the leader's commands unquestioningly, provide necessary service activities for the less committed clientele and a model of the distinctive mode of life favoured by the movement. This inner core would be largely insulated from the surrounding society, mediated to it through more accommodating and conventional personnel. In the Neo-Sannyas Movement, this elite role was played by the semi-permanent committed followers who lived in the Poona and later Rajneeshpuram communes, and in slightly attenuated form, the residents of the local communes established elsewhere.

Such a movement would provide world-accommodating facilities for those who wished to continue to live in the world, but to pursue a more zealous and enthusiastic spiritual life. In the Rajneesh Movement, the communes sometimes offered the opportunity for some people to live in while continuing conventional occupations in the surrounding society. They also offered facilities for those who had been initiated into Sannyas to visit for weekends, celebrations, parties and the like, and thus to recapture a sense of the

Rajneeshee lifestyle and their enthusiasm for it, before returning to the world after a visit.

It would also offer world-affirming facilities for those who wished for some elements of the movement's life or manner, while unwilling to commit themselves to all its requirements. In the Rajneesh Movement, this aspect was available through the Human Potential therapy and group activity, and other healing facilities and training.

This structure was particularly effective in that it provided a mechanism for supporting the world-rejecting elite from the gifts and fees of world-accommodating and world affirming members and clients, a graded rather than entirely discountinuous pattern of entry from less committed client to totally committed and deployable member, and also a protective periphery of more conventional personnel to represent the movement and speak in its defence in the wider society.

The modern world has elevated the rational at some cost to the affective life. Impersonality, bureaucracy, deferred gratification, long-term planning, rational cost accounting, job fragmentation and specialisation, and the pursuit of efficiency have developed alongside the democratisation of expectations and a mass consumption economy and culture. Not only do most adult individuals conceive themselves to possess the right to participate in the political process, but to a basic education, welfare, health and civil rights. The expectation of a satisfactory life and an equal right to life's bounty, has extended inward to the private life: a happy and sexually fulfilled marriage, a sense of personal fulfilment, of personal worth, have all come widely to be seen as individual rights, but they grow within a rationalistic environment sometimes incompatible with their achievement—even when those expectations were realistic in the first place. Achievement in the world may often only be acquired at the price of repression of the instinctual life and feelings, a learned incapacity for spontaneity and intimacy.

The cultivation of character is the attitudinal stance predicated upon the assumption of inequality and suffering, of bearing life's vicissitudes with fortitude. The cultivation and celebration of the self is an attitudinal stance predicated upon the assumption of a general right to happiness and fulfilment, and the belief that these should be and are attainable, if only the right means are found.

It is thus to be expected that there will emerge in advanced capitalist societies resources for attaining or recapturing a sense of spontaneity, emotional warmth, intimacy and community. Some people will wish to sacrifice achievement in the industrial urban environment almost entirely for these benefits, and they would gradually be absorbed into the inner movement cadre of deployable agents. Others will require only an occasional recourse to re-invigorate them to return to the rat race. They would be more attracted to occasional participation of the kind permitted through its world-accommodating and world-affirming facilities.

A differentiated structure of the kind elaborated above thus optimises the potential client and membership base, and is therefore particularly effective in a movement's early years, enabling rapid recruitment and the formation of a cohesive elite cadre while mobilising less committed followers and clients in the provision of economic support. It is a structure utilised by Scientology and (during its social movement phase) by Synanon, and to a lesser extent by Transcendental Meditation.

But there are inevitable tensions in such a structure. Maintaining a permeable boundary and a world-affirming clientele limits the extent to which firm social controls can be deployed to constrain participants without frightening them off. At the same time, the development of an effective cadre of deployable agents is likely to create an inner movement culture of an exclusivist kind. As numbers of committed adherents rise they will be likely to develop a sense of themselves as engaged upon a superior task than others, as spiritually more developed, possessing a clearer vision of the spiritual life, and thus a sense of their separateness and elite status. Those not prepared to commit themselves to the same extent are likely to be seen as missing the essential point:

> Alone you cannot go very high. Alone you are alone. Alone you have all kinds of imitations. When you are one with many, infinite energy is available. And many things will start happening which cannot happen alone (Rajneesh, quoted in Joshi, 1982: 146).
>
> .....work is a way to commune with me. The more you work for me, the closer you are to me (Rajneesh, 1983a: 16).

If the movement has a charismatic leader, moreover, he is likely to wish to constrain the dilution of his thought and practice, and the emergence of other leaders attracting their own personal following. He is therefore unlikely to inhibit the tendency for inner cadre elitism to spill over into sectarian hostility to the world and towards those who fail to commit themselves to the model they demonstrate in their lives. These developments are likely to be enhanced by continuing conflict with the outside world, leading to heightened group cohesion and an expectation that less committed members will stop sitting on the fence.

With the growth of the Rajneesh Movement, such tendencies began to manifest themselves during the Poona phase, with aggression towards neighbours and stricter regulation of lower level participants, but were developed further in Oregon. Somendra, a leading Sannyasin and hitherto favoured disciple who had built up a substantial centre in Brussels and an incipient personal following, but who displayed too independent a line (too much committed, it was said, to his own ego and thus to that extent insufficiently surrendered to Rajneesh) was excluded from the movement, and immediately abandoned by his erstwhile supporters. Somendra in an interview sometime prior to his exclusion from the movement set the scene while back in the West after a stay in Poona:

> I'm back here now because I still had some kind of thing in me which liked to be independent, some feeling of wanting to do things in my own way, and in new ways—the set-up in the Ashram didn't really permit this. I felt cramped, and because of this I became a bit rebellious in certain ways there towards the administration and so on (Somendra, 1980: 17).

Others too independent, not sufficiently yielded to Rajneesh, were declared to be "late sannyasins", officially dead to the movement.

Other evidence of growing centralisation and a more inward orientation, lies in the closure of the small local centres, with live-in Sannyasins being grouped together into larger Ashrams where more discipline can prevail, along with a more cohesive and integrated community life.

Such developments were unlikely while the movement possessed only an ideology of personal transformation, and the radically idealist conception that, "nothing needs to be done—all is and all is perfect as it is...." (Rajneesh, 1983: 117). The pursuit of personal enlightenment in the early years of Rajneesh's mission had little by way of social ethic or political vision, except to the extent of a critical view of those who maintained a less liberated stance. Rajneesh was essentially an exemplary rather than an ethical prophet. His message of acceptance provided no clear basis for social action. A certain attitude was enjoined upon the believer, but no guidelines for collective action could be found in this principle, other than passive withdrawal. But in its collective behaviour, particularly from the mid 1970s on, the Rajneesh Movement clearly did not adopt the policy of accepting everything that happened to it. In its collective behaviour the Rajneesh movement manifests many desires, and the motivation for its attitude towards its environment must clearly be sought elsewhere than the personal ideology of surrender. Rajneesh was to develop an apocalyptic vision that the conventional world would destroy itself by nuclear war or other disaster by the 1990s. In 1982, for example, Rajneesh said that:

> ...all the causes for a third world war have already happened. There is therefore only a very remote possibility that the conflict itself will not take place. It would take something totally unpredictable—such as, for example, contact with an intelligent life form from another galaxy—to change the direction in which humanity is heading...the third world war...will begin sometime between 1993 and 1999 (*Rajneesh Foundation International Newsletter*, 1, 14, 1st October, 1982: iv).

He had earlier, in 1978, spoken of the need to create "a new humanity":

> If we cannot create the new man in the coming twenty years...then humanity has no future...The old man is ready to commit global suicide. The

> third world war is global suicide; it can be avoided only if a new kind of man can be created (Joshi, 1982: 148).

Even as early as 1964, Rajneesh had said (1970:62) that, "The third and last war, is now on the way." By the early 1980s this had advanced to become the basis for a new exclusivism, a conception of Rajneesh as the only route to salvation:

> Man is now living in his most critical moment and it is a crisis of immense dimensions. Either he will die or a new man will be born. Rajneeshism accepts this challenge and is making the only worldwide effort to transform human consciousness... The period of this crisis will be between 1984 and 1999. During this period there will be every kind of destruction...Rajneeshism is creating a Noah's Ark of consciousness...I say to you that except this there is no other way (*Rajneesh Foundation International Newsletter*, 2, 14, 1st October, 1983: ii).

In 1984, Rajneesh also "predicted that AIDS will kill two-thirds of the world's population" (*Rajneesh Times*, 16-31st October, 1984: 6).

This apocalyptic theme, pressed harder in the late 1970s and early 1980s, generated a more disciplined atmosphere in Poona and later a sense of urgency in getting the Oregon commune established, and possibly created some loss of patience with those who were believed to have received so much from the movement in service and enthusiasm, but who failed to commit themselves whole-heartedly:

> The more you work for me, the closer you are to me...Otherwise how is this Buddhafield to be created? Thousands of people have to work...So

> everybody has to contribute and everybody has to contribute totally, absolutely (*Rajneesh Foundation International Newsletter*, 1, 19, 15th November, 1982: 8).

Rajneesh has also observed (*Rajneesh Times*, 26th October, 1984: 131):

> A man like me cannot remain unopposed. A man like me is bound to divide people into two categories: those who are with me and those who are not with me.
>
> Just the other day, an old friend wrote a letter to me suggesting...Right now there are only two kinds of people: one who are *(sic)* devotees, who are utterly in love with me, and the other who are enemies, full of hatred for me. He wants to create a third category of people who are neither devotees nor enemies, but impartial thinkers.
>
> His idea looks logical, but it is not possible...I am not interested in impartial people.

Having achieved a substantial committed membership and organised various business activities, and by 1984, having invested some $100 million in the Oregon property, by this stage in its development, the world-affirming and other less committed adherents may have been seen as less valuable than when membership was still being built up. Now the movement can concentrate more effectively on its fully committed ashram dwellers, and a more exclusive, world-rejecting stance seems a likely outcome.

The evidence for this claim lies in the formation of larger, more centralised Ashrams; the more actively oppositional stance to the surrounding society; the expulsion of those who displayed too great an independence of the growing centralised authority (such as Somendra); and the tests of loyalty placed on formerly high-ranking Sannyasins, once close to Rajneesh, but who were removed from positions of authority. For example, Shiva (Swami Shivamurti), once Rajneesh's bodyguard and leader of the Poona Ashram guards, was declared to be:

> no longer a disciple of Bhagwan...when situations change and a disciple who has been in a position of authority is suddenly without power, this is both a test and an opportunity. If the disciple can drop the attachment to power, then he, or she can easily transcend. If not, a great opportunity is missed (*Rajneesh Foundation International Newsletter*, 1, 19, 15th December, 1982; i).

A disciple who protested against this and was told that he had the same desire to be special as afflicted Shiva, recalled in his own statement of submission:

> ...five years ago when I had asked if there were any limits to surrender to the Master (I didn't want to work in the Ashram office)...he (Rajneesh) had said then, "Surrender comes only when things go against your own decision—not when they go with your decision. Then what is the point of surrender? Nobody is telling you to be in such trouble. You can drop Sannyas! Why create anguish unnecessarily for yourself?" (*Rajneesh Foundation International Newsletter*, 1, 19, 15th December, 1982: i. On "following blindly" see also Rajneesh, 1975b: 430).

In earlier years, at the Poona Ashram, Rajneesh had established the principle, even if it was not then enforced so rigorously:

> ...if anybody decided for himself, then the simple thing is that he should not be part of the commune.

> He can decide; then there is no problem in it...But if you want to be part of the commune the whole decision goes to me...I am not going to accept half-hearted people and I am sorting them out fast...(Yatri, 1980: 394).
>
> ...I am preparing something for the future, so I don't want any dissidents here in the way, because once things become bigger, if a few dissidents are here, they will create cliques and will disturb the work.
>
> I want it to be absolutely homogeneous—with one voice, with once direction, with one soul (Yatri, 1980: 453).

After the departure of a number of the old guard, Rajneesh described these events (as reported in *Rajneesh Foundation International Newsletter*, 1, 19, 15th December, 1982: iii), as follows:

> The Sannyasins who have been with Him in Poona are more likely to feel negative now than newer disciples—unless they can adjust to the changes that are happening. He said that if they want to cling to the old ways—seeking power, complaining, creating discontent in others—it is better for them to go. It would be more dangerous to keep them here for they would only pollute the new energy field He is creating here...Newer disciples come without any expectations. They have no demands. This is a period of transition, the move into the ultimate phase of the Master's work...He said that it is better to decide now than to linger on, so that those who *are* committed can go on with the work.

As in a number of comparable cases among the new religions (see, for example Ofshe, 1980; Wallis, 1982; Johnston, 1979), change, the deconstruction of established structures, the casting down of old leaders and elevation of new leaders, is both a means for infusing a new vigour and excitement into the movement, and a test of loyalty which, by provoking reaction and departures, will weed out those less than totally committed to the leader's changing vision and his need for complete surrender as an authentication of his unique spiritual identity, his charisma.

NOTES

1. This research on the Neo-Sannyas Movement was supported by the Nuffield Foundation and by the Queen's University of Belfast. The author is most grateful to both institutions for their financial assistance; to Dr Peter Clarke and the new Religious Movements Centre at King's College, London for allowing him to browse through its material on Rajneeshism; and to Dr David Taylor who both undertook Rajneesh meditations on which he provided reports and kept up a steady flow of Oregon newspaper clippings which proved most valuable. He is also grateful to the many Sannyasins and former Sannyasins who were willing to discuss their lives and experiences with him.

   There is a growing literature on Bhagwan Shree Rajneesh and his followers. Some of this has been written by Sannyasins and constitutes devotional work; among the more revealing of life in the Poona Ashram, and the thought of Sannyasins and those in the process of becoming Sannysasins, is Bharti (1980). The most insightful account of one Sannyasin's transition into and out of the movement is by Belfrage (1981). A useful, but entirely hostile work is by van Leen (1983). There is also the meretricious "sociological" study of Mullan (1983).
2. Rajneesh is not always consistent in the terminology he applies to this true identity, using a variety of terms such as "self", "Self", "soul", "Brahma" and "Authentic Being". Sometimes he refers to the ego as the "self" and therefore as what is to be dropped, but the principle seems reasonably clear even though the terminology varies.
3. We are grateful to Dr Edward Mann for stressing this point to us. We are obliged to him, to Dr B.R. Wilson and to Michael Barnett for their comments on this chapter.

(1986)

Chapter Seven

Asian Religions in Europe

REINHART HUMMEL AND BERT HARDIN

The religious groups with a Hindu or Buddhist background that reached Europe in the 1960s and 1970s[1] came without exception by way of the United States and thus penetrated the Old World in an 'Americanised' form. The aspects that struck people as objectionable—the commercialisation, the PR methods, etc.—were North American rather than Asian characteristics. Several features, such as the attempt of Transcendental Meditation to present itself as a purely secular technique of relaxation, were connected with the strict separation of Church and State in the USA and would probably not have come into being at all in Europe. To this extent the fact that these cults reached Europe via the USA worked against their chances of success. This makes it all the more interesting to study a movement which may have been strongly influenced by the psychological climate in North America but which nevertheless reached Europe directly from India. This is the movement led by Bhagwan Shree Rajneesh. This study will therefore focus on this movement as it is representative of more recent trends in the religious scene.

Typical meditation movements like TM and the Divine Light Mission had by the middle of the 1970s passed their peak and have since entered a phase of consolidation. One reason for this has been the campaign against youth cults and sects which was able to uncover a whole series of internal contradictions. What was involved above all was the gulf between claim and reality. These groups not only showed themselves incapable of fulfilling the almost paradisiacal promises they made: the techniques of meditation themselves that they used were often shown to be dangerous and sometimes lacking in intellectual and spiritual content. Many leading members remained discontented and found fulfilment in movements of more strongly Hindu character such as that led by Sathya Sai Baba.

The diffuse influence of non-organised forms of Asian spirituality such as *yoga* and Zen is, moreover, a characteristic of the intellectual and spiritual climate. Perhaps the dying out of humanist education is a reason for a monist attitude to life no longer relying on quotations from Goethe today but on passages from the Upanishads or from Buddhist writings.

Of recent years the focus has shifted from the soul to the body and geographically from India to China and Japan. What are sought today are techniques that serve the body's physical self-awareness and development such as T'ai Chi Ch'uan and Aikido. Bringing body and soul into harmony is meant to mobilise the primeval energy of the cosmos and enable one to experience it. This means that the time is also ripe for the dervish dances from the Islamic Sufi Movement and Tantra Yoga with its Hindu and Buddhist origins. Tantra Yoga includes the body and sexuality in the process of salvation. There is also an increase in interest in Tibetan Buddhism with its Tantric influences.

1. The Bhagwan Movement[2]

It is above all the Neo-Sannyas Movement led by Bhagwan Shree Rajneesh, at first in Poona but since 1981 in Antelope, Oregon that bids fair to rival the Volkswagen Beetle: it runs and runs. Far from indicating the end and dissolution of the movement, the breaking up of the Ashram in Poona introduced a new phase in its spread by bringing about the return to Europe and the United States of the elite of therapists and committed staff members. By 1981 the number of Rajneesh centres in Belgium had risen to seven, in France to eleven, in Great Britain to twenty-six, in Italy to eighteen, in the Netherlands to twenty-five, and in West Germany to fifty-seven. In Germany, on which our investigation will now focus, the movement's centre of gravity will in the future be the newly acquired Wolfsbrunnen castle in Meinhard-Schwebda. Here a city of Rajneesh is planned, an enormous centre for therapy and growth with an abundance of handicrafts and similar opportunities for the Sannyasis to translate their devotion to their master into actual work.

Previously the largest German Rajneesh Meditation Centre was Purvodaya in Margarethenried north-east of Munich. According to its own figures this 'centre for self-awareness and meditation' has shown the following increase in turnover: 1978, DM 205,000 (nearly £48,000); 1979, DM 725,000 (nearly £170,000); 1980, DM 2,632,000 (over £600,000); while that budgeted for 1981 was nearly five million deutschmarks (over £1,150,000). Sixty-seven per cent of the visitors were between 20 and 29 years old and 14 per cent between 30 and 39, with the rest being older or younger. Eighty per cent were classified as middle class (the majority teachers and students, very many from the field of social work, with the rest being officials and white-collar and manual workers). There is a certain noticeable tendency for leading members to be drawn from the aristocracy. Many of the newly opened centres operate under names drawn from the field of humanist psychology. They cannot be immediately recognised as Rajneesh centres. While the castle and its grounds have apparently been acquired for the new city of Rajneesh by the Rajneesh Foundation, most of the centres are independent. Their cohesion is guaranteed by the attitude of discipleship towards the Master Bhagwan Shree Rajneesh on the part of those running them. Looked at from the point of view of organisation, the Neo-Sannyas movement does not fit into the pattern of youth cults and sects among which it is often counted. Its organisational structure is heirarchical but not totalitarian. Many visitors to the Rajneesh centres come because of the therapeutic groups and leave when and how they want. Alongside these Bhagwan clients there are also Bhagwan believers for whom Rajneesh is a second Buddha or Jesus. This fits in with the fluctuating character of this movement which is at one and the same time a psycho-religious movement, a syncretistic Guru-cult and an esoteric school of the mysteries.

2. Rajneesh: From Rebel to Guru

Born in 1931, Rajneesh began his career not as the Guru of a predominantly Western flock of disciples but as a radical critic of his own culture, as a 'lonely enlightened rebel' (R. C. Prasad) against the taboos of Indian politics and religion. His offical biography, however, mentions religious experience during childhood and an experience of enlightenment when he was a student at the age of twenty-one. Obviously he went on to experiment with techniques of meditation and similar techniques of altering one's awareness and from 1964 onwards introduced his followers to these in meditation camps in Rajasthan. Here, too, he did not follow the usual pattern. He did not teach the usual forms of *yoga* but predominantly group meditation and dances that had been developed by Gurdjieff, probably relying on Sufi traditions. Parallel to his appropriation of new concepts and practice, a change came about in his own appraisal of himself. Up till the 1960s he was known to the Indian public as Acharya (teacher) Rajneesh: he finally became Bhagwan (God) and thus one of mankind's great enlightened ones. With this should be connected the withdrawal from public life that led to the foundation of an Ashram first in Bombay (1969) and later in Poona (1974 to 1981).

While Rajneesh was still teaching philosophy, Michael Murphy and Richard Price founded the Esalen Centre in California in 1962. With its remarkable blend of Western psychology and Eastern wisdom it was the model of other Human Growth centres. It was at Esalen that Fritz Perls, the founder of Gestalt psychology, came to rest in his old age; the pupil of Wilhelm Reich and the founder of bio-energetics, Alexander Lowen, and his pupil Stanley Keleman worked there; there too Alan Watts, the champion of Beat Zen, and Baba Ram Dass, alias Dr Richard Alpert, the former colleague of the apostle of LSD Timothy Leary, were able to teach their philosophies and practices inspired by the East. Towards the end of the 1960s the first European Growth centres appeared in London and Amsterdam and in them the name of Rajneesh first began to be secretly whispered. It was from these places and from German psychological centres such as ZIST and AAO that an increasing number of professional and lay therapists as well as adherents of this kind of psychological culture found their way first to Bombay and later to Poona. The first generation of people who today are aged around thirty-five[3] had for the most part experimented with LSD and similar drugs as well as with techniques of altering consciousness, and were acquainted with the ideas of Gurdjieff, Reich and others. For them what they were able to experience at the feet of Rajneesh was the crowning fulfilment of all their previous searching. Rajneesh, who from his reading was already familiar with the concepts of humanist psychology, had for his part no hesitation over enlisting in his service Western therapists and even artists like Georg Deuter and thus turning his Ashram in Poona into 'the greatest human growth centre of the world', as it liked to describe itself. To the extent that techniques of humanist psychology found acceptance, the Rajneesh Ashram became more attractive for Europeans and North Americans. In the second half of the 1970s this development led to the Ashram becoming westernised. There was an appreciable diminution in the part played by Indians, and perhaps it was ultimately only consistent for Rajneesh to move to the USA in 1981.

3. The Bhagwan Movement as a Psycho-Religious Movement

Most seekers arrive at the Bhagwan centres because they 'have problems' or want to 'change' themselves; after taking part for a shorter or longer period of time in the work of the groups and the meditation exercises they return to their normal occupations. In the introductory phase the function of the groups and the meditation exercises is above all to clear up unresolved conflicts and 'unfinished business', to liberate blocked energies and let them flow once more. In Rajneesh's monistic interpretation of the world there is fundamentally only one energy which, in the sense of humanist psychology, he is able to call 'bio-energy'. It is 'life' itself or 'love' or even the 'light'. Most practices and rituals of meditation are aimed at making it possible to experience this energy and become aware of it. The dance meditations, known as 'stop techniques', that Rajneesh had taken over from Gurdjieff, do this by following phases of extreme physical exertion and hectic ecstasy by complete rest. An important ritual is the energy *darśana* that in traditional Indian terminology is called *śaktipat,* that is the transmission of power by touch or glance. The ceremony of initiation or dedication includes, besides handing over the *mālā,* the wooden chain with Rajneesh's portrait, a transmission of energy of this kind by pressing the thumb on the so-called third eye. The mobilisation and experience of energy is also the aim of Buddhist exercises intended to increase one's attention and of Chinese physical techniques like T'ai Chi.

This conscious awareness of one's inner life ('Let it happen ....') is meant to help people to distance themselves from it. Eventually they become neutral, uninvolved, impartially observing 'witnesses'—the *sahshi* of classical Indian *yoga*. Awareness understood in this sense is a key to understanding Rajneesh's thought: it does not matter whether someone renounces sexuality[4] or 'accepts' it. Both lead to the goal, as long as it happens with awareness. A concept taken from the vocabulary of Western psychology is thus interpreted by Rajneesh against the background of Hindu and Buddhist ideas and elevated to beome the supreme value.

The stream of energy that has been liberated by group work and meditation and is now consciously perceived has its origin, according to Rajneesh, in the sexual centre, the *mūladhārā cakra* of the physiology of Tantra *yoga*. Most people are so 'deformed' by religious prejudices and social pressures that their energy is 'perverted'. But 'perverted energy cannot by transformed'. Hence the importance of the introductory phase in which the individual should learn to overcome his or her inhibitions and to let the stream of energy flow. Rajneesh recommends the Tantric way: acceptance and surrender. Because 'spirituality and sexuality are two ends of one and the same energy', one and the same business is involved in the mutual surrender of man and woman as in the relation of master and disciple. The relationship of the disciple to the master is a 'relationship of love'. Like Tantrism as a whole, Rajneesh has a divided attitude towards sexuality. On the one hand he stresses with tremendous anti-puritan emphasis, the divinity of the unique power of life; on the other he stresses the necessity for it to be transformed and transcended. What happens in practice is an increasing depersonalisation of sexual relations, which is clearly experienced by many people who are plagued by problems of personal relationships as a liberating breakthrough to the knowledge that everyone is irrevocably alone and must learn not to need anyone else. Corresponding to this is the repeated emphasis on everyone being exclusively responsible for himself or herself and for his or her inner development.

What stops people surrendering themselves in trust to the master and to the stream of life he personifies is the 'mind'. The 'mind' enables us to plan for the future or to play the 'games' of the past and keeps us from living with full awareness in the here and now. Following Gurdjieff, Rajneesh emphasises that the unawakened man or woman is only reacting like an automaton instead of living authentically on the basis of his or her own spontaneity.

4. The Bhagwan Movement as a Syncretistic Guru-cult

Rajneesh does not see himself as a Guru in the traditional sense of the word, and in fact he is not one. Nevertheless certain ritual elements of honouring the Guru are maintained in the Rajneesh centres: the main feasts are Rajneesh's birthday and the day of his enlightenment as well as *Guru-pūrṇimā*, the feast of the full moon. But Rajneesh is not to be equated with the guarantor of a particular doctrinal tradition since doctrinal traditions are something he fundamentally rejects. Even in Poona personal contact with his followers was reduced to a very low level and has ceased almost entirely with his move to the United States. In this way he pays no attention to many functions ascribed to the Guru by the classical tradition. Nevertheless his person assumes an extraordinarily important role in the life of his followers. To begin with, the master is for Rajneesh the object of that surrender without which it is impossible to overcome the ego and 'mind'. The erotic and sexual character of this surrender is clear to those affected: it is not by accident that Satyanada uses the metaphor 'becoming intimate with the master'.

A consistent trait in Rajneesh's understanding of the master's function is his stress on absolute passivity: 'No relationship exists on the part of the master because the master does not exist. . . . If your ego is there, project it too on to the master. It is your projection.'[5] What Rajneesh is describing is the condition of the person who is fully enlightened. The connection between his reinterpretation of the Buddhist ideal and his presentation of himself as a screen for people to project their ideas on to is unambiguous. Hence there is no lack of statements to the effect that the master's voice is fundamentally 'my own inner voice'. Even Rajneesh's physical absence does not make any essential difference to this kind of relationship between master and disciple.

The trust that is continually demanded in the master characterises the atmosphere in the Bhagwan centres and above all the works in the therapeutic groups. Readiness to abandon oneself to what happens in the group and to give up every kind of usual safeguard is demanded and guaranteed on the basis of trust in Bhagwan's omnipresence. This means, too, a substantial reduction in the burden of responsibility borne by the therapist: he or she can stop worrying about professional prudence because Bhagwan is responsible for everything.

Seeing himself as an 'enlightened master' also characterises Rajneesh's dealings with the religious traditions of mankind. He has indeed used the sacred writings of the most diverse religions as the basis for his lectures: from the Buddhist world a handful of *Mahāyāna Sūtras* and above all the literature of Zen, from the Chinese world a series of taoist writings, from the Indian tradition some of the later Upaniṣads, Patañjali's *Yoga Sūtras*, Tantric writings, the songs of the Bengali Baul, and especially the writings of Kabir, and in addition he draws on Sufic and Hasidic writings. It is thus above all the mystics of the different religious traditions that are expounded for his hearers and readers, admittedly in Rajneesh's uniform interpretation; and this in itself is an astonishing expansion of the usual Western intellectual horizon that certainly accounts for part of Rajneesh's attraction. Of course, in Rajneesh's interpretation they are all saying the same thing, with certain nuances. Similar, this brilliant assimilator, as R. C. Prasad calls him, slips easily into the role of the Zen master, of the Sufi Sheikh, of the Hasidic rabbi, and above all into that of the great founders of religion like Buddha and Jesus. What they said of themselves ('I am the way', etc.) are transformed almost without being noticed into statements by Rajneesh about himself, and his relationship to his followers covertly becomes the main theme of the history of religion. Fundamentally he is not the source of any new religious ideas. It is not a new idea but Rajneesh himself as the enlightened one and as master around whom the fullness of the various religious traditions syncretistically form themselves. To this extent one is justified in describing the Bhagwan movement as a syncretistic Guru-cult. The idea that as an enlightened one Rajneesh is talking 'on the same level' as Buddha and

Jesus serves as a legitimation for interpretations that depart from traditional ones. This is of course particularly the case with regard to the Semitic traditions.

5. Bhagwan Movement as an Esoteric School of the Mysteries

A fundamental principle with Rajneesh is that demands for faith are to be rejected and that all statements must be based on experience alone. Hence in his circle it is only with a certain uneasiness and an embarrassed smile that people admit to believing in *karma* and reincarnation and other esoteric dotrines. Clearly there are hopes of oneself reaching, under Rajneesh's guidance, the status of an enlightened one.[6] 'The Ashram is a nursery in which enlightened ones are produced, and Bhagwan is the chief incubator.' Connected with this are hopes of cosmic proportions, because with an increasing number of enlightened ones the 'entire state of vibration of the planet' is altered. In connection with certain astrological constellations of the 1980s and the hope that the 'age of Aquarius' is about to dawn, there arise expectations of a 'quantum leap' on the part of mankind and its being saved from a catastrophe of apocalyptic proportions. Against the bakground of the belief that Rajneesh was a great Tibetan master who lived seven centuries ago and has now returned in order to gather his former pupils around him once again, the traditional greetings used by Rajneesh, such as: 'Here you are at last' or: 'I've been waiting for you for a long time', take on a deeper meaning. Also to be included among these esoteric speculations are Rajneesh's statements about Hitler as a tool of the Great White Brotherhood who unfortunately ended by making himself independent and was thus the cause of the ruin of the Second World War. Clearly there are more speculations of this kind circulating around Rajneesh than have hitherto been made public.

In order to understand this fluctuating phenomenon as a whole it is important to bear in mind the wealth of different aspects under which Rajneesh presents himself. The traditions of West and East combine to provide a stream of water to drive his greedy mills. He has succeeded in satisfying equally such disparate needs as that for psychological relief and enrichment, that for the religious experience of being dissolved into oneness with the ground of all being, and that for the attainment of esoteric secret knowledge. He has succeeded in presenting himself in the role of the psychological healer, the religiously enlightened one, and the great initiate and adept. The boundaries between these different roles are fluid, and equally fluid are the distinctions among his followers. Alongside the great mass of Bhagwan clients is the band of Bhagwan believers for whom Rajneesh has become the symbol and embodiment of cosmic life and love, and finally there is the élite of those who have been initiated into the mysteries of the cosmos and its future. In the immense market-place of religions and pseudo-religions on offer there are at the moment no rivals who can cover so broad a spectrum of expectations and needs.

Translated by Robert Nowell

(1983)

NOTES

1. See Reinhart Hummel, 1981.
2. See R.C. Prasad, 1978.
3. See the seven interviews in Swami Satyananda, 1981. (Satyananda is the monastic name of Jörg-Andrees Elten, formerly well-known as a reporter on *Stern* magazine.) This also includes references to further literature.
4. For Rajneesh's attitude to sexuality see above all Bhagwan Shree Rajneesh, 1975.
5. Bhagwan Shree Rajneesh *Mein Weg. Der Weg der weissen Wolke* (Berlin, no date) p. 261.
6. For what follows, see Swami Satyananda, 1981: 128 f., 116 ff.

Chapter Eight

The "New Renunciates" of Bhagwan Shree Rajneesh: Observations and Identification of Problems of Interpreting New Religious Movements*

LEWIS F. CARTER

The Rajneesh movement is a changing melange of Eastern mysticism, personal development techniques and

*The initial field team included Masman Andara Donald Beck, Janet Lee, Quang Tran and Susan Weeks. Later field trips were assisted by Erik Carter. Appreciated is Lee Freese who "took a leap" in authorising two WSU vehicles for the first field contact. The Department of Sociology at Washington State University provided additional assistance with telephone calls and recording equipment. The Society for the Scientific Study of Religion provided a grant for summer, 1996 field expenses. Louis McNew and William Willard gave encouragement and guidance. Dave Frohnmayer, Marion Goldman, Vidanta Hanya, Barbara Hill, Armand Mauss, Prem Prasad and Clifford Staples read and criticised earlier drafts of this Chapter.

experimental "international communities", supported by contributions from clients and investors as well as royalties from an international network of schools, centres, hotels, restaurants, stores, and discotheques. The movement emerged in Manali, India in 1970, emphasising sudden personal enlightenment through meditation techniques. The classic Hindu tradition of "Sannyas" involves renunciation of much of the world (economic activity, sex, pursuit of comforts) usually accomplished by older, experienced people who have "transcended" such needs through protracted discipline. The Rajneesh "Neo-Sannyasins" are said to transcend prior socialisation much more rapidly by being "deprogrammed" so as to respond in daily life without resort to norms or patterns (Joshi, 1982: 96-97).

Meditation centres are located in Europe, Asia and North America (Gunter, 1979) and over one-hundred Sannyasin communes were claimed (Prasad, 1985). The financial centres appear to be in London and Zurich (Long and Zaitz, 1985) though there are many corporate identities in several countries. The symbolic centre of the movement is the person of Bhagwan Shree Rajneesh who has had difficulty establishing a permanent spiritual centre. The initial "Ashram" in Koregaon Park in Poona, India, antagonised neighbours, government officials and religious figures. Insider accounts emphasise political jealousies (Joshi, 1982) while outsiders point to moral, legal and tax problems (*Asia Week*, July 29, 1983; Mehta, 1987; Mitra, Draper and Chengappa, 1985). The "oasis community" of Rajneeshpuram in Eastern Oregon produced more conflict, investigation and media coverage than has any other contemporary American religious activity. After Bhagwan pleaded guilty to making false statements to federal officials and was expelled from the United States, the Oregon commune began dissolution. An initial thousand Sannyasins left within a month, followed shortly by another thousand, leaving approximately 200 followers to manage liquidation auctions and sales. The ranch and buildings are on the real estate market, maintained by a small staff of approximately 30. Bhagwan had been shunted from country to country (India, Nepal, Crete, Ireland, Uruguay, Jamaica) seeking permanent refuge and a place for Sannyasins to gather. Many ex-residents of Rajneeshpuram returned to their home countries. They and their American cohorts have estalished many new therapy centres and other businesses, typically living in "group homes" housing a dozen or so Sannyasins. Many await the next opportunity to again "be with Bhagwan", while an unknown number have disassociated themselves from the movement.

The goals of this paper are both descriptive and analytic: (1) to present a balanced documentation of the Rajneesh movement from the point-of-view of a non-involved outsider; and (2) to identify interpretive and data-access problems which complicate the study of such movements, often leading to polarised accounts, either celebratory or deprecating. Extant written accounts illustrate this polarisation. The mass of information generally falls into one of two conflicting traditions: the hundreds of promotional books developed by insiders arrayed against thousands of articles written by generally hostile outsiders.

Conceptual and Methodological Problems

The analytic task is complicated by the changing and inconsistent nature of the Rajneesh movement which makes no claim to consistency of ideology. Further, beliefs, practices and goals are extremely changeable, though a few enduring patterns can be abstracted. The Rajneesh movement appears to be totally "manufactured" in the sense that beliefs, practices, corporate identities, and physical location may be changed quickly to suit necessities and convenience of the moment. Just as Sannyasins are urged to live in the "here and now", their social systems and legal identities are impermanent.

No totally satisfactory conceptual framework has been developed for defining the new religious movements, especially those transplanted to the United States. Some scholars focus on personal crisis, disillusionment and rebellion in accounting for the growth of non-traditional involvements (cf. Wilson, 1981). Some journalists seek the exotic (cf. Greenfield, 1975). Critics (Mehta, 1979) focus on the absurd; followers emphasise satisfying aspects (Gunther, 1979). Robinson (1985) notes that interpretive controversies arise in part from differences in social positions of observers (therapists see people with problems; fundamentalists see "heathens"; satisfied converts see "enlightenment"), and in part because observers are studying different things (recruiters, ex-members, financial structures, security isolation mechanisms). It is possible to mitigate these complications by acknowledging that a "religious movement" may have many facets (inner circles, devoted followers, transient "groupies" corporate identities) and by integrating the "impressions"of observers who have varied backgrounds and motivations (critics, potential converts, ex-members).

Some difficulties in analysing "new religions" stem from attempts to see them as modern instances of historical immigrations or as small, physically isolated utopian groups. In the first instance, observers draw analogies to European immigrants who brought their own history, culture and institutions to the United States. In the second instance, modern movements are compared to the Shaker, Oneida or other utopian groups. The first comparison misses the importance of the fact that some new religions represent "manufactured" belief systems and cultural practices designed to satisfy certain client populations. While all religions may be viewed as "manufactured" in a sense, groups like the Rajneesh have rituals and institutions which may have histories measured in years or even days and this distinguishes them from practices that are changed over decades or centuries. The latter have the force of custom and tradition, while the new religions must draw on current authority and charismatic leaders in establishing practices. With the Rajneesh, a "clergy" was invented and repudiated within a two-year span. The second comparison misses the sophistication with which the new religions recruit members, disseminate practices and manage access to information as well as their mastery of techniques of group psychology. Isolated utopians did not have the power of press, production studios, legal consultants and marketing experts to spread their message and produce images of their movement.

What observers learn will depend on their own background and orientation as well as how they are viewed by the group to be studied. Early contacts with the Rajneesh were rigidly controlled by them, with a public relations person assigned to manage movement and contacts. Initially, we were treated as possible recruits, possible tourists and possibly as covert enemies. Later contacts were less controlled as the identity of "non-hostile" outsider was established through a longer-term relationship. What can be learned from a guarded visitor centre and tour van is quite different from what can be learned over dinner, while rock climbing or hiking, before coffee in the morning, or in other informal contexts.

Special problems are posed by the dispersal, rapid changes adapting to external constraints, and contact management of the new religions. With the Rajneesh it is especially difficult to locate the movement: (1) in physical space and ime; (2) in terms of formal and legal structures; and (3) in terms of ideology and historical-cultural perspective. Other new religions seem to share some of this movement's portability and heterodoxy, but the Rajneesh illustrate the research problems well, in that they are unusually mobile, legally creative and ideologically heterodox.

Dispersal in Space and Mobility

The Rajneesh are remarkably dispersed, with adherents spread over five continents. Meditation centres and businesses are similarly dispersed and have become more so since the "diaspora" following the expulsion of Bhagwan from the United States. Levels of involvement vary from those who gathered to live and work "with Bhagwan" in Poona and Rajneeshpuram, those who worked in Rajneesh businesses and still others who maintain personal identification as sannyasins but who live otherwise unremarkable private and professional lives. Since Sannyasins are concentrated in the professions and intelligentsia, individual adherents move about their countries and the world to a greater degree than most people. Sannyasins can move from careers "in the world" to the Ashram in Poona, back to careers to Eastern Oregon, back to careers and, presumably, on to a centre which might be established in any new location. Significant numbers of adherents travelled from other parts of the world to annual celebrations and relatively large numbers gather in any country allowing visitation with Bhagwan (India, U.S., Crete serve as examples, while a condition of entry to Uruguay was no visitation by Sannyasins).

There is yet another dimension of mobility by the Rajneesh. The group can marshal sufficient resources and co-ordination to build roads, housing and public services for a total community within two years (and sell much of it in one). They demonstrated the ability to collect 4000 disadvantaged people from across the United States and move them to sparsely populated Eastern Oregon within weeks.

Such dispersal means that an observer must focus on a small part of the movement at any given time or rely on personal networks and press accounts from across the world. The mobility means that demographic and other surveys depend entirely on local co-operation and may become out-of-date within days or months. Most demographic and other survey approaches to research assume that population characteristics change in an orderly fashion through operation of birth and death processes with minor perturbation through migration. Further, migration is assumed to be more or less atomistic, rather than the result of central planning. These assumptions are so at variance with the managed relocations and surges of Rajneesh populations that traditional demographic techniques are of doubtful utility. The movement can use survey techniques, but outsiders are greatly impeded in doing so.

Legal and Organization Identities

It is difficult to fix the legal identities relevant to a thorough description of this movement. Businesses are incorporated in several countries with several profit and non-profit corporations (co-operatives, foundations and trusts) operating in the same locations and resources transferred routinely among these. Each corporation has separate legal identity, somewhat distinct purpose and considerable interlock. As new challenges are encountered by movement, new legal identities are created to receive resources, dispose of resources, implement new policies, and obscure accountability.

In addition, contact with individuals is more difficult

because of the cultural practice of taking a new (Sannyasin) name upon initiation. Men take the title "Swami" followed by a generic name similar to a family name, followed finally by a name chosen by Bhagwan which is said to reflect their character. Women's naming rules are similar, though the courtesy title is "Ma". Some individuals maintain routine use of the original name. This practice makes the researcher unusually dependent on the goodwill of the Rajneesh in providing networked information about the location and contact procedure for Sannyasins. It causes some problems for Rajneesh "returning to the world" in occupations dependent on the continuity of a Vita or Resume (teachers, city planners, foresters) but seems an asset for those working in "New Age" or "Human Potential Movement" therapy contexts.

Ideology and Historical Cultural Context

Over 350 books are attributed to Bhagwan Shree Rajneesh addressing his views on all facets of human and cosmic existence. Virtually all of these are compilations of "discourses" usually listing a "compiler" and another person as "editor". The views are eclectic, endorsing some aspects of all major world religions. There is consistency in the goal of creating a "new human" combining the sensuality of Zorba-the-Greek with the spirituality of the Buddha. Followers are urged to transcend the "need" for the world but urged to remain in contact with the world. While outsiders have difficulty rationalising the term "Sannyasin" (with its historical reference to renunciation) with the openly affluent and sensual life-style of many Rajneesh, Bhagwan argues that denial of the senses is as contrived as is indulgence of them. He seems to believe that one must experience desires before they can be "transcended". This doctrinal permissiveness makes it difficult to generalise about

Sannyasin lifestyles, with some being quite permissive and indulgent while others seem austere and conventional. Doctrine is difficult for the rationally oriented reader because it is said that contradictions are of no importance. Indeed Bhagwan seems to delight in endorsing positions seen as opposites to the Western mind. The only attempt to codify Rajneesh beliefs and practices is the so-called "Bible of the Rajneesh" (Academy of Rajneeshism, 1983) which establishes levels of clergy and lifestage rituals (birth, death, marriage). This codification was repudiated by Bhagwan in October, 1985 as a creation of misguided followers.

Further difficulty is introduced by the fluidity of Rajneesh practices, with a pronouncement in the name of Bhagwan having been sufficient to cause abandonment of old practices and acquisition of new ones. When Bhagwan speaks personally he seems to urge followers to find their own direction, though his representatives were much more directive in their management of the Poona Ashram and the Oregon commune. The Oregon community was designed along lines very similar to the school of Gurdjieff (see Bennett, 1973 and Webb, 1980), though with less personal involvement by Bhagwan because he communicated initially mostly through intermediaries especially during his period of "silence" in Oregon. Bhagwan and many of his followers are aware of the Gurdjieff-Ouspensky tradition and cite with admiration Gurdjieff's unpredictability and outrageousness. The Oregon community was designed as a totally contained social system for members. It employed all but two of the mechanisms described by Kanter (1972) for maximising commitment (sacrifice, investment, renunciation, communion and mortification). The only important mechanisms omitted were celibacy and a detalied theology.

Attempts to establish patterns of cultural practice for

the Rajneesh will lead to transitory descriptions, unlike some other new religious groups. Followers are extremely diverse with little commonality of practice and belief beyond their commitment to identification with Bhagwan. Many have read little of his work and most, even those in a position to manage public relations, have little knowledge of external accounts of the group and sparse knowledge about cultural antecedents for some of their practices. Most commune residents had no interest in external relations, dismissing questions about current events with "we leave that to the lawyers".

The ideological and cultural shifts which the Rajneesh have accepted over the past three years call into question the appropriateness of the analytic concept "culture" when studying this group. Cultural practices are generally viewed as having developed over an extended period of time, exhibiting considerable stability and being resistant to sudden or repeated change. The history of the Rajneesh movement evidences a population of intelligent, externally successful people who retain little interest in ideology and little respect for authority, though many maintain an intense identification with Bhagwan who they see as having pointed the way for their liberation from both ideology and authority. Changes, even adversities and setbacks, are simply seen as instances of an uncaring universe and corrupt social systems. Though many Sannyasins were disappointed with the closing of Rajneeshpuram, they also express pride at being able to "simply walk away from" the community that they built, and apparently view this as indicative of acceptance/transcendence of change.

Information Collection Strategies

The problems encountered in locating the Rajneesh movement (physically, legally and culturally) plague many researchers of new religious movements.

Richardson alludes to the fable of the blind men trying to describe an elephant (1985: 132). On the one hand the problems involve limitations of researchers who deal with dispersed, varied and changeable phenomena which must be viewed, as least in part, through documents and the eyes of others. On the other hand, researchers also confront problems of the lack of coherence of the movement to be described. We sought to mitigate some of these limitations through the use of multiple data and research strategies, described below. The heterodoxy and change are characteristics of the Rajneesh movement and, while troublesome for the researcher seeking simplicity, must be reported and tolerated to avoid oversimplification.

Wallis' review of methods used to study new religious movements (1984: 132-44) emphasises validity problems posed by the status and orientation of the observer. Internalist accounts involve better knowledge of group practices, though this can be turned to celebration or indictment depending on motivation. Externalists have some advantages of perspective, but the outsider is not privy to many important private features of such groups.

The internalist/externalist distinction is valuable in assessing the credence to be given observations, but this dichotomy oversimplifies the relationship of many researchers to the objects of study. In our case, information was collected through a multiplicity of sources: first hand observation, collaboration with others in first hand observation, second hand accounts of members, neighbours and opponents, written accounts by members, ex-members, opponents, and journalists. Each of these approaches has limitations and advantages, some of which are discussed below:

First Hand Observation (alone and with others)

Direct observation included several trips to

Rajneeshpuram (April, 1984, August, 1984, and May, 1986), conversations with others, before and after visits, correspondence and telephone communication with commune representatives (March, 1984 through the present) and meetings with representatives of Rajeeshpuram at the annual meeting of the Society for the Scientific Study of Religion (October, 1985).

The initial visit to Rajneeshpuram was a team research activity in a graduate research methods course. I accompanied five graduate students to Eastern Oregon where we conducted informal interviews with people in communities surrounding Rajneeshpuram and spent two days in Rajneeshpuram proper. The study team consisted of individuals of varied personal orientations. National origins included the United States (3 members) and one member each from England, Indonesia and Vietnam. Two women and four men were in the group and personal religious identifications included Christianity, Islam, Buddhism, Pagan and atheist/agnostic. Diverse personal identities allowed us to cross-check our reactions and impressions.

We conducted informal interviews with commune residents, ate in communal dining facilities, slept in commune guest housing, photographed physical facilities, attended meditation sessions, visited the therapy centre (Rajneesh International Meditation University), and engaged in experiments testing reactions of the commune to us.

While nominally free to range over much of the commune, there was considerable guidance and control. For example, as outsiders, we were subject to search of gear and automobilies, relinquished control of automobiles, and wore identifying green wristbands. In addition, we were required to sign forms: (1) allowing the commune absolute discretion in our expulsion; (2) releasing the commune from all liability; and

(3) allowing unrestricted use of any photographs, audio or video tape which might be taken of us while visiting. After negotiation, we were given limited permission to photograph. Certain areas were designated "off-limits" and movement in other areas was closely monitored by observers with radio, telephone, vans and binoculars. Finally, we were told not to disturb individuals "at worship". Since worship has a special meaning at the commune, that is work is worship, this amounted to a restriction against talking to residents from around 7 a.m. to 7 p.m. We honoured the spirit of these restrictions and upon leaving, were told that no other outsiders had ranged so freely without complaints being lodged. Some residents who became talkative with us were "gently" reminded by others to return to worship.

Though some residents were annoyed by strangers outside "tour" boundaries, we were generally treated with courtesy or indifference. Our identity was candidly that of "sociologists from Washington State University" and our purpose was to "see how the Rajneesh live". This seemed novel for many commune members who view the world as consisting of Sannyasins, seekers after enlightenment and hostile ememies. On several occasions during this visit and subsequently, I had to reiterate that I was neither an enemy nor did I seek membership or therapy. This "identity" may have closed off some information available to a "seeker", but was easy to maintain with consistency and was ethically comfortable. Repeated invitations to return suggest acceptance of our stance as non-hostile externalist researchers.

On a second visit to Rajneeshpuram during August, 1984, my son accompanied me. We toured Antelope, Oregon and the public area of Rajneeshpuram, where I received criticism of an earlier draft of this paper. The community was preoccupied with an imminent subpoena for Bhagwan and contact was limited. While I managed to contact some acquaintances made earlier, I was hampered by security even more restrictive than before. Periodic contact with Rajneeshpuram has been maintained by telephone and letters, through much of the contact has involved recruitment offers.

More recent contact involved participation with two representatives of Rajneeshpuram in a session on the "new religions" at the annual meeting of the Society for the Scientific Study of Religion (October, 1985). Interviews and the tape-recorded question-and-answer period filled gaps in my understanding of the Rajneesh.

The next visit (May, 1986) contrasted sharply with earlier contacts in that my son and I were allowed freedom to roam virtually unguided, had unlimited use of our automobile and the opportunity to become personally acquainted with several Sannyasins. At this time commune residents numbered approximately 75. Most were occupied with sales of property and arranging their affairs for "returning to the world". Security was minimal and we seemed almost as "insiders" with little comment or note of our comings and goings. Tourists and buyers were still managed with routinised regulations, though these were less stringent than when Bhagwan was present. We visited school sessions, a meditation session, and had unregulated access to remaining commune residents, including several children. None of the remaining "hard-core" seemed to have lost their identification with the movement. All viewed the experiment as having had personal value, though several expressed regrets that the "management" had run afoul of Oregon sensibilities and law. We slept in the hotel, then occupied by remaining residents, ate in communal facilities, photographed and taped interviews freely, attended farewell parties and were generally treated as friendly guests.

Second Hand Accounts

Interviews have been conducted with Sannyasins and a few seekers (non-initiates) at Rajneeshpuram, seven other academics who have visited Rajneeshpuram, three Indians who lived near the Ashram in Poona, and with Oregon neighbours of the Rajneesh. While some of these personal accounts border on gossip and the Sannyasin interviews have tended to be testimonial, the cross-checking with other academics has been useful in guiding interpretation. The most important gap in information is the absence of defectors or people who no longer regard themselves as Sannyasins. Rajneesh might argue that enlightenment is an irreversible change, but it is likely that more "ex-Sannyasins" will be available with the recent dissolution of Rajneeshpuram.

Books by and About the Rajneesh

An attempt was made to include writings by both insiders and outsiders reflecting a range of orientations. Of the 350 English language books attributed to Rajneesh, I have read fourteen. Several of these reinterpret other traditions in the context of the beliefs of Bhagwan. *The Mustard Seed* relates Rajneesh's observations on Christianity, the *Psychology of the Esoteric* deals with Freudian, Jungian and other psychologies, and other books draw heavily on Zen, Sufi, Tao and Buddhist traditions. Several are more or less stream-of-consciousness renderings of taped "discourses" without unifying theme. Also included is *Rajneeshism: An Introduction to Bhagwan Shree Rajneesh and His Religion*, attributed to "Academy of Rajneeshism", (1983) which purports to summarise beliefs and ceremonies of the religion. This book was marketed at Rajneeshpuram for over two years as an official synopsis, but repudiated by Bhagwan who ordered the burning of all copies at the ranch, saying, "That was not my book. I've never read it.

I am not a saviour. I am not a prophet. Nobody has ever been a saviour" (*Spokesman-Review*, 1985a).

At the time of writing this account, works by others included a celebratory biography by Vasant Joshi (1982) and an attempt by Ram Chandra Prasad (1970, revised 1978) to systematise the thought of Rajneesh. Prasad's admiring treatment was useful in organising major themes developed by Rajneesh, but should not be viewed as objective assessment. Accounts of the Ashram life in Poona include a poetic portrayal with photographs of therapy and ceremony by Bernard Gunther (1979). The only systematically developed book in counter-point was *Flowers of Emptiness: Reflections on an Ashram* (Belfrage, 1981). Ms. Belfrage detailed her skepticism, subsequent recruitment to the Ashram, and resulting ambivalence. She recounted daily life at the Ashram, and described therapy and patrons as well as the human conflicts and stresses of her experience.

There was, at that time, no English language book devoted to outsider accounts of the Rajneesh, though there was mention in several summaries of contemporary movements and several books were in preparation. Extremes of existing reports were anchored by Aubrey Menon's (1974) spectacular description of a mass meditation conducted by Rajneesh and by Gita Mehta's (1979) acerbic ridicule of Rajneesh. In *The New Mystics*, Menon expresses admiration for Rajneesh and sees his practices as a simpler and practical way to glimpse the enlightenment of classical sages (1974: 201). In stark contrast, Mehta expressed contempt for Rajneesh as well as for Europeans who seem drawn to India for "....enlightenment and dysentery".

Newpaper and Magazine Articles

Thousands of popular articles report activities of the movement over the past three years. Some coverage has been stimulated by Rajneesh with press releases and news conferences. Remaining coverage is of four types: (1) neighbours' anxious reaction to perceived threat; (2) human interest reports of flamboyant aspects of Rajneeshpuram; (3) serious investigative reporting of legal and financial arrangements; and (4) public relations coverage of staged events. A handful of articles are pleas for tolerance by regional scholars or liberal religious figures. Until recently, West German accounts focused on the financial success of Rajneesh enterprises while Indian newspapers and magazines take snickering pleasure in the troubles of the Rajneesh with barely restrained contempt for the gullibility of the West.

Articles were systematically collected from major regional newspapers in the North-west supplemented by articles from communities nearest Rajneeshpuram. Reports were checked against issues of *The Rajneesh Times,* a paper published by the commune. After the arrest of Bhagwan in Charlotte, North Carolina, a sampling of Southern newspapers was included. Finally, systematic monitoring of English language publications from India has yielded a collection of accounts from *India Today, Asia Week, the Times of India, and India Abroad.*

Data Problems

Observational data are distorted by the frame-of-reference of the observer and by security and other constraints on observers. The research team sought to reduce these problems by making contacts at different hours, locations and settings at the commune. We reported observations to each other and had verifications or cross-checks. We pushed our entree as far as we dared to ascertain reactions, including minor norm violations and talking with people until others interrupted us. To some extent, our diverse backgrounds tempered some of our more idiosyncratic interpretations. For example, security was seen as less obtrusive by the Indonesian than by Americans, and the Buddhist was less surprised by ideological inconsistency than were the Christians. Sannyasins were more candid in the presence of Third World researchers than with those who appeared to be American. These differences in reactions gave us more confidence in our interpretations where we had consensus (e.g. the extent of social control, isolation, and dedication of Sannyasins; ethnic composition and social class; discontinuity between current and prior identities of Sannyasins; general contentment of followers; internal social stratification; evasiveness and elusiveness of respondents in certain content areas; and absence of extreme displays of sexuality or drug use in the commune).

The books examined pose some special problems of interpretation, as most of them are represented as "official" (by copyright or authorship). Still, the books of Bhagwan can be analysed for continuities and theme. These and other promotional materials display the public face of Rajneeshism which attracts some to become seekers and repels others to the point of attack. Repudiated books point to important deviations during a stage of the movement. The paucity of hostile insider accounts may be due to the youth of the movement, to success in transformation of initiates, or to fear. Mehta's (1979) open contempt raises questions about her interpretations, but some observations concerning clientele and practices may be valid. Especially where accounts of insiders and outsiders are consistent, we may place more confidence in them.

Interpretive problems are most severe with critical newspaper and magazine accounts. Early and local newspaper accounts displayed a level of mistrust regarded by many as overdrawn at the time, though some concerns were susequently substantiated. Later accounts (1983-1984) emphasize exotic though superficial aspects of Rajneeshpuram (Rolls Royces, celebrants dressed in red, oddities of language). Accounts from this same period are shaped by the public relations skill of the Rajneesh who moved reporters and visitors through media events. By 1985, several newspapers shifted to serious investigative reporting, most notably, the *Portland Oregonian*. Accounts focused on verifiable facts detailing contractual arrangements, corporate structures and financial dealings. In spite of the limitations of newspaper accounts, conclusions are facilitated by following specific developments over several months or years. The litigiousness of the Rajneesh caused many reporters to be more cautious in backgrounding and verification procedures.

History and Analysis of the Rajneesh Movement

The following discussion provides a history of the Rajneesh movement and is an attempt at a balanced history from the point of view of a non-hostile outsider. The historical account synthesises official biographical information with information from Indian sources and accounts of investigative reporters. Descriptions of interactions of group members rely on personal observation, interviews with Sannyasins and insider accounts. Problems of studying such groups are inferred from personal observations, accounts of other reporters, and analyses of shifts in official positions.

Background in India

The religious movement called the "Rajneesh" began as the Neo-Sannyas International movement in 1970 in Manali, India led by Mohan Chandra Rajneesh. Educated at Saugar University (M.A. in Philosophy), Rajneesh was employed briefly in a Sanskrit University and subsequently as an instructor at the University of Jabalpur (1958-66). He travelled about India, conducting "meditation" camps and criticising traditions of Hinduism (Joshi, 1985). Around 1970, he introduced "dynamic meditation", a whirling active form of dance, followed by silence. (Descriptions and portrayals of these exercises can be found in Menon 1974: 201-14; Gunther 1979: 15-27; a variation in Belfrage, 1981: 169-71; instructions in Rajneesh, 1976a: 232-48.) The researcher could best describe the procedure as a combination of vigorous "jazzercize" with a "primal", followed by a period of quiet passive meditation.

The first attempt to establish a spiritual centre was a farming community established in Maharashtra State (O'Sullivan, 1983) followed by the establishment of a school/residence/therapy centre in Koregaon Park in Poona, India. By 1974, the movement had grown to include several thousand members and attracted wealthy patrons who assisted in development of publications. In the next five years, the movement built a commune outside Poona, called Rajneeshdham (O'Sullivan, 1985) and developed a clientele drawn from the intelligentsia (Belfrage, 1979) and aristocracy of Europe (Joshi, 1982). These were joined by advocates of the Human Potential Movements from California, and encounter groups, rolfing, primal therapy, and rebirthing were added to the various meditation offerings (Gunther, 1979).

By 1981, the Ashram hosted 30,000 visitors per year. An authorised biography details violence and assassination attempts preceding the move of Shree Rajneesh to the United States (Joshi, 1982). Allegations of unrestrained sex, drug use and violence marred the image of the Ashram (Mitra, Draper and Chengappa, 1985). There are conflicting reports about injuries in encounter groups (Karlen and Abramson, 1984; Prasad, 1985). India cancelled the tax exempt status of the Ashram and serious conflicts emerged with religious leaders (Mehta, 1979). Ill health is cited by followers as the reason for the immigration of Bhagwan to the United

States, but others attribute the move to these conflicts (*Asia Week*, 1983).

Sannyasins contacted several governments to explore the possibility of immigration and Rajneesh came to the United States with the sponsorship of follower Ma Anand Sheela. Close aides also moved to the United States, followed by some wealthy initiates; others were left to fend for themselves in India. Rajneesh entered a period of silent retreat shortly before leaving Poona on June 1, 1981. He initially entered this country on a three month medical visa, thought he later claimed sanctuary as a religious leader.

The Centre in Eastern Oregon

Rajneesh waited in a Montclair, New Jersey castle owned by the movement while disciples searched for a place to site the new spiritual centre. In August, the Chidvilas Rajneesh Meditation Centre, a New Jersey Corporation headed by Ma Anand Sheela, purchased the Big Muddy Ranch, a 64,000 acre tract in Eastern Oregon for $5,750,000. Anxieties expressed by locals were dismissed by Rajneesh representatives who indicated plans for a small farming commune of approximately 40 residents. By October, the population had grown to 170-180 people and the group sought more building permits (Carter, 1981). Citing need for services, all 150 registered voters on the ranch voted to incorporate Rajneeshpuram, which was accomplished in May, 1982. Incorporation freed the ranch from building permit constraints by the surrounding county and construction began in earnest.

The Rajneesh took control of the nearby community of Antelope, Oregon by purchasing all commercial properties in the town and electing members to the mayor's post and to five city council seats (Nikelani, 1983). Taxes were raised, most old-timers moved out, all public positions were replaced with Rajneeshees, and the town was renamed Rajneesh. Rajneesh (Antelope) and

Rajneeshpuram were linked by commuter vans with Antelope serving as an outpost for Rajneeshpuram.

At peak (approximately October, 1984), Rajneeshpuram and Rajneesh had approximately 5,700 residents (2,000 Sannyasins and 3,700 "street" people), though facilities for 12,000 to 15,000 were under construction and temporary housing accommodated up to 15,000 visitors during festivals. The town, now on the real estate market, is located in a valley through which a large creek flows to the John Day River. There is a collection of townhouses in the main canyon and complexes of A-frame lodges in side canyons. The Valley floor included a hotel, airport, casino, Rajneesh International Meditation University, city halls, and maintenance facilities. A gravel county road passes through the town and a shopping centre adjacent to it was open to visitors. The shopping centre included restaurants, a beauty shop, a book and record store containing exclusively Rajneesh media, a clothing store specialising in red clothing, a discotheque, post office, bar and Peace Force Office.

Outside the shopping centre and county road was regarded as "private" communal space by the Rajneesh and entrance was by permission only, requiring a rigorous security check and paid registration. Guard posts were prominent and were visible from most points in the commune. By August of 1984, security surveillance began with Peace Force cars 18 miles away in Rajneesh (Antelope) and was repeated at intervals along the county road, as well as in Rajneeshpuram proper.

Basic community services were well off the county road. Rajneesh Mandir, a two-acre meditation centre dominated the north-western end of town. A sewage plant, cement plant, recycling centre, warehouses, shops crematorium, water storage tanks, martial arts centres, and electrical distribution centres were spread through side canyons. A large dairy herd, avian farm and truck farm were located in the four miles between the town and the John Day River. The community and much of the county road was surrounded by a barbed wire fence labeled "electric", though not acually charged during our visits.

Transportation was efficient and multiplex. Airplanes (Air Rajneesh) and chartered buses brought visitors and guests from nearby communities and Portland. Buses and vans transported visitors on a guided tour, while outsider automobiles were restricted. Internal transportation was provided by several bus lines linking all points to the "Zen Connection", a transfer point with covered waiting stations. School buses were used during peak hours and vans during off-peaks. Scheduled lines, once the fourth most extensive in Oregon, were supplemented with automobiles, vans, security vehicles, motorcyles and bicycles.

The goal was a permanent, self-sufficient community. Estimates of the investment vary widely and are difficult to fix because of a complex corporate structure. Legal arrangements are described in detail by investigative reporters Long and Zaitz (1985) who note the conversion of the Chidvilas Centre into a church, Rajneesh Foundation International, which then established two corporations responsible for development. One of these, the Rajneesh Investment Corporation, became sole owner of ranch property, and the other, Rajneesh Neo-Sannyas International Commune, was to manage construction and living arrangements for residents. The commune provided free labour and completed facilities became property of the investment corporation. No residual rights were guaranteed to members of the commune, a feature allowing rapid clearing of the ranch as it moved into liquidation in late 1985.

While the community had some features of an

ordinary Oregon town, challenges to its incorporation were eventually upheld on the basis of the intimate church-state connection. It is interesting to reflect on what "ordinary" features were missing from this town. There were no children in residence, though a few were housed in Antelope. There were very few people over the age of 40 and almost no one was impaired. Most residents were in the 25-35 year range. In April, 1984, White Americans predominated, with most others of Northern European derivation (Germany, Switzerland, Holland, England, and some White Rhodesians and South Africans) and a small minority of Eastern Indians. Also startling was the lack of diversity in housing, commercial activities and publicly available facilities. Exclusive ownership by Rajneesh Corporations meant that housing was uniform. The usual small town varieties of churches were absent as well as many businesses (grocers, automobile dealers, hardware, etc.). Outside magazines, newspapers, books or television were not publicly available, media were virtually restricted to Rajneesh produced messages. No gasoline was readily available to passers-through. While a hotel suggests public services, access was limited to those willing to undergo rigorous security checks and sign away normal legal rights. The town was an exclusive (almost reclusive) total society with restricted outsider contact, limited to catering to spiritual and therapeutic needs of well-to-do "seekers". Routine tourists or travellers were discouraged.

Conflicts and Controversies

The desert community was the centre of heated controversies for its four-year existence. Some conflicts stemmed from the attempt to protect the controversial Guru and foreign followers while securing a financial and political presence in a hostile environment. These include immigration problems, zoning and development problems, conflicts with the town of Antelope and the 1984 importation of indigents to balloon local voting strength. Other problems stem from security concerns and an inner circle who acknowledged no constraints in achieving expansive goals. These latter include wiretapping, eavesdropping and alleged weapons violations, poisonings and plans of assassination and arson.

Immigration charges were the eventual downfall of Bhagwan Shree Rajneesh. He entered the country on a limited medical visa. Protecting his stay required a shift to claiming sanctuary as a religious leader. Rajneeshees oscillated on this issue. At times they claimed Bhagwan as leader of the group and then, in 1985, asserted that he had no knowledge of the directions of its development and that it was not a religion. Presence of foreign nationals, many recently married to Americans, prompted INS (the Immigration and Naturalisation Service) to investigate the possibility of a "marriage market". Bhagwan pleaded guilty to two charges of making false statements to federal officials (of 35 charges raised), though he denied guilt after his return to India. His penalty was a $400,000 fine, a suspended 10-year sentence, and five years of probation.

Other conflicts centred around expansion of the community. Some were of a narrow technical nature: zoning, permit and land use conflicts. The ranch was zoned for agricultural use, yet plans required reservoirs, wells, streets, houses and community buildings. Other conflicts can be viewed as either taxation or church-state issues, e.g. tax exemption of the meditation centre as a "public religious building". While security required stringent limitation of access.

One of the most dramatic moves involved recruiting of "street people" to Rajneeshpuram shortly before the 1984 elections. The "Share a Home" programme was billed as a philanthropic gesture to spread the abundance of Rajneeshpuram to the homeless of America (Worthington, 1984). Travelling through major American cities, recruiters offered a warm place, three meals a day, a couple of beers and cigarettes. Outsider accounts (Senior, 1984; Dietrich, 1984) are supplemented by one "insider" account from a journalist who posed as a street person to join the commune (Ray, 1984). Locals feared an election takeover of the county and arriving indigents were given instruction in voting laws of Oregon and assistance with registration (Ray, 1984). It appears that approximately 4,000 indigents were recruited with up to 2,000 residing at the commune at a single time. Oregon officials reacted by establishing special registrars after a temporary suspension of registration.

The upper-class Rajneesh and the new recruits were housed separately and soon encountered cultural difference, though serious conflict was largely avoided. Control plans included purchase of large quantities of tranquillizers. The stay was brief for most, with over half the recruits departing within a week. Some people were given return tickets to their homes and others were transported to Portland or nearby towns (Ray, 1984). Several welfare organisations provided for additional return tickets and representatives of The Guardian Angels travelled to Rajneeshpuram to demand an end to recruiting of urban indigents (*Lewiston Tribune*, 1984a; Ulrich, 1985). When massive voter registration was blocked, the Rajneesh ceased recruiting and boycotted all but local elections. An interesting side effect was the highest voter turnout in history for traditional Wasco county residents (92 per cent).

For the next eleven months Rajneeshpuram seemed to turn inward, with little media coverage and no new programmes. It appeared that Oregonians and

Rajneeshees had finally come to a grudging accommodation, though several lawsuits were pending. However, state and federal officials continued investigations of immigration and other issues, the community showed signs of financial strain and there is evidence of an insurgent internal struggle. Most significantly, the incorporation of Rajneeshpuram was declared invalid.

Disintegration began when Ma Anand Sheela, the key financial figure in many Rajneshee corporations and undisputed dominant at the commune, left for Switzerland on September 14 with three other commune leaders. The next day, ten other leaders followed. In the following week Bhagwan denounced his previous intimates, charging them with poisoning his physician, bugging his living quarters, drugging street people, embezzling 55 million dollars, attempting to poison a neighbouring community's water system and other serious crimes (McCarthy, 1985; McCoy, 1985). A federal-state investigative task force moved to Rajneeshpuram. That investigation produced evidence of widespread bugging of communal facilities, wiretapping of telephones and immigration violations, and stimulated new testimony concerning alleged conspiracies to murder political figures and burn public buildings.

Motivations are difficult to read in such contexts, but it appeared that every effort was being made to normalise relations with neighbours as rapidly as possible. Within a few days, Bhagwan encouraged the restoration of Antelope's original name, offered to sell commune properties to original residents, abolished the distinctive dress code for followers, repudiated the book defining the Rajneesh religion, and declared that Rajneeshism was not a religion. He contended that the "religion" was established without his knowledge or permission, in fact, running counter to his philosophy. Followers claimed that Sheela "and her gang" turned the commune into a fascist state and expressed hope for a bright future. Celebration followed with the burning of Sheela's robes and belongings along with all available copies of the "Book of Rajneeshism".

Officials continued investigation of charges and a new corporation was formed to guarantee Rajneeshees legal representation. Bhagwan's attorney, Prem Niren, claimed that arrest of Bhagwan was planned, though officials sought to dispel this notion. On October 27, Rajneesh and close associates left the commune suddenly in two Lear jets and flew to Charlotte, North Carolina, where he was arrested for attempting to flee prosecution. He was denied bail, and moved across the country for the next week, held briefly in several detention facilities. After a subsequent guilty plea, Bhagwan Shree Rajneesh paid his fine and left for India. Sheela and others were arrested in West Germany and are now serving prison terms in California.

For a few days, the commune maintained that it would continue, but frozen bank accounts and the absence of Bhagwan soon made it apparent that the commune would be closed. Shortly most of the remaining residents left. The fleet of Rolls Royces was sold to a Carolton, Texas car dealer and other portables at the ranch were sold in an auction. Some Sannyasins who deposited money with the Rajneesh Financial Services Trust reported being unable to retrieve their money, though Prem Niren, the new chief attorney for the enterprise, expressed confidence that all claims would be paid. These claims are now the subject of a complex agreement to be implemented when the ranch is sold.

The North-western press now treats Rajneeshism as finished, ignoring that the movement antedates Rajneeshpuram by a decade and is likely to persist after liquidation of the commune. Rajneesh returned to India, renting the Span Resort near his home area of Manali. India revoked the visas of the foreign members of his personal staff. He moved rather precipitously to Crete, but was expelled at the urging of the Greek Orthodox Church. Subsequently, he was allowed a brief stay in several countries, finally appearing to settle in Uruguay, and negotiations were underway to allow visitation by Sannyasins and establishment of a "mystery school". Subsequently, he left Uruguay and was reported in Jamaica, then Pakistan and finally in India, where he resides in Poona.

Most of the portable assets of Rajneeshpuram have been sold; the ranch is offered for public sale. Many businesses in other countries have been sold to Sannyasins who continue to operate them much as in the past. Disciples in India, the United States and Europe express hope for rebuilding after finances are cleared (Mitra, Draper and Chengappa, 1985). Residents of Rajneeshpuram have "returned to the world" except for a small maintenance staff. Many live in group housing with other Rajneeshees and a number have established Rajneesh-oriented therapy centres and businesses. Some have returned to prior occupations though several report initial problems in securing interviews because of their association with Rajneeshpuram. Others have been placed in appropriate jobs through Rajneesh networks.

Structure of the Rajneesh Movement

The Rajneesh movement is a loose collection of identities and institutions, beliefs and practices, communities and living arrangements, financial structures, businesses, and political and social goals. Rajneesh and his followers are fond of pointing out that Western observers are confounded by their own preoccupation with consistency, though some Eastern observers also seem troubled by Rajneeshee claims that "contradictions are of no consequence". Rajneesh (1985) asserts the absurdity of "objective" study of religion, as the experience is totally subjective and accessible only by meditation. He acknowledges that one can use other means to study externalities of religion (adherents or followers, beliefs and practices, relationships), but argues that this amounts to studying the "corpse" of religion. While I cannot attest to the internal experience of Rajneeshees, certain consistencies can be abstracted concerning the movement.

Recruiting and Initiation

Initiates are almost uniformly drawn from the apparently successful, either aristocratic Europeans or accomplished professionals from Europe, the United States, Canada, Japan, India. Members include attorneys, physicians, writers, artists, academicians and other professionals. Many Sannyasins characterise themselves as "drop outs" from the top of society and indicate disillusionment with bureaucratic institutions and industrial societies. Rajneeshees tend to be young, most in the range of 25-40, though there are a few older members. Some writers (e.g. Levine, 1984) make the mistake of assuming that Rajneesh recruitment follows the pattern of groups like the Hare Krishnas and Children of God. Levine argues that new adults are "stopping over" in unconventional religious movements as a stage in growing up. Rajneeshees are almost uniformly older and at later stages in their lives before turning to the movement and rather than chance recruitment by strangers, as described by Levine, Sannyasins indicate active pursuit of Rajneesh training after referral by friends. Some have been drawn by advertised therapies. Most have travelled widely and report earlier experiments in other religions and therapies.

Becoming a "Sannyasin" involves few overt

commitments from individuals and no commitments from Rajneesh, though Sannyasins report an overwhelming sense of being "unconditionally loved". Conversion involves contact with Bhagwan and experience with meditation practices (extensive for some and brief for others). Commitment is indicated by a decision to use four "devices" separating Sannyasins from others: (1) dressing in "sunrise"colours (originally orange at the Poona Ashram, but changed to red, purple, pink in Rajneeshpuram); (2) wearing a "mala" in visible display (a necklace with 108 beads and a picture of Bhagwan); (3) using the new Sannyas' name, given by Bhagwan upon initiation; and (4) to continue meditation practice as appropriate.

Recruitment to Rajneeshpuram was more complex, with seekers undergoing extended oservation before admission to the commune. Some described the selection by current members and others claim that membership decisions were virtually in the hands of Ma Anand Sheela, who was so empowered by the By-Laws of the commune. No "price" was assigned to membership (Hanya, 1985), but many gave gifts and others seem to have been selected on the basis of wealth or special skills. Internal politics determining the inner circle of intimates to Bhagwan remain hidden to outsiders, but he has retained a core of intimates for over 15 years, with stresses among Indian, European and American patrons in terms of control of the movement.

The Rajneesh are a genuine "mixed type" in terms of Wallis' (1984) classification of new religious movements. In some respects the movement approximates Wallis' "world affirming" type (1984: 20-35), emphasising personal enlightenment and individual self-realisation. The goal is to "de-programme" individuals so that they may behave without reference to norms (oughts or shoulds). At times this sounds very like the notion of a "clear" in Scientology. Wallis characterises such movements as appealing to middle- and upper-class individuals who continue to function in the everyday world enhanced by their training. Such movements lack developed theology and collective rituals of worship. The range of commitment among Sannyasins poses a problem for classification. While some Sannyasins continue to function in the everyday world, even these view the prevailing social order with contempt. Others, like residents of Rajneeshpuram, withdraw rather completely. This orientation is more in keeping with Wallis' notion of "world rejecting" religions, usually thought to draw members from lower socio-economic groups. Further, the Rajneesh, while lacking developed theology, had collective rituals of meditation and distinguishing manners of dress, though these are now optional. Wallis notes that world affirming adherents pursue self-interest and world rejecting ones pursue service to a Guru. Most Rajneeshees pursue self-interest but retain contempt for the arena in which they do so. Commune members identified "work" with "worship" and eschewed self-interest. Nor do the Rajneesh clearly fit Wallis' final category, the "world accommodating" religion. While emphasising individual growth, Rajneesh are explicit in protest against conventional religious institutions and society and this rejection of conventions seems strongly directed toward the political goal of a new social order. Bhagwan speaks of creating a new human, capable of Eastern mystical insight and Western material accomplishment. In a sense, Rajneeshpuram was viewed as a demonstration project (Prasad, 1985).

Few Rajneeshees expect the world to be accommodating and none are promised support or protection from the movement. Consequently, events seen as devastating by outsiders (e.g. the dismantling of Rajneeshpuram) may dishearten some Sannyasins, but will be seen as of no consequence by others. As one Sannyasin told me after Bhagwan's arrest, "Life is full of surprises when you are with Bhagwan."

Belief System and Practices

Followers of Bhagwan Shree Rajneesh view him as an "enlightened master" (comparable to Jesus, Buddha, Lao Tzu) who can guide others to enlightenment. All are capable of enlightenment, merely blocked by conditioning and socialisation in a distorted society and debilitating religious traditions. Writings based on discourses of Bhagwan explore his core ideas, linking these to selections from different religious traditions. The writings are eclectic, ranging across Christianity, Buddhism, Tantra, contemporary and 19th-century psychology. Most are neither indexed nor organised into sets of related topics. He has said that critics will go crazy trying to systematise his thought. The books are readable, with sharp insights and dramatic parables, marred by appeal to "secret" and uncited manuscripts providing new insight into teachings of other religious leaders.

While Sannyasins readily admit that the movement has no shared belief system (Prasad, 1985), certain recurrent themes appear. The universe is seen as a cosmic whole, without goal or purpose. Humans are seen as complete and perfect aspects of this universe, though constrained and distorted by human cultures. The bifurcation of eastern consciousness rooted in intuitive, direct experience and Western preoccupation with objective, rational analysis is seen as artificial. A goal of enlightenment is to produce a "new human" who is more whole because he or she will represent a synthesis of these dualities; eastern mysticism and Western materialism, rational and intuitive thought, spiritual and sensual.

The goal is described as a quiet, centred state from which one can act with intuitive assurance, taking absolute responsibility for one's action without recourse to norms, rules or a system of values. The cosmic view is decidedly "monistic" (Robins, Anthony and Ricardson, 1978) with its' denial of polarities. The Rajneesh push "monism" a step further than these writers, who distinguish groups as "technical" or "charismatic". The Rajneesh fall at both poles, using technical devices in meditation and therapy, while maintaining the value of discipleship, learning from an enlightened master.

The disciple-master relationship varies. Bhagwan's descriptions of the relationship emphasise independence and recalls Zarathustra's caution to potential believers that they must seek their own path (Nietzsche, 1954b: 82). While some disciples accept the risks of independence (Prasad, 1985), noting that Bhagwan has no responsibility to care for followers, interviews at Rajneeshpuram indicate that others seek a dependency relationship. Bhagwan describes his position as a charismatic leader as "the best showman in the history of mankind......." and followers as ".......my circus, my carnival" (Lattin, 1985).

Rajneeshees view enlightenment as achieved suddenly when one is ready, not requiring withdrawal or extended discipline. They distinguish no stages of enlightenment and thus are a "one-level movement" (Robbins, Anthony and Richardson, 1978). Members express a sense of relief and comfort at meeting other Sannyasins; all are seen as equal on a spiritual level. This is not to say the Rajneesh do not have invidious distinctions, but merely to say that richer, more skilled, more honoured, or more powerful Sannyasins are not more advanced in a spiritual sense. Seven "levels of consciousness" are mentioned in *The Psychology of the Esoteric*, but these ideas have not been elaborated nor are they prevalent enough among Rajneeshees to characterise the group as "multi-level".

Anthony and Robbins (1981) explore motivations for alternative communities created by "civil religion sects". Many monistic movements have no commuities but draw followers from everday society. While this is true for the majority of the Rajneesh, some devotees retreat to small residential communes and most prefer association with other Sannyasins. The Ashram in Poona and Rajneeshpuram were special cases of these alternative communities. Disciples at Rajneeshpuram claimed that concentration of enlightened people (and the presence of the Bhagwan) created a "Buddhafield" in which an ideal society could by built, attributing the general health, productivity, happiness and success of their community to this Buddhafield. While the Rajneesh currently have no spiritual centre, many small (50-350) alternative residential experiments remain (*Spokesman-Review*, 1985b).

There are some millenarian aspects to the movement with a recurrent assertion that civilisation faces impending destruction through nuclear war or pollution (*Rajneesh Times*, 1984b) or when AIDS kills two-thirds of the world's population (*Lewiston Tribune*, 1948b; *Rajneesh Times*, 1984a). Collapse of civilisation is seen as imminent (1984-1999) and Rajneeshism has been presented as a "Noah's Ark of consciousness" to focus efforts of survivors (*Rajneesh Times*, 1984a; Academy of Rajneesh, 1983, 56-57). Some followers view the alternative communities, especially Rajneeshpuram, as holocaust survival training (Lattin, 1983, Ritter, 1983).

Two Western influences are reflected in the Rajneesh philosophy. The view of man as tortured into a machine by social institutions draws heavily on Gurdjieff (Prasad, 1978: 14-17: Rajneesh, 1973: 100). Rajneesh's view of the "new human" who transcends the constraints of convention is reminiscent of Nietzsche's *Beyond Good and Evil* (1954a). His view of disciples as independent, forceful, highly competitive survivors is similar to Nietzsche's "superman".

The Rajneesh are criticised for indulgence of the senses, especially by Hindus who object to the Sannyasin (renunciate) term as it is used by the Rajneesh. Traditionally, a man who had achieved a full life, with business affairs settled and family matured (after extensive search and meditation) might come to a form of enlightenment through renunciation of the material and sensual aspects of the world. Neo-Sannyasins come to renunciation through experience. Rajneesh says: "I preach neither suppression (of passions) nor indulgence. I preach knowledge of suppression and indulgence. Suppression and indulgence are both ignorance, both are injurious" (Rajneesh, 1979b: 98). Critics see the indulgence, with Rajneeshism as a pretext for the indulgence, while ignoring the claim that *both* indulgence and repression are to be transcended. While Rajneesh advertising can titillate, observation at Rajneeshpuram suggested a population which was industrious, spontaneous, and outgoing, but not particularly licentious.

Mention should be made of the so-called "Book of Rajneeshism" (Academy of Rajneesh, 1983), representing Rajneeshism as a religion with ministers of different levels empowered to perform ceremonies of marriage, birth, death, initiation. This book, and other literature produced during the 1982-1984 period, was obviously an attempt to routinise what had been to this point a strongly charismatic movement. Establishing the title "Acharya" would have provided for others (or one other) to assume Bhagwan's initiation function. Ministers would have moved the group toward a more secular religion which is antithetical to the Rajneesh distrust of social institutions and organised religion. More consistent with his earlier discourses, Bhagwan renounced organised religion, claiming that materials written during this period did not reflect his views. While most copies were burned in a bonfire at the ranch, a few still exist and many of the ideas can be found (Snell, 1984). These may or may not portend future institutionalisation of Rajneeshism. Since this is a religion of recent manufacture, future models may differ in important respects.

Finally, one sometimes learns about a belief system from the "silences", from what is not said. Rajneesh has little to say about how Sannyasins should relate to other human beings. Absent is any code of behaviour or guide to living. Also absent is cosmology. While attention is given to the relationship of Christian, Judaic and Islamic traditions to Rajneeshism, the ethical/moral content of these is not incorporated. Sannyasins are seen as "beyond morality" in much the way that Nietzsche's "superman" was beyond good and evil. The Rajneesh have no shared beliefs about the origin or fate of humans, the world or universe. There is no cosmology, unlike most other religions. From their point of view, the cosmos simply "is".

Conclusion

The United States has a long history of settlement by religious groups which are locally unconventional. Drawn by a religious pluralism and some separation of church-state affairs which would seem to provide an environment open to innovation, most exotic religions have encountered hostility and suspicion from their neighbours. Resistance to small communal groups (e.g. Amana, Oneida, Shaker) has been somewhat localised, but extensive conflict has attended settlement of larger groups (Calverton, 1941). Eventual accommodation with the larger society seems to be enhanced if the group is either fairly conventional in social terms (e.g. Seventh

Day Adventists) or physically isolated to the extent of being more or less invisible to outsiders, as with the Mormon migration and contemporary rural communal settlements (Calverton, 1941; Bouvard, 1975; Kanter, 1972).

The fate of the Rajneesh American experiment was sealed by their unconventionality combined with their visibility. The choice of a rural commune may have been informed by the early experiments, but the survival benefits of isolation were foregone by the publicity and media exposure sought by these very urban people. At times, the leaders, and to a lesser extent, ordinary members, seemed to delight in their notoriety. Events were staged to mock neighbours and surrounding social systems in the apparent belief that the group was immune from sanction. Members expressed the view that "attorneys would take care of that". In a sense, the movement was caught in the dilemma of selling their outrageousness to clients so that the very publicity which fed the businesses and therapy centres served to inflame their neighbours. They could not at the same time claim the quiet and privacy of an Amish community while flaunting their unconventionality on national television.

During the course of this study it became clear that there was no single phenomenon that one could call "the Rajneesh movement". As with all closed groups, outsiders tended to see what they sought to see: a haven from a disturbed society, a centre of immorality, gentle and industrious utopians, dangerous fanatics. As noted earlier, study of this group is complicated by their dispersal and mobility, the many and changing corporate facades and the heterodox collection of beliefs and practices. To some extent, these problems face researchers interested in many of the new religious movements. The dispersal and mobility forced considerable reliance on the reports of others, which requires the researcher to cross-check sources and to attempt to discount known biases. The many corporate faces require attention to documents and cautious evaluation of the investigative work of others. The cultural and ideological heterodoxy could only be verified through extensive reading of materials produced by the movement and first hand encounters with members.

More fundamental, it should be noted that the character of such movements is in part a function of the social location of the observer and the observer's relationship to the movement. There is no single objective, external phenomenon which constitutes this movement. Not only do different observers seek and document different things, but the phenomenon itself is different for observers with different relationships to it. The behaviour of any given group of Rajneesh will be quite different when viewed by a member observer, a scholar observer, or a hostile observer. Richardson (1985) refers to this problem in his discussion of the interaction between the social location of the observer and those being observed. His insight becomes critical when we encounter articulate, sophisticated members of such groups who quickly assess the investigator and his or her stance toward the group before deciding what direction their interaction may take. This paper is a narrative of my reading of Rajneesh literature, encounters with individual Sannyasins and assessment of the accounts of others. Other narratives will differ markedly depending on where the observers stand and how they may be perceived by those studied.

While there is a general philosophical sense in which each observer's mental constructs of "The Rajneesh" are unique, there are modal response patterns among people in contact with the movement. Sannyasins tend to characterise members as enlightened, playful and open, some adding with obvious relish the adjective "outrageous". Neighbours, from Poona and Oregon, tend to use adjectives like authoritarian, sinister, and irresponsible while agreeing to the term "outrageous". (The most extreme added the term "evil").

In spite of extreme differences in culture and socialisation, all members of the original field research team share the impression that the Rajneesh of our experience are: (1) intelligent; (2) articulate; and (3) manipulative. The eclectic Rajneesh offerings in philosophy, therapy and lifestyle options contained features attractive to one or more team members and other elements which repelled one or another of us. While we debated heatedly about some details, our recorded debriefing around the teepee campfire on the Warm Springs Reservation concluded with prolonged silence following the question, "Would anyone like to spend a month alone in Rajneeshpuram?" For some time, while the adventuresome young social scientists reflected on the question, the tape contains only the sound of Tamarack logs crackling in the fire ring.

Epilogue

Of the many questions remaining, one that seems especially critical is why Rajneeshpuram collapsed after such an exuberant beginning. Subsequent field research from Summer, 1986 suggested tentative answers to this question. A grant from the Society for the Scientific Study of Religion allowed me to interview many Sannyasins remaining through May at the ranch, as well as scattered Rajneesh in the Willamette Valley, Portland and Seattle areas. In addition, I acquired first-hand knowledge of the opposition who pressured the Rajneesh to the point where they would display their intemperance and trigger legal reactions. Opponents included ranchers, loggers, lawyers, public officials, professionals, liberals, conservatives, fundamentalists, aquarians, cowboys, academics, ministers. Like the Rajneesh, the prior residents of Eastern Oregon employed several organisational structures and identities: "The 1000 Friends of Oregon," "Concerned Oregonians". It was at first puzzling that these many groups consisting of Oregonians who usually war (or at least contend) with each other (e.g. environmentalists and ranchers) could develop coalitions of such strength and focus.

Ranjeeshpuram was an attempt to transplant an exotic religious system and social structure into Eastern Oregon. The area has been the site of many transplants, each accompanied by some resistance and conflict, as is well-documented in the collective memory of the Warm Springs Confederation of Tribes. The short life of Rajneeshpuram is attributable to consistent and coordinated pressures from coalitions of existing residents, each group of which seems to have been offended by different facets of the Rajneesh (e.g. environmentalists focused on land-use and water issues, the Albany group on tax issues, some Christian groups on moral issues). Each of these groups, and others, seem to have had a different threshold, and the coalitions formed sequentially as new groups were alarmed or offended. The basic incompatibility of the Rajneesh with Eastern Oregon can be accounted for in terms of the cultural orientation of the movement, the social structure of Rajneeshpuram, and the personal orientations of Sannyasins. The tension produced by these orientations was exacerbated by tactical errors.

The fundamental flaw leading to rejection of Rajneesh communities, probably in Poona and certainly in Eastern Oregon, appears to lie in the religious orientation of the movement. Bhagwan Shree Rajneesh is a Tantric Guru; followers would probably add the prefix "neo" to this chracterisation. The tantric tradition is bifurcated into a right-handed and left-handed form. Left-handed tantrics outraged traditional Hindus by incorporating violation of fundamental taboos into their sexual practices (e.g. eating of meat). While some individual Sannyasins are quite inoffensive in their practices, the movement teaches disregard for offense given to others. The behaviour of some Sannyasins further suggests the "intention to offend". The disdain for the surrounding normative systems which the Rajneesh share with classic left-handed tantrics appears to have triggered a broader range of opposing groups than would ordinarily be possible in a region of such cultural diversity. Defensive moves on the part of the Rajneesh eventually exceeded the range of tolerated behaviour in American political systems (e.g. targeted poisonings, apparently by arsenic, and generalised salmonella poisonings). It is not clear whether the motivations for these tactics lie in a cultural affinity with Kāḷī (the bloodthirsty Hindu goddess), a political grounding in the state of Gujarat, or the "deprogramming" of individual followers.

Rajneeshpuram's internal social structure was described as "communal", but my "outsider" observations suggest that it was highly stratified, totalitarian in control structure and developed strong indications of a caste system. As Rajneeshpuram moved toward political action in Wasco county, these structural features produced initial fear, followed by anger, in prior residents. A gauge of this response is provided by the unprecedented voter turnout in the 1984 elections (92%). It is possible that the cultural diversity of Eastern Oregon was misread as an indication of unrestrained tolerance or disorganisation by Rajneesh leaders who selected the Big Muddy ranch as the site of their experiment. While the region has great diversity, Oregon has some of the strongest laws in the United States dealing with church-state separation. These stem from a stormy earlier history and reflect the uneasy accommodation forged among diverse and hostile groups. The region's traditions, both cultural and legal, are particularly inhospitable for religious based mono-cultural communities.

Sannyasins speak of having been "deprogrammed", which means that they have divested themselves of prior socialisation, normative rules and guidelines for behaviour. This is seen as desirable in that it frees the individual to "open or close" at any stage of an interaction or relationship (Prasad, 1985). While "deprogramming" appears to be of value to the degree that it frees individuals from possibly dysfunctional and neurotic facets of their histories, it can also strip individuals of useful normative response patterns which allow adjustment to sensibilities of neighbours and strangers. Some Sannyasins of my acquaintance are still unable to see poisonings and other extreme tactics as anything other than elaborate jokes or justified political action.

Finally, the Rajneesh ideology which describes non-Sannyasins as inferior and subhuman led to a fatal tactical mistake. Neighbours were seen as "hicks" or "monkeys" who could not effectively marshal resistance to the sophisticated legal and media moves of the Rajneesh. This contempt for neighbours led the Rajneesh to grossly underestimate the capacities of traditional residents. Though slow to organise, prior residents eventually developed sophisticated systems of surveillance, telephone trees to focus public participation, and legal mechanisms for challenge of the Rajneesh. These counter moves goaded the Rajneesh into excessive defensive responses for which some are now serving prison terms.

The uninhibited exuberance of Rajneesh celebrations and media events was initially attractive to many reporters and served almost as entertainment for the general population. But for those who were taxed or harassed from their homes, poisoned in their restaurants, and threatened in their political structures, the "playfulness" and "antics" of the Rajneesh took on more sinister tones. On the surface, Rajneesh playfulness reminds this observer of the "be-ins" from the 1960s. The difference lies in the fact that the Rajneesh, older, richer and more powerful than isolated groups of flower children, could threaten their neighbours in ways which triggered survival responses. A full accounting of the Rajneesh incident in Eastern Oregon will show documentable damages in excess of five million dollars.

The permissive behavioural system embraced by Rajneesh is almost an echo of the 1960s Aquarian production, *Hair*: "You can do anything you want to do, as long as it doesn't hurt anybody." An unfortunate feature of all echoes, including cultural ones, is that reflection of the first part of the message obscures the qualifying conclusion.

(1987)

Chapter Nine

Who Lives in Utopia? A Brief Report on the Rajneeshpuram Research Project

CARL A. LATKIN, RICHARD A. HAGAN, RICHARD A. LITTMAN, NORMAN D. SUNDBERG

In the summer of 1981, the followers of an Indian religious leader purchased a large tract of land in central Oregon and proceeded to the establishment of a community. They were followers of Bhagwan Shree Rajneesh, who had previously led a large Ashram in Poona, India, some 90 miles South-west of Bombay. A variety of factors, including alleged public harassment and poor health, led Rajneesh to move to the United States in 1981. Soon thereafter, he accepted an invitation to live at the new site, now named Rajneeshpuram.

Once "the ranch" became Rajneeshee property the occupants rapidly developed many of the amenities of a modern city. Although initially a small community, by the spring of 1982 over 500 people called Rajneeshpuram home. The population continued to skyrocket: approximately 4000 people had relocated there by winter, 1985. The extensive building programme needed to accommodate these people, along with the Rajneeshee presence in general, sparked serious objections from environmental leaders in the state and from inhabitants of the neighbouring communities. The result has been a steady stream of legal battles ever since.

By the winter of 1982, we had learned enough about the community to realise that an extraordinary event was taking place. Here was a social system in the making that was guided by a set of explicit beliefs and principles about people, personality, work, community, and religion. It was a human potential movement in the seclusion of the high Oregon desert. Social scientists may have fantasized about such a social experiment, but here it was. We began a study of them, and this is a report of our initial findings.

Although our research is to the best of our knowledge the only longitudinal study of the commune, Rajneeshpuram has not been wanting for publicity. The Rajneeshees were big news. In fact, they were a media event. Rajneeshpuram was a regular feature on both national and local television, and rarely a day went by that a major article did not appear in the state's larger newspapers. Unfortunately, coverage focused almost entirely on legal suits brought by or against the commune, the conflict between the commune and the "old-timers" of Eastern Oregon, and, in the fall of 1984 the influx of the homeless under the commune's share-a-home project. There are other written sources of information on the Rajneeshees, but it is almost all either anecdotal and frequently polemical, historical, or analytical and textual, the latter especially by those interested in the religious and philosophical nature of Bhagwan's thoughts (Clarke, 1983). To our knowledge, the data reported below are the only source of information collected through empirical methods; for this reason, our findings will be useful to anyone interested in the demographic question of who becomes a follower and the personality question of what these people are like. We have included details of the collection procedure(s) and data from the beginnings of our project; the effort was centred around learning more about the background characteristics of the Rajneeshees.

Procedures

Two surveys were administered at Rajneeshpuram, one in August and the other in October, 1983. The first survey was administered through Rajneeshee work groups (or temples, as they referred to them), which held regular meetings to discuss work-related issues. Each group included people who were working on the same type of project (i.e., all the people in construction in one group). Each group had a co-ordinator, and a meeting of all co-ordinators was held weekly. At the co-ordinator meeting prior to our arrival, a city official announced the intent and plans of our study. The co-ordinators were instructed to pick up the necessary number of forms from a central location, where three members of the research team had delivered packets of questionnaires and instructions. The co-ordinators then handed out the questionnaires to members of their respective work groups. Once a meeting ended, the co-ordinator returned all forms, completed and uncompleted, to the central drop location.

The questionnaires were prenumbered from 001 to 999 and a 3 × 5 identification card had been stapled to each copy. To insure anonymity, the identification cards, which included both the participant's names and subject numbers, were removed and stored at Rajneeshpuram. The answer sheets and forms did not include the subject's names, but subject number, sex, and age were included on the answer sheets. All materials except for the identification cards were taken back to Eugene the same day. A total of 732 people completed the first survey, a very high percentage of the estimated 800 people who were living there at the time. Of these, 635 fully completed questionnaires were analysed.

In the second survey, 200 people were chosen from the 635 who had successfully completed the first form. Subject numbers were randomly selected and a list of these numbers was then phoned to Rajneeshpuram. The numbers were then matched up to names, and these individuals were contacted concerning the possibility of completing a second form. Those who agreed to continue were asked to report to the commune cafeteria after work on Friday. Two members of the research team were on hand, and administration took approximately 45 minutes. Only 75% (150) of those asked to fill out the second form actually did, and we were concerned that these people might differ from the larger group which completed the first survey. To test this we looked to see if there were any differences in how the second-timers and the larger sample responded to the items on the first questionnaire. No significant differences were found, which is somewhat surprising given that a few differences might have been expected by chance alone.

Results

Demographics

The surveys emphasised two sets of information: demographics and psychological well-being. The first survey focused solely on demographics while the second stressed both forms of information. Data reported below on the first survey are based on the 635 respondents who completed the form without major error. It should be noted that not all totals come out to 100%, due to occasional unclear markings by the respondents or to the rounding of numbers on our part. The second survey started by asking more demographic questions. Of the 150 who filled out the second form, the data reported here are based on a random selection of 100 questionnaires. Data from the second questionnaire are indicated with an asterisk.

Age and Sex: Fifty-four per cent of the respondents were female with an average age of 33.9 years. Forty-six per cent were male with an average age of 34.7 years.

Family: Seventy-four per cent of the respondents reported they were married, 14% single, 10% divorced, and 2% widowed or separated. A minority of the Rajneeshees have children: 25% reported having children and 11% stated their children were living at Rajneeshpuram.

In the second survey we asked the question, "Are you presently living with your spouse?" Sixty-five per cent responded that they were. This question is similar to the question used in the first survey, "Does your spouse live at Rajneeshpuram?" to which 67% of the participants answered yes, indicating some consistency in responses.

Religious Orientation: Table 1 presents religious and ethnic background information. About half of the respondents were Sannyasins for 5 years or more and about two-thirds (63%) were living at a Rajneeshee centre prior to moving to Rajneeshpuram. Forty per cent characterised themselves as religious prior to becoming a Sannyasin and 60% did not.

In response to the question, "How did you first hear of Rajneeshism?" 40% mentioned friends, 30% books or taped materials of Bhagwan, and 10% through visiting a Rajneesh centre. No other specific source was mentioned in more than 3% of the cases.

TABLE 1

Member Characteristics

Length of time spent prior to moving to the ranch	at a Rajneeshee Centre	as a Sannyasin
1-3 months	6%	1%
3-6 months	8%	1%
6-12 months	13%	1%
1-2 years	10%	9%
2-3 years	8%	13%
3-5 years	8%	26%
5 or more years	8%	49%
never	37%	

Ethnic Background		Religious Background	
White	91%	No religious background	14%
Black or Negro	1%	Roman Catholic	27%
Hispanic/Spanish/Latino	2%	Jewish	20%
Other	6%	Hindu or Buddhist	4%
		Protestant	30%
		Other	4%

Education: Ninety-five per cent of the respondents graduated from high school and 64% from a university. We asked participants to "Please list degree(s), diploma(s), and certificate(s) you have received from high school, secondary school and beyond." Table 2 lists this information for a random sample of 100 along with academic area of degree.

Place of Residence: Table 3 presents size of community from which the participants came. About half (48%) were from cities of 100,000 or greater. This is in sharp contrast to their present situation; the nearest town of 10,000 or more is about 100 miles away.

TABLE 2

Academic Background

Highest Degree Obtained

None or unclear	8%	
High school/secondary	17%	
Community or junior college (AA)	6%	
Bachelor's degree (BA, BS)	33%	
		75%
Master's degree (MA, MS, MFA, etc.)	24%	
Doctorate (PhD, JD, MD, etc.)	12%	
		36%

Academic Area of Degree

Arts and Humanities	27%
Social Sciences	33%
Natural Sciences (Inc. Math)	10%
Professions	10%

TABLE 3

Community Size Background

Size of community in which participant spent most of time prior to age 18:

Farm	5%
Town Less than 5,000	10%
5,000—20,000	16%
20,000—100,000	22%
100,000—500,000	13%
More than 500,000	35%

Income and political orientation: Table 4 gives data on political orientation and income. We thought the question of highest income would be a good indication of previous income because many Sannyasins were living at Rajneeshee centres before coming to Rajneeshpuram and making little or no money.

TABLE 4

Political and Economic Background

Political Background

Categorized as	Per cent
Radical	11
Very liberal	31
Somewhat liberal	20
Somewhat conservative	2
Very conservative	0
Neither liberal nor conservative	36

Economic Background

Highest Income per year	Per cent
Less than $ 10,000	16
$ 10,000 – $ 20,000	26
$ 20,001 – $ 30,000	24
$ 30,001 – $ 40,000	15
$ 40,001 – $ 50,000	10
$ 50,001 – $ 75,000	4
$ 75,001 – $ 100,000	2
Over $ 100,000	3

Psychological Well-being and Mental Health

Along with some demographic inquiry, the second survey included a number of psychological inventories and questions directed at assessing mental well-being.

Inventories on perceived stress, social support, self-esteem, and depression were included. The scales were selected using several criteria, including reported validity and reliability, ease with which they were completed, and the consideration of what we believed to be key dimensions of psychological well-being. Several questions on life satisfaction were asked. Information on past and present life satisfaction is presented in Table 5. Before becoming a "Sannyasin", life satisfaction varied widely; few, however, were extremely satisfied. At the time of the survey, 93% reported being in the top two categories of life satisfaction.

TABLE 5

Life Satisfaction

Scale	0	1	2	3	4	5	6	7	8
	Extremely dissatisfied; never worse			Neither satisfied nor dissatisfied			Extremely satisfied; best ever		
Now	2%	0%	0%	0%	1%	0%	3%	11%	82%
Previously	10%	2%	10%	13%	23%	11%	22%	3%	5%

Perceived stress: The Perceived Stress Scale, developed by Cohen, Kamart, and Mermelstein (in press) is a 14-item global measure of stress level experienced during the last month. Items were designed to tap dimensions of unpredictability, uncontrollability, and overload experienced in participants' lives. The Rajneeshee mean on the Perceived Stress Scale was 15.22 (N = 79, S.D. 7.64; low score indicates low perceived stress). Cohen *et al.* report a normative mean of 23.34 (N = 543, S.D. 7.62).

Social support: Social support was measured with the Interpersonal Support Evaluation List (ISEL) (Cohen and Hoberman, 1983). This scale is comprised of a list of 40 statements to which the respondent answers true or false based upon perceived availability of social resources (e.g., "There are several different people with whom I enjoy spending time"). The Rajneeshee sample had a mean score of 37.91 (N = 78, S.D. 1.51; high score indicates a high perceived social support). Cohen and Hoberman report a normative mean of 36.5 (S.D. 7.4), a figure lower than that of the Rajneeshees. (One problem with this scale is a ceiling effect. The maximum score is 40.)

Depression: The measure of depression we selected was the Centre for Epidemiological Studies Depression Scale (CES-D scale). It was developed for epidemiological assessment in the general population. The CES-D is a 20-item, 4-point scale which asks about depressive symptomology during the past week (e.g., I had crying spells). The Rajneeshee mean was 5.86 (N = 86, S.D. 5.55; low score indicates low levels of depression). A study by Radloff (1977) reports means for three all-white samples ranging from 7.94 to 9.25 and standard deviations from 7.53 to 8.58, N = 4996.

Self-esteem: Self-esteem was measured with the Rosenberg Self-Esteem Scale (Rosenberg, 1965). Consisting of 10 items, four points each, the scale was developed as a measure of global feelings towards self. The subject is asked to respond to such statements as "I am as good as most people." The Rajneeshee mean was 35.71 (N = 87, S.D. 5.53). For comparison, Yancey, Rigsby, and McCarthy (1972) report means of 29.82 (N = 1179, S.D. 4.24; high score indicates high self-esteem).

Discussion

There are definite similarities between individuals who resided at Rajneeshpuram and members of other new religions: affluent, well-educated, and around thirty years old (Bird and Reimer, 1983; Volinn, 1985; Melton and Moore, 1982). As Kilbourne and Richardson (1984) point out, these types of individuals have the economic means to try out new religions. With Rajneeshees, finances may have been an especially important factor in joining; many followers travelled to India, saw Bhagwan, and then became Sannyasins. Although the Rajneeshee demographics resemble those of other new religions, there are substantial differences. The most notable is education.

The graduate educational attainment of the Rajneeshees is extremely high. As mentioned earlier, we do not know if our results represent Rajneeshees in general. It may be the case that highly educated Rajneeshees were more inclined to quit their jobs and go to the ranch, believing that if they so desired they could always leave and obtain a decent job elsewhere. It is possible the commune systematically selected Sannyasins with advanced education. One other explanation for the high level of education, and one that several Sannyasins espouse, is that these were individuals who had already reaped society's material rewards, became bored, and subsequently sought spiritual fulfilment.

The results from measures of self-reported psychological well-being differ from data compiled on other new religions. Galanter, Rabkin, Rabkin and Deutsch (1979) found that although joining the "Moonies" did increase levels of psychological well-being, the mean score of converts was still below the norm. This is not the case with Rajneeshees. They score well above average. Galanter's data indicate that a higher sense of well-being is not simply the result of the methodological problem of mortality. Low scorers do not drop out. Indeed, Galanter found that they were more likely to remain.

One should be cautious in interpreting the Rajneeshee responses by comparing them with those of other groups. This is particularly true with the mental health data, where several methodological/practical ambiguities exist. First, these inventories are only one form of data, i.e., self-report. Second, one cannot assume items will have the same meaning in different cultures. Third, the results are confounded with the Rajneeshee philosophy of emphasising the positive elements of life. The scales could be tapping philosophy instead of mental status; however, from our observations individuals at the ranch appeared in general to be happy and well-adjusted.

(1987)

III

MEDITATION AND THERAPY

Chapter Ten

Rajneesh: Meditation in Bombay

AUBREY MENEN

Before I write about Bhagwan Rajneesh I must, as they say in the British House of Commons, 'declare my interest'. That is to say, I must confess any personal matter which might prejudice my judgement.

Rajneesh began his career as a professor of philosophy, taking up that of a Swami only after a deep study of comparative systems. In his Ashram he has an enviable library of books. He advises his disciples which of these they should read, and to which passages they should pay attention. He marks these passages with scholarly neatness: one dot for a notable passage, two dots for those which are very notable. He has one of my books on his shelves. In it I describe my own experience of the Upanishads. I value the fact that I have several dots, single and double, and I feel that it is generous of the Swami to give me this *nihil obstat*. The experience I describe is that of Raja Yoga, the purely intellectual approach to the discovery of the true self, and I describe the path as long and hard. For me, it was. Rajneesh's own thinking is firmly based on the austere principles of the original sages, as my own is. But he has invented a simpler way of at least getting a glimpse of what the original sages were talking about. I think it interesting, practical, and spectacular.

In my book, *The Space within the Heart*, I describe how, during my experiment, I was quite alone. This is perhaps not so trying for a writer as it would be for others: he spends most of his day alone. But Rajneesh saw that it was fear of loneliness that made people seek him out, as thousands do. He therefore invented 'mass meditation'. I have attended one of these sessions, not to meditate, but to observe.

It took place at 9 a.m. under the dazzling, but still tolerable, morning sun of India. The site was a large open space, the garden of some institution unconnected with Rajneesh. There was nothing very private about the garden: a wall bounded one side of it on which were perched urchins and fisherboys ready to watch the fun. When I arrived, on time, it already held some two-thousand people. The entrance fee was nominal—12 cents—which was not always collected.

On a platform at one end was a revolving chair, covered in fawn leather. It was a luxurious affair, of the sort that one would expect to find behind the huge desk of some top American executive. On this chair sat the Swami, relaxed as no top executive ever is. He gazed at the audience as though there was nobody at all. It was composed mostly of Indians—clerks on their way to the office, housewives on their way to the shops, some neatly suited businessmen, university students, and a few old men in retirement. There were some foreigners, Americans and Swedes in the main, and a scattering of those young people in scanty Indian dress who come from abroad, seeking wisdom. I saw no Dharma-bums or their successors. All sat on the ground, with a fringe of standing people who, like me, were interested spectators.

A little group of women carried a parcel to the dais, unwrapped it, and showed it briefly to the Swami. It was a plaster model of his feet, gilded, and intended, I was told, for some South American Ashram. Then the mass meditation began.

Speaking first in Hindi and then in excellent English, the Swami told us with the utmost brevity what was going to happen. For the first twenty minutes the audience was to let itself go. 'Do exactly what you like: shout, dance, sing: just as you please. For the next twenty minutes meditate in absolute silence: meditate on whatever you choose. I shall be here to help you. For the last twenty minutes be happy: let me dance in your hearts.'

I noted particularly that in his whole brief address—he made no other—only this last sentence had any touch of rhetoric. This was a rare thing in India, where to speak in public without lengthy preambles, turgid prose and portentous but empty similes is considered almost an insult to the public.

A brisk rhythm from an expert drummer (on tape, the machine being clearly visible together with a worried recording engineer) roared from powerful loud speakers. For a few moments nobody moved. Then the Swami swivelled his chair round to the left. He held out his hands, palm upwards, fingers wide apart. His head leaned gently to one side, in a gesture of gentle, almost feminine, invitation. Slowly he swivelled round a full-half circle. As he moved, pandemonium broke out under his abstracted gaze.

I have seen hysteria in crowds. I have followed the fortunes of an Italian boxer in Rome from his beginnings to the time when he became world champion and the Romans made so much noise they would have terrified lions in the Colosseum; I have attended Nazi rallies; but

I have never seen anything like this. People were shouting, singing, and performing the most extraordinary actions all over the place, but there was absolutely no sense of a crowd. Each person acted completely on his own, glancing neither right nor left. Some followed with their eyes the man with upraised hands who was slowly, very slowly, turning on his chair. Many did not. His tranquil expression, the controlled beauty of his gesture, was a pleasure to watch, but there was no magnetism about it. As for me, I thought of a play by Sophocles performed in classic style, where the actors spoke lines filled with passion from behind immobile masks. The contrast between the Swami and his audience had something of the same effect.

One man flung his arms repeatedly in the air, singing tunelessly. Another danced round and round, a beatific expression on his face, not with the hop, skip and a jump of the Hare Krishnaites, but with graceful, ballroom steps. He was dancing, I thought, with the girl of his dreams. Another young man took off his jacket, and with jabs of his right and left fists fought an invisible antagonist with all the joy of a boxer punching his way to victory. An American woman, grey-haired, squatted on the ground with her eyes closed, clapping her hands with voluptuous movements. A man who was obviously an office clerk, stripped his coat, shirt and vest, and stood, immobile, clad only in his flimsy *dhotī*. At his feet a man flung himself on the ground and rolled about there, like a child on a soft carpet. A pretty girl gyrated slowly, her hands in a seductive gesture, as though she were a fashion-model. One old woman turned her face to the sky, weeping profusely and laughing at the same time. From all over, as the drum pulsed without stop, came a confused sound of voices as people shouted meaningless syllables. Nobody, as far as I could hear, was chanting a *mantra*. To the rhythm of the drum one man gave violent jerks of his head, left, right, left, right, till I thought he would break his neck.

The drum stopped. Everybody stood or sat still. 'Now', said the Swami, 'twenty minutes of meditation. Be still, be silent, close your eyes'. A hush spread across the assembly, which deepened into complete silence. The noises of the city crept back into my consciousness. Some people closed their eyes, others just stared into vacancy. The boxer relaxed his muscles visibly, the frantic dancers sat in utter stillness. There were no whispered prayers, no *yoga* postures, no mystic gestures of finger and thumb. Only stillness and a great quiet.

The drum started again, a softer, tripping rhythm this time. 'Now', said the Swami, 'joy, let us be happy'. The dancers got to their feet and danced but without frenzy. The boxer stood up, spread his arms, and smiled. The man who had rolled on the ground, stretched himself, still lying horizontal, and laughed. The pretty girl composed her face into an infant's smile. The man who had stripped half-naked rubbed his torso admiringly.

The drum stopped for the last time. The Swami left his chair and moved to his car, people crowding round him to touch his hands or feet. Assistants moved his chair and put it on the top of a taxi. The Swami drove away. An American girl burst into violent sobbing, while her companions watched her with amused smiles. The place of assembly was dotted with prone men and women, exhausted by their experience.

One of the most notable things at the meeting was the respectability of the response to the invitation, 'Do what you like.' Carnival time in a Catholic country invariably sees some sights that cause raised eyebrows in even the broad-minded: so much so that Carnival is forbidden in Rome because it might shock the pilgrims. But this criticism is not quite fair to Swami Rajneesh. The mass-meditation I saw was in a big city. Nudity (for instance) is forbidden within city precincts, even to fakirs. When Rajneesh holds his meetings in more secluded places such as the holy hill called Mount Abu, some of his followers strip naked with all the nonchalance of Western actors and actresses.

His invitation to freedom should not be taken with undue gravity. It is more like packing the kids off to the swimming hole for the summer afternoon. What is remarkable and new is the second twenty minutes. Whether the audience really meditates or not I cannot say. I can confirm that after the drumming and the frenzy there is that sort of silence which only a great solo musician can command. Even he could not produce that utter stillness: no coughing, no fidgeting. Like the soloist, Rajneesh is there on the platform, gyrating in his chair. But a large number of those in an enviable state of calm relaxation were not even looking at him. I have heard John Kennedy address a joint session of Congress, my seat being to his right behind him, so that I could observe the audience. He did not produce the stillness of Rajneesh, except from the Justices of the Supreme Court. But they were sitting in the front row, right underneath him and they had longer experience in suppressing yawns and the furtive scratch.

Nevertheless, Rajneesh's meeting was a public show, as much as those of Billy Graham, though mercifully less verbose. In private, he is close to the true teachings of the Upanishads. He is at pains to point out that to gain the knowledge of the real self, one must be alone. Like the sages, he attacks society in words that are a good deal sharper than those of Marcuse:

> Every type of social institution is a means to kill the individual and convert him into a machine. All our universities are factories to kill the spontaneous—to kill the spark, to kill the spirit and change man into

> a machine. Then society feels at ease with him. He can be relied upon. He can be predicted. Man becomes predictable as soon as he becomes a machine. We can predict a husband, a wife, a lawyer, a scientist. We know who they are and how they will react. We can be at ease with them.

He argues that we are all too rational, a philosophical word which is a little too worn to have much meaning. He has improved upon it. He says we *over-do.* "In the world in which you are proficient," he says, "you tend to over-do. This over-doing is the problem. One must not be an expert all the twenty-four hours. One must also do something in which one is no one. One must also do something about which one knows nothing. One must be a child, playing sometimes, immature, unknowing, ignorant".

It recalls Ramakrishna asking Vivekananda to explain 'logic' and then not waiting for an answer.

(1979)

Chapter Eleven

Rajneeshpuram: Hound Dogs with the Scent

WILLIAM T. DRENNEN

The "new age" community of Rajneeshpuram, near Antelope, Oregon, was initially formed in 1981. In July 1982, I attended the first annual celebration there, along with approximately 11,000 people who came in for this celebration from all parts of the world.[1]

Most people who came were Sannyasins, followers of Bhagwan Shree Rajneesh. The following is my story of this relatively new and very vibrant movement, and a partial view of Rajneesh's teachings. Some of his existential concepts are similar to modern holistic growth psychology, especially that of Carl Rogers (1961, 1980), Fritz Perls (1971), and Roberto Assagioli (1971). I also found similarities in Rajneesh's writing to many other humanistic, transcendental psychologists, and many familiar aspects of the older writings of Carl Jung (1968) and Wilheim Reich (1973). However, Rajneesh (1977d: 87) has discounted perceived similarities, saying:

> Yes, I don't give much value to Freud, Jung, Adler

> or Assagioli. Freud, Jung, Adler and others, are just children playing on the sand of time. They have gathered beautiful pebbles, beautiful coloured stones, but when you look at the ultimate, they are just children playing with the pebbles and stones. Those stones are not real diamonds. And whatsoever they have gained is very, very primitive. You will have to go slowly with me to understand.
>
> Man can be physically ill; then the physician, the doctor is needed. Man can be psychologically ill; then a little help can be given by Freud and Jung and others. But when man is existentially ill, neither a physician nor a psychiatrist can be of any help. Existential illness is spiritual. It is neither of the body nor of the mind, it is of the total—and the total transcends all parts.

Rajneesh feels that Freud and Jung were geniuses who had gone astray, both "ego realised", not "self-realised". Both are viewed as ordinary men with jealousies, competitiveness, fears and resentments. (I do not agree that this describes Jung.) Neither had cured themselves or resolved their relationship with existence itself. They were merely adjusted with some ego contact between the conscious and the unconscious. They were not Buddhas—awakened ones (Rajneesh, 1977d).

Thus, as a self-proclaimed Buddha, Rajneesh views his psychology as transcendent to that of the West. Rajneesh never pulls punches; he is dogmatic, confrontive, and humorous. The way to self-realize, he states, is not to analyse but to drop the mind and the ego entirely. For Rajneesh, even the efforts of the transcendental/spiritual psychologist, Assagioli, fall short. He states:

> The Western attitude has become very efficient in analysing, dissecting, taking things apart. Even a

> movement like the Psychosynthesis of Assagioli is not a real synthesis, because the very standpoint is missing. First Freud and Jung have taken things apart, they have broken the whole, and now Assagioli is trying to put those parts together somehow.
>
> You can dissect a man into parts, he was alive; when you have dissected him, he is no longer alive. Now you can put the parts back again, but the life will not come. It will be a dead corpse. And even parts put together again will not make it a whole. What Freud and Jung did, Assagioli is simply repenting for. He is putting the parts together again but it is a corpse. There is no synthesis in it (Rajneesh, 1977d: 89).

For Rajneesh, the purpose of life is to become conscious, fully conscious in the "here and now" (that is, much like Perls, 1971). Then, with a method of meditation or technique that fits you, you can transcend consciousness about anything to become consciousness itself—the drop becomes the ocean. The evolution of awareness without duality, without subject/object differentiation, is the very *purpose* of life (Rajneesh, 1977 b).

For this qualitatively different leap into "pure consciousness", the state of true meditation is required, and many methods of *yoga*, Zen, Tantra and other paths to this state are described in Rajneesh's transcribed discourses (for example, see Rajneesh, 1976b; 1981).[2] What is termed here as "true meditation" is best described, in terms of Wilber's (1982a) recent theoretical and experimental clarifications, as the final peak of many hierarchial levels of meditation—for example, from a simple relaxation response (TM), to the subtle realms of mind transcendence with witness awareness of fascinating phenomena (Bucke, 1923; Muktananda, 1974), to the *witlessness* being of pure, living consciousness (Walsh and Vaughan, 1980). Just as in Piaget's (1963) stages of cognitive intellectual development, there are qualitative leaps from one stage to another. Descriptions and conceptualisations differ, depending on the perceiver. As Vaughan (1982) recently summarised from Wilber (1977), Tart (1975), and other writers, there are three realms of knowledge: the empirical (sensory, EMG, EEG, and so on) the mental (such as logic/reason), and the spiritual or transcendent (such as highest intuition, ultimate truths, pure consciousness).

As is evident, Rajneesh focuses only on two basic states: ego consciousness-spiritually asleep versus meditation-spiritually awake. However, before offering more substance and reaction to his conceptualisation regarding the meditative state and many other transpersonal insights, let me give more of the experiential happening at Rajneeshpuram this past July (1982).

On the Road Again

Before I went to Rajneeshpuram (formerly a huge ranch), I had only read six or seven of Rajneesh's books (there are over a hundred). The books struck me as discourses by either one of the biggest egotists in the world or a person transcendent to all false humilities and probably enlightened. Such was their assertive impact—*I am the Gate* (1976c), for example. Since I had delved deeply into personality theories and was interested intellectually and existentially in Western/Eastern mystical, esoteric, and spiritual psychologies, I was fascinated with his brilliance, his humour, and his complete frankness.

Prior to my trip, I had come to view Rajneesh as extremely insightful with regard to universal principles of holistic personality, and perhaps more than just another spiritual/existential Guru. For example, his ability to confront/accept and synthesise human sexuality with spirituality seemed unique. However, I was not prepared to encounter the happenings that occurred in the previously deserted community near the little village of Antelope, Oregon.

In the Atlanta airport, I first encountered a small group of Sannyasins—people dressed in shades of red and orange ("fire" colours), all wearing *mālās* consisting of 108 beads (for the different names of God) and small, plastic-encased pictures of Bhagwan Rajneesh.

The red/orange wearing apparel and *mālā* are their symbolic gesture of the surrender of the ego to a *higher self* via their guide and catalyst, Bhagwan. Wearing such apparel makes one stand out and invites suspicion, fear, and even hostility from the public and former friends. All women are called Ma (Miss/Ms/Mrs) and all men are addressed as Swami (Mr).

In Seattle, we changed planes and met with a large group of Japanese Sannyasins; the other people on the plane were becoming curious about the red/orange dress. In the Portland airport, red-dressed people were everywhere, from many countries, and special buses were waiting. I really stood out in my green shirt and tan trousers; there were now very few people around who were not dressed in red/orange shades. Suddenly, I realised the reversal effect of being dressed differently. Now the looks of curiosity were being directed toward me! The "dress impact" continued to be important during my stay and will be discussed more later.

We stopped at the little township of Antelope at a small road stop that was run by swaying, smiling Sannyasins with rock music blaring in the background. We had been briefed on the bus that we might want to get something to eat as we would not be in time for supper at Rajneeshpuram. They served coffee, cookies, cheese sandwiches, and vegetarian hot dogs. I realised that I would have no more of my usual meat-based diet for a while.

Sannyasins are usually vegetarians, supplemented by milk and egg products. However, this health orientation stops short—they love cigarettes, tea, and coffee. No other drugs of any kind were permitted, and I failed to observe the presence of anything like alcohol or hashish during my stay. We had so many "Rajneesh cheese" sandwiches for lunch, it became a joke. (Later, when I returned home, a colleague happened to ask about TV news coverage: "Why did so many people stand by the roadside everyday just to see that *Big Cheese*?" All I could reply was, "Well, he had a great smile.")

I wondered, being a typical booze-and meat-hound psychologist, how I would fare without such habitual indulgences for two and one-half weeks. Actually, I did not miss them at all with so many activities attracting my attention. I learned that probably nothing is more effective than a new setting, strong consensus, and many activities to extinguish old habits. Of course, the return to the old setting fosters regression.

I could describe my first night at Rajneeshpuram as somewhat hellacious, not a walk over fire, but over mud[3] to a distant tent that was already full of Japanese Sannyasins; and as we tried to converse in our two languages (at 2.00 a.m.), someone shouted for us to "be quiet!" By the time I got back on one of their school buses to return to the reception centre, I was in a state of foul humour. I was ready to leave this muddy scout camp, overburdened with thousands of "red" people, many of whom were still coming in. It was chaos—wet and cold; I began to feel like a masochistic fool.

In one of his books, Rajneesh (1977d: 5-10) dichotomises people into three types: (1) the sadistic type, who is the politician—controlling, manipulating, competing, and sometimes evoking pain in those around him or her; (2) the masochistic type, who "enjoys" suffering, being the martyr, suppressing all emotions, inhibiting all desires—becoming the dogmatic religious *corpse* (as Fritz Perls would agree) for the sake of salvation; and (3) the type (Bhagwan and others) who is neither sadistic nor masochistic, who expresses needs, takes risks without the need to torture him or herself or others, lets go of ego achievement/esteem needs, and mainly *celebrates* life as the song and dance of existence. As with all polarities, the Sannyasin ultimately moves to synthesis or to the TAO, the transcendental centre, and joins the living current of cosmic life, love, power and wisdom.

After my torturous night, I awoke to a clear day and a new age community. Early that morning, I climbed the nearest mountain, had an emotional fantasy of being there before as an American Indian, and then took a bus to Buddha Hall for the first *satsanga* (music, readings, and silence) with Bhagwan and more than 10,000 others. We joined in long lines to first check in our shoes, and then walked or sometimes ran into the huge unwalled arena to the sound of greatly amplified live music.

Because of a serious illness, Bhagwan had been in seclusion for over a year. His Sannyasins were emotionally pitched for his arrival, but, after joyful shouts of greeting, settled down into silent meditation "in the presence of the awakened one"—the meaning of the name Buddha. For Bhagwan Rajneesh, this was his Buddhafield and he was there, not to be worshipped, but as a Buddha to facilitate those, sleeping in this dream, to awaken to what they really were—divine, eternal beings of God.

They did worship him, however; they loved him dearly throughout the week whether he was near or not. As one of his devotees' songs goes: "Wherever I go . . . there is your fragrance in the air."

Truly, his fragrance, his vibrations, seemed to have resonated with his Sannyasins. They seemed to have picked up on his *scent* to ultimately follow it hopefully through the halls of initiation to their awakening as Christ/Buddhas all. This message and its rhythmic "entrainment" (Leonard, 1981) sank into me during the week. This man was very possibly a living manifestation of love/wisdom—a complete gestalt, a synthetic self-reflective essence, a perfect circle, vibrating in the exact harmonic overtones of the perfected marriage within, in tune with the cosmic music of spheres. The attraction to this man transcends any usual transference phenomena; the call is to all receptive pilgrims of something within which pulsates in them as the very heartbeat of God. The prodigal sons and daughters sense, or get a glimpse of, their divine touchstone, their home—"the goose is out", as Bhagwan's (1982b) last discourse reads; and the tiger knows it is not a goat (as I will explain later).

A Selective Analysis

In his talks about the sayings or *sūtras* of Jesus (for example, see Rajneesh, 1974b), Bhagwan makes clear that real initiation, being born again, is not becoming the child again but becoming the sage. Children's innocence is present because of their lack of life's "lessons", conditioned attractions and aversions. The sage's innocence is earned through transcending anger-compassion, love-hate, happiness-sorrow, sexual aversion-sexual attraction; in fact, all conditioning and polarities.

There are two major conceptions here on which I would like to comment. The first, that the child becomes the sage (not that the adult becomes the child) seems to be in accord with Wilber's (1982b) thesis regarding what he terms the "pre/trans fallacy". Briefly, there are three human developmental stages of consciousness in evolution: (1) prepersonal (for example, an infant is reflexive, instinctive, non-ego reflective or aware); (2) personal (self-aware adult ego, differentiated, proactive); and, (3) transpersonal (ego awareness is not destroyed, but transcended to self; spirit returns from alpha to omega; Hegel, 1949). Thus the sage is both the transformed child (infant) and adult (ego).

However, in contradiction to this differentiation of the child/normal adult/sage, Bhagwan Rajneesh conveys in many discourses that utilitarian conditioning has so corrupted the adult that the person must let go of his or her ego (including its computer like mind) and get in touch again as an adult with his or her authentic, spontaneous "child" in mind and body. In terms of Transactional Analysis (Berne, 1961), I feel that Bhagwan has mixed up the adult ego state with the "sick" adaptive child state. The "ego" is not the culprit; it may be corrupted, however, by accepting conditioned messages from the fearful/hateful/conformist "child" as real. As Rogers (1980) concluded, the self-concept and the authentic organismic self have become incongruent. Conditions of worth lead to inner war, one ego state rejecting another (Berne, 1961). Also, in stating that all we need do is wake up to know our already present divinity, Bhagwan is coming logically from the second world view discussed by Wilber (1982a); that we have suffered involution from a divine heritage—the ego is regression. There is not only confusion in these views, but even the positive aspects of the ego are considered barriers to becoming "awakened" to our spiritual self.

The second point concerns polarities. Rajneesh (1974a) states that polarities are really complementaries: one needs the other (light/dark). But then he also states that only the positive side has substance and is real (light); the negative side is the positive side's *absence.* This seems contradictory, as do many other concepts, *when taken out of context.* For example, one Sannyasin asked him:

> Bhagwan, I have heard you say that knowledge is useless. Then, what is needed to guide us to the ultimate goal? (Rajneesh, 1982b: 51)

Bhagwan gives appreciation first to the phrase "I have heard you say," explaining how often what is heard is not what was said (or perhaps meant).

He adds:

> No, I have not said that. Knowledge is very useful—wisdom is useless! Knowledge is needed in the market place, in business, in politics. Everywhere knowledge is needed—in technology, in science—everywhere....wisdom is absolutely useless, but that's its beauty....it does not belong to the utilitarian world; it is a flowering (p. 52).

He adds that such things as love or the bird's song are also useless. However, in another context—that of becoming awakened, of self-enlightenment, of the trip within to join in communion with the higher self—wisdom and love are essential; knowledge is useless.

He explains:

> My whole message is that you can eat the cake and have it too, so why go for half? Knowledge is useful in the outside world, in the inside world it is a hindrance. And the same is true about the inner wisdom; it is of immense joy inside but don't try to use it outside (Rajneesh 1982b: 54).
>
> We need a new kind of human being who has both wings: the wings of knowledge, science, technology, and the wings of meditation, enlightenment, love, freedom. When both wings are functioning in a deep synchronicity, in a deep togetherness, in accord and harmony, then only man is complete, total (p. 55).

Thus one must be careful in trying to construe this man's many discourses; one is easily led astray by one's own perspective and by not grasping the contextual gestalts.

THE BASIC HUMAN DUALITY

In the discourse on *The Mustard Seed* Bhagwan suggests seven dualities, but the basic human duality revolves around the issue of sex. He feels that each of us has a sexual polarity of maleness and femaleness; we are two sexual beings (as Jung has written, 1968). This polarity represents our *incompletion,* our basic conflict within and the source of sexual "love" without. For the male, a particular woman keys with or completes the *circle* of his masculine energy with her reciprocal feminine energy. This can cause irrational attraction, dependency, and the misery of disillusionment. The woman provides an external key to the music of the spheres. However, for completion, the man must focus only enough on this external energy to gain contact and communication with his own internal, feminine energy field (*śakti*) within. The sexual dance is a potential means to lose the mind, become an energised circle, and thus enter the true meditative state. The woman is only a catalyst; and, I might add, so is Bhagwan. Both males and females must ultimately become androgynous and harmonious sexual beings. They must learn to complete their own circuit of life's energy without sexual union with another and, therein, be in resonance with the cosmic, oceanic energy field always present. Then the feelings of sex are transcended; one is *in love* with all that is.

In *The Goose is Out,* Bhagwan (1982b: 7-8) talks of the similarity of love and enlightenment. He states:

> Enlightenment is almost like a love affair. Just as you fall in love—you cannot rationalise it; it is below reason—in the same way you fall into

> enlightenment. It is above reason: you fall above words.
>
> It is a beautiful story. Enlightenment is falling upwards just as love is falling downwards. But something is similar in both; the falling—unreasonable, unexplainable, inexpressible. Only those to whom it has happened know, and even when it has happened you cannot explain it to anybody to whom it has not happened yet.

You fall into both, down into love for a mate, up into enlightenment with the oceanic cosmos as you circle within and become a complete gestalt—a self-generating circuit of life's energy, love, awareness, its celebration!

Bhagwan warns that to force the marriage within prematurely is dangerous; you could fall from the peak of enlightenment to the valley of madness, with an eruption of overwhelming dissonant energy. He adds that this is why the goal of completion is given, but the method is kept secret—a master guide is needed. This was, from Bhagwan's view, one secret Jesus had with his disciples. From my view, the mystery of the pentecostal or flooding of the disciples with the Holy Spirit is contained in this secret. Others, Eastern writers, refer to it as the awakening of the serpent power within, the *Kuṇḍalinī* for the marriage of Śiva and Śakti (Muktananda, 1974). You may awaken or go mad. Risk is very apparent (Krishna, 1972).

Let me express it this way—as long as two energy fields (+ and –) are separated in some major way (for example, through suppression or insulation), very little energy is flowing between them; it is dead or flowing outward. But, if the "circuit" within is opened, one of two things happens: harmony and enlightenment or chaos and madness. The energy fields within must become joined with complementary resonance; otherwise entropy results. Scientific investigations of related phenomena are being conducted by Motoyama (1981).

In America, biofeedback and related sensory/neurophysiological research has addressed itself to concomitant changes in the body's physiology during differential states (some viewed as meditative) of stress/relaxation and consciousness (see, Pelletier and Garfield, 1976; Walsh, 1982). For sometime in this country, alpha training (EEG 8-13 Hz) was thought to be our Western panacea for relaxation and transpersonal "meditational" states. Bluntly stated, alpha biofeedback training was oversold. Recent reviews (for example, Plotkin and Rice, 1981, p. 590) have questioned whether there has ever been any published evidence of "actual" alpha enhancement above optimal prefeedback baseline levels. Also, there is no substantive evidence of alpha changes directly (other than placebo) covarying with other indices such as mood or state of relaxation.

The whole area of biofeedback (that is, the Western "hope" for quick *nirvāṇa*), which is my current field of basic and applied research, is being scrutinised very critically after much false optimism (Simkins, 1982). TM training suffered a similar fate (Drennen, 1978; Smith 1976). However, the baby is not yet "thrown out with the bath water". There is still a possibility that certain synchronistic brain wave patterns may differentiate specific states of consciousness along with other metabolic indices.

The Hypnagogic/Hypnopompic States

Elmer and Alyce Green of the Menninger Foundation have reported a number of extraordinary experiences of people while in the theta state (EEG 4-7 Hz) (Green, Green, and Walters, 1979). It is a state reported by some *yogis* as noisy, and by others as full of hypnagogic images, creative intuitions, and "peak" experiences.

When theta brain waves are dominant, most people are in light sleep. (Theta dominance in one who is normally alert sometimes suggests brain dysfunction.) Also, Pelletier and Garfield (1976), in a review of a number of studies, reported the presence, in "transcendental" states of awareness, of either slower, higher-amplitude alpha (8-9 Hz) or theta (4-7 Hz).

I suspect that the hypnagogic (going into sleep) and hypnopompic (coming out of sleep) states, which occur between REM and stage one NREM sleep, are only indirectly related to a deep state of meditation. However, these states may be *one gate* to meditative dimensions. They are frightening states for most people. The brain is highly excited, firing off synchronistic, theta EEG rhythms in certain regions. The voluntary motoric system is cut off and, if you are "aware", you experience floating sensations, helpless paralysis, and possible auditory and visual hallucinations, with electriclike sensations throughout the body." You may subjectively even join the rising energy and leave the body (OOB) to find yourself in a rather strange dimension called the subtle or astral realm (Moss, 1974).

I had been familiar with this initially awesome state for over ten years before going to Rajneeshpuram. I had come to enjoy the body electric and the OOB peak experiences, which were more "real" than a very lucid dream. I had never had anything like this state during "awake" daytime hours, even with or in lieu of sexual orgasm, and I had concluded that I was never relaxed enough to melt into the flow of existence (known as tantra—the path of surrender; Rajneesh, 1976b, Vol. 2). However, during my stay at Rajneeshpuram, I was a participant in a dynamic body work group. We went through some gruelling bioenergetic exercises. On the fifth day, we did deep breathing, sitting up, for an hour or so, making an auditory sound on the in breath. This technique did something to my system. When I lay back exhausted, I went into a pleasant state, blissfully witnessing a body, now completely singing electric, with intuitive thoughts passing through my mind. When I got up I could still maintain this dissociative, holonomic (Leonard, 1981) state for about an hour. This experience probably was not the highest state of meditation (Wilber, 1982a) but I think it is the closest I have been to the blissful nectar of pure witness awareness during the day. I am not now really sure what a truly meditative state is, where "spirit" knows itself as spirit (Wilber, 1982a). But when I was in the state I have just described, I seemed to "know" and "be" in oceanic cosmic communion without needing any substantive verification. Such was my glimpse into a truly wondrous dimension of oneness with the flow, bliss, and intuitive wisdom of living existence. Time seemed almost to stop; there was nothing to do, just being and witnessing simultaneously (Walsh and Vaughan, 1980).

However, enough about my own experiences; let me continue with my story of the Sannyasins—hounds with the scent.

The Sannyasins

From my observational perspective, the red/orange people were generally bright to very bright, well-educated, economically independent, with vocational or professional training and skill, and represented many races. The ages were well distributed, with a majority being between 25 and 35 years old. They were healthy, and enthusiastic, and loved to dance and sing. They were mostly warm and considerate, but also obviously assertive. Sometimes they were insensitive and aggressively broke into food or bus lines with egocentric impatience. It was also obvious that being a Sannyasin was only a beginning—the usual characteristic fears, inhibitions, anger, and jealousies that typify most of us humans were apparent.

Sometimes I felt avoided because of the obvious difference in my dress. In fact, after a week I bought a red shirt so as not to stand out so much. No one was hostile with regard to my dress, but at times I did feel quite alone in the crowd. The few who dressed differently would at times seek each other out. No one "recruited" me or tried to convince me to take Sannyas. In fact, when I did ask about the possibility, I was told to consider it more deliberately on my return home. I am a very deliberate considerer. To realise "you are a tiger, not a goat" is not easy.

Rajneeshpuram: The Community Experiment

There are now about 300 permanent residents living at the new township of Rajneeshpuram. A descriptive brochure is available upon request. The community is nothing short of a miracle in terms of what they have accomplished in only one year.

They live mostly in mobile homes, work hard at assigned tasks for long hours, and all share a dream to build a permanent new age community. They have now completed their own water and irrigation/sewage disposal systems from wells, streams, small artificial lakes, and a mountain river. The place is extremely muddy when it rains, and desert dry/hot most of the remainder of the time. They have planted gardens and fruit trees and have horses, cattle, chickens, and other fowl. The farms there will definitely become greener and very fruitful. The huge Buddha Hall will become a permanent controlled atmosphere plant house. The residents are looking toward having their own source of energy supply, including solar heat and electricity generated by a new lake system. Rajneeshpuram is 100 square acres in size, with mountains and valleys reminding one of scenes from *Close Encounters* or, in winter, *Lost Horizons.* They bought the former ranch for $6 million, and the budget is quite large—$1 million being budgeted, for example, to crush rocks to cover their roads. There are plans and hopes for up to 4,000 permanent residents. Next year, they hope to attract 50,000 friends and Sannyasins for the second annual celebration.

Last Reflections

"It takes one to know one," as the saying goes. I really cannot adequately summarise or evaluate this possibly enlightened man and his new age community. All my life I have been open to all possibilities, accepting nothing without the cold objective appraisal reflected by my middle name—"doubting" Thomas (see Kopp, 1976).

Frankly, what has struck me as I have read more and listened (videotapes and audiotapes) to Bhagwan Rajneesh's many discourses is a synthetic mind/heart/body/soul feedback of affirmation. He has spontaneously and beautifully expressed many of my deepest, most experiential, transcultural views of the human being in evolution.

However, there are areas of disagreement, especially the way he denigrates the mind (ego) as a major hindrance, a computer without any creativity, a sick computer out of touch with or suppressing feelings (valued as more authentic). Therapy or growth intervention, as Wilber suggests, needs to assist a weak ego to become flexibly strong and *then* become transcended with the type of meditational method right for a particular person.

As Wilber (1982b) concludes and I agree, many world views are only half right. One view is the orthodox Western scientific fallacy of starting with the primitive and evolving to the developed rational ego; the other is the spiritual one of "involution" or the fall from the highest Self to the insightless, heartless, selfish ego. Evolution and involution are one cycle of relative awareness, unawareness, as the drop relates to the ocean of God (Hegel, 1949; Meher Baba, 1958). It is a dance; to stay in one state, as Bhagwan has suggested, would be a perfect bore. God loves to play.

Much of what I have read in Bhagwan's discourses about therapeutic interventions strikes me as a compelling concept of a highly eclectic nature. The basic problems of much of human misery are the dissociations of the ego (Wilber, 1982a) from the body. A sick, fearful, old age survival-oriented society breeds this madness. As Rogers and Perls have agreed, we have been conditioned to be split by having to fit into a rather sick system of receiving esteem and love. I disagree that the objective mind or the positive ego is the culprit and must be put only to utilitarian use—the new age mind has heart, is creative, and can facilitate the voyage within for its own transcendence.

Related Growth/Therapeutic Institutes

One of the major reasons for my initial interest in Rajneesh about three years ago was the indirect knowledge that a great deal of eclectic psychotherapy and growth interventions were taking place in Poona, India, where he resided before coming to the United States. With my own holistic interests, I have explored numerous growth and therapeutic interventions for groups and individuals for over twenty years. All therapies have their particular applications and limits, both in terms of the therapist and the client.

There are now many Sannyasins who were once involved in previous orientations I would label as "neo"-Reichian, Jungian, Adlerian, Rogerian, Perlian, and the like—who now do Rajneesh Therapy (Rajneesh

Meditation and Growth Institute at Geetam, 1982; Medina Rajneesh, 1982). Their brochures feature a large variety of techniques. From a few personal observations, I would venture that they are confrontational, intuitive, warm, confident, and value action/emotion over words or analysis.

There is much emphasis on body work, breathing, expressing in sound, bioenergising, releasing, catharting, contacting, being authentic, loving, playing—celebrating. The closest of three combinations of previous movements would be encounter, Gestalt, and the transformed, more authentic, more participating client-centred therapies. In the brochure describing Medina (1982: 8-9), Ma Anand Poonam sums it up this way:

> Ultimately there are three things that make a good therapist. The first is the ability of the person to stay open and vulnerable in themselves. The second is the knack, the insight, the intuitiveness that is either there or isn't. That isn't something you can train anyone in. The third thing is the technique. It's the least important. If somebody has the insight, perceptiveness and ability to get out of the way and see another person, and the openness to continually look at themselves and see themselves, then the technique and practice can very easily be taught—they are just by-products. The main thing I look for in a therapist is a lack of judging. As soon as the therapist judges, he becomes a parent, an authority, someone is saying "This is right and this is wrong." In Rajneesh Therapy there isn't any right or wrong, there is simply the understanding of what is. When there isn't judgement, there is love, understanding and compassion. And love and compassion are where the real healing is.
>
> Rajneesh Therapy is a sharing. There isn't a

> client and there isn't a therapist, but two people sharing an experience. It's as if the therapist first invites the client to share in that experience, the two come together and there isn't a separation. Then there isn't a client-therapist relationship any more, there are simply two people understanding each other. At that moment there is total love, total trust, and total understanding—a glimpse of oneness.

One major difference on the part of Rajneesh Therapy was expressed by one of the body work facilitators; work was in communion with Bhagwan, his spiritual guidance. This vibrational bond is one of a disciple to a master.

The goal is transformation. For this there are also techniques of meditation from the East. Bhagwan talks of 112 ancient methods contained in his discourses (1976b). His own contributions also include what is called "dynamic meditation" and "Kuṇḍalinī meditation," described in the famous *Orange Book* (1981a), among many others. Dynamic meditation is especially wild and vigorous, with chaotic breathing, cathartic movement, sounding "hoo" and jumping and stomping, a dance of celebration. Sannyasins love to dance and sing above most anything else; this is their communal celebration of life and love. There are also "quiet" techniques and, finally, life becomes one meditative experience.

I will not here attempt further to evaluate Rajneesh-based therapy; that lies in the future. For further descriptions, see Amitabh (1982).

Synchronistic Events

The American Indian has an age-old myth that whenever a highly spiritual event is to take place, there will be a shower for purification of the local atmosphere. On July 6, for the only time there, Bhagwan was to come at 7.00

p.m. for a *Darśana* or special master's day celebration, with singing and the like.

That evening's celebration was really the climax of the week's festivities. We were singing our special songs composed for this event and Bhagwan, awaiting his arrival. Not a drop of water had fallen since that first muddy night (July 2). At exactly 7.00 p.m., the thunder and lightning bolts began, with hurricane winds and rain for about fifteen minutes before and during his arrival. Shortly after he arrived, the sky cleared and the calm was very serene. Some purification that was! There were other synchronistic happenings—just chance?

To have witnessed the first great celebration with these new age people together in an obvious synergy of community relationships did my heart good. My mind's computer suffered from an overload—"it does not compute".

A Basic Message

There is a story about a young tiger living with goats. The story was a favourite of the Indian saint Ramakrishna, and is also cherished by Bhagwan. The young tiger felt and behaved like a goat. For example, he was vegetarian. An old tiger came by and, shocked by the young tiger's behaviour, confronted him, dragged him to the lake to view himself, taught him to eat meat—and eventually to roar. The old tiger is now played by Bhagwan; the Sannyasins are being dragged by him to the lake; the rest of us tigers in goats' skins await either this old tiger or another one of our choosing—*perhaps the one within* (Kopp, 1976).

The other basic message I would like to highlight is from Bhagwan's last discourse, *The Goose is Out* (1982b: 4). The basic Zen koan, or unresolvable riddle, is this: "If a man puts a gosling into a bottle and feeds him until he is full grown, how can the man get the goose out without killing it or breaking the bottle?"

The answer defies logic, you ask the question, the Zen master knocks you on the head, gets your undivided attention, and says: "You see, the goose is out." The answer is really that you are the goose and you have never been in the bottle, only asleep:

> It is only a question of becoming alert, awake, it is only a question of waking up. The goose is in the bottle if you are in a dream; the goose has never been in the bottle (Rajneesh, 1981a: 3).

Rajneesh (1982b: 2-3) comments further:

> All of the philosophies of the world and all the religions of the world create duality; howsoever they may go on talking about non-duality, they create a split personality in man. That has been the greatest calamity that has befallen humanity; all the do-gooders have created a schizophrenic man. When you divide reality into means and goals you divide man himself, because for man, man is the closest reality to man. His consciousness becomes split. He lives here but not really; he is always there, somewhere else. He is always searching, always inquiring, never living, never being, always doing, getting richer, getting powerful, getting spiritual, getting holier, saintly—always more and more. And this constant hankering for more creates his tense, anguished state, and meanwhile he is missing all that is made available by existence. He is interested in the far away and God is within him. Hence the most fundamental thing to understand about Zen is: The goose has *never* been in.

In conclusion, all this means is this: You are already one, you are Buddha; but you are asleep—wake up, dance and sing, celebrate as one with life's existence. Let me put it this way:

COMMUNION

Truth met Truth
Along the road
And said—
Yes

They shared together
Along the road
And met—
Life

Truth and Life
Danced and sang
Along the road
And met—
Bliss

Truth, Life and Bliss
Celebrated
Along the road
And met—
Love

Bhagwan smiled
Along the road
And so did
Will.

NOTES

1. For a different perspective, when the Rajneesh Ashram was located in Poona, India, see Amitabh (1982).
2. For other views regarding meditation, see Pelletier and Garfield (1976), Chitrabhanu (1979), Shapiro (1980), and Walsh (1982).
3. The ranch that had formerly occupied the site was referred to as "Big Muddy" in a movie with John Wayne.
4. However, the subtle sexual-like energy reverses its usual flow downward (the usual genital sexual release for males) and flows upward, sometimes with a beelike buzzing sound.

(1983)

Chapter Twelve

Therapy, Charisma and Social Control in the Rajneesh Movement

SUSAN J. PALMER AND FREDERICK BIRD

More than most new or old religions, the Rajneesh movement (currently known as the Osho Friends International) has incorporated therapies into its programme as a vital, if not essential, part of its spiritual life. Therapy groups, which were an important source of fund-raising in the group's original Ashram at Poona (1974-1981) and in Rajneeshpuram (1981-1985), offered an eclectic range of techniques including gestalt, encounter, bio-energetics, primal, massage, rolfing, and others. In the course of researching the Montreal Rajneesh community between 1978 and 1986, the authors noted that many of the disciples interviewed described their spiritual path in therapeutic terms—as "personal growth".

Frances Fitzgerald, in her article on Rajneeshpuram (the movement's utopian city in Oregon), comments: "The place was awash in the human potential movement." There is evidence that many members of this new religious movement were previously involved in various branches of humanistic psychology. In the University of Oregon survey on Rajneeshpuram it was found that 11 per cent of residents had graduate degrees in psychiatry or psychology, while another 11 per cent had B.A.s in these subjects, and yet among them all "there was not a single Freudian or behaviourist" (Fitzgerald, 1986: 67). We also noted a preponderance of therapists and people from the "helping professions" among the Montreal Sannyasins. Eight out of the twenty Sannyasins interviewed made a living (or partial living) through massage, breath therapy, or counseling. Braun's portrait (1984) of the residents of Rajneeshpuram corresponds closely with Stone's description (1976: 107) of participants in the Human Potential Movement: "The survey showed that the average age was 35, that they are better educated than the Bay Area residents with the same incomes. Politically they are liberal to radical . . . . Some of the lifestyle characteristics that appear are never having married . . . and experimenting with drugs."

In many respects, however, the Rajneesh movement is very different from those NRMs which originated out of the Human Potential Movement (HPM). Examples of these are est, Arica, Psychosynthesis, and Silva Mind Control. Unlike these NRMs which bear the hallmarks of multiple participation, a transient membership, and fee-for-service course work emphasising individual development, the Rajneesh movement demands from its members total commitment or "surrender" to Rajneesh and his charismatic community.

The prominence of therapy in this movement is thus balanced by a veneration for the leader who (until 1987) was honoured by the highly religious name of Bhagwan, the "Blessed One", a title of divinity. The Rajneesh movement appears to correspond to two different kinds of religious movements, those described elsewhere as being constituted of apprentices learning personal skills through therapy and purification rituals, and those constituted of devotees who submit to the sacred authority of their revered Lord or Truth through initiations and meditation (Bird, 1978). These two types of NRMs are quite different. The first views the sacred as a quality within each person, to be realised through training, purification, and self-knowledge. The second views the sacred as a self-transcending other that becomes present and empowering through devotion. Typically, apprentices learn their skills and their ability to tap "powers within" through classes or training programmes. Devotees, on the other hand, are expected to submit to the authority of the group, which represents the sacred other and is often symbolised by the person of the leader. In many respects Rajneesh espouses what Durkheim predicted would become the religion of the future: a "cult of man" philosophy. He preaches a kind of self-deification through meditation and presents his initiation into "neo-Sannyas" as an acknowledgement of the divinity of the self (Westley, 1983).

In other respects, however, the Rajneesh movement corresponds more closely to the "devotee" type NRM, whose aim is "to become one with the revered Lord or Truth" (Bird, 1978). Rajneesh "Himself" is clearly perceived by his followers as being a locus of the sacred. This notion was expressed during interviews in such terms as, "He is Life Itself" and "When He came out of silence, he realised He was One with the Absolute."

A close study of Rajneesh therapy illustrates the tension existing in the movement between individualism and collectivism: a tension between an Esalen-style humanism and an oriental-style Guru devotion—and yet, our data suggest that one of the functions of these "groups" was to provide a forum wherein the conflict between these apparently irreconcilable foci could be resolved. The purpose of this study, therefore, is to explore the role of therapy in the Rajneesh movement, concentrating on the problem of how this tension between the therapeutic focus and the devotional focus in the movement was resolved. Finally, the hypothesis will be presented that the particular kind of therapy which evolved in the Rajneesh movement and the peculiar type of veneration which Rajneesh inspires are to some extent compatible, and that "He" united in his person the "real self" which is the goal of therapy, and the Bhagwan or "godman" who demands veneration.

In order to explore the relationship between therapy and devotion in this NRM, and to support this argument, our strategy will be as follows:

First, to present a brief history of the movement; second, to demonstrate the function of its therapy groups: (a) as a form of social control; (b) as an initiation into the charismatic community; and (c) to argue that Rajneesh unites in his person the exemplary prophet (or example of the "real self" which is the goal of therapy) and the "Bhagwan" who demands surrender.

Methods

This study is based on research conducted in Montreal between 1984 and 1986. The Montreal commune, Grada Rajneesh, numbered seventy-odd residents when it disbanded in April, 1986. The local meditation centre still continues to serve the 200-odd Montreal Sannyasins. The information on Rajneesh therapy was collected by Palmer through participating in five "groups" directed by therapists from Rajneeshpuram, and through interviewing twenty Sannyasins, many of whom were local Rajneesh therapists.

The History of the Rajneesh Movement

The founder-leader of the movement, Mohan Chandra Rajneesh, was born in 1931 to a Jain family in Kuchwada, India. A former philosophy professor who claimed to have achieved enlightenment at the age of twenty-one, Rajneesh travelled throughout India giving lectures in which he expounded his eclectic and controversial ideas. Statements like "Never deny the body" and "Sex is the first step to superconsciousness" led the Indian press to dub him "the sex Guru". He settled down in an Ashram in Poona in 1974 where he attracted large crowds of Western disciples. Visiting therapits from the human potential movement were invited to set up "groups". Among them were Paul Lowe, founder of Europe's first growth centre, "Quaesitor", Michael Barnettt, author of *People not Psychiatry*, and Leonard Zunin, a Californian psychologist on the American Board of Psychiatry and Neurology. Their Sannyasin names were, respectively, Teertha, Somendra, and Siddha. According to Rajneesh's devotee-biographer, "These therapists had given up all the rewards of wealth and prestige ... because they found in Bhagwathe only spiritual master who fully understood the concept of holistic psychology ... a means of bringing individuals to higher levels of meditative consciousness" (Joshi, 1982: 124). In 1975 the Ashram offered encounter and gestalt groups. By 1979 sixty different therapies were offered as well as Eastern meditations like *yoga*, vipassana, sufi dancing, and tai chi.

The therapy groups were a major source of income for the movement. *Time* (16 January, 1978: 57) reported that between 1975 and 1978 more than fifty thousand "seekers" had visited Poona to try out the famous groups. According to a lengthy study in the *Oregonian* newspaper, "For Love and for Money" (1985), they drew from one to two thousand participants a year, and claimed in a financial statement filed with Maharashtra state charity officials in 1980 that therapy accounted for $188,253 of the movement's savings.

In 1981 Rajneesh withdrew his physical presence from the evening *darśana* and went into silence. The Ashram's head therapist, Swami Anand Teertha, began to perform the initiation ritual of "taking Sannyas", and presided over blessings and "energy *darśana*" as a "medium for Bhagwan".

In 1981 Rajneesh and his core group moved to the United States where they purchased a ranch in Oregon and began to construct the city of Rajneeshpuram based on the utopian ideals of sharing, equality, meditative consciousness, ecological harmony, and sexual communism. It was woman-ruled and grew at an extraordinary rate in terms of land cultivation, tourism, and building construction, mainly due to the regimen of "worship"—the twelve-hour day of unpaid labour in which not the task itself, but the consciousness brought to a task was emphasised. Sheela, Rajneesh's personal secretary, took over the leadership of the commune after he became silent and apparently attempted to usurp his spiritual authority, conferring upon herself the title *Boddhisattva* and wearing what were later burned as "Sheela's Pope's robes". The twenty-seven head therapists raised money for the city by conducting groups at RIMU (Rajneesh International Meditation University) for visitors to Rajneeshpuram. They also toured the international Rajneesh communes which had begun to sprout up in 1983 in Germany, Japan, Australia, Holland, England, and Montreal, where they were enthusiastically received as ambassadors of the utopian society at Rajneeshpuram. They offered groups that were attended by local Sannyasins, commune members and outsiders. These therapy groups were not unlike revival meetings, and the therapists inspired and revitalised the local religious communities as mediums of "Bhagwan's energy".

In 1984 Rajneesh came out of silence and began to predict the death of two-thirds of humanity through the disease AIDS by the year 2000. Sannyasins were advised by the Rajneesh Medical Corporation to wear condoms and rubber gloves while lovemaking, and to refrain from kissing.

Rajneesh held a press conference on September 4, 1985, in which he announced that Sheela had defected after attempting to poison three core group members, bugging his private chambers, and leaving the commune $55 million in debt (*Rajneesh Times*, 1984a: 1) The movement went through profound changes, and these changes were reflected in the form and function of its therapy groups.

Therapy as Social Control

There were at least three ways in which the Rajneesh therapy groups functioned as a form of social control: through promoting identity change by means of the ritual breaking of taboos, through educating members in a new system of ethics and new patterns of self-other relating, and through initiating members into the charismatic community.

The Ritual Breaking of Taboos

The groups in Poona achieved a certain notoriety because of the high incidence of nudity, sex, and violence in the years 1975 to 1978. As Rajneesh's biographer expressed it: "They transcended the usual limits set by society and personality because they functioned in freedom and with greater intensity." The *Oregonian* (1985: 6) is more critical: "To the uninitiated, reports of nudity, rape, and broken bones in some sessions seemed like bad publicity. The promise of no-holds-barred encounter groups, however, proved a powerful lure for the dissatisfied and unfulfilled. Word spread that therapy in the Poona commune would top anything allowed in the West."

Fitzgerald (1986: 83) states, "There were several cases of rape in the sessions, there was also a broken leg, several broken arms, and various other injuries." Van Leen (1980: 193) relates lurid tales of "pack rape", "enforced sex", and the "mysterious death" of Prince Welf of Hanover in 1980.

Fitzgerald (1986: 83) explains the violence as a taking of Reichian therapy to extremes:

> The theory behind "dynamic meditation" was that people should give physical expression to their repressions and frustrations in order to get rid of "emotional blocks". Teertha and Somendra... merely extrapolated on this notion in the groups and being rather literal people, they encouraged participants to act out all the emotions... including the desire to inflict grievous bodily harm.

Worseley's interpretation (1968: 251) of ritual obscenity among the cargo cults in Melanesia perhaps offers a more adequate explanation:

> If we examine the many cases of "sexual excess", "erotic communism", "morbid asceticism" and all the other labels pinned to ritual obscenity and sacrilege, it becomes clear that we are not dealing with unbridled lust or with ascetic perversion. We are dealing with the deliberate enactment of the overthrow of the cramping bonds of the past, not to throw overboard all moralities, but in order to create a new brotherhood with completely new moralities... Sexual communism and sexual asceticism, both so common in millenarian movements, are thus two sides of the same coin—the rejection of outworn creeds.

The following account of a neo-tantra workshop attended by a journalist appears to be a clear example of the ritualised breaking of sexual taboos:

> Suddha...one of the top international therapists...was late...Her first words were "What, haven't you got your clothes off yet?" and we dutifully stripped...(S) he got us to line up, men facing women, and the women had to sniff our armpits and genitals and *vice versa*....We break for the night and Suddha tells us to find a person to stay with for the night, even accompanying the other to the toilet (Nicholas, 1982: 11).

Rajneesh's own explanation (*Book of Books*, 1980: 3) for sex and violence in therapy suggests his underlying intention was to break old patterns in order to create a "new morality":

> In my commune it is a totally different phenomenon. Centuries-old taboos are broken, centuries-old inhibitions are thrown to the winds. I am all for freedom, particularly sexual freedom, because all other freedoms are rooted in that... This commune is a pond, and I am training female fish to embrace every male fish.

Rajneesh claimed the purpose of the therapy groups was to purify Western disciples of neurosis. He often stated in his discourses that Westerners find it difficult to meditate because they are too tense, extroverted, and worried about their relationships. Therefore, a catharsis is necessary before they can even begin to sit still in meditation: "They will help you unburden the garbage that you have repressed within yourself. They will clean you and only in a clear, clean heart is prayer possible.......Therapy is catharsis. It brings you face to face with your own unconscious" (quoted in Van Leen, 1980: 117).

The theories of Wilhelm Reich have strongly

influenced Rajneesh therapy, as the following pamphlet (quoted in Belfrage, 1982: 22), circulated by the London centre in 1980, indicates:

> In most of the techniques devised by Bhagwan, there is strong emphasis on using physical energy. Bhagwan stresses that there can be no separation between mind and body and that by clearing energy blocks in our body we become integrated human beings again. Basically.......the concepts will be familiar to anyone who knows something of the work of Wilhelm Reich. All our neurosis is rooted somewhere in the body. At some point in our childhood we decided that in order to survive, in order to get the love we needed to exist, it was necessary to stop being ourselves—we had to be the way others, usually our parents, wanted us to be.........We couldn't allow ourselves to feel, and to stop the feelings we tensed our bodies, suppressed our needs, and stopped breathing. In Bhagwan's meditations we start to breathe again........of course we resist because it may be painful.........But if we can persevere.........we gradually come to realise the vastness of our potential as human beings and the ultimate bliss which is possible for us all. To help us on this vast inner journey, we need a...........teacher who has made this journey himself and now is able to communicate this to others. Bhagwan is such a teacher.

Rajneesh therapy appears to function as ritual of purification whose manifest ritual objective might be negative: "to clean out alien, external forces"; or positive: "to reorder the self in relation to a particular vision of self" (Bird, 1980: 29). Negative rituals often prepare the way for positive rituals, and this appears to be the case in Rajneesh therapy, since one of the conditions for initiation is for the aspirant to perform the cathartic dynamic meditation daily for a month, and to enrol in a number of therapy groups until the local director judges him or her sufficiently free of "rubbish" to qualify for the positive ritual of "taking Sannyas". Thus, there is a relationship between the ritual taboo-breaking in the therapy groups and the aura of charisma surrounding Bhagwan. One former Sannyasin commented on her visit to Poona, "There was truly something extraordinary about Bhagwan...But my experiences in the groups were very intense, and I think they somehow prepared me for Bhagwan. I thought then it was just Him, but maybe it was also the groups which made me feel that way."

Many of the techniques employed in Rajneesh therapy groups conform to Kanter's theory (1972) of commitment mechanisms as examples of *mortification*. Mortification enhances the individual's commitment to the community in that it "provides a new identity for the person that is based on the power and meaningfulness of group identity; they reduce his sense of a private, unconnected ego. Self-esteem comes to depend on commitment to the norms of the group" (1972: 103). Kanter notes that sensitivity training groups employ mortification processes that "can be a sign of trust in the group, a willingness to share weaknesses, and one's innermost secrets with others. People often come to such groups... deliberately seeking the identity involved in mortification. They may call it 'personal growth' instead".

Education in New Ethics and New Relationships

One of the functions of Rajneesh therapy groups, particularly during the Rajneeshpuram phase of the movement, was to educate members in the highly developed alternative patterns of sexuality and spiritual family life of the commune. Thus the purpose of many of the exercises employed in the "groups" attended by Palmer appeared to be the following: to encourage sexual communism or sharing inside the commune; to discourage what Kanter calls "dyadic withdrawal" from the group by censoring possessive feelings and exclusive sexual relationships; and to provide a forum in which members who were having difficulty adjusting to these new patterns and ethics could express their jealousy or other emotional dilemmas and receive counselling and support from the group. The events related below, witnessed by Palmer in five different Rajneesh therapy groups, demonstrate how this was done.

On April 8, 1985, Palmer attended an evening "minigroup" given by the therapist Vasumati. There were sixty-odd Sannyasins wearing red, and the majority were commune members. Vasumati began by expounding Bhagwan's philosophy of love:

> We were brought up to think of love as what our parents had. It was permanent—and dead! First comes love, then comes the games, and then the end of love...Your parents felt things like possessiveness and jealousy: "Stay with me Baby, I need you." Does that sound familiar? "If you leave me, Baby, I will die!" How many people here ever felt that one? If your lover goes to another's bed, you feel a lot of energy for him, right? Why experience that energy as pain? It comes from our expectations of what love should be. The moment you try to manipulate that energy, to cling to it, it goes dead. If marriage really were permanent, and led to happiness, then no one would ever become enlightened. If we were all happily married, we would never feel the need for Bhagwan.

Vasumati gave a series of exercises which encouraged physical and emotional intimacy between sexes, and then ended the workshop with the following drill: Men and women lined up facing each other. The men she picked had to cross the room, face the woman they found most attractive and ask her, "Would you like to be with me?" If she said "Yes," they walked to a corner and sat on cushions. If she said "No," the man must join the other men who were "wallflowers". "And get in touch with that feeling of what it's like being a wallflower." Then the women had to choose the men. The people who had been the most demonstrative during the workshop seemed to be the chosen ones, not necessarily the most ornamental participants.

The following account of a workshop which took place on August 30, 1985 demonstrates how the Rajneesh therapists exorcise jealousy which threatens the social cohesion of the commune:

> A young woman stood up in front of the group and spoke of her jealousy. Her boyfriend, it turned out, had spent the night with another woman in the group. Purna, the therapist, invited her to bring her boyfriend into the middle of the circle and "act out" her feelings. She clutched him and shouted, "Nobody look at him! Go away, you (women), especially you! (pointing to her rival) He's mine, he belongs to me!" Her boyfriend began hamming it up and assumed the posture of a dog begging, tongue hanging out. Purna asked, "Is this the way you like him?" "No" admitted the woman, "I don't like him like this," and she began to laugh. "You are a beautiful woman" said Purna. "How many men here think she's beautiful?" (She was, and there was an impressive show of hands.) "You should come to the Ranch," said Purna. "You'd soon find out you didn't need him." It was clear the woman, having expressed her jealousy and received sympathy from

the group, was now reconciled to her boyfriend's infidelity and encouraged to try other lovers as a panacea. Later she was walking hand in hand with her rival.

The therapy groups were also a place where members who were poorly integrated into the commune could receive help and advice from the therapist. In Rafia's group on October 27, 1985, one woman confessed how, since she had moved into the commune a few months ago, "I find it difficult being open with so many people." Rafia responded, "What I hear you saying is you feel you're not getting enough love from others." She burst into tears, and admitted she felt excluded and shy. Then Rafia turned to the group and asked if they had anything to say to her. One Swami spoke up, "I used to think you were a juicy woman, but then you seemed to close up and I was afraid to touch you." Rafia said, "Look, if you feel you're not getting enough juice from the commune, you have to ask for it. Who would you like to hug right now?" The woman looked around began to giggle shyly. "Juicy woman" called out a Swami. "Which of you Swamis out there want to give her a hug, which of you Ma's? Well, go on, the love is there, you just have to relax and be open to it." The woman was then embraced by all the members of the commune in turn, and it seems reasonable to assume that, having expressed her feelings of alienation to her fellow Sannyasins, her life would improve in the commune.

A comparison between the Rajneesh "groups" and the Mutual Criticism Sessions of the Oneida Perfectionists might contribute toward an understanding of the social function of therapy in the Rajneesh movement. This intentional community was founded in the 1830s by John H. Noyes and settled in Oneida, New York. Their commune was based on the utopian ideals of sharing, equality, the striving for individual perfection, and a kind of pantagmous system of "free love" called "complex marriage". There are striking affinities between the Oneidans and the Rajneesh. Both communes banned procreation, sought to undermine sex distinctions in labour, dress codes and social life, and attracted members of the intelligentsia, artistic community, and upper-class. Both leaders equated marriage with the selfish hoarding of private property and regarded the sex act as sacred.

The Oneidans regularly held what might be described as Victorian versions of the "lemon session" or "T-group" which they called "Mutual Criticism". According to Foster, "Mutual Criticism served the same function for the Oneida community that confession of sins to the elders did for the Shakers. It provided the basic means of encouraging the desired character development and commitment to the community and its principles." Accounts of these sessions by Victorian travellers indicate that Mutual Criticism was a mechanism for discouraging exclusive sexual relationships or close interpersonal bonds (termed "selfish love") which might threaten group cohesion. Foster explains it as "a form of social control which helped to prepare the way for complex marriage and the close community life associated with it" (1981: 98-99).

A ninteenth-century researcher (Nordhoff, 1966: 292) offers an account of a Mutual Criticism session in which a young man who has recently impregnated a female member in the "stirpiculture" experiment is reprimanded for showing sings of "selfish love" toward her. Similar events were observed in Rajneesh therapy, where faithful couples would be warned against "clinging" or " getting stuck" and encouraged to "follow the yes" and "let the energy flow".

Therapy and Charisma

Therapy in the Rajneesh movement also served as a

means of cultivating personal charisma, Rajneesh "groups" in this sense can be viewed as ordeals which individuals undergo in order to learn to identify and express extraordinary powers residing within. This cultivation of personal charisma can occur only by interacting with others who acknowledge its presence. The cultivation of charisma has several features which include learning to *recognise* spiritual dimensions of ordinary realities, learing to *display* this charisma in front of the group, and learning to *receive and pass along charisma*—i.e., share it with others.

Lucy DuPertius' study (1986: 119) of the Divine Light Mission analyses the recognition of charisma as an "active, conscious social process involving the confirmation of belief through non-cognitive methods of altering perception". Her descriptions of the processes whereby DLM Members are educated in charisma and taught to generate it within their circle would apply to the Rajneesh therapy groups. It could be argued, therefore, that one of the important functions of therapy in the Rajneesh communes was to provide a forum in which charisma could be contracted, transmitted, and displayed.

Throughout the Rajneeshpuram phase, its 27 head therapists would arrive at the local centres filled with "Bhagwan's energy" and set up "groups" in which individuals could "open up" and "receive juice" from both the therapist and the other participants. Therapists were described in interviews as "channels for Bhagwan". One Swami said, "They have to put their own egos out of the way so that you can feel Bhagwan working through them." The difference between Rajneesh therapy and "ordinary" therapy was explained by a Montreal Sannyasin as follows, "In a sense they are like mediums. Therefore, they can go deeper and afford to take more risks. They tend to confront you more heavily, but they have Bhagwan behind them so you can feel His love coming through."

A second locus of potential charisma is the individual, whose inner spiritual identity is called "the energy," and is encouraged to "flow", to "rise", and to "move" by the therapists.

The group itself is the third locus of charisma in the sense that it is an extension of the "Buddhafield" (the community of souls surrounding Bhagwan). One Sannyasin explained the Buddhafield as "an electrical current you plug into when you fall in love with Bhagwan". Therefore, to participate in Rajneesh therapy groups is to participate in the *saṅgha*, and one way of understanding these groups is to regard them as an ordeal of initiation into Rajneesh's charismatic community.

The following account of events observed by Palmer in the course of participant observation in "groups" is meant to demonstrate how charisma "operates" in Rajneesh therapy and how Sannyasins are taught to recognise, display, and share "Bhagwan's energy".

Confessions to the group of personal problems—particularly sexual problems—was a common exercise, and the therapists would often interpret these in an occult fashion. Conflicts between lovers were viewed as impediments encountered on the spiritual path. For example, one Swami's longing for a departed girlfriend was interpreted as evidence of spiritual desire—i.e., the need for his "energy" to "connect" with Bhagwan. Confessions of the most intimate sexual difficulties were encouraged by the therapists and endowed with a weighty, cosmic significance. One woman's inability to achieve Reichian-style orgasms was diagnosed as "stuck energy"; and she was advised to "Stop trying, just relax, and open your heart to Bhagwan." She spent the rest of the afternoon seated and breathing deeply before the six-foot photograph of Rajneesh that dominated the room.

Many groups featured what Kanter would term the communion mechanism which "reinforces the notion that members are equal, undifferentiated parts of a whole". Many Rajneesh weekend workshops conclude with a ritual called "melting" in which everyone lies on the floor in a mass embrace. Circle dances, ritualised eye contact, and touching could all be interpreted as symbolising the individual's surrendering his or her private identity to the group and, in turn, receiving its charisma.

Certain exercises gave individuals the chance to test and display their charisma in front of the group. One common pattern was to shift from the confessional mode to a ritual mode and for the therapist to identify signs of charisma in the ritual actor's behaviour that would be confirmed by the group. For example, a young Swami began to speak of how his lover had rejected him and became inarticulate with weeping. The therapist instructed him to "get in touch with" his feelings of rejection, so he stood up and began to shake violently. "Feel the energy rising," she prompted, and he started jumping and panting "Hoo! Hoo!" (The techniques of shaking, jumping, and panting are part of the daily meditations practiced in Rajneesh centres.) "Isn't he beautiful?" the therapist asked the group: "Which of you ladies feel attracted to him right now?" Several raised their hands. He began to laugh, and she said, "See! You may be all alone, she may have left you, but you are alive and beautiful just as you are now. You still have yourself. Now, look at these woman, you're turning them on! Who do you feel energy for?" He pointed to one. Well, what are you waiting for?" The Swami leaped across the room and curled up in the woman's lap. Everyone laughed and hugged him and each other. "Beautiful!" the therapist pronounced.

Palmer received the impression in the course of her participation that it was the Sannyasins who "acted out" the most violent rages or revealed their most intimate problems who were given the opportunity to test their charisma. Those who just sat and watched, or presented uninteresting problems were seldom told they had a "beautiful energy".

As the examples above indicate, the ultimate aim of Rajneesh therapy is to invoke the master's presence. Thus, a successful "group" has much in common with ecstatic religions. The experience of "Bhagwan's energy" resembles the forms of possession found in Voodoo ceremonies and in the Shaker communities in the 1830s. During the Era of Manifestations, Shaker brothers and sisters would shake in order to enter a trance state in which they could receive "gifts" from the spirits. These would often take the form of possession and would be manifested by irrational behaviour such as visions, glossalalia, or an "Indian" dance step. In a similar manner, Bhagwan's presence would often be manifested by an exaggerated show of sexual attraction to other members of the group, a form of irrational behaviour defined by the group as charismatic, since Rajneesh equated spirituality with sexuality.

Bhagwan, the "Ultimate Transferance"

Rajen, a Rajneesh therapist, described the relationship between Rajneesh and his disciples as "Transference, but transference onto a master. The final transference, Bhagwan says, is always onto a master" (quoted in Fitzgerald, 1986: 83).

This passage suggests that the particular type of veneration Rajneesh inspires is not incompatible with the quest for the "real self" which is the goal of the transpersonal psychology emerging from the HPM. Thus, although a tension between collectivism and individualism can be detected throughout the history of the movement (as in any intentional community), these tensions seem to be resolved in the person of Bhagwan.

On one hand, Rajneesh conforms to Weber's model of the exemplary prophet demonstrating to his disciples that it is possible for them to become *real selves*. He says, "Look at me, the roses have bloomed" (quoted in Joshi, 1982: 114). He represents the rebellious child, playful and curious in its sexuality. He is the eternal *enfant terrible* whose discourses are filled with provocative statements, risque jokes, and antinomian messages. Thus he is the example of the Reichian-style "real self" his followers experience in therapy as they "get in touch with" sexual and aggressive impulses censored by previous authority figures.

Rajneesh tells his followers that they are perfect, beautiful exactly as they are, and does not recommend any discipline of mind or body; on the contrary, he tells them to "loosen up", "let it all hang out", and accept themselves in the "herenow". He is a warrant for distancing themselves from the authoritative claims of parents, teachers, priests, and for dismissing the judgements of others. In the place of these external authorities from the past, the inner authority of feelings and impulses is evoked in the therapy groups.

Besides modelling the "real self" Rajneesh is also regarded as its *source*. He is "Pure Love", "Life Itself", and also "The Absolute". As "The Enlightened One," or the reincarnation of Gautama Buddha who reappears thoughout the millennia, he represents for his disciples a rare and irresistible opportunity to embark on the "vast inner journey" toward their potential as human beings. Thus, by rejecting the claims of their previous relationships, by recognising "His" superior claim, his devotees are at once pursuing their own freedom and autonomy and yet "surrendering" to the Blessed One.

Bhagwan, therefore, represents the two poles of the movement: the radical individualism of those who reject or relativise the normative claims of others and, at the same time, the collectivism of those who find their true identity by submitting to the authoritative claims of the group. In this manner, the individualism is reinforced by therapies that loosen exclusive diadic bonds and family ties. Bhagwan represents the ultimate individual, but he is also a symbol of what all his disciples have in common: a new vision of themselves. They are joined together as parts of a whole in their "connection to the master". In this way, therapy fosters a collective consciousness by cultivating a shared sense of charisma.

A Postscript to the Role of Therapy in the Post-Communal Phase

Three events since the disbanding of Rajneeshpuram illustrate how therapy has continued to evolve in response to the needs and new directions of this NRM. These three events are: the RIMU marathon, the "therapists' controversy", and the formation of "new style" therapy groups.

The RIMU Marathan

Shortly after Sheela's defection and following Rajneesh's announcement that he was not a Guru but a "friend", the Rajneesh International Meditation University (RIMU) held a week-long free therapy session for commune residents in which they were encouraged to express all the "negativity" they had kept bottled up under Sheela's "fascist regime". A testimonial to the cathartic efficacy of this event was offered in the *Rajneesh Times* (1985c: 5) "after eighteen hours of the most intense thunderstorm of my being...the sky cleared, and through it all the RIMU folks were just there—accepting, supporting and encouraging".

A special therapy group was organised for the sixty-odd children living in Rajneeshpuram who appeared to be exhibiting anxiety at the prospect of leaving their "kids commune" which had fostered strong peer attachments and discouraged the parent-child relationship. Therapist Rajen (quoted in the *Rajneesh Times* (1985b: 8) reports his insights on directing this group, "I spent a couple of hours with about sixty or more of our younger commune members, their ages ranging from ten to eighteen. It was an exciting happening that brought a startling revelation: Our kids are conditioned! Our meeting produced a remarkable, graphic demonstration of the emotional amouring they acquired under Sheela's influence."

The Therapists's Controversy

Teertha and other head therapists established the International Academy of Meditation in Sicily in the spring of 1986, and Teertha began touring the Rajneesh communes that were disintegrating in the wake of Rajneeshpuram and offering workshops designed to drum up business for his new Academy. Palmer, who attended Teertha's Montreal therapy workshop on April 3, 1986, received the impression that he was claiming an independent status as an enlightened spiritual master. Many of the participating Sannyasins appeared to be confused by the new directions of their movement and disheartened by the collapse of their utopian dream, and were willing to support his claim. One Swami, who had been saving money to "be with Bhagwan" in Poona, confided in Palmer that he had decided to take Teertha's course in Sicily instead because, "I need a master I can sit and talk to, and Teertha is enlightened, for sure." This threat of schism was reported in an article entitled "The Therapists' Controversy" (*Rajneesh Times,* 1986) citing Teertha's manifesto, and Rajneesh's response:

> He'd played the master-disciple game long enough; that Bhagwan was exploiting Sanyasins and that he

> left them in financial misery: that he appreciated Bhagwan's silence, but did not want to be involved with His actions; that he was on the same level as Bhagwan and was happy doing his own thing.

Rajneesh responded through his secretary, Ma Prem Hasya:

> We ourselves were going to tell all Sannyasins not to participate in any of the therapy groups of Teertha, Amitabh, Somendra, Rajen, Poonam, and anybody who has betrayed Bhagwan.
>
> And Teertha has never been a disciple, but only a politician hoping to succeed Bhagwan. As far as his therapy is concerned, it is nothing but a mindgame. Bhagwan has allowed these phony people as therapists to clean the minds of those who have never known the art of meditation. But now that the therapists will not be doing their therapies in the context of a master and meditation, they can prove immensely dangerous. Their therapies can create a kind of addiction. They cannot help anyone to transcend mind.
>
> These therapists are full of mental problems. The rate of suicide and madness in therapists has risen: it was twice as much as other professions, now it is thrice.

Another head therapist, Michael Barnett (Somendra), also claimed he was enlightened and subsequently founded the MB Energy University in Zurich. He advertised Zen courses especially designed to propel disillusioned "Buddhafield" dropouts rapidly toward the individual goal of *satori*. Barnett's message in his brochure (*No Nation News*, July, 1988: 6) is carefully anti-collective and anti-institutional:

> I'm not interested in building a movement called the Wild Geese Company of which I am the great leader internationally known...(T)he Wild Geese Company is an Energyfield...a teaching...designed to enable enlightenment to happen for all who make contact with it and only that.
>
> I'd rather have one person who meant business about their enlightenment than a hundred thousand people who thought the WGC was a great thing to belong to.

The "New Style" Groups

In June, 1986, "new style" therapy groups began to replace the more highly structured, ritualised and authoritarian therapy of the Rajneeshpuram era. Rajneesh therapists now refused to direct their groups or to intervene in participants' interactions. The motto for the Montreal Rajneesh centre at this time read, "Community allows the seed of individuality to flower." Poona therapists, Maitri and Bayanand in their new role as "fellow travellers" conducted a weekend workshop which one participant described as follows:

> They've moved to a higher level. There was no structure, no techniques—just being there.
>
> The therapists didn't try to control what was happening, so you were just thrown back on yourself and totally responsible for what happened. They said, "It's time you took responsibility for your own process of waking up"—so, they would respond, but they refused to provoke.

There appear to have been mixed reactions to this workshop. Another participant described it in more critical terms as "pure chaos. It was as bad as a John Cage concert". Other Sannyasins expressed their distaste for the manipulative style of certain therapists, and one woman, who had just ended her relationship with a "tantra sex" therapist, began referring to him disparagingly as "Psycho-the-rapist".

Conclusion

A close study of the Rajneesh movement reveals an NRM remarkable for its commitment to the experimental mode, and for its divagations in locale, authority patterns, and social organisation. The ongoing innovations in forms of therapy throughout the movement's history can be interpreted as both reflecting and facilitating a tension between collectivism and individualism, between surrender to the Guru on one hand and the quest for autonomy on the other. In the Poona era, between 1975 and 1978, the ritual breaking of taboos in encounter groups served to undermine old patterns and old indentities in order to forge a unique society based on new ethics and new loyalties. When the Rajneesh movement moved to Oregon in 1981 and Rajneesh retired into silence, the therapists assumed a priestly role as part of the process of the institutionalisation of charisma. They travelled among the international communes educating members in charisma and in the alternative patterns of sexuality modelled by the exemplary society in Rajneeshpuram. Therapy within the walls of Rajneeshpuram was packaged and sold at RIMU to paying visitors while the local communards engaged in work as "worship". Once Rajneeshpuram was disbanded, and Rajneesh announced the death of "Rajneeshism" and bid his disciples to stop wearing red and living in communes, the movement began to lose many of its "devotee" characteristics. Former commune residents began to pursue secular careers, and the movement became less sectarian in its attitudes toward the larger society. The change in name from the "Rajneesh Foundation International" to "Friends of Rajneesh International" in 1985 reflected this trend. The priestly authority of the head therapists became obsolete once Rajneesh decided to "de-institutionalise" his religion (Palmer, 1988), and those who refused to be shorn of their charisma resorted to apostasy and schism. Therapy no longer functioned as a commitment mechanism for budding communards, but continued as a means of raising funds and providing recreation for temporary visitors to Poona.

It is interesting to note that the Oneida Perfectionists also resorted to a kind of therapeutic group confession when faced with external threats to their community. While on trial before the Utica Grand County Jury for their unconventional sexual practices in 1852, they held a year-long marathon of Mutual Criticism during which they reviewed their individual and collective failures. This marathon, which they labelled the "Abolition of Death", was an important step toward their voluntary disbanding as a religious commune (Foster, 1981: 113).

It has been demonstrated that both the Rajneesh and the Oneidans employed therapeutic techniques of "mortification" to educate their members in their precarious etiquette of sexual communism. When confronted with external persecution, the same techniques of confession and criticism functioned as a kind of "de-commitment mechanism" in order to facilitate a relatively smooth transition from a commune to a looser type of social organisation.

In their post-communal phase, the purpose of therapy for dedicated Sannyasins (as for HPM participants) is to peel away layers of false identity to discover the "real self". In the Osho Friends International today, this inner self or "energy" is still identified with the late spiritual master, Osho.

(1992)

Chapter Thirteen

Jealousy and the Abyss

SWAMI ANAND VEERESHWAR (WILLIAM PENNELL ROCK)

Imagine this: you're very much in love with someone, and you have to go out of town. You know your lover's habits; you know he or she likes to go to bed fairly early, and that he or she gets up and goes to work in the morning. So you go away on your trip. You're gone for about a week, and then one evening you call, and there's no answer. Awful pictures rush into your mind. With great forces of will you stop them. The next morning, you call at eleven in the morning. His or her roomate answers the phone and says, "Gee, I'm sorry, She's not up yet. She's sleeping late." Oh god! Something is fishy. Something's going on. You don't know what it is, but your stomach is starting to churn. You're jealous.

What do you do when you're jealous? In a fever, you may try to find out if your lover has been with someone else. If he or she has, you go into a rage, a frenzy of blame.

It's an immediate response. You are angry. You feel violated. You want revenge. You want to stop what is happening, control the situation, manipulate whatever is necessary to protect yourself.

If you can cool down, if you can get hold of the internal automatic reactions that accompany jealousy, you might find out that you can indeed fix the situation. Often, what comes up as jealousy can be eradicated by simple communication. "I need to have more time with you." "When we go to a party, I don't want you to be with anybody else." "I need to have sex outside the relationship." When we leave these needs unspoken, they lie in wait until a situation exposes them. It is essential to get very clear and explicit with your partner about your needs and expectations.

Such solutions of diplomacy are important, but they remain superficial. A deeper opportunity is missed. Things are happening in this odious passion that present the possibility of entering new levels of self-understanding, to see who you are and what is the source of suffering.

The first step is to clarify what you are about in the relationship. If you and your lover want to evolve into more awareness; if somehow, somewhere, the glimmer of enlightened consciousness attracts you and you want to move in that direction, then you can make an important choice. What you choose is not just to increase your pleasure together, not even necessarily to protect the relationship or to secure it in some way, but to use the relationship as a means of coming to a deeper and more fundamental understanding of what is so.

Relationship for Truth

How you see the relationship will affect matters from the beginning; for instance, what you share with each other about your realities. If both of you are there to create a safe and secure relationship, you will tend to conceal anything that might threaten it. Many couples come to live completely mendacious lives together. Gradually they smother themselves in compromises. Love energy—

eros—cannot pass between two lives lived in lies. Only truth is erotic.

If the relationship is seen as a means to knowledge, the paradigm shifts: The discipline is to learn to live uncompromisingly in your truth and to love the other without qualification. No easy task, but there is no higher. What you are loving together is truth. Everything real has to be shared; everything else has to be dismantled.

Here is a simple test to see where you are in this matter of relating. Write down all the things you have not shared with your partner. Contemplate this list, and there you will see the limits you place on the relationship, the degree of your commitment to the way of the lover.

Love and Attachment

Now, on the path where relationship is a means for coming to self-understanding, it is necessary to clarify the difference between loving and being attached. This is a most basic distinction, because so much of what we experience as attachment, we *call* love. In fact, most of the institutions around love, such as marriage and family, are actually ways of protecting our investment in attached situations.

Loving someone is glorifying who they are in their uniqueness. Consider a flower. You see a flower that is really beautiful to you. You want to glorify that flower in its own natural setting, or else you want to pick it and posess it. Those are two entirely different ways of being. Love creates a thankful glorification of the flower. You love the other—you want to see the other thrive, enjoy, and grow. You want to see them become more of who they are, no matter what that entails. That's the truth of love. It is unconditional.

Attachment is quite different. You want to pick the

flower, sever it from its roots, and make it yours. You want to appropriate the beloved, make him or her be what *you* want them to be, conform to what is convenient for you in the relationship. Attachment is not care for the other; it is care for oneself. The distinction has to be understood: Are you loving, or are you attached?

If you are attached, you are going to experience the pain of jealousy. It follows that jealousy becomes the opportunity to see within yourself the truth of attachment. Not theoretical understanding, but existential awareness of attachment at its very roots. Only through this awareness can jealousy be really transcended.

Penetrating to the Core

The most extraneous and irrelevant way to deal with jealousy is trying to control your partner. It is also the least effective. Whatever illusions you may have as to who is to blame or who is at fault, jealousy is within *you*; not within the relationship. Manipulating your lover is a poor palliative. To control outer circumstances by making your lover behave or toe the line in a certain way is to miss the opportunity. You always miss the opportunity of jealousy—indeed, of any pain—if you blame others. It is not that the other may not be to blame, but that in the matter of inner realities, *blame is always irrelevant.*

Manipulation of the other is external. Moving inward, we use the situation that created the jealousy as the occasion for clarifying communication and for negotiation. To do so is constructive for the relationship, but still peripheral, still not touching upon the real opportunity presented by jealousy. Moving further inward towards the core, we come to the personal level: yourself and your own reactions. This is the real field for dealing with jealousy: not trying to blame or fix your partner, but seeing who you are.

Really, jealousy is like an onion—so overwhelming, so pungent, so difficult to be near. It cannot be ignored. It makes you cry. Yet the onion is an important food. In blaming and controlling, you are refusing to see that there is an onion. You are trying to avoid. In trying to see who you are, you take the onion in hand. You take a radical, internal view of what happened to you in jealousy. Now you peel off layer after layer of the onion until you reach its centre. There at the core is the possibility of freedom.

Dysfunctional Beliefs

The first layer of the onion is your unexamined notions about how one should be in relationship. What are your beliefs? Do you believe that if you're in a relationship with someone, you should be with them exclusively and they should be exclusively with you? Well, where does that belief come from? Is it based upon some hidden idea that the other is your possession? Is the other an object to be arranged in a way that is suitable to you? Only if you possess the beloved can you tell them how to be. So, if you're inclined to manipulate and control in this way somehow subconsciously you have already made the lover into your possession. This is something to look at. Can one person be the possession of another? What beliefs do *you* carry about relationship?

The fact of the matter is, you are not actually in a loving relationship if you think that you possess the other, because the essence of the other is basically free. Whatever peripheral control you may exert, you cannot touch that inner freedom that a human being is. You may control your lover so that he or she appears to love you, but you cannot make a person love you.

Moving inward, look at the situation rationally or

realistically. We each have our own sexuality, and we each have to take care of it as we can. Only some people can fit their sexuality into one relationship. So to have the belief that your lover should be able to so conform may already be erroneous. You are not responsible for the sexuality of the other. You cannot take control of their sexuality. You do not own it. It is their own. And what they do about it is in a real sense their own affair.

This insight has probably helped me in my own dealings with jealousy more than any other. Somehow I had the idea that my sexuality and her sexuality were tied up as one. That is a beautiful experience. In fact, the relationship may go through a long period where there is a pure union of two sexualities. But to say that is how it must be forever and oblige the other to behave in accordance with that belief will not work.

Erroneous beliefs inevitably contribute to the pain of jealousy. Take stock of your beliefs, and drop the ones that aren't functional. That's the first skin of the onion.

Projection

The second layer is projection. Sometimes we suspect that our partner is being untrue to us. For instance, that night you called your lover, a thought immediately came to mind: "Oh, she's got somebody with her." One reason that you may have these perceptions is because you yourself are harboring thoughts of being "unfaithful". In fact, if you are in a relationship where you have an agreement not to be sexual with anybody else, you will almost inevitably start having feeling of wanting to be with others. Sooner or later, if you don't share those thoughts, or if you're not up front about the fact that you have such feelings, you will imagine that your partner is having them. This is projecting. Your jealous feelings may come from the fact that you feel like you want to play around, and so you suspect that your partner is doing it because you refuse to be aware that you are entertaining such a temptation yourself. A projected perception and a real one *feel* differently. We can learn to discriminate between the two. Again, the challenge is to be aware, to examine oneself.

Envy

Another level that we have to peel off is envy. Envy is often mistaken for jealousy. I have experienced what I thought was tremendous jealousy, when in fact what I was feeling was envy because my partner was having a ball and I wasn't. Well, she's off having a good time with a boyfriend in New York, and I'm out here sitting alone. I want to have a good time with somebody. Envy is the frustrated longing for the other's experience. It is a different, more superficial phenomenon than jealousy.

Guilt

Another layer is guilt. Guilt can afflict you if you feel bad because you're jealous. Since the sexual revolution, some would-be liberated people think it is wrong to feel jealous. We are told that we shouldn't feel jealous, we should rise above it. So if you have this belief and you feel jealous, you're going to experience shame and guilt. But judgement is truly irrelevant. Jealousy is jealousy. It is neither good nor bad. It simply is, and it is an opportunity.

We must learn to peel away the skins of illusion, and get to the core. Really, what I'm talking about is awareness. The discussions of projection, envy, and guilt are pointers, but you have to bring to your own internal situation of jealousy *your* awareness. Ask these questions and investigate the reality of your feelings. In order to transcend a negative feeling, you must move deeper and deeper into your own authentic experience of it. Not what you read in a novel or saw in a movie. Not what someone has said you should feel. What you are actually feeling.

Becoming aware of the actual feeling and the true source often alleviates the feelings. You may experience what you describe as jealousy, but when you really examine the feelings, what is really there is anger that you were being left out of something that was fun—envy. There's your partner taking a trip with someone else. You would like to go on that trip and you're being left out. Those are not really feelings of jealousy. They are simply feelings of sadness or anger at being excluded from something that's happening, something that you feel, you belong to in some ways.

The outer layers of the onion of jealousy really aren't jealousy at all. They're reactions belonging to other complexes. If you can see them, and separate them out from what you're really feeling, you can sometimes relieve the pain without ever coming to jealousy. What was really going on was moral indignation, envy, guilt or fear, or some other kind of feelings.

Up to this point in peeling the onion, the primary emotions are sadness or anger. Both are created out of expectation. You are angry with your lover, you are sad because he or she has violated your expectations. But *you* are responsible, because *you* have created and are holding those expectations. Desire, according to the Buddha, is the source of suffering. A tension is created in your consciousness between whatsoever is and what you would have it be. That tension in the basis of all suffering.

Once the anger and sadness resulting from our fractured expectations are peeled away, once blame is removed from the other and anger disappears, once we see the superficial feelings around ourselves that aren't really at the core of jealousy, we come to fear.

Fear and Anxiety

The first fear we come to is fear of loss. Jealousy sees many things that can be lost. The fear of loss of the lover is the greatest. The rest of the fear around jealousy is in fact anxiety; that is to say, it does not have a real object.

The first anxiety comes from the loss of self-esteem. All kinds of self-doubt come up. You don't have enough money. Something's wrong with your body. You start projecting your own inadequacies on the other's actions. If your self-esteem is low, a jealous episode is going to be used as an occasion for proving that you are unlovable.

Examine the ideas that you have. You'll notice that they belong to all the old mechanisms by which you put yourself down. In other words, you were putting yourself down for these things long before the beloved came along to give you an excuse for doing so. Now you're just using him or her as a pretext.

So here's something else that you can do about jealousy: Start being aware that you are putting yourself down and that the inclination to do so is there independently of the jealousy-producing situation. Own your own tendency to put yourself down. Learn to deal with it yourself, and don't lay it on your lover.

Deeper than fear that comes from a loss of self-esteem is fear for the nest. One of two lovers is usually more concerned about the security of the relationship. Often it is the woman. Usually the function of the female in nature has been to keep the nest. It's almost as though nature gave her that fear out of protection of its own. The woman fears for her home, fears that the source of biological or family security is threatened. A man can also be possessed by security obsession. As women have become freer and more assertive men experience jealous insecurity more often. This is a deeper level of this onion of jealousy.

Infantile Anxiety

Deeper than fear for the nest—and closer to the core, are anxieties from infancy that are quickened by the present situation. Often, such jealousy is delusional—there whether or not there is any occasion for it. We can come to terms with many of these fears by looking deep inside and finding memory traces from our childhood—of being abandoned, for instance. These memory traces come from various losses or threats, beginning at birth. Later, you may want to win the special love of the parent of the opposite sex, but you may not achieve this primitive goal, so you feel constantly frustrated and inadequate. Or you become morbidly guilty and conclude that you *should* lose your oedipal goal because your incestuous wishes are bad.

You carry within you for the rest of your life memories of these early childhood traumas. Later, as soon as your lover goes for someone else, all that early trauma is triggered. Now if you move into a deep awareness, you can actually experience those childhood traumas, you can see that what you're experiencing in this present situation actually comes from a deep residual memory of abandonment.

All of these levels of the onion have to do with illusion, not with realities. They're from the past, from childhood, or they're illusions about the present, beliefs that are illusory, that don't relate to here/now reality. This is a very significant aspect of these anxieties that come with jealousy. If you have jealous feeling, and you start looking at them, suddenly you begin to see that they're not real, you are torturing yourself with unreal fears. What does this mean? What does it come from?

The Core Illusion

We are coming closer to the core of the onion. Reactions that are peripheral, the more superficial skins of the onion, are resting upon the core. The core is the source—the first illusion. The core has to be there for the other illusions to be there.

At the core is fear of a deeper kind. In its first aspect, it looks like fear of aloneness. This fear, too, comes from a childhood situation, from memories of when your parents left you alone. There you were, freaked out in your crib, crying, and nobody heard you.

This core fear has also the aspect of fear of death. Again, something is going to be taken away—your own *being*! That's how vulnerable you are. There's something about jealousy, that gut feeling, that is like the fear of death. It's that immediate, it's that real.

Something that's very like fear of death, interestingly enough, is fear of love. When we love, we move so much into the other that we lose ourselves. We use the expression "falling in love" because it's like falling into a great abyss. You lose your identity, your sense of autonomy. And that is exactly what happens when you fall in love. You lose your autonomous sense of who you are.

The fears of aloneness, of death, of love, all have the aspect of fear of abysmal nothingness—the fear that there isn't anything. Death suggests this to us. When we die, we don't know what's beyond. The only thing we know is that it's not like here. So as far as we're concerned, it's just oblivion. Nothingness is there in our consciousness all the time. Jealousy brings us immediately to this fear of oblivion.

All these fears—of death, love, aloneness, and nothingness—all are *like* the core of the onion. In fact, they all point to this core. The core itself is existential. It has to do with your existence. Thus jealousy is not fundamentally a problem of relationship, not a problem of love, but a problem of religion. Jealousy is basically, fundamentally, a spiritual problem.

What I mean by "religion" here is not belief or morality. I mean religion in the fundamental sense of how you rate to your own existence—your feelings, your senses, your inner aloneness—all of those realities that you experience but can never really communicate. Every human being relates to his or her own existence. Existence is God. In that relationship you're totally alone. In that you have no company. That is what it is to be a human—relating alone and reflectively to your own existence.

The truth of your religion has little to do with going to a church or temple, but with how you relate to that which you can't articulate, which is within you, and true. The way you relate to this existence is the basis of religion, and this religious matter is the core of the onion. Jealousy in its core exposes how you, as a human being, relate to your existence.

The Ego

Basic to the question of existence is the question, who is this "I" that's doing all of this feeling? Who is this "I" that loses self-esteem, that has a nest to protect, that is afraid? Who is this "I" that says "mine"? Who is this conglomerate of expectations? *Who is this I?*

In the East, they call it the ego. We use the word "ego" in the West in the sense of self-esteem; or in psychoanalysis, it is your capacity to cope with reality. When I talk about ego, I'm talking about something more fundamental. It is that which identifies, that which feeds on self-esteem, that which is the composition of all your expectations, that which perpetuates itself by possessing. In short, ego is that which can become jealous.

Ego and jealousy are both illusory. In your experiences of jealousy, you come to an insight that it is not real. You were jealous, and then all of a sudden you're not jealous any more, and you look back to when you were, and you feel that it wasn't real at all. It disappeared because it had no basis. That's what I mean about ego. Ego is that which we experience which is not real. Jealousy is also not real. Becoming aware is the joy you feel when you actually experience that unreality.

Let us consider envy again. Like all the skins of the onion, envy stands on ego. See how illusion works in envy. First of all, how do you know if you can be envious of another person? You see only outer circumstances and objects. You don't really know if the other is really happy with what they're experiencing. When you look at the other, what you perceive is your own projections. Don't even suppose that you can see another person's reality sufficiently to compare with yours in the first place. There's no way—until we reach utter, silent awareness within—that we can go into another and truly know their reality. But the illusion goes deeper.

In envy you are comparing the I—which is your ego—with the ego presented by someone else. Your comparison is based on an illusion that you are one entity and the other another entity, and you can compare the two. Only ego is "comparable". Only if you see yourself as an ego can you compare yourself in the first place.

Your comparison is based on illusion. The "you" object that you're comparing with some objectified person out there is really a subject—internal, hidden, uniquely, incomparably yourself. All your subjective reality is being objectified and then judgement compared with an object out there that you perceive to be a certain way.

With envy, possessiveness, jealousy, ego itself, we are not dealing in moral or ethical issues. It is irrelevant whether these or any acts they come from are wrong or right. It is a matter of reality or illusion, of authenticity, of phoniness. When I talk about peeling away the layers of the onion, what I am asking you do is to become aware. Through awareness *only* can we drop the illusion. And that which has illusions, that which can be jealous, is ego.

The feeling of abysmal jealousy is an eruption, a deep catharsis of ego. That's why jealousy is the great opportunity to stare ego right in the face. But it is difficult. It requires ruthless awareness, because ego is usually concealing itself. With deadly subtlety it masquerades as comparison, as blame, as the fault of the other, as problems that you have. It's hard even to have any grasp of it, because its hold on you is so subtle, so magical. It's always casting a spell over you. In fact, *you* believe you *are* ego. That's why it's so hard to see. Thus, when jealousy presents the source of suffering itself directly before you, there is great possibility.

What creates ego in the first place? Existence takes care of me as a child in a womb. It keeps "breathing" me. Then why do I develop this illusory me that—in the name of protection—keeps me in pain, keeps me alienated, isolated, separated from others, and unable to trust in existence? Why am I unable to trust that I'm taken care of by the whole, by all that is? All of us live in fear, and that which lives in fear is the same as that which is jealous: the ego.

The Abyss

To understand the ego, we must return to the core of jealousy. We "fear" the same in love, death, and aloneness. It is existence, or God, pure being. But because it is not a thing (only ego sees things), it has been called in the East, "nothingness" and "emptiness".

Let me give you an experience that might give you some sense of this nothingness. When you're waking up in the morning you are in a twilight. You're just coming out of sleep, before your thoughts begin to form, some ground is there. Like a tremendous empty vessel, it's there prior to your thoughts. Things bubble up in it and become realities. They congeal, take on an identity, and form the ego that you think you are.

The words "vessel of emptiness" or "nothingness" sound as though they are describing something that is devoid of content. They don't have that meaning. They mean that for existence there are no things that are real. In other words, existence presents us with an undifferentiated flow of experience welling up out of a void, an abyss of the unknown. Only with our minds do we pick out things, interpret them, and say that they are real. Our minds say that things out there really exist in the meaning context and values we assign to them. What we actually experience is a moving kaleidoscope of uninterpreted fullness. And this moving, everchanging phenomenon over which we have very little control, really, is a nothingness. It is a fullness in which there is no thing. So when you get right down to the basic religious question raised by jealousy, you have to question whether or not you really even exist.

In his great work *Being and Nothingness,* Sartre said that we as human beings so dread this ground of consciousness, this nothingness, that we have to create ourselves to be something. We are nothing. We are undifferentiated out of the great emptiness. We have no content. But this is so frightening, so abysmal, that we create ourselves to be something—namely, an ego. Being and nothingness is ego and existence, jealousy and the abyss. We are something fearful created out of nothing. Since somewhere we always know the something to be unreal, nothing is always present to us threateningly. My sense of my death is that it is always presented because nothingness is always there. Death is an accession to nothingness, a return to the source. So here we are, and basically what we come from is emptiness or nothingness. This is our basic angst.

A friend of mine experienced a lot of pain in her relationships. She was very compulsive, and possessive. She asked her teacher, Bhagwan Shree Rajneesh, about her pain, and he told her this: The ego, which arises out of the nothingness that we basically are, can have a negative or a positive response to the nothingness. The something that we are knows deep down that we're standing on nothingness. All of you know, deep down, that before the whole, you aren't anything. The negative response is subliminal terror. Against this fear of nothingness, you create the illusion that you are something. You back this project by preoccupation with realities, accumulating and possessing. That something illusory that you are is the one that suffers in jealousy. The entire structure is a negative or fearful response to nothingness.

But Bhagwan told my friend that this something-ego can also relate positively to nothingness. Only then can we move out of attachment into prayerful gratitude and heartfelt celebration of the other's being. Only then are we capable of real love. Only by saying a deep yes to nothingness, existence, the whole, do we come to be at home in nothingness. Eventually the positive response enables us to drop the something in favour of nothingness.

You are just a bubble. You were nothing before; you are nothing now. An enlightened bubble is not concerned with its bubbleness. It just is. It doesn't appear anything special, yet it feels all, sees all just as it is. That's why it is said to be enlightened. This is a positive, pure response to our given existential situation.

False Idols

Most of us don't react positively. Instead, we shore up our ego realities and live in fear. But death goes on reminding us of nothingness; aloneness goes on reminding us of nothingness; and love reminds us of nothingness. All three of these are ways that we experience nothingness right here and now, and they are frightening. If you have a fear response to nothingness, you will cling in your relationships, you will have to be possessive. You will have to control others. These are all tensions and compulsions that reflect this fundamental fear—this negative response to nothingness.

Thus ego in its fear protects itself from truth. This is the core of the onion. It is this core that you're really dealing with in jealousy. Many illusions are there, many external circumstances distract you from this core, but this is what jealousy is.

Given what is so, you have to turn yourself around completely and fall in love with nothingness. This turning brings with it the greatest religious insight: Nothingness is there to be relaxed into and loved. This is what they call in religion, surrender. You surrender to the nothingness and when you do so, it begins to give forth what you need. You have no control. There is no you that can control.

The 'you' that controls is exercising the illusion of the ego. We are all in it—all of us running around filling our lives with possessing, controlling, and manipulating. We are not really in control. Our manipulations are only superficial, but the ego would have us believe that we must be in control or else there is chaos. If you have much insight into how things around you really are, you will come to see this control for what it is. It is like a molecule thinking it controls the universe.

The whole organism of existence is moving in its own way, and we are just nothing. Nothingness is the organism that is the whole. You are not separate from that organism, and the sense that you are separate from it is the basic illusion of ego. It prevents the richness that the whole gives forth when we let go to it.

You can become possessive about God as you can about a lover. If you become possessive in religion, you lay a trip on God. He will be Rāma, he will be Jesus, he will be dialectical materialism, he will be the state, he will be *your* God. "My religion is the only true one." "The God I believe in is the one and only." Anyone who is very rigid in his or her beliefs is manifesting the same principles as that which creates jealousy. In other words, the possessive person and the fanatic are involved in the same game. They build up the same kinds of resistance to the same primordial fear. So, if you are in negative response to nothingness, you'll become preoccupied with material possessions, you'll become obsessed with controlling a lover, or else you'll become very religious and rigid about your beliefs.

When you possess you become possessed. You live in a deep vulnerability based in illusion. The stomach-churning pain of jealousy comes from that vulnerability. That's what you're experiencing. The jealous moment is the essential catharsis of this existential complex.

To the Core

Now, a relationship with a lover or a relationship with God can reveal the ultimate. Through loving a lover or an image of God you can experience pure nothingness as bliss. But if you possess, if you have a God that you have fixed beliefs about, or if you have a lover that you jealously control, what you're actually doing is blocking your realisation. Out of fear you are misusing that which can give you an experience of bliss. You are so controlled that you cannot be overwhelmed. And the ultimate can only make itself known when you allow yourself to be overwhelmed.

If you have this negative response to nothingness, the very base upon which you are standing is false. That false base is ego, the seat of jealousy. The possessed person, or the God or principle that you believe in, is only a projection of that ego. It is not real. You are relating to an illusion, a projection that you created to keep yourself from experiencing fear. Your eyes are closed, you can't really see the beloved.

And this is what happens to us. This is why we don't communicate in love. Because the lover is a false idol. Whether it's the person or whether it is a God, somehow it's false. Our eyes are closed to the reality, and what we're relating to all the time is our own illusion.

This is the basic mechanism that creates jealousy in the first place. What you really want from a lover, what you really want from God, is bliss. If you possess them, if you lay your trip on them, if you're relating to your own projection, you're stopping yourself from experiencing this bliss. If you can't know joy through the lover, or through God because of the illusion that you've created, you can't really experience the bliss of love. You have to see this basic mechanism that is happening in your relationship to existence and know that as a jealous person you are making a choice.

Love cannot be channeled to one object. If you have one love object and channel all of your love there, what you are experiencing is attachment. Similarly, if you are jealous, you are not experiencing love, you are experiencing attachment. If you *really* love, then you'll experience an overflowing, you will experience love for all. It's natural consequence of loving. It is not a natural consequence of attachment. In attachment, you've channeling all of your love in one direction. In love you're experiencing something in one direction that frees you in all directions. It's as if you threw a stone into a pond. Where the stone hits the water, radiations ripple outward. When you really love, it may be directed toward one object, but it radiates into love for all of existence. That is why love is said to be divine.

So this is the possibility that you have as a jealous person. When you work on jealousy, forget the lover and deal with your own relationship to existence. Go deep inside of yourself, slowly peel away the outer layers of the onion until you come to the core that is your own relationship to existence. Then you will free yourself to love more.

My own love relationships have been guided by my teacher. In the last five years he has shaped all the significant factors in the development of my love life, because he wants me to reach beyond the neurotic needs of relationship. There was a time when I experienced a lot of pain in loving, a lot of jealousy. I felt that I was always living in fear of loss. I felt like I couldn't hold on, and I was in constant pain because of it. So I went to my teacher and asked what to do. His answer cut through to the core. "Simply love more," he said. "To cut right through fear of loss which is infantile in its source, right to the core of the basic relationship that you have to existence, go into more loving." In other words, if you love someone, go deep into your own unique experience of what that love is, and just let that be who you are. Surrender to it. Build your identity upon it. You are not a person who is jealous. Not someone who's trying to control. Not even someone who's fearing. You are love experiencing itself deeper and deeper within its own fullness.

"Your love is a boat," Bhagwan said. "Just go on, enter loving more, tending, penetrating—and the boat, of its own volition, will carry you to the other shore."

(1983)

Chapter Fourteen

From Device to Vice: Social Control and Intergroup Conflict at Rajneeshpuram

CARL A. LATKIN

The building of a new community allows researchers to observe a variety of unusual social phenomena. The diverse ways that members of unconventional groups interact, cope, and function in work, play, and religion is not only of academic interest. Investigations of such communities also help us to understand our own societies; by standing out in sharp relief to our own practices, these groups give us a vantage point from which to examine ourselves.

Most new communal societies are short-lived. Kanter (1972) found that the average life expectancy was a mere five years. In this article we will examine the social-psychological dynamics of the former commune of Rajneeshpuram in Central, Oregon. With the advantage of hindsight, I will delineate a set of hypotheses on the antecedents and consequences of social control and intergroup conflict at Rajneeshpuram. Then, we will analyse, first, both situational and belief factors that interfered with followers' ability to judge their leaders' and their own behaviour, and second, how those factors allowed the leaders to exert strong social controls. Many of these dynamics led to and exacerbated the conflict. We will also examine how isolation, fear of assassination, external threats, status as a minority, and identity abetted the conflict.

Rajneeshpuram is not the only new religious commune in recent years to have been devastated by conflict (Robbins, 1988). The Jonestown tragedy has left a deep impression and raises the haunting question: Is there anything inherent in the beliefs and structure of new religious movements which disposes them to conflict and violence? Some of the causes of the fall of Rajneeshpuram were idiosyncratic, whereas others were cross-situational. The inter- and intragroup conflicts were dynamic processes. As they escalated, the tactics, perceptions, and behaviours changed. Although it is impossible to sort out the links in the causal chain of the conflict, I will describe some of the underpinnings.

Research on the Rajneeshees

The Rajneeshees, disciples of the Indian religious leader Shree Rajneesh, who was also known as Bhagwan and Osho, purchased the 64,229-acre Big Muddy Ranch in Eastern Oregon in July, 1981. The Rajneeshees immediately began setting up the Rancho Rajneesh commune, later incorporated as the city-commune of Rajneeshpuram (Braun, 1984; Mullen, 1983). What Rajneesh's followers, who are called Rajneeshees, Sannyasins, and Neo-Sannyasins, developed was not a small rural settlement; by 1985 over 4,000 were living on the ranch.

The research of the Rajneeshees and Rajneeshpuram upon which this article is based began in 1982. It continued through the break-up of the commune (see Latkin, 1987; Latkin *et al.*, 1987). We collected a range of data on the commune and on the public's perceptions of it. Social-psychological surveys and individual interviews conducted at Rajneeshpuram and a statewide survey on attitudes toward Rajneeshees comprise the bulk of the data. We conducted interviews throughout the study; however, the majority of the interviews occurred in late 1985 and early 1986. The administration of surveys and interviews occurred after the investigators had had prolonged contact with the Rajneeshees. None of the investigators was a Rajneeshee.

Interview Procedures and Subjects

Forty interviews were conducted over a six-month period from November 1985 to May 1986. These interviews, ranging from one to three hours, were taped. The major topics were background, daily events, and reactions to recent stressful events. Subjects for the interview were volunteers. While some respondents were chosen on the basis of availability, we endeavoured to select individuals from a range of work areas. Many of the interviews took place after the commune's chief spokesperson, Ma Anand Sheela, left the commune. This was a period of intense introspection and evaluation after her departure, and most of the interviewees expressed misgivings about, as well as praise for, the community.

The interviews were semi-structured or focused interviews (Denzin, 1978). All interviews covered a basic set of questions; however as individuals varied in occupations held and in length of residency, there were variations in the details obtained on each topic. To reduce the possibility of memory distortion, probes were as specific as possible. One of the more common methods of analysis is a matrix process in which topics or symbolic relationships are arranged on one axis and situations or individuals on the other axis (Spradely, 1979). A matrix of seven topics was derived from the interview schedule as follows: background, taking Sannyas (the initiation ceremony), life on the ranch, Rajneesh philosophy, language analysis, and crimes and power.

History of Rajneeshpuram and the Conflict

When the Rajneeshees first arrived they made peaceful overtures to the surrounding communities; nonetheless, within the year they became embroiled in battles with their neighbours. The principal conflict was over land use: the ranch land had been zoned agricultural, and the Rajneeshees wanted to establish services and activities more common to a town. This conflict quickly escalated into bitter hostility. The Rajneeshees took an aggressive stance, became exceedingly litigious, and sued dozens of groups and individuals (Androes, 1986).

One of the many manifestations of hostilities arose when a local fundamentalist preacher and his parishioners protested Rajneesh's daily drive into the town of Madras, which is about 50 miles from Rajneeshpuram. The Rajneeshees responded by busing their followers to counterdemonstrate. The demonstrations escalated as did the number of protesters on each side. They were defused by the district attorney, with the Rajneeshees agreeing not to drive into the town of Madras.

A bombing of a Rajneeshee-owned hotel in Portland in August of 1983 heightened the tension, and at Rajneeshpuram the increasing display of semi-automatic weapons by the commune's "Peace Force" created a picture of imminent battle. Concomitantly, on the legal front, the commune was embroiled in a series of legal battles. Suits were brought against the commune, declaring that the City of Rajneeshpuram was illegally incorporated, and on December 11, 1985, the State Supreme Court proclaimed that the city's very existence was a violation of the constitutional separation between church and state (Manuto, 1987; Shay, 1985).

Ma Anand Sheela, the *de facto* commune leader, who had the title of chief spokesperson and Rajneesh's personal secretary, did little to foster co-operation or ease the conflict. Her speaking style was sharp, fiery, crude, caustic, arrogant, and defensive. Her posture not only inflamed the hostilities but also helped bring the media, who came in droves, to Rajneeshpuram.

Abruptly, on September 14, 1985, Ma Anand Sheela and 15 to 20 other officials left the commune. They were immediately denounced by Rajneesh, who accused them of perpetrating serious crimes inside and outside the commune. It was revealed that unbeknown to government officials, and nearly all commune members, a secretive group had master-minded a series of illegal activities, ranging from the poisoning of a salad bar with Salmonella in a nearby community, to wiretapping and attempted murder within the commune. After Sheela and two other leaders were extradited from West Germany, they plea bargained to a range of charges, including the attempted murder of Rajneesh's physician, Swami Devaraj, a.k.a. George Meredith. According to a chronology provided by the Office of the Attorney General, the blatantly illegal and criminal activities, such as the wiretapping, did not begin unitl the spring of 1984, three years after Rajneeshpuram began—they did not become public until the fall of 1985. After Sheela's departure Rajneesh declared that his disciples were no longer required to wear their distinct "colours of the sunrise" and that his followers were no longer to be called "Rajneeshees"—he did not want to establish an institutionalised religion. At the time of our study they called themselves Rajneeshees, as did the public, hence in this paper I will use the appellations "Rajneeshees" and "Sannyasins" interchangeably.

A month after Sheela's departure, Rajneesh was arrested in Charlotte, North Carolina, as he was purportedly fleeing the country. On November 14, 1985, Rajneesh left the United States in accordance with a plea bargain on charges of arranging fraudulent marriages to enable foreign disciples to stay in the United States. About two weeks after Rajneesh departed, commune officials decided that Rajneeshpuram was no longer economically viable, and members were asked to leave as soon as possible. The commune was finally sold, in December 1988, for 4.3 million dollars (see FitzGerald, 1986, for a more detailed account). In January 1990, Rajneesh died at his Ashram in Poona, India.

Problem of Judgement

Situational Ambiguity

At Rajneeshpuram there were a number of dilemmas facing Sannyasins; one was the question of which standards to use in judging their own behaviour and that of their leaders. The community professed to have a new set of values; beyond good and evil. Old standards were not to be trusted—this was a new society, a new humanity—yet new standards had not been formulated. The result was a paradox: How do you judge new behaviours without relying on old norms? What are to be the standards when you are changing? Who is to judge these new behaviours?

Rajneeshpuram had a self-generated cryptic countenance. In fact it was called by Rajneesh "a mystery school"—for inner transformation. The second dilemma

Rajneeshees faced was how does one judge events or behaviour in a mystery school? They may well have meanings beyond rationality. Rules of logic do not necessarily apply. If something at Rajneeshpuram appeared to be peculiar, such as the busing in of thousands of street people, it could be seen as part of this great and mysterious lesson. Moreover, the Rajneeshee practice of focusing on "being in the here-and-now", rather than concentrating on goals and on the future, further hindered members in assessing their situation. Thinking about why you're doing what you're doing—What are the reasons? Do they make sense?—implies focusing on the end-product, the goal. Such planning for the future was discouraged at Rajneeshpuram. These two conceptions, a new society and a mystery school, made it problematic for Sannyasins to assess the behaviour of their own group. This, in turn, gave the leadership freedom in decision making and diminished the ability of Rajneeshees to question their leader's bellicose acts.

A third complication was the dilemma of how to judge Rajneesh himself. Many Sannyasins viewed Rajneesh as an enlightened being, one of only a handful, such as Jesus or Buddha, who had ever walked on earth. Being in the presence of such a figure was a once-in-a-lifetime opportunity. How could they—on a lower level of consciousness—judge his behaviour? Many assumed that he had a masterplan for the development of the commune, one that they simply could not comprehend; consequently, odd and troublesome policies were easily attributable to such an unknown masterplan. It should be noted that there was a vast spectrum of views on Rajneesh's powers, which ranged from seeing him as a good friend to revering him as a God-like being with supernatural powers.

Ingroup Bias

Both cognitive and psychological biases affected the community's ability to assess self and others. Rajneeshees strongly believed that their group was composed of superior beings. The belief in superiority of one's own group is axiomatic; one would not be likely to join a group that one did not think was superior in some fashion. In addition, there is a consistent finding in the intergroup conflict literature that assigning people to groups, even randomly, produces ingroup biases (Tajfel, 1981); each group perceives itself as superior. Ingroup bias has been found to be stronger in cohesive gorups (Janis, 1972), and conflict enhances cohesion (Worchel and Norvell, 1980). Although belief in the superiority of one's own group is a normal product of social cognition, at Rajneeshpuram this process was exacerbated by the Rajneeshees' world view. One of their prevailing beliefs was that the world was heading toward destruction, and implicitly—at times explicitly—that the Rajneeshees were the only sane individuals in an otherwise insane world. Rajneesh himself talked at great length on how the world was in a disastrous state, and when he began speaking publicly again in 1985—after three years of silence—he made disparaging comments about Oregonians and other non-Rajneeshees. If others are stupid, ignorant, and at a lower level of consciousness, then it makes no sense to listen to them and take their concerns seriously.

Several Sannyasins mentioned that the commune developed an air of superiority. One commune member, who was interviewed several months after the demise of the commune said, "I guess that's part of our arrogance.... that we believed in or bought into, you know, about being better than whatever, the rest of Oregon or humanity." Because the group believed it was superior, naturally what they did was likewise superior, and so there was no need to scrutinise or question their actions. This attitude was a barrier; it prevented Rajneeshees from obtaining feedback about their behaviour.

There was another motive for the disparaging comments that Rajneeshees made about government officials and others. These comments were, in part, a reaction to the public's negative depiction of them. The media had presented a highly unfavourable image of members of New Religious Movements (van Driel and Richardson, 1988). The Rajneeshees were portrayed as cult members, freaks and deviants. These labels were a threat to their self-esteem. When self-esteem is threatened individuals attempt to bolster their self-concept (Willis, 1981). For the Rajneeshees there were two logical tactics for deflecting the negative labels and bolstering their self-esteem: denigrate non-Rajneeshees and glamorise their own image. They employed both. The contents of their weekly newspaper, *The Rajneesh Times*, was an excellent example of both. The paper's sub-heading read "The world's best newspaper in the world's best city," while many of the articles denounced and ridiculed Oregonians and other non-Rajneeshees for their prejudices and stupidity. The psychological phenomenon of ingroup bias, combined with the Rajneeshees' arrogance and with the group's attempt to buttress its self-esteem, led to group-wide condescension and overconfidence, which impaired the Rajneeshees' judgement and helped to alienate them.

Social Control Factors

Freedom and Ambiguity

All organisations develop methods of making decisions, dealing with conflict, and checking deleterious behaviour. They may explicitly draw up and formally agree upon a set of rules and procedures to govern and regulate behaviour. Rules and policies may also evolve over the course of time without any explicit process or written record (Schein, 1985). From the interviews, an interesting picture emerges of the socialisation and social control process in Rajneeshpuram. Receptivity to socialisation began at initiation. It was later fostered by the leaders with various forms of social control, including threatening Sannyasins with expulsion, keeping information about the commune organisation relatively secret, and using the concept of "personal growth" as a controlling device.

It is reasonable to assume that Rajneeshees knew more than non-Rajneeshees about how to be Rajneeshees, yet many of those interviewed said that when they joined, although they were intrigued by the movement, they really did not understand it. One woman said she wanted to be a good Sannyasin but did not know how to be one. There was no rule book outlining how one ought to act, how one should be. Paradoxically, this lack of structure became a coercive force; it made it easier for the leaders to control behaviour. Freedom from rules proved problematic in several ways. Given the lack of agreed-upon behavioural standards, it was difficult to judge the behaviours of others or to object to what appeared to be inappropriate. This was exacerbated by the community's lack of history. As previously mentioned, members saw the commune as a model for a new society, so the rules which applied to the "old" society did not necessarily apply in this new setting.

The newness and accompanying ambiguity heightened conformity. In a review of the research on organisational conformity, Nemeth and Staw (1989) contend that ambiguity of performance criteria contributes to conformity. At Rajneeshpuram no one knew what to do, but assumed that the leadership did, and hence followed their dictates: freedom from the past thus gave way to overpowering social control by the leaders.

Festinger (1950) argued that within groups there is a general proclivity toward conformity. He postulated two intergroup forces. The first is the social comparison process—others' beliefs and perceptions are used as a guide to validate one's own views—which restricts choices and options. A second impetus is that groups are motivated to attain goals and, hence, to avoid incapacitating discord—members are willing to submit to the will of the group and its leaders. Both forces were at work at Rajneeshpuram. Moreover, in ambiguous settings such as Rajneeshpuram, individuals are more likely to engage in social comparison to assess their own behaviours (Schachter and Singer, 1962). As the Rajneeshees were eager to build Rajneesh's visionary community, they submitted to the will of the group.

Leadership Socialisation

This lack of structure and the absence of a codified belief system gave those in power a free hand in designing the commune's culture. Those who entered and found themselves in mid-level leadership positions did not know the "correct" way to lead, so they would look to others for guidance. The most logical individuals to copy were their own superiors—since they assumed there was a valid reason for them to be supervisors. One woman, who was the commune's major luxury car purchaser, freely admitted that she copied Ma Anand Sheela's aggressive leadership style. A second woman also said she tried to use the same style of leadership as that of her co-ordinator, but when she went on exchange to a German Sannyas commune, this style was, much to her surprise, seen as overly harsh and authoritarian. A third woman, who described the leadership style as "straight", said, "The other people who were in a position of power had ways of being very hard and very direct with people, and I thought I needed to learn that [method]." Wanous

(1980) proposes that when newcomers enter organisations one of the most effective coping strategies is to observe and practice the behaviours of others. This strategy was abundantly apparent at Rajneeshpuram.

Once norms are established, even arbitrary ones, they tend to take on a life of their own and become resistant to change. New members are most susceptible to the influences of group norms. Sherif (1966) demonstrated that once people make judgements in a group setting they adhere to the group's norm even after departing from the group. Jacobs and Campbell (1961) found that once an arbitrary norm was instilled it persisted even after old group members exit and new members are added—provided that the old members do not all leave at once. In an organisational context, Zucker (1977) reported that norms are most resistant to change in a hierarchical organisation, less resistant in a non-hierarchical organisation, and least resistant in a non-organisational context. It was by no means inevitable that the strict controls and methods of regulating behaviour evolved as they did at Rajneeshpuram, but once they were in place they became self-perpetuating.

Ma Anand Sheela's harsh and often combative style was also accepted and copied simply because she was Bhagwan's personal secretary, and many believed that Bhagwan directed her to behave the way she did. In the interviews, several respondents said that since Bhagwan picked Sheela, and since he is enlightened, there must have been a good reason for anything she did. Furthermore, since few commune members knew how decisions were made, there were no available methods or processes for rejecting or appealing a decision. Often a request would be followed by the phrase "the commune needs this". Such a request was difficult to question or ignore. Indeed, several studies have found that wording a request in an impersonal fashion increases compliance (Langer, 1989).

Beliefs and Control

Besides the above-mentioned socialisation process, there were several other factors that allowed the commune to be tightly controlled. One social control device was the unacceptability of negative feedback. The commune's philosophical emphasis on enjoying life became expressed as a desire to emphasise the positive in life. On many occasions this translated into the suppression of legitimate criticism. If one voiced a criticism, one could be accused of being negative and told that this negativity should be "dropped". One woman who worked in the central records office gave the following scenario to describe "negativity":

> The first week or so I would bicker with her about it: "Come on, why don't we do it [file records] this way.....and it's all clear and you can find this and I'll know where that is, and if I put this here....." And our co-ordinator [supervisor] said, "Look, just drop all that stuff. Just do it the way she wants it done." That was negativity; having a creative idea was being negative.

The Rajneeshee emphasis on being positive had a naive or innocent quality. Most Sannyasins assumed that they were all at Rajneeshpuram for the same spiritual reasons. They did not realise that the quest for power and notoriety, not spiritual fulfilment, may have motivated some of their comrades. This unquestioning demeanor interfered with their ability to assess accurately the leadership's behaviour and motivation.

A third method of social control was what was known as a "device", a Rajneeshee method for personal growth. A device is a Buddhist technique for focusing one's energy on the self in order to learn about the self. For example, an event that one felt to be upsetting could also be used as a path toward self-understanding. One woman describes Sheela this way:

> And so I saw Sheela's being horrible as sort of a device for me—getting angry at all authority figures in my life. And it's not that I agreed with her, but I could think, "Boy this makes me mad, boy that kind of stuff makes me mad, this is a way of knowing myself."

A classic example of events being explained away as a device was the importation of several thousand homeless street people to live at Rajneeshpuram before November 1984 election. Many saw this act as a device for Sannyasins to examine their prejudices toward the poor.

Self-blame and Fear of Expulsion

Social control was not only externally imposed by the leaders; it was also internalised by the members. Over and over, respondents said that when they would sense something amiss, they would blame themselves. A typical response was, as one woman said, "I felt uncomfortable, but I didn't know what it was, and since I was not involved [with the illegal activities] I thought maybe it was me." According to attribution theory (Heider, 1980), Rajneeshees were making internal attributions for the problems that they detected. This self-blame was reinforced by what was called "cleaning up on people". This activity was done by the leadership and directed toward others in leadership positions and also toward subordinates. It entailed criticism, often harsh, of those who had been critical of the system.

In addition to self-blame, those who objected to what was going on around the commune were told that the problem lay within themselves and was not due to the leadership. A guard who protected Rajneesh's car by riding next to it with a sub-machine gun was asked if any commune residents ever objected to his carrying such a powerful weapon. He responded by saying:

> No, not that I know of, not that I can remember. For a lot of people a part of it was jealousy [of the honour of being one of Rajneesh's personal guards] and part of it was probably valid. They didn't really understand or they didn't like the way it was going, but I wasn't interested in that, that wasn't the concern, if you didn't particularly like it, it wasn't my problem, it was your problem.

Another means of social control was the fear of being asked to leave the commune. Those who did not like what they saw felt that they had two choices: they could either toe the line and be allowed to stay with Bhagwan, or they could say what they honestly thought and be asked to leave. Several individuals expressed the opinion of one woman who said, "A lot of people were sent away, or they were put into other positions, and if you wanted to stay here and be with your family and friends and with Bhagwan, you shut up because these people were in power." A Sannyasin who said that he was prone to get into trouble, stated:

> In no uncertain terms they made it clear to certain people that unless that line was toed, that they would be living somewhere else. And so people had to look at that and the main interest was to live around Bhagwan, and to be around Bhagwan. And because we trusted him, we trusted them. And it was fine. And it still is fine. I mean there's no regrets about anything that happened here.

This last statement of there being no regrets should be taken seriously. A theme often expressed by Sannyasins is that regrets are futile. One should endeavour to enjoy whatever one is doing and not dwell on past mistakes.

This philosophy, in the context of work behaviour, was translated into the prescription that it was up to each individual to make work a positive experience. This could be done with the "right approach". This prescription, however, was contradicted by the practice of giving menial jobs as punishment to individuals who were a threat to the system or who had been "negative".

Structural Characteristics

As the ranch grew so did security. An elaborate system was erected to monitor and control the street people, including patrolling the grounds and setting up a pass system based on commune resident status. There were coloured bracelets that indicated whether one was a visitor, a short-term resident, or a commune member. Throughout the ranch there were restrictions on travel that were based on resident status. Even though most of the street people stayed at Rajneeshpuram for only a few weeks and even after 90 per cent of the street people had left, these security structures remained. Once in place they were difficult to dismantle. Furthermore, as the ranch grew it was impossible to know everyone personally. This growth made it easier for strangers to slip in undetected and made the security system seem imperative. One can only speculate as to whether such social controls would have been possible without an enemy, and whether they would have been accepted without the powerful desire of Sannyasins to be near Bhagwan and without belief in his omniscient powers.

Physical and Psychological Isolation

One of the structural attributes of the conflict was the secluded setting. Due to their isolation, the typical Rajneeshpuram residents saw only a restricted range of acts toward and beliefs about them. In the evenings they saw the television news clips about themselves. What they did see was most often negative, and some of the media reports were factually inaccurate. On weekends fundamentalist Christians from nearby towns would drive down the main street of Rajneeshpuram, get out of their cars, read from their Bibles, and make pronouncements about how Rajneesh was the devil and that Rajneeshees would go to hell. From these limited and skewed samples of observations, the commune members' belief that the outside world was hostile and antagonistic toward them was strengthened. This limited perspective led to the further alienation of Rajneeshees from the larger society.

Rajneeshees were not only isolated due to their physical location, but they also began to lose contact with their friends outside of the commune, a psychological isolation. They felt that their friends no longer understood them, and life outside of the commune seemed distant, not relevant to life at Rajneeshpuram. One example of the outside losing its relevance was that although *The Oregonian*, a daily, statewide newspaper, could be purchased on the ranch, few Sannyasins chose to read anything other than the weekly *Rajneesh Times*, which had little coverage of state, national, or international news. What was reported in newspapers was not felt to be relevant to ranch life. The loss of contact with friends and the media further exacerbated the problem of judgement. To whom could Sannyasins turn for feedback about the community's behaviour and that of commune officials besides other Rajneeshpuram residents?

Feedback from outside residents could have helped to alert Sannyasins to the deterioration of inter-and intracommunity affairs. Those Sannyasins who continued to communicate with family and friends said that they did it out of obligation and that their phone calls and letters were usually superficial. A woman who worked on Rajneeshpuram's farm commented that if one saw someone writing a lot of letters, something was wrong with that individual. It indicated that his or her energy was no longer focused on the ranch. Lack of communication with the outside further hampered obtaining feedback from the outside and was thus a means of social control—the leadership became the sole legitimate source of information and of interpretations.

CONFLICT

The Role of Beliefs

Many of the beliefs that interfered with Sannyasins' judgement and abetted social control were factors in the intergroup conflict. The commune leaders capitalised on the belief that Rajneesh was an enlightened being. The leaders demanded, in Rajneesh's name, obedience to them, which on occasion included hostile acts toward outsiders (such as harassing public officials who came to examine city records). What sacrifice would be too great to make Rajneesh's dream come true? What did it matter if they bent or broke a few laws to build Bhagwan's vision? After all, it isn't everyday that a Jesus or a Buddha comes along. In the Rajneeshees' view an enlightened being is a phenomenally rare occurrence. Again, not all Sannyasins accepted the leadership's prescriptions. Some were appalled at what they saw and left. Others questioned the wisdom of the leadership. Often they were asked to leave to commune.

Tittle (1977) found that one of the strongest impediments to engaging in deviant behaviour is fear of social sanctions. Those who consciously and explicitly remove themselves from society may feel less constrained by societal norms. As the Rajneeshees professed to care little about what outsiders thought of them, they were less restrained from engaging in deviant behaviour. In new communities such as Rajneeshpuram, creative and innovative organisational structures and social behaviours can emerge, yet—without the fear of social sanction—so can deleterious ones.

Another precipitating factor, which in part stemmed from the Rajneeshees' beliefs and in part from their backgrounds, was that the Rajneeshees would not and did not play the role of accommodating newcomers or of a complacent minority. They made few attempts to fit in or to assimilate. Many of the Rajneeshees had previously held professional, high status occupations, and they were used to being leaders. They were not accustomed to either a subordinate or conciliatory role. Refusal to accept this role undoubtedly exacerbated tensions.

Conflict was exacerbated by a prevalent Rajneeshee belief in the possibility of Rajneesh's assassination. In an interview with the author, Ma Anand Sheela said that Ranjeesh, on several occasions, proclaimed that he would be assassinated, most likely by one of his own followers. The fear of his assassination created an atmosphere of paranoia; no one could be trusted, not even the closest disciple. As conflict with the outside escalated, the Rajneeshees construed the hostility as proof that people were bent on destroying Rajneesh. In intergroup conflict it is common to find that each side's perceptions are altered by the conflict (Pruitt and Rubin, 1986). Negative attributes of the opposite side are magnified, and ambiguous events are interpreted as hostile.

As the community focused on this perceived threat and how to prevent it, the problem became magnified. Detailed files were kept on hate mail. Phones were tapped. Along with guardposts, two large fences were constructed around Rajneesh's house, and Rajneesh's house was guarded and his grounds patrolled. By directing the commune's energies to this protection, the perception of hostility and conflict were brought to the foreground of commune life.

Leadership

The methods of leadership and the ensuing events did not simply result from a few individuals grabbing the reins of power overnight. The group's philosophy, the lack of initial behavioural standards, the desire to be with Bhagwan all led to a situation in which the leadership steadily amassed great power. The leadership structure, along with the community's arrogance and the lack of external feedback, provided fertile ground for the commune's demise. The methods of social control that have been described do not imply that residents found the work or leaders to be oppressive. Many of those interviewed had the highest regard for the top leaders. They felt that they had integrity, tried to do what they perceived to be best for the commune, and that without them the city would never have been built.

At Rajneeshpuram, the harsh and sometimes oppressive actions of the leaders that led to such bizarre behaviours as wiretapping and poisonings inside and outside of the commune cannot be attributed simply to those in power wanting more power for their personal gain. The leaders saw the outside world, i.e., government officials on all levels, the media and surrounding communities, as dangerous. To reduce the external threat, the leaders felt they needed more control and became increasingly paranoid and coercive. The commune leaders thought that by becoming more aggressive toward the outside, they would ward off potential enemies—the deterrent theory. In this atmosphere a siege mentality began to develop: criticism was no longer legitimate. In a state of war one does not question authority—one obeys. In the interviews it was revealed that a whole filing system of information on enemies and a catalogue of all the hostile letters received were developed. This system amplified the perception of hostilities by focusing attention on the conflict. The increasing fear that hostile outsiders would infiltrate or invade gave the leadership a rationale for strict control of the ranch. A tyrannical system was accepted by the members because they thought that the leaders had some spiritual authority.

It has been shown that external threat increases group cohesion (Wilder and Shapiro, 1984), which has been hypothesized to be beneficial for group survival (Kanter, 1973). This linkage raises the question, did the leadership instigate conflict to build group cohesion? Was there a conscious manipulation of attitudes toward outsiders in order to enhance group solidarity? Nesbitt and Wilson (1977) have demonstrated that we are much less aware of our behaviour than we think we are. It is likely that individuals found the tactics that enhanced solidarity rewarding and effective rather than having consciously manipulated the situation in order to enhance group solidarity. In addition, intense group loyalty, and the concomitant socialisation processes aimed at achieving loyalty, are not the sole domain of religious groups; they have been observed in a variety of non-religious organisations (Alder and Alder, 1989).

Group cohesion, however, is not always constructive; it can be deleterious. It can increase the chances of intergroup conflict and suppress dissension. A constellation of behaviour of highly cohesive groups that results in the suppression of dissent has been entitled "Groupthink" (Janis, 1982). Symptoms include an illusion of invulnerability, unquestioned belief in a group's morality, stereotyped views of opponents, conformity to pressure, self-censorship, and an illusion of unanimity. Each of these symptoms was manifested at Rajneeshpuram as the commune became embroiled in conflict.

Conclusion

The lack of questioning of leaders was due in part to the failure to understand the overwhelming impact that situational structure had on behaviour—in the present case, the effect on leadership behaviour of a hierarchical, non-democratic, organisation coupled with external hostility. A prevailing assumption of commune members was that "aware" individuals would make good decisions regardless of the situation and regardless of the organisational structure. However, it had been consistently demonstrated that strong situational forces may overpower personality factors. The classic Milgram study of obedience (1974) and the Zimbardo prison study (Zimbardo *et al.*, 1977) clearly show that manipulating a seemingly innocuous situation can induce stable, normal individuals to engage in aggressive and potentially harmful behaviour.

Although some Sannyasins felt they were living under a despotic regime, most did not—or chose to stay and to be with Bhagwan anyway. Still other inhabitants chose to see the commune as a positive, loving, utopia, and saw Ma Anand Sheela as a protector of the commune. This diversity of perspectives is a good example of how one's environment is actively "enacted" (Weick, 1979). The degree to which perceptions may be determined by social factors is further evident in that most individuals at Rajneeshpuram were unaware of the dubious activities going on around them. Few Sannyasins interpreted events, such as the busing in of the homeless to increase the number of city residents in order to "stuff the ballot box", as a symptom of corruption; rather, they saw it as some part of the master's plan for utopia.

The Rajneeshees saw politics as evil and believed that politicians act solely in their own self-interest. The ideal Rajneeshee society would be free of political institutions. They believed that if people lived with awareness and in harmony there would be no need for politics. Rajneesh argued that social change is not brought about by changes in the social structure or by a political process. Change results from personal transformation; change is an internal process, not externally imposed. When people become more aware and true to their nature there will be societal and world harmony. Only then will political problems be solved. Rajneesh's views on politics stem, in part, from Taoism, Buddhism, and Hinduism. His perspective does not, however, fit well with American political culture. Indeed, political institutions and social controls are essential for the survival of any large group. It is ironic that the Rajneeshees' antipathy toward political institutions resulted in the establishment of a maladaptive and authoritarian political system.

The fall of Rajneeshpuram leads to several questions about communes and new social organisations: If one wants to create an experimental society how much contact should there be with the outside world? Too much may stifle change, and too little may result in the inability to judge internal behaviours. Another set of questions concerns the Rajneeshees' naivete. There is evidence that focusing on positive life events and being optimistic is an effective and beneficial coping strategy (Lewinsohn *et al.*, 1980); however, can one emphasise the positive without becoming gullible? A final question is, how have the Rajneeshees changed? Although Rajneeshpuram collapsed the group did not disband—they are now back in Poona, India. Did their views and beliefs change as a result of their experiences at Rajneeshpuram? Their behaviour is not set in stone. Have their methods of social control changed? Which ones have remained? (1991)

IV

CONFLICT AND RENEWAL

Chapter Fifteen

Seeing Red: A Social-Psychological Analysis of the Rajneeshpuram Conflict

CARL A. LATKIN

From 1981 to 1985, Sannyasins, followers of the Indian religious leader Bhagwan Shree Rajneesh, inhabited the commune in Eastern Oregon that they named Rajneeshpuram. During their stay in Oregon, the Rajneeshees gained wide publicity from their innumerable conflicts. Throughout the United States and around the world, Rajneeshpuram was prime time television and front page news. Everyone in Oregon knew about the Rajneeshees, and few had anything good to say about them. This dislike of the Rajneeshees was not a mild annoyance. The Rajneeshees enraged the people of Oregon. It is surprising that the tension did not fulminate, boil over, and culiminate in bloodshed. From a social-psychological, information processing perspective the following questions about the

Rajneeshpuram conflict will be examined: why did this group catch the public's attention? Why did the public react so strongly to them? Why were they feared and despised? And, why did the Rajneeshees become so hostile and bellicose toward outsiders?

I will present the results of a state-wide survey on the public's attitudes toward Rajneeshees and address the question of how the public received information, processed it, and made inferences about the Rajneeshees. There are three salient components of this information-processing framework: Lazarus' stress and coping paradigm, which helps to explain why information was sought; the construct of "level of abstraction", which clarifies how individuals ascribed meaning to the material presented; and finally, the construct of scheme, which can be used to examine how individuals remembered information about the Rajneeshees.

In analysing the Rajneeshees' role in the conflict I will use the construct of "moral exclusion" and assess how this process amplified the conflict. In addition, the Rajneeshpuram conflict allowed the opportunity to study the content of social cognitive processes related to conflict: how the Rajneeshees' beliefs and values fostered hostilities, and how they themselves were transformed by the conflict.

Social psychology has generated many mini theories. Often these mini-theories are held in abeyance, removed from the context of specific historical events (Gergen, 1978). In this article mini-theories are used to explain, understand, and integrate the dynamics of the Rajneeshpuram conflict. What is meant by "understanding" can be best explained by the dichotomy of scientific knowledge proposed by Dubin (1969) of predicting versus understanding. Understanding can be conceived as similar to the Gestalt principle of "good fit" (Kohler, 1947).

History of Rajneeshpuram and the Conflict

The Rajneeshees purchased the 64,229-acre Big Muddy Ranch in Eastern Oregon in July, 1981. The closest city was Antelope, which was 18 miles away and had a population of fewer than 50. The Rajneeshees immediately began setting up the Rancho Rajneesh commune, later incorporated as the city-commune of Rajneeshpuram. What Rajneesh's followers or disciples (who are called Rajneeshees, Sannyasins, or Neo-Sannyasins), developed was a small city. By 1985 over 4,000 Sannyasins were living on the ranch, and they had built a hotel, shopping centre, airport, dam, sewage reclamation plant, townhouses, and many other amenities of a modern American town.

When the Rajneeshees first arrived they made a few peaceful overtures to the surrounding communities; nevertheless, within the year they became embroiled in a series of battles with their neighbours. The principal conflict related to land use. When the Rajneeshees first arrived, they stated that they were planning to build a small farm—the ranch land had been zoned for agricultural use. It soon became apparent that the Rajneeshees wanted to establish services and activities more common to a town. This conflict over land use quickly escalated to bitter hostility.

A focal point of conflict was the town of Antelope. Initially the Rajneeshees purchased only a few lots in Antelope. After a dispute with the public interest landuse group, the 1000 Friends of Oregon, over establishing the commune, and after Antelope denied the Rajneeshees a business permit for their mail-order operation, more Rajneeshees moved into town. In April 1982 the town of Antelope voted on disincorporation, to prevent the Rajneeshees from taking over the town. By this time enough Rajneeshees had moved into Antelope to defeat the measure. The following November,

Rajneeshees were elected to all but one seat on the Antelope city council. In May of 1982, the residents of Rancho Rajneesh (the commune) voted to incorporate the city of Rajneeshpuram. The control of the Antelope city council and questions of land use were not the only points of strife. The Rajneeshees aggravated the situation by raising city taxes and gaining control of the Antelope public school. They took an aggressive stance on many issues and became litigious, suing groups and individuals.

The Rajneeshees did not receive a cordial welcome to Oregon. Soon after the Rajneeshees arrived in Oregon, church leaders began denouncing Rajneesh and his followers. Petitions were circulated to rid the state of this supposed public menace. Letters to the editors in newspapers around the state reviled the Rajneeshees. One such letter on 15 April, 1982 stated, "Are we going to stand by and see another Sodom and Gomorrah rise, or are we going to make a stand for morality and our children's futures?" Another letter in March of that year declared, "It [the Rajneeshees] is a cancer in our midst and like a cancer will spread beyond control throughout the whole state."

Hostilities arose out of Rajneesh's daily drive into the town of Madras, which is about 50 miles from Rajneeshpuram. Awaiting his arrival at the edge of town, where Rajneesh would turn around and head back, was a group of protesters led by a local fundamentalist preacher. The Rajneeshees reacted by bussing in their followers to counterdemonstrate. The hostilities escalated, as did the number of protesters on each side. This specific confrontation was defused by the district attorney, who served as a negotiator, when the Rajneeshees agreed not to drive to Madras. This episode highlights the growing tension between the Rajneeshees and their neighbours.

A bombing of a Rajneeshee-owned hotel in Portland, in August of 1993, heightened the tension, and at Rajneeshpuram, the increasing display of semi-automatic weapons by the commune's "Peace Force" created a picture of imminent violence. There were rumours around the state that the National Guard would be sent in to arrest Rajneesh—the National Guard did survey Rajneeshpuram, as a first step, in case the were ordered to storm the commune. Concomitantly, the commune was embroiled in a series of legal battles. Suits were brought against the commune declaring that they city of Rajneeshpuram was illegally incorporated and that the city was a violation of the constitutional separation between church and state.

As Rajneesh did not speak publicly and gave few interviews—until October 1984—Ma Anand Sheela, the chief spokesperson and Rajneesh's personal secretary, became the *de facto* commune leader. She did little to foster cooperation or ease the conflict. Her speaking style was sharp, fiery, crude, caustic, arrogant, and defensive. Her posture not only abetted the hostilities, but it also attracted the media to Rajneeshpuram. Abruptly, on 14 September, 1985, Sheela and 15 to 20 other top officials left the commune. They were immediately denounced by Rajneesh, who accused them of perpetrating crimes inside and outside the commune. It was revealed that, unbeknownst to government officials and nearly all commune members, a secretive group had masterminded a series of criminal activities—including wiretapping, poisonings, arson, and attempted murder—that precipitated the largest criminal investigation in Oregon's history. According to the Office of the Attorney General, the blatantly illegal and criminal activities, such as the wiretapping, did not begin until the spring of 1984, three years after Rajneeshpuram began. After Sheela and two other leaders were extradited from West Germany, they entered a plea bargain on a range of charges; the most serious was the attempted murder of Rajneesh's physician, Swami Devaraj, a.k.a. George Meredith.

A month after Sheela's departure, Rajneesh was arrested in Charlotte, North Carolina, as he was purportedly fleeing the country. On 14 November, 1985, Rajneesh left the United States in accordance with a plea bargain on charges of arranging fraudulent marriages. These marriages were arranged so that foreign disciples could circumvent visa restrictions and remain in the United States. Two weeks after Rajneesh departed, commune officials decided that Rajneeshpuram was no longer economically viable, and members were asked to leave as soon as possible. The commune was sold, in December 1988, for 4.3 million dollars. Rajneesh returned to India after a controversial and circuitous world tour and died there in 1990. There are several accounts of Rajneeshpuram and the Rajneesh movement, including Abbott (1990), FitzGerald (1986), and Palmer (1988).

Before examining the question of why the public reaction to the Rajneeshees was so intense and negative long before the revelations of illegal acts, it is essential to assess whether the public actually had such strong feelings. It is possible that a few vocal individuals distorted the public sentiment and that the public was mildly opposed or indifferent to the Rajneeshees.

History and Methods of the Research Project

Our study of the Rajneeshees and Rajneeshpuram began in 1982. It continued through the break up of the commune (see Latkin *et al.*, 1887). We collected a range of data on the commune and on the public's perceptions of it. Social-psychological surveys and interviews conducted at Rajneeshpuram and a statewide survey on attitudes toward Rajneeshees comprised the bulk of the data. The majority of the interviews occurred in late 1985 and early 1986. The Rajneeshees strongly believed in what they were doing and that research would bring credibility to their enterprise, hence—after a lengthy process of negotiating and building rapport—agreed to our study of them. The administration of surveys and interviews reported here occurred after the author had spent a month as a participant observer and after months of observations, informal interviews, and focus groups.

Interview Procedures and Subjects

Forty interviews were conducted from November 1985 to May 1986. These interviews, ranging from one to three hours, were taped. Subjects for the interview were volunteers. The interviews were semi-structured or focus interviews (Denzin, 1978). The interview data were approached from the perspective of grounded theory (Glaser and Strauss, 1967). Many hypotheses associated with the interview materials arose out of a seminar approach to the analysis of qualitative data, as delineated by Strauss (1987). A more detailed description of the interview procedures has been reported elsewhere (Latkin, 1991).

Survey of Attitudes Toward Rajneeshees

From the summer of 1985 to the spring of 1986 we conducted a statewide telephone survey on attitudes toward the Rajneeshees (Katsikis and Laktin, 1988). Interviewers were trained using a standardised training and testing procedure developed by the University of Michigan's Survey Research Centre. To ensure reliability, a supervisor randomly listened to calls and filled out a reliability check list.

The target population of the survey was adult Oregonians. The cities selected for the study were restricted to those having a TIE line—the Oregon state system of higher education's low-cost telephone network. However, both high and low population areas were represented by the ten communities selected. The survey was intended to explore several hypotheses including: Are media habits related to attitudes? Are attitudes related to demographic factors? Are specific emotions such as fear and anger strong components of attitudes? And, is knowledge about Rajneeshees related to attitudes?

Survey Results and Discussion

Over 99 per cent of the 742 respondents had heard of the Rajneeshees, and the overwhelming response to the survey's attitude questions was negative: 80 per cent of the respondents agreed with the statement "Rajneeshees are a cult"; 69 per cent agreed that "Rajneeshees are brain-washed"; 75 per cent saw Rajneeshees as "outsiders", and 75 per cent of the respondents said "no" to the statement "I like Rajneeshees."

Respondents were well-informed about the Rajneeshees. Knowledge about the Rajneeshees was tabulated by the number of correct responses to five factual questions, such as the name of their spiritual leader (Rajneesh or Bhagwan) and the colour of their clothing (colours of the sunrise or red). One point was assigned for each correct answer. The mean score on knowledge scale was 2.88. Only 2.5 per cent of the respondents missed all the questions, and only 4.5 per cent responded correctly to all five.

It has been proposed that the antagonism toward new religions is in part due to competition between established religions and new religions (Kilbourne and Richardson, 1984). If this were the case, then it would be expected that highly religious individuals would have negative attitudes, for their church would be integral to their identity. We did find partial support for this theory.

People who reported themselves as having no religion had significantly fewer negative opinions, as did Jews and Mormons, but by no means did these groups hold positive attitudes. Catholics were the most negative. Religiousness, as measured by the frequency of church attendance, was only marginally correlated with negative attitudes toward Rajneeshees ($r = .10$, $p < .04$). Political conservatism, measured by a standard one-item question, was highly correlated with negative attitudes toward the Rajneeshees ($r = .25$, $p < .001$). Although on the level of analysis of the individual there was not a strong relationship between religiosity and attitudes, religion was a factor in the controversy. Some of the most vocal opponents of the Rajneeshees were Christian ministers.

The Rajneeshees believed that hostility toward them stemmed from bigotry and envy. This lay analysis is in essence a weak frustration-aggression based on deprivation hypothesis (Berkowitz, 1978). The Rajneeshees believed that the public was envious of their wealth, life-style, and level of happiness. We do not have any data to address this hypothesis.

Another explanation for the public's dislike of the Rajneeshees is that the Rajneeshees were engaged in unscrupulous activities, and therefore, the public's reaction was reasonable and logical. Interestingly, we found that once the actual criminal activities were disclosed, in late 1985, respondents became slightly more positive toward the Rajneeshees. If attitudes were solely based on actual behaviour of the Rajneeshees, then the disclosure of the illegal activities should have produced more negative attitudes—not more positive. This positive change in attitudes may have been due to Sheela becoming a scapegoat.

Cognitive Processes and the Public's Reaction to the Rajneeshees

The public's reaction to the Rajneeshees can be better understood in light of Lazarus' stress and coping paradigm. Lazarus (1966) has hypothesised that coping is a dynamic process, in which events are first appraised to determine whether they are benign-positive, irrelevant, or threatening. If they are seen as threatening the situation is reappraised—secondary appraisal—for possible actions. Coping responses are then invoked. Coping is not always constructive; often it involves managing emotions and can include such diverse behaviours as denigration, anger, humour, and information seeking. Lazarus' paradigm has been researched on three levels: interpersonal, intrapersonal, and physiological (Folkman and Lazarus, 1980). I am proposing that coping also occurs on a group level. In the present case, the Rajneeshees were new and an unknown entity. They needed to be assessed for potential danger. The government and especially the media are charged in American society with primary appraisal (Patterson, 1980); others have described this governmental role as that of consumer protector (Beckford, 1986; Richardson, 1986). The outcome of the appraisal process was that the Rajneeshees were seen as threatening.

Gathering information on the Rajneeshees was a form of both primary and secondary appraisal. This information was negative and indicated that the Rajneeshees were threatening. Many Rajneeshees' behaviours were unpredictable (the Rajneeshees relished behaving this way), and one of the most stressful conditions is that of lack of control or unpredictability (Cohen, 1980). The public then engaged in secondary appraisal and coping. Actions by the government were means of behavioural coping: handling the threat of the Rajneeshees by investigating Rajneeshpuram, enforcing the laws, and making new laws. In fact, the office of the Attorney General and other state offices were barraged with phone calls and letters asking them to do something about the Rajneeshee problem.

One threatening aspect of Rajneeshpuram was that it was perceived to be an all-encompassing social structure—an institution that serves all domains and needs, e.g., employment, spiritual, leisure, and social (Goffman, 1963). Except in extreme situations such as mental institutions and hospitals, these types of institutions are seen as too powerful, over controlling, and diminishing of individuality (Robbins, 1988).

Some forms of coping were those of problem solving; other forms were palliative, such as emotional discharge—as seen in the letters to the editor about the Rajneeshees—and were invoked to reduce unpleasant feelings. One coping response was a legal remedy: the claim that Rajneeshpuram violated the separation between church and state, was illegal, and therefore should be dismantled. The stress and coping process was cyclic. The Rajneeshees were seen as threatening; more information was gathered, but cognitive processes of cult schema and level of abstraction amplified the Rajneeshees' negative characteristics, which heightened concern and elicited hostile actions.

The Cult Schema

The concept of schema is a useful heuristic for understanding how the public process information about the Rajneeshee, and the ensuing antipathy to them. Schemata are cognitive representations of information, which contain both attributes and relationships among the attributes. Research on schemata has posited that they guide perceptions, memory, and inference of social situations. One of the most studied schemata are role schemata. These are frameworks for processing information about the members of a social group such as men, women, athletes, introverts, or computer programmers. Schemata can bias perceptions. Once a schema is activated, there is a tendency to look for confirming evidence that coincides with the schema, even to misinterpret events or have faulty memory of them to make them fit. For example, Sagar and Schofield (1980) found that both "black" and "white" subjects rated the ambiguous acts of blacks as meaner and more threatening than when the same acts were performed by whites. Sagar and Schofield interpreted these results to support their contention that, since there are more negative traits in the black schema (for both blacks and whites) than in the white schema, ambiguous events involving blacks are more likely to be perceived as negative. Schemata are enduring structures. Memory for information consistent with the schema has been found to be better than memory for inconsistent information (Fiske and Taylor, 1984).

We did not conduct a rigorous, experimental assessment of the components of the cult-member schema; however, we believe that it contains the notions of brain-washing, gullibility, dangerousness, and being susceptible to manipulation. There have been several salient events and groups in the last few decades that may have had an indelible influence on the cult schema. The label of "cult" has been applied to followers of Charles Manson and the Reverend Moon. Both groups have been portrayed highly unfavourably. The Jonestown mass suicide and murders are also woven into the cult schema. Perhaps the reason researchers of new religions shy away from the label of "cult" is that they recognise the strength and negative valence of the cult schema. New religious movements do have a highly negative image in the print media (van Driel and Richardson, 1988).

The cult schema affected the way Rajneeshees were

perceived and treated by the press and other outsiders. People looked for and interpreted behaviours that confirmed their cult schema. A byproduct of their cult schema (Fiske and Taylor, 1984) was observed in the survey results: respondents consistently reported that Rajneeshees were forced to give up all their worldly possessions in order to join the group, which was not true. In a study of perceptions of Rajneeshees, we asked three classes of university students the open-ended question, "When you think of the word 'Rajneeshee' what comes to mind?" The word "red" was given 30 per cent of the time, "Rolls-Royce" 18 per cent, and "cult" or "brain-washed" 20 per cent.

Level of Abstraction

Another useful heuristic for understanding the public's processing of information about the Rajneeshees is that of level of abstraction. It is often difficult for the public to evaluate the behaviour of members of new religions. One reason for this incomprehensibility is the level of abstraction used to understand behaviour. Not only can an event have a variety of interpretations, but it can also be interpreted on a variety of levels of abstraction. The act of writing on paper, while listening to a speaker, and later re-examining the paper, is abstracted to be called studying; sometimes it is characterised as learning. People tend to abstract their own actions to the highest possible level of identification (Vallacher and Wegner, 1987). For the Rajneeshees, the wearing of the colour red and other colours of the sunrise was identified as a re-affirmation of their spiritual search and quest for personal growth. But to the public it was simply seen as wearing red. It was considered bizarre, deviant, and threatening. The public did not construe such behaviour as spiritual.

Another method of conceptualising this difference in perspective can be seen in the role of symbols at

Rajneeshpuram. Geertz (1973) states that symbols are quintessential to religion. They provide order and motivation. Yet for individuals outside the religious system, the symbols lose their power and meaning, and are interpreted out of context and without their original significance (Johnson, 1985). For example, the Rajneeshees' *mālā*, which was a necklace with 108 beads (one for each type of meditation) and a picture of Rajneesh, was seen by the Rajneeshees as a tool for meditation and as a source of inspiration. To non-Rajneeshees the *mālā* was seen as proof that Rajneeshees were automatons controlled by their master.

The Rajneeshees' Role in the Conflict

As delineated above, the conflict was not a one-sided affair. The Rajneeshees were active participants. A letter dated 12 January, 1985 by the mayor of Rajneeshpuram exemplifies the antagonism the Rajneeshees vented toward government officials. In responding to a letter written by the state Director of Building Codes—that was addressed to the "Putative City of Rajneeshpuram"—the Mayor of Rajneeshpuram, Krishna Deva, states, "Knowingly or unknowingly, you have taken a role in the Attorney General's fascist play, which assumes this City's guilt [of the legality of its incorporation] before it has been proven." The Mayor goes on to say, "In the future please address mail according to reality, which is that the City of Rajneeshpuram exists, and not according to the distorted fantasies of a man [the Attorney General] attempting to use this community as a stepping stone to fulfil his personal political ambitions." Other acts of hostility included harassment and poisonings of townspeople in Antelope and of government officials who came to Rajneeshpuram to review city records.

On the level of analysis of the individual, there were several reasons to expect that the Rajneeshees would work to minimize conflict. First, the vast majority of Rajneeshees were from middle-class and upper-middle-class backgrounds. In one survey, 81 per cent of the respondents characterised their families as white collar or professional, and over one-third of the Rajneeshees had advanced degrees (Latkin *et al.*, 1987). Such a well-educated group would, presumably, place a premium on conflict resolution, discuss their grievances rationally, and settle disputes diplomatically. Second, as the Rajneeshees placed a high value on interpersonal sensitivity—over half had been in psychotherapy—it would be expected that they would be highly empathetic and not degrade others. Third, one of the group's strongly professed beliefs was individuality; this value should have aided in immunizing them to the effects of pressure from other Rajneeshees to be hostile to non-Rajneeshees; and finally, as they were the subject of discrimination, one would anticipate that this experience would sensitise them to prejudice and discrimination.

Considering their level of education, psychological sensitivity, valuing of individuality, and experience of prejudice, the Rajneeshees' role in the conflict seems paradoxical. It is plausible that the leadership of Rajneeshpuram was hostile to outsiders, whereas most Rajneeshees were not. We did not systematically survey the residents of Rajneeshpuram on their attitudes toward outsiders; however, our data suggest that the leadership's antagonistic rhetoric was consistent with members' attitudes.

Rajneeshees' Attitudes Toward Outsiders

There were three sources of data suggesting that the Rajneeshees held negative attitudes toward non-Rajneeshees. First, when asked what they planned to do after leaving Rajneeshpuram, Rajneeshees consistently said in the interviews that they wanted to be around other Rajneeshees and did not look forward to interacting with non-Rajneeshees, whom they regarded as intolerant, bigoted, and materialistic. Second, a consistent response to both survey and interview questions on how they reacted to Rajneesh's departure from the commune was that although they were personally sad to see him leave, they were glad that he was finally free from the injustice, bigotry, and intolerance that he was forced to suffer in America. They believed that Rajneesh had been persecuted by narrow-minded, prejudicial Americans, who were out to destroy him. Third, in a follow-up, post-Rajneeshpuram mail survey, many respondents expressed surprise that outside the commune they had met good-hearted individuals who were not Sannyasins. From the interview materials and the follow-up survey, there is unambiguous evidence that the prejudice toward non-Rajneeshees spread beyond the leadership to the other commune members.

As previously mentioned, the Rajneeshees' view of the outside was not purely illusory. Indubitably, hatred of and prejudice toward Rajneeshees did exist. The community received hate mail; bumper-stickers declaring "bag the Bhagwan" and "Antelope, better dead than red" could be bought in neighbouring towns; road signs to Rajneeshpuram were fraught with bullet holes; fundamentalist Christians would drive down the main street of Rajneeshpuram, get out of their cars, read from their Bibles, and make pronouncements about how Rajneesh was the devil and that Rajneeshees would all go to hell; Rajneeshees were often portrayed in the press as manipulated stooges; and as our survey discovered, around the state there was a strongly negative attitude toward them.

The Role of the Media

The Rajneeshees, naive to the nature and habits of news

reporting, assumed that the media would be dispassionate and report on their praiseworthy activities, such as their land reclamation and high yield farming practices. The Rajneeshees held the belief that the media was impartial and objective, i.e., there is one-to-one correspondence between what is reported and the event itself, and the proper place for reporters' opinions is on the editorial page. This view of the media is common (Smith, 1979). The Rajneeshees were shocked and upset by the coverage they received, which focused on conflict and the negative. The Rajneeshees would regularly view television news clippings of them, which were almost uniformly negative and at times highly inaccurate (Myers, 1986). This portrayal led them to believe that the media and the state were prejudiced, bigoted, and out to destroy them. Furthermore, as the news reports were at times inaccurate, the Rajneeshees tended to discount the accurate reports as well.

Rajneeshee leaders did little to foster a positive media image. They believed that there was no such thing as bad publicity; all press was good press. In an interview with the author, Sheela stated that Rajneesh himself had taught her this—using Richard Nixon's career as an example. Sheela stated that Rajneesh claimed that the negative publicity Nixon received as a senator and during his first presidential campaign helped him in his subsequent presidential race.

Negative publicity did serve as advertising, a vehicle to get their message across to society. Media attention also helped to legitimise the commune to its members: if someone or something is receiving media attention there must be a reason for that attention; it must be important. This media attention became addictive. Consequently, Rajneeshees had to think of more and more grandiose ways to get media coverage. This media craving was amplified by the Rajneeshees' belief that if they were to keep a low profile the state of Oregon would trample over their rights. In an interview, one commune leader stated that during a period when Sheela purposefully kept quiet, legal decisions suddenly began to go against the Rajneeshees.

Moral Exclusion

In the midst of hostilities the Rajneeshees were unable to see that they held their own stereotypes and had engaged in the process of "moral exclusion". Moral exclusion has been defined to occur "when individuals or groups are perceived as outside the boundary in which moral values, rules, and considerations of fairness apply". De-individuation, condescension, transcendent ideology, and derogation, which are hypothesised to be involved in the process of moral exclusion, were all apparent at Rajneeshpuram. Individuals "who are morally excluded are perceived as non-entities, expendable, or undeserving; consequently, harming them appears acceptable, appropriate, or just" (Opotow, 1990: 1). This rubric of moral exclusion readily applies to some of the more heinous behaviours the Rajneeshees committed, such as the poisonings and arson. Since non-Rajneeshees were not fully human, they became expendable, objects to be used as part of the leaders' masterplan.

Moral exclusion was evident in how the Rajneeshees viewed themselves and non-Rajneeshees. Rajneeshees clearly felt that they were superior beings on a higher level of consciousness. Several Rajneeshees mentioned that the commune as a whole developed an arrogant countenance. One commune member, who was interviewed several months after the demise of the commune said, "I guess that's part of our arrogance . . . that we believed in, or bought into, about being better than the rest of Oregon or humanity or whatever." The Rajneeshees saw themselves as happier and better adjusted than outsiders. This ethnocentric view was not merely the result of feeling satisfied with their lifestyle and values, but they constantly compared themselves—favourably—with others.

One antecedent of moral exclusion was the strong cognitive and affective bond the Rajneeshees had with their group. Social identity theory, based primarily on the work of Tajfel (1978) and Turner (1981), states that when individuals identify with a group this group becomes part of their self-concept. A link between the self and the group arises as does a re-definition of self, in which the individual's behaviour becomes congruent with the group goals and actions. The literature on social identity theory postulates three conditions that enhance group identity: distinctness of the group's values and practices, prestige in belonging to the group, and salience of the outgroup. All three conditions were present at Rajneeshpuram. Distinctness was augmented by the Rajneeshees' dress and physical isolation; prestige was apparent in the belief that their group was spiritually elite, and from what they saw of how they were characterised in the media, the outside was "worlds" apart.

Often the Rajneeshees would defend the outlandish and childish acts of their leaders, such as swearing on prime-time television. Why did they support such antics? According to social identity theory the individual Rajneeshees identified with their group and representatives of it; so disciples felt that an attack on their leaders was an attack on them, and therefore, they rallied to defend the leaders, the group, and, in turn, themselves.

Another dimension to moral exclusion is stereotyping. The Rajneeshees stereotyped politicians as one-dimensional, shallow, unfeeling, and stupid—as seen in the letter to the Director of Building Codes. In general, outsiders were seen as inflexible and immutable, so there was no rationale for reasoning with them. According to attribution theory (Heider, 1980), Rajneeshees made stable and internal attributions to outsiders' hostile acts: outsiders had been and would always be prejudiced. (An unstable attribution would be, for example, anger, and an external attribution would be that some action by the Rajneeshees made outsiders angry.) These stereotypes and attributions helped to justify the Rajneeshees' hostile behaviour; there was no sense in trying to reason with outsiders or treat these "rednecks" equitably. Much has been written on how degrading the enemy, portraying them as homogeneous and less than human, disinhibits aggression (Allport, 1954; Zimbardo, 1970). Few Rajneeshees could see that they had articulated a stereotype of outsiders, were engaging in moral exclusion, and that this process facilitated aggression and prevented interaction or accommodation.

Content Specific Beliefs and Conflict

The intergroup conflict advanced and reinforced beliefs and values that were consonant with the Rajneeshees' perceptions of the conflict. Often beliefs were integrated into tactics. One such belief was that of "shaking people up" by acting outrageously. The Rajneeshees believed that shaking people up had a beneficial effect of forcing a new perspective, thereby gaining a new insight. For example, when a county inspector came to view the city records, a group surrounded and began chanting and harassing him. It was felt that this strategy would catch their opponents off guard, eliciting a hasty and rash reaction, one that was unwise and would expose their opponents' prejudices, thus giving the Rajneeshees a tactical advantage. What was thought to be outrageous was often debasement and facilitated moral exclusion. Several studies have found that once individuals display hostility or debase others, the aggressors rate the victims less favourably (Berkowitz, 1972; Cialdini, 1980; Zimbardo, 1970). With the Rajneeshees, this tactic of shaking up intensified hostilities. It reduced the Rajneeshees' opinions of their opponents, enhanced psychological distance, and helped to promote conflict.

Calling government leaders such epithets as "bigots" and "narrow-minded" illustrates another of the Rajneeshees' beliefs. They maintained that it is of the utmost importance to be candid and state even the most unpopular opinion. This tactic of name calling allowed the Rajneeshees to portray themselves as an oppressed minority and garner sympathy. Here again is an example of venting hostility leading to degradation of the adversary.

Although the Rajneeshees believed that the govenment was determined to destroy them, they held the belief that of all the government institutions the judiciary would treat them the most equitably. They believed that the courts would be less prejudicial, less political than the other branches of government, and more likely to give them a fair hearing. They also reasoned that they had the advantage in this arena: several Sannyasins had been prominent lawyers; they had the financial resources to hire the "best" outside legal counsel, and could—and did—train many Sannyasins to be paralegals. This legalistic method of conflict resolution often led to a heightening of tension. Instead of exploring avenues of compromise, the Rajneeshees would build a legal case that emphasised how they had been unfairly singled out and harassed. The judicial method of conflict resolution facilitated a win-lose dynamic (Blake and Mouton, 1979). The concern at Rajneeshpuram became winning, not negotiating or attempting to resolve differences. This legal remedy did not reduce discord.

Much has been written on cognitive processes and

biases and their role in conflict, e.g., selective memory for negative outgroup behaviours, attribution errors, failure to attend to disconfirming information, and stereotyping (Pruitt and Rubin, 1986). Social perceptions are not only cognitive processes; they also fit into the group's beliefs and values. As conflicts evolve it becomes difficult to distinguish the interplay between cognitive processes that bias information, and values and beliefs. Moreover, as values and beliefs are not always internally consistent, those that conform to the pressures of the social space become dominant.

Conclusion

One criticism of social-psychological research on conflict is that most studies use college students, who have little knowledge of or concern for the issues (Pruitt and Rubin, 1986). This was not so at Rajneeshpuram; both sides were intensely preoccupied with the conflict. The Rajneeshpuram conflict provided evidence of external validity for the role of social and cognitive processes in exacerbating intergroup conflict.

I have endeavoured to present factors that contributed to the public's antipathy of the Rajneeshees, and how the Rajneeshees' beliefs and perceptions fostered the hostilities. The present case study highlights the fact that cognitive biases are subtle, blurred shadows, based, in part, in truth. By no means have I presented an exhaustive list of social-psychological elements in the Rajneeshpuram conflict. For example, I have not touched on any of the cultural differences that may have contributed to the conflict or on the role of a charismatic leader (Johnson, 1992). Galanter's (1989) social system perspective also could have been applied to Rajneeshpuram. The emphasis placed on the psychological, subjective aspects of the conflict does not negate the objective roots, such as the Rajneeshees taking over the town of Antelope. It is important to note that understanding the causes of the hostilities is by no means an excuse for the Rajneeshees' behaviour. Let us not forget that the people in the neighbouring town of Antelope lived in terror of the Rajneeshees, that Rajneeshee leaders admitted responsibility for poisonings within and outside the commune, and that the state spent millions of dollars on the Rajneeshee legal cases.

Throughout this article I have described how the Rajneeshees' views of outsiders became a self-fulfilling prophecy. Early in our research we interviewed the mayor of Rajneeshpuram, Krishna Deva, about the hostilities and means of conflict resolution. The mayor stated that it was impossible for the Rajneeshees to accommodate; the other side was prejudicial and intent on destroying them. The mayor felt that the Rajneeshee must aggressively defend themselves. The Rajneeshees' view of the public as hostile contributed to their antics and tactics, led defenders of the Rajneeshees to withdraw support, and encouraged anti-Rajneeshee groups to become outspoken—fulfilling the Rajneeshees' prophecy. In addition, the Rajneeeesheess' antagonistic behaviour increased the public's overt animosity, which confirmed the Rajneeshees' view about outsiders.

The public's views about the Rajneeshees also became a self-fulfilling prophecy. The public initially viewed the Rajneeshees as deviant, brain-washed, and untrustworthy. This attitude was communicated to Rajneeshees. To protect themselves from these dangerous outsiders, the Rajneeshees' leadership demanded strict obedience, diminishing individual liberty, so that indeed the Rajneeshees did give up many individual liberties—just as the public suspected.

Although I have discussed the explanatory power of social psychology in analysing intergroup conflict, this does not negate the role of religion on both sides of the conflict. It was Christian leaders who were the most vocal in opposing the Rajneeshees. Fundamentalists stood on Main Street and preached that Rajneesh was the devil, and signs on land adjacent to Rajneeshpuram made similar pronouncements. Though the Rajneeshees claimed that they were not a religion, the violence was in part due to their commitment to a spiritual leader, and the Rajneeshees' beliefs about human nature led them to design an organisation that fostered conflict.

The enormity of the crimes perpetrated at Rajneeshpuram surprised many individuals. Although there were discussions about storming the commune to arrest Rajneesh, the precipitous fall of Rajneeshpuram and the revelation of the enormity of crimes committed by the Rajneeshees came as a surprise to scholars, law enforcement officials, and the news media. This failure to predict the intensity of Rajneeshpuram conflict might be due in part to a tendency to underestimate the power of religious beliefs to influence behaviours. This article provides an analysis of several features of the Rajneeshpuram conflict, yet the role of religiosity in the conflict has not been fully elucidated.

A final caveat is that although the Rajneeshees held negative attitudes toward outsiders, most Rajneeshees at Rajneeshpuram were indifferent to the intergroup conflict. It was not real to them. They were unaware of criminal activities and unconcerned about intergroup tensions. For example, although Sannyasins at Rajneeshpuram could buy a daily Oregon newspaper, few did. The outside world, the political world, was not relevant to their spiritual pursuits and yearnings for personal growth.

Though Rajneeshpuram was a source of bitter conflict, what the Rajneeshees built during their short stay in Oregon was extraordinary. It is unfortunate that they were forced to abandon the commune they worked so hard to build. A greater misfortune is that the Rajneeshees and the public helped to strengthen and perpetuate stereotypes and pejorative images of groups that deviate from the mainstream.

The Rajneeshees' headquarters is now back in Poona, India, and their leader, Rajneesh, has died. In the ensuing years it will be interesting to see how and if the group modifies its behaviours. How will it assimilate its experience in Oregon? Will it develop a system of internal and external conflict resolution, or will the Rajneeshees remain antagonistic to outsiders? (1992)

Chapter Sixteen

Charisma and Abdication: A Study of the Leadership of Bhagwan Shree Rajneesh

SUSAN J. PALMER

A study of the career of Bhagwan Shree Rajneesh, the 55-year old Guru from India, reveals a leadership which constantly fluctuates in its style and in its authoritative claims. The history of his movement, the Rajneesh Foundation International (RFI), is remarkable for its abrupt changes in policy, and the varied and contradictory demands made upon its members. Due to his considerable personal charm and a certain dramatic flair, Rajneesh was able to render these divagations coherent and meaningful to his disciples for whom their leader's inconsistencies were an integral part of his charisma. As one member explained:

> When you are with Bhagwan you never know what to expect. He takes you on a journey that is full of surprises and mystery. He says what he is

> experiencing at that moment, so he might say the opposite the next day. If you are looking for a dogma, a creed, you are wasting your time. He is a reflection of life itself which is a paradox and full of contradictions.

In order to interpret this pattern of unpredictable and apparently arbitrary change which has characterised Rajneesh's leadership, I will refer to Roy Wallis' theory of relationships between charisma and institutionalisation which is outlined in his paper, "Charisma, Commitment, and Control in a New Religious Movement" (1982).

Wallis attempts to refine Max Weber's theory of charismatic authority, which he finds "relatively brief and not entirely lacking in ambiguity" (Wallis, 1982: 73). While Weber's theory traces the various routes to bureaucratisation or traditionalisation after the leader's death, Wallis is concerned with the living leader's struggle to keep his or her charismatic authority untrammelled by the forces of institutionalisation. Wallis focuses on the career of Moses David, the prophet-founder of the Children of God, a deviant Christian group which originated in California in 1968, and then analyses the relationship between charisma and its "nemesis", institutionalisation, by identifying four possible responses of charismatic leaders to this problem. The responses are: Encouragement, acquiescence, Displacement, and Resistance. Wallis then argues that the seemingly erratic behaviour of "Mo" David can be interpreted as an example of Resistance, a deliberate strategy intended to undermine the attempts of his followers to stabilise and institutionalise his movement. He describes this response as follows:

> ....in which the charismatic leader foresees the threat of institutionalisation subverting his

> authority and takes active and effective steps to forestall it (Wallis, 1982: 119).

In attempting to explain Rajneesh's leadership as an example of Resistance, I encountered a series of obstacles which suggest that the relationship between charisma and institution building is more complex than Wallis' four categories allow for. Although Rajneesh employed the strategy of Resistance at many points in his career, he also adopted the strategy of Encourgement. Wallis describes Encouragement as a process:

> in which the charismatic leader embraces the possibilities involved in institutionalisation and actively directs the process in such a way as to control it and utilise institutionalised structures and procedures to buttress his authority, rather than allowing it to constrain him (Wallis, 1982: 117).

In outlining the seven phases of Rajneesh's career, I have attempted to show that he vacillated between these two extremes. On the one hand he encouraged strong leaders within his movement and conferred upon them considerable power in decision-making. On the other hand he occasionally challenged them or destroyed their institutions if they were steering the movement in a direction not to his liking. Since these two policies are apparently contradictory responses to institutionalisation, it is clear the Rajneesh's case represents a different relationship between charisma and institution building than Mo's.

The second difficulty in fitting Rajneesh's case to Wallis' model of Resistance, is that Rajneesh did not appear to share Mo's desire to control and direct his followers' lives. The outstanding example which illustrates this is Rajneesh's announcement on September 26, 1985, that he was renouncing his role of Guru and ending his religion, Rajneeshism. He advised his followers on this occasion to stop wearing red and the *mālā* (necklace bearing Rajneesh's photograph) which were symbols of initiation into the master-disciple relationship. This extraordinary gesture might appear to be an extreme case of Resistance, as it delivered the death blow to the institutions of the movement, but instead of strengthening the leader's authority over his followers, it weakened it (see phase seven). Therefore I would like to propose that a fifth category be added to Wallis' four which represents a new relationship between charisma and institutionalisation. This I shall call Abdication. In order to explain the vacillations in Rajneesh's leadership, to interpret the meaning of Abdication, and to explore the inner logic of this new category my strategy will be as follows:

(1) To describe the peculiar nature of Rajneesh's charisma, and to examine the mechanisms whereby he protects and enhances it.

(2) To describe seven phases of Rajneesh's career, which represent different strategic responses to the problem of institutionalisation and exhibit his tendency to vacillate between the two extremes of Resistance and Encouragement.

(3) To argue that a close examination of Rajneesh's career reveals that his incompatibility with the process of institutionalisation arose not from his desire to exact total obedience from his followers (as was the case with "Mo"), but rather from a reluctance to assume the responsible, authorising role. By distinguishing between two aspects of charismatic authority, (i) Performance, and (ii) Responsibility, I will attempt to prove that Rajneesh's behaviour indicated a desire for the adulation, deference, and fame that come with performance, but a dislike for the responsibility that leadership entails. I will then argue that Rajneesh was a brilliant performer but a weak or recalcitrant pastor, and that he chose to delegate

the responsible role to various members of his core group. His final gesture of Abdication I interpret as his solution to the problem of responsibility and of institutionalisation, in that it enabled him to get rid of his fully committed followers, or "flock", while retaining his devoted (and rotating) audience.

Methodology

This study is based on my involvement with the Montreal Rajneesh centre as a participant-observer from October 1984 to September 1986. During this period I interviewed ten Sannyasins and attended five therapy groups and various ritual and social events at the centre. Initially my aim was to collect data for my Ph.D. dissertation on women in spiritual communes, but when Rajneeshpuram fell I became fascinated by Rajneesh himself. Throughout the exercise I managed to remain impervious to his charisma, but not to his charm. I feel it is important to note that while Wallis' theory is a useful tool for interpreting the history of the RFI, it is inadequate as a means of fathoming the inner workings of the complex and creative mind of a spiritual master. That is to say, this study is not meant to imply that Rajneesh is acting out of secular motives rather than responding to an inner religious drive.

The Nature of Rajneesh's Charisma

Rajneesh was born in 1931 in Kuchwada, India, to a Jain family of wealthy cloth merchants. While teaching philosophy at the University of Jabalpur he laid the foundation for his career as a spiritual leader by giving lecture tours in which he expounded his eclectic and controversial ideas. He conducted meditation camps, and in 1966 resigned his teaching post to travel across India criticising local religions and preaching that the individual was his own religion or god. In 1968 he delivered a series of lectures on sex as a meditative first step on the path to enlightenment, which attracted a large following of American and European tourists. By 1970 he had settled in Bombay and begun to initiate a group of disciples, which marked his transition from an intellectual critic of religion to a spiritual master.

If a leader's charisma can be measured by the number of his followers, Rajneesh's authority has been considerable, extending to approximately 350,000 Sannyasins, or initiates, according to the claim of the *Rajneesh Times,* October 14, 1983. The *Oregonian* notes, "Figures supplied by Rajneeshee officials and by outside observers..... were often wildly different" and quotes an "insider's figure of 60,000" (*Oregonian,* 1985: 3). Rajneesh manifested his charisma through his "discourses" or public lectures, which have been transcribed into several languages in over 350 books and also recorded on videocassette. These discourses have had an extraordinary effect on his followers. Several Sannyasins I interviewed said they "fell in love with Bhagwan" through exposure to his discourses. Even his critics attest to the power of Rajneesh's presence. Sally Belfrage, who wrote a rather disparaging account of life in the Rajneesh Ashram in India, confessed on viewing him in person, "He was AB-SO-LUTE-LY-R-IVET-ING" (Belfrage, 1981: 131). The *Oregonian* claims it is his message rather than his presence which has attracted disciples:

> Their Guru's lectures... tell his disciples to live life to its fullest, to abandon their own egos in favour of a communal consciousness and to view sex as... creative energy leading to enlightenment. Sin and guilt are not worth worrying about and everyone has the potential to realise a personal divinity through daily meditation and worship (*Oregonian,* 1985: 2).

Rajneesh, however, corresponds to Weber's model of

the exemplary leader, not the ethical prophet:

> ...the prophet may be an exemplary man who, by his personal example, demonstrates to others the way to spiritual salvation, as in the case of the Buddha. The preaching of this type of prophet says nothing about a divine mission or an ethical duty, but rather directs itself to the self-interest of those who crave salvation, recommending to them the same path as he himself traversed (Eisenstadt, 1968: 263).

Rajneesh is the living example of his message of self-realisation:

> I am absolutely content. If I were to die this very moment my life would be complete (*The Way of the Heart*, 1984: videocassette).

His charismatic authority is based on his claim to be the "Enlightened One" who returns throughout the millennia to awaken spiritually an elite group of seekers. Many of his disciples believe they have resumed work with him begun in a previous life. Rajneesh stresses the notion that the master-disciple relationship transcends even the limitations of death.

Weber states:

> The...leader may be required periodically to offer miraculous signs as proof of his powers in order to maintain [his followers'] commitment (Weber, 1947: 359).

A testimonial to Rajneesh's power of maintaining relationships through the reincarnation cycle is offered by Ma Anand Vivek, an Englishwoman who has lived with him since 1971, whom he describes as his "caretaker". Rajneesh claimed she was the reincarnation of his childhood sweetheart, Sashi, who, before she died in 1947, made him promise to wait for her return, Vivek states:

> One of the first things Bhagwan said to me... was, "Do you remember me?" I went click! "I remember that you're someone I loved very much" (Joshi, 1982: 107).

Unlike many well-known spiritual leaders who assume the role and image of father in relation to their followers (as, for example, Reverend Moon), Rajneesh is described by his disciples as a lover, and, paradoxically, a child. Although he appeared to be, at age 55, a frail old man with long white hair and whiskers, his personality was that of a mischievous and intellectually precocious child. He was surrounded by his core group of attractive women who played the role of the doting (but sexually liberated and expressive) mother to the brilliant, capricious prodigy.

Wallis notes:

> Since the charismatic identity is precarious, it must be protected against subversion or challenge by hiding the prophet away from general contact, carefully vetting all who may come into his presence, and immediately excluding those who do not display complete surrender (Wallis, 1982: 5).

To this end the core group at the Ashram in India created a distance between Bhagwan and the large mass of his following. A bodyguard controlled access to the Guru's presence. Sally Belfrage describes the procedure governing admission to the evening *darśana* at Poona:

> At least half a dozen people are turned away from *darśana* every night, it seems, for failing to pass the sniff-at-the-gate test, which has become more stringent lately because one woman slipped through with a perceptible odour of perfume and it

> made Bhagwan sick the whole of the next day. Some people have been turned away....I have washed my hair eight times....Śiva, a red-bearded Scottish Sannyasin who seems to be his chief bodyguard intones the drill before the smelling starts. Personal questions about Bhagwan are not permitted. Do not go nearer to Bhagwan Shree Rajneesh than a meter. Do not touch him except his feet. If you are turned away, wash harder next time (Belfrage, 1981: 137ff.).

An important feature of Bhagwan's special status (and regarded in the RFI as a sign of enlightenment) is his reputed autonomy and self-sufficiency. Throughout the RFI literature this notion is stressed. Stories of his childhood picture him as an independent, anti-authoritarian being who was impossible to influence or control. Even in infancy he was supposedly not dependent on his mother:

> It is said that the child neither cried nor accepted any milk for the first three days (*Sannyas* 5, 1980: 8).

Bhagwan has described himself as follows:

> I have never been initiated into society. I entered as an individual, and I have remained aloof and separate like an island (*Sannyas* 5, 1980: 10).

In this respect he remained distant from his Sannyasins, whose communal lifestyle and encounter group experiences encourage gregarious behaviour and physical and emotional intimacy.

The Seven Phases of Rajneesh's Career

Phase I—Initiation and Discipleship: Claiming Charisma

In 1970 Rajneesh created his ritual of *initiation darśana* or "taking Sannyas", in which he touched initiates on the "third eye", endowed them with Sanskrit names, gave each a *mālā* (necklace of wooden beads bearing Rajneesh's photograph) and required them to wear orange (later changed to red).

Through this ritual Rajneesh established a following and claimed a charismatic status as an enlightened master. He explained the meaning of initiation as a surrender of the ego to the master:

> When you become a Sannyasin I want to destroy that identity... When all these identities have been destroyed you will know who you are: the unidentified, the nameless, the formless, the indefinable (Joshi, 1982: 17).

Rajneesh began to live in a close community of devoted followers which he termed his "Buddhafield":

> To create a Buddhafield, to create a *saṅgha* means you are now creating an alternate society. You are no longer a single individual; you are gathering power... .Now you can create a revolution (Joshi, 1982: 100).

Robin Theobald had observed that an "Attitude of complete submission is what is required of disciples who from part of the *Gemeinde*" (Wallis, 1982: 107). The Buddhafield corresponds to Theobald's description of the *Gemeinde* or household living in "an emotional form of communal relationship" with the leader. Spheres of authority are not clearly defined and the leader assigns duties on an *ad hoc* basis and intervenes at will. Members are chosen not for their skill or training, but rather, Weber argues, for their charismatic qualities. Wallis adds that an equally important quality is the intensity of their devotion. Rajneesh's core group of women invariably described themselves as "in love with" their leader.

Phase II—From Acharya to Bhagwan: Building Charisma

In 1971 Rajneesh changed his name from *Acharya* (which

means teacher) to *Bhagwan* (which means "blessed one" or "God"). Joshi narrates the event as follows:

> I was known all over the country as Acharya... I was teaching and travelling. That was just the introductory part of my work...one day the word teacher will not be enough...Find something which is universal...And then he found "Bhagwan" (Joshi, 1982: 112).

This change in title implies not only that he was claiming greater charisma, but that he affected a change in type as a spiritual leader. According to Frederick Bird's typology of new religions (Needleman and Baker, 1978: 173), there are three types: Devotee, Apprentice, and Disciple, each of which features a different type of leader-follower relationship. The role of the apprentice leader is to be a teacher of techniques which the apprentice learns in order to tap a source of sacred power which is perceived as located within the self. The devotee type leader is looked up to as a lord, *avatāra*, or Second Coming and is perceived to be the transcendent source of sacred power to which the devotee must surrender in order to find salvation. What is interesting in the case of Rajneesh is that he managed to retain some of the characteristics of the apprentice group, such as each individual being the source of sacred power, while raising his own status to that of the most powerful type of leader, the devotee type. His reply to the question, "Why do you call yourself Bhagwan?" demonstrates this:

> Because I am—and because you are—and because God is....When I call myself God, I mean to provoke you, to challenge you. I am simply calling myself God so that you can also gather courage to recognise it. If you can recognise it in me, you have taken the first step in recognising it in yourself (Joshi, 1982: 114).

Like the initiation ritual, this move was effective as a test of loyalty and served to weed out the less committed of his members:

> ...people who used to come to me to gather knowledge they stopped. The day I called myself Bhagwan they stopped. It was too much for their egos, somebody calling himself Bhagwan (Joshi, 1982: 113).

Phase III—The Poona Ashram: Encouragement

In 1974 Bhagwan moved from Bombay to Poona where he founded the Shree Rajneesh Ashram. The daily programme began with the Dynamic Mediation, and in the evening Bhagwan would deliver his increasingly famous discourses. By 1975 Western-style therapy groups were incorporated into the programme and drew an international crowd of one to two thousand participants a week, according to the *Oregonian. Time* magazine reported that between 1974 and 1978 more than 50,000 seekers had tried the therapies at Poona (*Oregonian*, 1985: 9). The fast-growing membership and the transient population meant that the leader could no longer be personally available to his Sannyasins, except for a small core group. Thus the problem of institutionalisation arose. Bhagwan's response at this point of his career fits Wallis' category of *Encouragement.* Bhagwan encouraged growth and approved the efforts of his "power ladies" to establish an efficiently run Ashram while trying to imbue the growing superstructure with his own personal mystique. The ubiquity of his photograph served this purpose. Besides being displayed on every disciple's chest in the *mālā,* his smiling visage decorated the walls of the Ashram, inviting Belfrage's comparisons to Orwell's Big Brother. Another strategy was to insist that Bhagwan was even *more* present to his disciples in his absence. For example, an empty chair was placed on the podium when he stopped directing the Dynamic Mediation. Joshi explains:

> The master was present—but now his disciples had to feel Him on a more subtle level.

Bhagwan reassured them: "even if I am not here in the body, the contact will not be lost". This placed the onus on the followers to cultivate their awareness of his occult presence, and constituted a test of faith.

A strong core group of what Wallis would term "institution builders" ran the Ashram with maximum efficiency—and they were sufficiently high-handed and dictatorial in their *modus operandi* to be labelled the "power ladies", and by a disgruntled ex-Sannyasin, as the "dowager duchesses". These women were chosen for their charismatic qualities which, in Bhagwan's terms, meant receptivity to his "energy". He explains in *The Book* that women are superior to men because they are more receptive, less aggressive, and the essence of the mystic is receptivity. The *Oregonian* suggests that he preferred to work with women because they were more obedient than men and offered no competition.

Unlike Moses David, Bhagwan allowed his core group a considerable degree of power in decision-making and leadership, but at the same time he found ways to undermine their complacency and to maintain their dependence on his charisma, so as to discourage any tendency to develop independent signs of charisma. Of his personal secretary, Laxmi, who became the managing trustee of the Rajneesh Foundation, he said:

> "Always remember that Laxmi never does anything on her own. She is the perfect vehicle, that is why she is chosen for this work...Whatever is said she does" (Joshi, 1982: 102).

According to the *Oregonian* there are many indications

that Bhagwan took care to keep his core group under control:

> He chose the Ashram's department heads and pitted them against one another.
>
> Although he delegated office duties to Laxmi, he was known to countermand her decisions.
>
> There was a hierarchy, but no one was protected... He was always the final word (*Oregonian*, 1985: 5).

At the early period of Poona, Bhagwan appears to have been in close touch with every aspect of the Ashram. He would listen to reports from the individual therapy groups, offer personal advice, and perform the initiation *darśanas* himself.

Bhagwan encouraged a healthy rivalry among his power ladies and prevented the formation of permanent offices (one of the perennial symptoms of institutionalisation) by allowing them to oust each other from their posts:

> Ex-Sannyasins said Sheela edged out Prem Arup for the number two spot on Rajneesh's office staff.
>
> Bhagwan appeared to encourage competition and quarrels among the power ladies and allowed Sheela to oust Laxmi as his personal secretary (*Oregonian*, 1985: 7).

This strategy resembles Moses David's tendency to demote or rotate his leaders, and is an example of Resistance to the process of institutionalisation.

In the last two years of the Poona era, Bhagwan played a less active role in Ashram life, due to his declining health. Afflicted with asthma, diabetes, and back pains, he temporarily stopped giving discourses and *darśanas* in 1979, and substituted silent meditation. In 1981 he withdrew his physical presence from these sessions, and it was announced that "Bhagwan is entering into the ultimate, silent stage of his work" (Joshi, 1982: 155). Three core-group members were appointed to perform the initiation *darśanas* as "Bhagwan's mediums" and in May, *Satsaṅga* was introduced; "the silent communion between master and disciple". The empty chair strategy was reintroduced:

> The day you are able to see this chair, this body empty, this being empty, you will have seen me... that's the real moment when the disciple meets the master. It is a dissolution, a disappearance...the dew dissolving into the ocean...And there prevails profound silence (Joshi, 1982: 158).

The *gacchāmmi* ritual was incorporated into the *satsaṅga* meeting at this time, which involved bowing to Bhagwan's empty chair or photo while chanting the Buddhist creed:

> *Buddhaṃ śaraṇaṃ gacchāmi*
> *saṅghaṃ śaraṇaṃ gacchāmi*
> *dharmaṃ śaraṇaṃ gacchāmi*

This is translated by Sannyasins as "I go to the feet of the Enlightened One. I go to the feet of the community of the Enlightened One. I go to the feet of the Ultimate Truth of the Enlightened One." This is clear indication that the institutional charisma of the *saṅgha*, or community, now equalled the personal charisma of the master, and that due to his physical inaccessibility Bhagwan was in danger of being reduced to a symbol, or (in Durkheimian terms), a totem of his community.

In 1981 Bhagwan left the Shree Rajneesh Ashram in Poona and flew to the United States. The move to America appears to have been a unilateral decision on the part of Sheela, who claimed it was for medical reasons. She oversaw the buying of the 64,229 acre ranch in Oregon and began to supervise the building of what would soon be the city of Rajneeshpuram.

Phase IV—The Silence: Acquiescence

Bhagwan's silence began in the spring of 1981, and ended in October, 1984.

During the silence the institution builders were active, and Bhagwan's response at this time appears to conform to Wallis' description of Acquiescence, "... in which the charismatic leader, finding himself trammelled and constrained, acquiesces to the situation with more or less good grace" (Wallis, 1982: 117).

As Bhagwan withdrew into self-imposed solitude and silence, and made Ma Anand Sheela his representative, he became increasingly unaware of the administrative decisions, the political struggles with local authorities, and even the innovations in religious life taking place in his commune. In 1981 Rajneesh granted Sheela limited power of attorney, and removed the limits in 1982. In 1983 Sheela announced that "He" would only speak with her. At this stage it appears that his knowledge of goings on in the commune was exclusively derived from Sheela. He claimed in a later press conference that she kept him in ignorance:

> When I was in silence I was completely unaware... for eight months I supported Sheela... All things came to my knowledge yesterday... I was in isolation (September 16, 1985).

The rapid development of institutions can be observed during this phase. Sheela's book, *Rajneeshism* (1983) is a striking example of the routinisation of charisma. It describes the newly created Academy of Rajneeshism as an "ecclesiastical organisation" in which there are three categories of ministers: Acharyas, Arihantas, and Siddhas. A symptom of creeping institutionalisation for Wallis is the appointment of officials "on the basis of their qualifications and experience rather than on their inspirational virtues" (Wallis, 1984: 116). *Rajneeshism* stipulates:

> To be eligible for the ministry, a person must have the following experience and training: a minimum of:
>
> —two years as a neo-Sannyasin
> —two years of participation and practice in meditation
> —one year of worship-meditation or apprenticeship in Rajneeshism
> —specific orientation for the ministerial duties *(Rajneeshism,* 1983).

Aside from creating a "charisma of office", Sheela seemed to be claiming a charismatic status by conferring upon herself titles like "Boddhisattva" and dressing in long red silk robes in her office as Chancellor of Rajneeshism. She declared in an interview, "I am the head of a religion" *(Oregonian,* 1985: 16). The head therapist, Swami Anand Teertha, performed most of the Ranch initiations and began to exhibit signs of independent, non-Bhagwan-derived charisma—it was rumoured that he was enlightened.

Another sign of the routinisation of charisma was the creation of permanent offices. Weber notes that it "takes the form of the appropriation of powers of control and of economic advantages by the followers" (Weber, 1947: 367). Wallis adds that the officials "hope to preserve their hitherto *ad hoc* status and enjoy a commensurate lifestyle and thus press for some tenure of office and the regulation of office-holding in a non-arbitrary way" (Wallis, 1984: 116). Rajneeshpuram was governed by an efficient hierarchy of female coordinators called "moms" who were in turn directed by a small core of "supermoms". The *Oregonian* contrasts the luxurious lifestyle of the supermoms with the ascetic regimen of the rank-and-file Sannyasins. Sheela kept her office as Bhagwan's personal secretary for almost five years and held executive positions in all the major organisations of the city. "I am going to live like a princess. That's my style!" (Sheela, interviewed in the *Oregonian*, 1982: 16).

Wallis notes that "to pay for the 'permanent routine structure'... some form of rational fiscal basis for the movement must be secured" (Wallis, 1982: 116). A host of small chain businesses were established out of Rajneeshpuram, such as boutiques, restaurants, discos, therapy centres, and bookshops. An interesting effort was made to imbue these rational workday ventures with mystery and humour (Rajneeshee charismatic qualities). The twelve hour day of unpaid labour expected from all residents was described in *Rajneeshism* as "An abundance of creativity" and was regarded as a form of meditation-in-the-world called "Worship". The Rolls Royce collection was a wise investment of the commune's money but explained to a skeptical public as "a sign of the great love between master and disciple", or, alternatively, as a "joke":

> Bhagwan is like a child who delights in his toys. He has 92 Rolls Royces, the most expensive car in the world, and yet he.... can only drive one at a time, and for only half an hour a day. For us, it is a great paradox, a great joke.

Sheela organised a Rolls Royce Raffle for which every Sannyasin was expected to buy tickets, and the winner invariably gave the Rolls back to Bhagwan. In Rajneesh's system gambling can be a spiritual exercise as it involves "taking a risk" (in the language of Encounter). The Rajneeshpuram City Council passed an ordinance in September 1982 requiring that a joke be told at the beginning and end of every meeting. This appears to have been an attempt to retain an atmosphere of spontaneity in the face of an increasing tendency-toward organisation.

Phase V—Prophecy and Resistance

When Rajneesh came out of silence in October 1984 his first discourse was what Weber would call a "charismatic display". Having had the good fortune to be present at the Montreal Rajneesh commune on this occasion, I witnessed the extraordinary effect on his disciples of their master's (taped) voice. Approximately 300 people wept, laughed uncontrollably or sank to the ground as if in a swoon. It was clear from his words that he was claiming an increase in charisma. He said that he had travelled so deeply into the Absolute through his silence that he was now virtually indistinguishable from it.

Bhagwan announced on this occasion that there was no God, which had the effect of elevating his own status to the next best thing. The convention of referring to Rajneesh as "He" and "Him" in the RFI literature certainly implies this. Bhagwan proceeded to denounce great religious leaders to whom he had referred favourably in the past. He then claimed to have founded "the first and the last religion", Rajneeshism, and explained how it was superior to all previous attempts:

> Rajneeshism is a kind of religionness, not a dogma, cult, or creed, but only a quality of love, silence, meditation, and prayerfulness. Hence it can never end... Jesus did not know about Buddha, Buddha did not know about Lao Tzu... I have travelled all the paths.... What I am saying is going to last forever because nothing more could be added to it.

This move can be interpreted as a strategy of Resistance. Rajneeshism was contradicting previous statements. In Poona he had often referred to God and had declared in 1971 that all religions were acceptable paths leading to the superconsciousness.

Wallis explains how Mo of the Children of God constantly contradicts himself in order to resist institutionalisation:

> Thus the prophet's charisma is further heightened through the fact that the only certainty left is himself. The arbitrariness of his statements entailed that one should not even be committed to any particular thing he said but to Mo *regardless* of what he said.

Rajneesh also attempted to de-institutionalise Rajneeshism by explaining it as "the laughing religion", a "religion-ness", "the religionless religion".

In March 1984 Rajneesh prophesied the death of two-thirds of humanity from AIDS, the "spiritual disease". As a result, Sannyasins were required to wear rubber gloves and condoms while making love and to refrain from kissing. This development resembles Moses David's millennarian prophecies which Wallis interprets as examples of Resistance. Certainly the newly instituted sexual taboos were a Resistance strategy insofar as they served to break down exclusive ties between couples and emphasised the ritual function of sexual activity. I have argued elsewhere that the AIDS threat encouraged Renunciation, one of Kanter's six commitment mechanisms (Palmer, 1986).

Rajneesh undermined the claims to charisma among his core group in the following manner: two Sannyasins interviewed described his reading out a list of one hundred people in the commune whom he pronounced enlightened. This caused a sensation, and excited rivalry and argument until Bhagwan admitted later the whole thing had been a joke. One Sannyasin who described the incident to me saw it as a test:

> It was to show what big egos people had, that they could ever imagine they were on the same level as Bhagwan.

Rajneesh began to oppose Sheela's efforts to build a solid institution to survive his death, and to ensure her succession. Over the summer of 1984 she had announced that Rajneesh had created three *saṃsads* to offer spiritual guidance after his death. On August 19th of the same year Rajneesh flatly contradicted her in a deposition filed in Multnomah County Circuit Court:

> I am not making anybody head of my religion because I don't want any books to be followed by me exploiting people in my name. I am not going to be succeeded by anybody. The day I am dead I am dead. There is no question of any succession.

Phase VI—Sheela's Betrayal: Attempted Displacement

On September 16, 1985 Bhagwan held a major press conference at Rajneeshpuram in which he revealed a series of crimes allegedly carried out by Sheela and her "fascist gang". These alleged crimes included three poisoning attempts, salmonella food poisoning in The Dalles, wiretapping, bugging rooms, and financial abuse which left the commune $55,000,000 in debt.

From the evidence at hand it appears that Sheela's alleged crimes (of which she is now convicted and serving a prison sentence) were the end-result of an unsuccessful Displacement attempt. Wallis describes the response of Displacement as follows:

> A third case is that which institutionalisation proceeds without clear recognition by the charismatic leader of what is occuring until too late for him effectively to reverse the situation despite a strong antipathy towards it (Wallis, 1984: 118).

A close look at her alleged crimes suggests that she

was attempting to preserve her exclusive access to the Guru, which she had enjoyed during his silence. Her three poison victims were the only Sannyasins who were close to him. The bugging devices found in his rooms suggest she wished to control his sources of information. Some of her statements from prison indicate that she might have intended to displace Rajneesh as the head of Rajneeshism:

> She said the allegations were merely a device used by Bhagwan to keep the Sannyasins movement united behind Him. Otherwise it would have split into two camps, one following her and the other staying with Bhagwan... "I'm still your Mom. You may not have a Dad my more but I'm still your Mom" (*Rajneesh*, March 11, 1986).

Rajneesh appeared to regard her actions as a displacement attempt:

> It seems these people could have even killed me. If I was dead they could have worshipped my dead body and have full power to do whatever they wanted to do (September 1986 press conference).

He ascribed her motives to jealousy of his charismatic authority:

> As I started to speak again, a strange thing happened. Sheela became very sad. Everyone was ecstatic that I spoke again except Sheela. Strange! Within a few days it became clear. While I was in isolation she had become a celebrity through the news media. She was famous all over the world. When I started speaking again Sheela's swollen ego started shrinking. If I speak myself there is no need for a mediator, a messenger, a representative. I said..."You have become addicted to being famous....the worst drug in existence" (September

16 press conference).

Bhagwan's first reaction to Sheela's displacement attempt was to protect his own charisma. He disassociated himself from her activities by publicly denouncing her. This laid him open to the charge of irresponsibility and weak leadership in remaining ignorant of her abuses. However, he deported himself with his characteristic charm and managed to tread the fine line between accepting responsibility and disclaiming responsibility for the unfortunate events. On one hand he showed concern over the gravity of the situation:

> They were absolute criminals, inhuman, fascist in outlook!

On the other hand he joked about it: "Adolf Hitler has died again!"

He promised to take responsibility for the welfare of his commune in the future:

> I am going to continue to speak for the rest of my life. I will be here!

—and yet disclaimed responsibility for Sheela's behaviour: "One can never really know another human being."

Another strategy (eagerly embraced by his Sannyasins who wished to preserve their absolute faith in their leader's infallibility) was to blame everything on the followers. Bhagwan hinted that he had allowed the situation to develop as a learning "device":

> People were almost asleep. Unless something really shakes them up they don't see much. We have seen in time!

One Sannyasin echoed this notion:

> We thought we were surrendering to Bhagwan, but

> it turned out we were obeying Sheela. It was our own fault what happened. Bhagwan has always warned us not to give up our independent judgement, not to be blindly obedient. He allowed Sheela to go crazy with power and it was a great learning experience for all of us.

Phase VII—"I am not your guru": Abdication

On September 26, Bhagwan told his Sannyasins to stop wearing the colour red and the *mālā*, their traditional symbols of initiation (*Rajneesh Times*, 1986: 27). All *mālās* were to be sent back to the ranch. When his followers protested, Bhagwan relented and allowed them to keep the *mālā*. He announced the end of Rajneeshism, saying "A religion has died." A celebration of the death of Rajneeshism took place at Rajneeshpuram in which a bonfire was made of copies of Sheela's book *Rajneeshism* and her "pope's robes". The *Rajneesh Times* of October 4, 1985 offers Bhagwan's explanations which reveal his acute concern for the problem of institutionalisation:

> In an interview with Bill Graves of *The Bulletin*, Bhagwan said he decided to take these steps in an effort to keep his movement from becoming institutionalised.
>
> The book and the word "Rajneeshee" were developed by Ma Anand Sheela against his wishes during his three-and-a-half years of silence.
>
> "I hate the word 'ism'. "

Bhagwan continued to deliver blows to the institutions of his movement. The *Rajneesh Times* of October II reports that he abolished the daily "gacchamis" or bowing ceremony "which he said was too similar to ritual Christian and Mohammedan prayers" and at the same time he put an end to the terms "worship" and "temple" which were to become plain old "work", and "department" again. He attacked the large international communes by declaring "I am absolutely against centralisation" and invited his Sannyasins to start new communes.

On October 18 the *Rajneesh Times* announced "Friends of Rajneesh International is born" meaning the name of the movement was no longer The Rajneesh Foundation International. This move was inspired by Bhagwan's statement that he was not a Guru to his Sannyasins, but merely a friend.

On October 27 Rajneesh boarded a Learjet on what he claimed was to be a vacation, but he was forced to land, was arrested, jailed, and charged with arranging "sham marriages" among his disciples in order to bypass U.S. immigration laws. He entered a technical plea of guilty (while privately denying the charges) and on November 14 was deported from the United States. Rajneeshpuram officials decided to close down their utopian city, since Sheela's alleged "financial abuse" had left them 55 million in debt, and Rajneesh would no longer be in residence to attract thousands of visitors to the summer festivals which were the city's main source of income. The international communes began to disband, the Montreal commune following suit in April, 1986.

Performance and Responsibility: Two Aspects of Charisma

In order to account for the divagations in Rajneesh's career and to explain his abdication it is useful to distinguish between two aspects of charismatic authority: (1) Performance, and (2) Responsibility.

Performance. A charismatic leader's authority rests on his ability to demonstrate "exceptional powers or qualities", to convince others of his "supramundane power or knowledge for which [he provides] the channel of which [he is] the source" (Wallis, 1982: 2). In this capacity his role is not unlike the inspired performer or the creative artist who receives adulation from his audience or fans.

Responsibility. This role demands the leader's willingness and ability to provide a direction for the movement, to set policies and handle administrative decisions. It also entails giving counsel to his followers, and settling conflicts arising within the group and also from without: in confrontations with the larger society. In this capacity the leader assumes the role of the pastor who protects and guides his "flock".

The portrait which emerges from a close study of Rajneesh's career is of a man who excels as a performer but is weak or recalcitrant as a pastor. Although Rajneesh showed considerable leadership ability in phases 1, 2, and 3 of his movement he demonstrated an increasing unwillingness to assume the responsible, authorising role after 1980 and appeared to shy away from the active exercise of power, leaving the direction of his movement in the capable hands of Sheela. Many of the changes in his movement correspond with shifts that allowed him to back away from assuming the authorising, responsible role. The effect has been to preserve his personal, exemplary charisma as an object of devotion and to avoid institutional restrictions on this authority.

Interviews with Montreal Sannyasins supported this view of Rajneesh's leadership. His gifts as a performer were praised:

> Bhagwan would get up there and just do his own thing. You could tell he was having a ball! —The first thing I thought was, "This guy is a brilliant comedian!"

He was often described as childlike, innocent, carefree:

> Bhagwan is like a child, awake in the moment and

> filled with the wonder of life...Even when he found out he was going to jail his reaction was, "What fun! Will they put handcuffs on me? I've never tried handcuffs before!"

Many disciples did not appear to expect concrete guidance from their leader:

> Bhagwan never tells us what to do.
>
> After you took Sannyas, it was up to you. Whatever you chose to do with Bhagwan's energy, it was your affair.

This analysis of Rajneesh's leadership explains his tendency to vacillate between Resistance and Encouragement. His aversion to the pastor role led him to delegate the responsibility of leadership to Sheela and her core group of "supermoms" who were energetic and determined institution builders. Rajneesh appeared to view his female leaders as receptacles of his own charisma. His writings stress the passive, receptive qualities of women, and his policy of making a woman-ruled commune was a means of extending his charisma into the government of his movement through the channels of women devotees who were filled with his "energy". Free from the constraints of responsibility, Rajneesh could pursue an untrammelled career as the performer whose gestures of Resistance were often his most exciting acts. Thus his jokes, tantrums, and shock tactics were a means of pruning the institutions to his own taste without necessitating an active involvement in decision-making procedures, and at the same time a means of entertaining his disciples, who interpret his more outrageous moments as "a device to wake us up".

It could be argued, therefore, that Resistance and Encouragement are not necessarily contradictory strategies, and that Rajneesh's case challenges the assumption underlying Wallis' theory; that the process of institutionalisation *inevitably* constitutes a threat to the leader's charisma. Even in his example of Mary Baker Eddy as a successful case of Encouragement, Wallis sees her institution-building as "a process of bureaucratisation" in which "some charismatic elements were retained" whereas "initially Christian Science was emphatically charismatic" (Wallis, 1982: 117). Weber, however, does distinguish between several typical patterns. There can be institutionalisation that amounts to an eclipse of the charismatic quality of devotion to authority: this occurs with bureaucratisation and traditionalisation. There are also forms of institutionalisation that attempt to (or are able to) preserve the charismatic qualities. Weber discusses these in relation to the terms "routinisation of charisma" and "hierocracy". Rajneesh's strategies of Encouragement and Acquiescence, therefore, could perhaps as better described as the routinisation of charisma.

Throughout this study I was confronted with the difficulty of distinguishing between the "pure" type of personal charisma and the slightly institutionalised form which serves to buttress it. In other words there is no clear boundary between charisma and institutionalisation. The relationship between the two is a subtle one, for charisma cannot exist without institutions, and the process of institutionalisation is fed by charisma. There were indications that Rajneesh's charisma was enhanced by some modes of institutionalisation but threatened by others. For example, one Sannyasin claimed "Bhagwan was at his most powerful during His silence." Another complained about Sheela's book *Rajneeshism* as "a Mickey Mouse version of Bhagwan's religion". When Rajneesh destroyed the institutions in his movement by abdicating, he inevitably undermined his own charismatic authority. Swami Prem Amitabh is quoted in *Rajneesh* (July 16, 1980) saying Bhagwan has "lost it". Many former disciples interpreted his act as a loss of charisma, and some are writing books with titles like *Bhagwan, The God Who Failed* and *Oranges and Lemmings.* Certainly in terms of possessing a visible following with a distinctive philosophy and lifestyle, Rajneesh's authority is diminishing. These examples suggest that the relationship between charisma and institution building is more complex than Wallis' model permits.

Abdication. Rajneesh's decision to abdicate is in part to be understood in relation to his being a prophet of the exemplary type. He lacked a world historical mission and thus failed to satisfy some Oregonians' expectations of another Jonestown. Instead of urging his followers to defy state authorities unto death he remained true to his claim as the "Enlightened One" to being "aloof and separate as an island", and therefore simply negotiated for the lightest sentence and skipped the country leaving his flock to fend for itself.

Rajneesh's abdication has met with widely varied responses from his Sannyasins. Some, like the therapist Amitabh, feel "He" has "lost It". Others expressed in interview the notion that Bhagwan had proved himself to be an authentic spiritual master by cutting his disciples off. This was explained as the final stage of a spiritual path in which the disciple has to prove himself or herself by continuing alone, giving up dependence on the Guru. Some Sannyasins referred to Krishnamurti, who established his credentials as a master by in fact disclaiming the role of *avatāra* which Annie Besant had prepared him for. Others referred to the Russian mystic, Gurdjieff, whose style of spiritual teaching often involved shocking his students or sending them away. It is perhaps significant that recent editions of *Rajneesh* have contained frequent references to Krishnamurti and

Gurdjieff, who both abdicated from positions of responsible leadership. One article describes how Gurdjieff closed down his community in Fontainebleu in 1924 and concludes: "any resemblance between their experiences and our life... may be coincidental. Be aware, however, that the Master's ways are many" (*Rajneesh Times*, September 8).

Rajneesh, Krishnamurti and Gurdjieff share similar characteristics. They are all examples of what R. S. Ellwood would term the "hermetic magus" type of leader, representatives in their own way of the gnostic tradition (Ellwood, 1973: 49). The spiritual paths they outlined emphasise liberation from mechanical patterns of thought and behaviour. The source of the sacred is perceived to lie within the self and the function of the master is to awaken the disciples from sleep, or to shock them out of their preconditioned patterns. This is achieved by putting disciples through ordeals or stopping the mind through outrageous behaviour (as in the case of Gurdjeiff) or destroying rational thought processes through paradox (as in the case of Krishnamurti and Rajneesh). In this sense their philosophies could be described as individualistic and antinomian.

These masters exhibited an aversion to institutions and an impatience with routine patterns of economic and social life. The *modus operandi* of each leader could be interpreted as an extreme example of Resistance.

Each master stressed the impermanence of life and the importance of learning to live in the present moment. Rajneesh calls it the "herenow", Krishnamurti the "eternal present." They possess a certain detachment from or self-consciousness towards their role as spiritual master, an elusiveness and a shamanic ability to disappear or to change shape. For example when Rajneesh adopted the name, "Bhagwan", he called it a "device" which he could "drop" when the time came.

Conclusions

Thus far I have attempted to establish that Abdication does represent a new relationship between charisma and institution building and that the meaning of this strategy in Rajneesh's case can be understood by distinguishing between two aspects of charisma: Performance and Responsibility. Having shown by my examples that Rajneesh is strong in the first aspect but weak as regards the second, I will conclude by arguing that his abdication solved the perennial problem of institutionalisation in several ways:

First, it enabled him to renounce the responsible role of pastor, while retaining the role of performer. He relinquished his followers but kept his audience and devoted "Friends".

Second, it was undoubtedly a step to salvage his reputation and protect his personal charisma which Sheela's scandalous behaviour threatened to discredit. Thus he disassociated himself from the organisation and religion, Rajneeshism, which had suffered in institutional "loss of charisma".

Third, it served as a sort of shaman's ordeal of initiation, a symbolic death which enabled him to change shape. Rajneesh chose to become a disembodied symbol, a mythic figure, on par with Gurdjieff and Krishnamurti who, even in death, resist attempts to systemise or institutionalise. Thus his Abdication was a means of transformation from one type of charismatic leader to another: in Fred Bird's typology it would represent a transition from a Devotee-type to an Apprentice-type leader. Instead of presiding over a utopian city, Rajneesh has become an itinerant performer, and is producing philosophical literature. (Krishnamurti and Gurdjieff wrote or dictated prolifically after they abdicated.)

Recent editions of *Rajneesh* have compared their leader to "The Unknowable Gurdjieff" (Bennet, 1973). Both masters are mysterious, unattached, and elusive "teachers" who communicate their vision through verbal performances and cryptic behaviour rather than through the creation of coherent belief systems or the building and governing of utopian societies. (1988)

Chapter Seventeen

Feelings after the Fall: Former Rajneeshpuram Commune Members' Perceptions of and Affiliation with the Rajneeshee Movement

CARL A. LATKIN, NORMAN D. SUNDBERG, RICHARD A. LITTMAN, MELISSA G. KATSIKIS AND RICHARD A. HAGAN

Several early studies of former members of new religious movements (NRMs) or cults reported that participants experienced high levels of psychological distress after departure (Clarke *et al.*, 1981). These studies have been questioned on their scientific rigour (Kilbourne and Richardson, 1984). Richardson *et al.* (1986) suggest that means of departure is strongly associated with attitudes toward the group; those who are "deprogrammed" have more negative views. A detailed study by Wright (1987) found that defectors hold a variety of opinions, with most former members valuing their participation. Other studies also report that former devotees have a diversity of opinions about their experiences (Galanter, 1989; Rothbaum, 1988). In this research note we report on a study of former Rajneeshpuram residents and examine affiliation with the Rajneeshee movement and their perceptions of it.

The Rajneeshees' sojourn in Oregon began with the purchase of the 64,229 acre Big Muddy Ranch in eastern Oregon in July 1981. The ranch was renamed "Rancho Rajneesh." Rajneesh's followers or disciples, who are called Rajneeshees, Sannyasins, or neo-Sannyasins, developed a commune, Rajneeshpuram, with facilities of a modern American town, including a hotel, shopping centre, airport, dam, sewage reclamation plant, and the third largest public transportation system in the state. By 1985 several thousand Sannyasins were living on the "Ranch". In November 1985 Rajneeshpuram disbanded, and the Rajneeshpuram residents, who considered the commune their home, were suddeniy asked to leave and to fend for themselves. The commune collapsed shortly after many top leaders fled the state, including its charismatic leader Shree Rajneesh, also known as Bhagwan. Several of these leaders pleaded guilty to criminal acts. It was anticipated that, due to these revelations of criminality and the methods of social control used at Rajneeshpuram, many former members would hold negative views of the movement after leaving Rajneeshpuram.

As Rajneesh's spokesperson, Ma Anand Sheela's rule of Rajneeshpuram was hierarchical and tightly controlled. Many Sannyasins resented this authoritarian leadership, and after Sheela's departure, Rajneesh sought to change the movement. Sannyasins were told that they no longer needed to wear the colours of the sunrise, the special necklaces called *mālās*, or use their Sannyasin names. These three items had been the overt symbols of their affiliation. Our research sought to examine former residents' retrospective views of Rajneeshpuram and to assess their present affiliation with the Rajneeshee movement.

METHODS

Beginning in July 1986, about seven months after the large exodus from the ranch, a follow-up study of former residents of Rajneeshpuram was undertaken. Approximately one thousand letters were sent. Half the letters were returned "address unknown", "forwarding address expired", "moved—left no forwarding address", or "not deliverable". This lack of valid forwarding addresses is understandable. Many Sannyasins left Rajneeshpuram hastily, and many, after leaving the ranch, moved several times within the space of a few months. By December 1986, 362 former residents of Rajneeshpuram had responded and agreed to be in future follow-up studies. Of these 362 individuals, 231 responded to the second survey. The questionnaire sent with the initial letter was only one page. The follow-up survey was 12 pages, assessing beliefs, personality, and mental health. One question from our 1985 survey (see Latkin *et al.*, 1987; Latkin, 1989) was repeated, an open-ended item on relationships with Rajneesh. Answers to this question were compared to reponses to the same question in the follow-up survey.

RESULTS

Out of the 231 respondents who filled out the follow-up survey, 60 per cent were female, with 1946 as a median year of birth (mean = 1945 sd = 11). The males' median year of birth was 1948 (mean = 1948, sd = 10). Table 1 presents demographic characteristic of the repondents. Of those who obtained college degrees, 37.2 per cent reported their highest degree as an Associate: 36.7 per cent, Bachelor; 20.5 per cent, Master; and 5.6 per cent held a Doctorate.

TABLE 1

Background Characteristics of Religion, Marital Status, Income, and Education for 231 Respondents who Completed the Survey of Former Rajneeshpuram Residents**

Marital status	*(%)*	*Income*	*(%)*	*Years of college*	*(%)*		*Religion*	*(%)*	
Married	29.7	<$ 5,000	9.9	None	11.4	6.2*	None	14.5	14.2*
Separated	21.8	5-10K	13.5	1-3	21.9	24.0*	Catholic	17.4	30.2*
Divorced	33.6	10-20K	18.8	4	24.1	23.4*	Protestant	41.9	36.4*
Widowed	0.4	20-30K	21.2	5-7	34.3	37.3*	Jewish	12.8	8.2*
Never		30-40K	8.6	8 or			Other	13.2	10.6*
Married	14.4	>$ 40,000	8.1	more	8.3	9.1*			

* Data from 1985 survey.

** Percentages rounded.

For comparison purposes, data on previous religious affiliation and years in college are presented in Table 1 from a sample of 225 Rajneeshpuram residents who filled out a social-psychological survey in October 1985. One noticeable difference between the two samples was the higher per cent of Catholics in the 1985 survey. Fifty–four per cent of the respondents to the 1985 survey were female, whereas 60 per cent of the respondents to the follow-up and survey were female. The median year of birth was 1948 for the follow-up and 1949 on the 1985 survey. On the follow-up survey respondents and on the 1985 survey, the adjusted duration of time spent at Rajneeshpuram was 31 months. As marital status at Rajneeshpuram was confounded by the arranged marriages of foreign disciples to United States citizens to circumvent visa restrictions, any comparison of marital status between the Rajneeshpuram and follow-up surveys would be misleading.

In comparing those who returned the follow-up survey (N=231) with individuals who did not (N=131), there were two marginally significant differences (Table 1). There was a difference on present life satisfaction; those who returned the follow-up survey scored slightly higher (6.5 versus 6.2 [range 0.8] $t = 1.90$, $p < .06$) and were more likely to be employed, 89 per cent versus 82 per cent ($X = 3.62$, $p < .06$). Table 2 presents the proportion of respondents to the follow-up who exhibited overt affiliation with the movement. The mean score on present life satisfaction on a scale of 1-8 was 6.32 (sd = 1.6), while their retrospective rating of satisfaction at Rajneeshpuram was 7.25 (sd = 1.1). This latter score differs little from a survey given at Rajneeshpuram (mean = 7.14). In the first post–Rajneeshpuram questionnaire, present satisfaction correlated with overall satisfaction at Rajneeshpuram, $r = .27$ ($p < .01$). The follow-up surveys were returned from 16 to 24 months after Rajneeshpuram had disbanded. At this time, 68 per cent of the former residents reported living with other Sannyasins, and 49 per cent meditated, which was a former requirement for Sannyasins. As seen in Table 3, respondents report that they frequently thought about Rajneesh.

TABLE 2

Per cent of Respondents who Reported Wearing Colours of the Sunrise, Use of Sannyasin Name, and Frequency of Contact with Sannyasins (N = 231)*

Wearing of Sunrise Colours		*Use of Name*		*Contact with Sannyasins*	
Always	7.0	Always	23.3	Every day	19.4
Usually	61.0	Sometimes	64.5	A few times a week	40.1
Rarely or never	32.1	Never or rarely	11.8	A few times a month	25.3
				About once a month	8.3
				Less than once a month	6.9

*Percentage rounded.

Table 3

Respondents' Evaluation and Recollections of the Ranch Experience (in per cent; N = 231)

	Almost everyday	*A few times a week*	*A few times a month*	*Less than once a month*	
1. How often do you think about the ranch?	16	32	34	18	
2. How often do you think about Bhagwan?	61	20	16	3	
	Strongly agree	*Agree*	*Don't know*	*Disagree*	*Strongly disagree*
3. I learned a lot about myself on the ranch	79	19	1	0	0
4. I am extremely glad I lived at Rajneeshpuram	90	8	1	0	0
5. I'm sure Bhagwan didn't know about what Sheela was doing	3	8	47	25	18

Included in the survey administered at Rajneeshpuram and the follow-up survey was the open-ended question "please describe your relationship with Bhagwan". This question was asked before and after the break-up of Rajneeshpuram. The responses were coded by the key theme in the opening phrase. If the first phrase was subsequently contradicted or if the remainder of the response incorporated a persistent and dominant theme that was different from the first phrase, then the response would be coded by the dominant theme. If there was no key theme in the first phrase, then the whole response was coded for a general theme. Three coders established the themes by an iterative and consensus process and then proceeded to code the materials (Strauss, 1987). Coding issues were resolved by consensus. The themes derived from the two surveys, which were coded separately, are presented in Table 4. The question on

TABLE 4

Theme Coding with Examples to the Question "Please describe your relationship to Bhagwan" (calculated to the nearest per cent)

Survey I (N = 110)	*Survey II (N = 193)*
Master-disciple, guide or mirror (25%) "In his eyes I see the infinite"	Master-disciple, guide or mirror (12%) "An enlightened master"
Friend (14%) "Non-personal friend...inspired me more than anything else put together"	Friend (6%) "A fellow traveller, a friend"
Heart-to-heart connection (9%) "A deep connection no words can describe"	Heart-to-heart connection (4%) "A deep, silent meeting of the hearts"
I love him (13%) " I love him. Not in the sense that I need him ...it is just a great joy... to be with him"	I love him (12%) "I love him deeply"
Love affair (13%) " It is a love affair on a non-physical plane...the orgasms start in my heart, not in my genitals, and are as intense as genital orgasms"	Love affair (7%) "Love not like to the opposite sex or a lover. But like to existence, life itself"
Defies description (5%) "It is not describable; it is not intellectual"	Defies description (10%) "Indefinable but very deep in my consciousness"
Laconic (4%) "Hah!"	Laconic (2%) "!"
No relationship (5%) "He tells the truth and I try to hear it"	Change (less intense or distant) (8%) "It feels finished, but at the same time I really feel that he is enlightened."
	Grateful or respect (13%) "No other human being has given me so much"
	Poetic description (3%) "I am a river. He is an ocean."
Other (7%) No response (4%)	Other (10%) No response (3%)

relationship to Rajneesh was included on approximately half the first surveys (N =110). On the follow-up survey, the first 193 surveys returned were coded. On both surveys the vast majority of descriptions were positive.

The predominant themes were those of teacher or master, and love or love affair. Few individuals harboured unfavourable sentiments toward Rajneesh. Many responses had multiple themes. One respondent, who was coded under the rubric "love" wrote, "I admired, respected, and loved the master of Rajneeshpuram, as I do today. Bhagwan is an infection that has settled in my heart...often disturbs me...also keeps me aware of the important things in life. Single most important person in my life."

Although most respondents viewed Rajneesh favourably, there were a few who expressed feelings of anger and bitterness. One man reported that his relationship with Rajneesh was, "Very intense. Mixed up at best. At times I think he is on a global ego trip. That he needs Sannyasins as much as (some) Sannyasins need him. He is a phenomenon, but nevertheless a human being with ego, etc. Enlightenment is nothing but wishful thinking. Maybe he is a dreamer *par excellence*." Out of all the surveys the harshest statement was that of a woman who said, "He loved people with money and gave them lots of attention. He is an antisocial personality, and even if he is enlightened he's still the same rotten personality." The woman who gave this response also indicated that she had been in psychotherapy. According to Richardson *et al.* (1986), her negative views might be due to the labelling that occurred in psychotherapy of her experience in the movement. There were systematic differences between the two surveys. On the second survey there was a greater tendency for respondents to report that they felt distant from Rajneesh; such as one individual who stated:

> Right now, I feel he is my teacher, but I feel like he is off in the distance...I used to feel very strongly that he is my master and I am his disciple but I'm

> not so sure anymore of that. I feel our closeness has been diminished, but I still love and respect him and am grateful for the light he has shed upon me.

The theme of personal responsibility for one's life and personal happiness was more prevalent in the second survey than in the first. Another difference between surveys was that in the second there were numerous reports of feeling grateful to Rajneesh. Those who reported that they were grateful varied in their attitudes toward Rajneesh. The responses varied from, "No other human being has given me so much," to "grateful...yet hate his personality; his lies and his manipulations. I never loved him as many did. I remain fascinated by him".

Many respondents reported a diminution in their feelings toward Rajneesh. One individual stated that "my relationship was strong...now I have little connection". A similar response was, "I am not zealous now...Bhagwan's impact was profound on me ... an era in my life that has passed." Others indicated greater change in their relationship, such as the response, "I still 'feel' when I see a picture of Bhagwan ... I became disillusioned after what happened at the ranch." The eight participants who did not affiliate with Sannyasins, use their Sannyasin name, or wear colours of the sunrise did not exhibit hostility in the descriptions of their relationship with Rajneesh. One of the eight stated that he had no relationship with Rajneesh except "the enjoyment of watching a man as a master actor".

In a final set of analyses, the opinions of those who believed that Rajneesh was aware of the criminal activities at Rajneeshpuram were evaluated. Respondents who stated that they "strongly disagreed" with the statement that implied Rajneesh was unaware of Sheela's criminal activities (Table 2, item 5) were compared with the other respondents. There were no statistically significant differences between these two groups on reports of living with other Sannyasins, frequency of use of Sannyasin name, or frequency of contact with other Sannyasins. The only statistically significant difference was that this subgroup thought less often about Rajneesh ($t = 2.76$, $df = 2.26$, $p < .01$).

Discussion

Over a year after the departure of Rajneesh from the United States, former members of the Rajneeshpuram commune were questioned about their relationship to Rajneesh. Although some respondents reported that they felt distant, the majority reported a high positive regard for Rajneesh. Most Sannyasins indicated that they believed that Rajneesh knew about Ma Anand Sheela's illegal activities, yet most maintained a deep, personal connection with him. The predominant themes that summarise their relationship to Rajneesh were those of gratitude, teacher, master, lover and a special bond with Rajneesh. Only a few respondents reported that they were disillusioned, and even those who harboured negative feelings toward Rajneesh felt that living at Rajneeshpuram was a great experience and were grateful for it. These data coincide with Wright (1987), who found that 67 per cent of defectors from new religious movements felt "wiser for the experience".

The differences in responses from the first to the second follow-up indicated that members' relationships with Rajneesh had become less intense. There are several explanations for this change. After Rajneesh was arrested, the leadership was unable to control Rajneesh's image. Under these conditions he may have begun to appear more human and less godlike. Another explanation is that of charismatic leadership (Hunt, 1991). The nature of Rajneesh's relationship to his disciples might have been unstable, and without his presence the emotional bond between Rajneesh and his disciples began to dissipate. A third explanation is that activities unrelated to the movement became more important after leaving the commune, and therefore Rajneesh was no longer the central figure in their lives.

Respondents reported a wide-range of levels of affiliation with the movement. There was no evidence that once outside the protective confines of Rajneeshpuram members made a sharp break and disavowed their affiliation. The continued association may be due to their method of exit, the locale, and the belief system. Richardson *et al.* (1986) mark the distinction between disengagement from communal versus non-communal settings and report that withdrawal from non-communal organisations is less traumatic. The Rajneeshee movement was communal, but after Rajneeshpuram it became less communal and much more decentralised. This change in organisational structure also may help to account for the lack of a strong shift in perceptions after leaving Rajneeshpuram.

Richardson *et al.* (1986) and others have demonstrated that labelling is an important determinant in reports of perceived experience with new religious movements. In our study participants were not labelled by themselves or by non-members as defectors. This lack of labelling also may help to explain why respondents were generally positive about their experiences. It is likely that former Rajneeshpuram residents' opinions of the movement were more positive than if they had become cut off from other Rajneeshees and were surrounded by individuals who lack understanding of their experiences. The positive regard for Rajneesh may have also been related to affective ties with friends in the movement. The reports of frequent contact with other Rajneeshees suggests that the group continued to fulfil affective needs and provide social support. Others have found that defectors maintain positive regard for members (Wright, 1987). Beckford in his study of ex-Moonies (1985), found that a major problem for defectors arises when they return to their parental home, where they are pressured to disavow their former group and lack a well-developed friendship network. As most Rajneeshees continued to live with other Rajneeshees both stressors would be, in part, alleviated.

In general, perceptions of the movement and Rajneesh were robust. Even after Rajneesh's ignominious flight from the United States, his followers did not have a sudden change in attitude, nor did they exonerate him from any wrongdoing. One common explanation for favourable attitudes of former members of new religious movements is to invoke the theory of cognitive dissonance (Festinger, 1967); that is, in order for members to reduce feelings of dissonance they praised and overrated their experiences. Our data suggest that respondents could acknowledge inconsistencies. Wright (1987) also found that former devotees had complex views of their experiences in new religious movements.

The positive responses exhibited by former Rajneeshpuram residents are consistent with their beliefs about human nature. The Rajneeshees believed that all life events can be used as learning experiences. The authoritarian structure of Rajneeshpuram and the disbanding of the commune were regarded by many as opportunities for learning and self-understanding. Another adaptive belief was the view that all being is transitory; nothing is permanent. Many Rajneeshees' beliefs overlapped with New Age beliefs or a mystical meaning system (Wuthnow, 1976). This overlap may have aided in adjusting to life outside Rajneeshpuram, for their beliefs would not appear bizarre or aberrant to the subculture of non-Rajneeshees who are also mystically inclined. The survey data support the position that retrospective assessments and social interaction play a strong role in crystallising experience of new religious movements (see Beckford, 1985).

In conclusion, 16 or 24 months after the break up of Rajneeshpuram most former residents who were surveyed continued to think about Rajneesh almost every day and were living with other Sannyasins. Most reported that their present relationship was positive, and only a few respondents expressed anger or hostility toward Rajneesh. The relation between Rajneesh and his disciples has been permanently altered. After returning to India in 1987, where he took the name "Osho", Rajneesh died in 1990. In light of Rajneesh's charismatic leadership, it will be interesting to see in the ensuing years if disciples' affiliation with the movement strengthens, dissipates, or remains the same. (1994)

V

POSTSCRIPT

Chapter Eighteen

Osho Commune International

ROGER HOUSDEN

The Indian on the black gates—the kind that protect mansions in Mill Valley or Hampstead Heath—looked just like the rogue Guru himself: long, flowing beard, large doe eyes, a woolly hat on his balding head. He directed me round to the side entrance where, he said, I would have to take an AIDS test before being allowed in. That would be 200 rupees, plus 20 rupees standard entrance ticket. Though there were plenty of Indians outside the gates, watching the foreign girls, there were none to speak of inside—£4 is more than most of them earn in three days.

My AIDS negative confirmation in my hand, I was finally greeted by one of the team of twelve who manage this most Western and opulent of all Ashrams in India. I mentioned the uncanny resemblance of the man at the gate to Osho himself.

"That's his brother," she explained. "His family is very involved here."

There is nothing remotely Indian, however, to be

found in this exquisitely designed and landscaped 'Buddhafield', as Osho called it. Not even Indian currency is allowed, since it is a common way for diseases to spread—you buy coupons to use in the various facilities. The Ashram at Poona which repeatedly captured the world's headlines in the 1970s and 1980s has undergone an extraordinary rebirth since Osho's death in 1990. Japanese gardens, swimming pools, a health club ('Club Med'—get it?) and Western restaurants, have been added to the existing alternative university, and the tent-like structure in steel and glass known as 'The Buddha Hall'. The university has many more courses available, the restaurants have their own organic vegetable gardens, the Ashram has its own wells and rigorous hygiene testing systems. Most of the buildings are in black and white, and—appropriately—have an air of the post-modern look of corporate architecture. These people mean business. As a mid-1980s bumper sticker said, 'Moses invests, Jesus Saves, Bhagwan Spends.'

Now Bhagwan is dead: long live Osho. With the troubles of Rajneeshpuram, Oregon, far behind them, Osho Commune International in Poona can only be delighted at the way business has gone over the last five years. Far from dying along with the Guru, the Osho Commune is receiving more visitors than ever before. (Though it is called a Commune, hardly anybody actually lives on the premises.) Since 1990, the number of new disciples, Sannyasins, has been increasing fourfold each year. Osho's books are going through a worldwide publishing explosion. In 1993, over 640,000 Osho books in English were sold worldwide. In the same year, 120,000 were sold in Russia, and over 300,000 in India in six languages. Two of Germany's largest health insurance companies are buying hundreds of Osho's meditation CDs for use in their health care programmes, and in Asia, a satellite channel covering 38 countries now regularly beams Osho's discourses in English.

Why? One can only presume that the cliche has been confirmed yet again: the more someone—especially in religion—achieves notoriety in his lifetime, the more he will be revered as a prophet after his death. Osho was risky territory while he was alive. Many who may have been sympathetic to his teaching would never have wanted to associate themselves with a cultish following whose antics and scandals were railed against the world over. Now he is dead, people are free to use his teachings as they wish without the stigma attached to them in the 1980s, and without the need to belong to a group. You just buy the courses you want at the Commune, watch a video of Osho at your leisure, and get on with your life.

This, perhaps, is the other main reason for Osho's success in the 1990s. He appeals to the instant gratification mentality. He used to say that his disciples wanted instant enlightenment, so that is what he offered. Cynics might quip that an instant high may have been a more accurate description. His Dynamic and Kundalini meditations are aimed at rapidly stimulating the psychological organism and to provide the kind of relaxation that comes after any strenuous physical effort. Businessmen can practise them before work and get through their day with more ease and vitality than otherwise. His techniques, introduced by Osho trainers, are used in corporate management throughout the world. Bus drivers in Stockholm have regular Osho meditation courses financed by the local government. As stress management tools, these methods are undoubtedly effective. A large proportion of the visitors to Poona are people with a busy and successful schedule. What could be better than to come to a beautiful, pollution- and disease-free zone in India—the only one in the subcontinent—and cool out with friends in a warm and meditative atmosphere while imbibing the spiritual ideas of a brilliant orator? Osho always said that while Jesus spoke to the poor, his audience was the rich. The affluent West has time on its hands to attend to spiritual matters. The poor, East and West, can only think of survival. Osho's point was, you do not have to change your life to practise his methods and subscribe to his ideas; you do not have to give up your wealth, you have to learn how to enjoy it and lighten up. Nowadays, this is truer than ever—no mandatory orange clothes, such as were commonly seen in the 1980s; no group to lean on the individual, not even a Guru to tell you to drop this or take up that. Just a message of pleasure, meditation and self-loving. Few people would argue with it, not even in India, where Osho's books are now to be found on every newsstand.

Yet Osho Commune International is not the place of free love it was in the seventies. On the contrary, since the AIDS scare, sexuality is now seen as an energy to transmute into personal aliveness, not to waste in gratuitous licence. There is plenty of affectionate hugging, but that is as far as it goes. The whole way of life in the Commune is in fact highly structured to maintain the atmosphere of a sacred space—to preserve the 'Buddhafield', as Osho put it. All visitors wear a statutory maroon robe while in the Commune; at certain times during the day, everyone will stop what they are doing for fifteen minutes and dance to loud music, or stand like statues in silence. As in Aldous Huxley's *Island,* a cock crows on the hour to remind people to recollect themselves. There are meditation sessions throughout the day for people to choose from.

One evening I went to the meeting of the Osho White Brotherhood, the main event of the day. Everyone had changed from maroon to white. Fifteen minutes before the meeting started, people were walking along the paths to the Buddha Hall in silence. There must have been almost 1,000 people sitting on the marble floor in front of a stage. Two men appeared from the wings, carrying a white armchair, which they sat down in the middle of the stage. This was the chair from which Osho used to give his discourses. Music started up on the loudspeaker system, and more and more of the meditators began to sway and dance on the spot. Suddenly, after fifteen minutes or so, everything stopped and the entire crowd let out a yell of 'Osho!' with their arms in the air, as if his presence were still among them. The same routine was repeated four times, and then a giant video screen was let down over the stage. For the next hour, everyone sat in rapt attention as Osho, in top quality close-up, gave one of the discourses he first offered ten years before. At the end, still in silence, everyone filed outside, collected their shoes, and went off into the night.

The event was stage-managed to perfection. Osho Commune International offers a haven for those who have time to review their values and the way they are using their lives. It offers skills and techniques to enhance the quality of life and to be a more open and loving person. As such, it is performing a valuable service for a pressed and anxious world. Osho must have known that the revolution in consciousness implied by a spiritual path is neither to be confused with personal development nor to be won lightly. Yet he gave people what they wanted, and spoke to the values of his time in the way he was able. Poona is his living testimony.

(1996)

The Contributors

Robert M. Birnbaum (Swami Prem Amitabh) holds a Ph.D. in Clinical Psychology. He has worked in this area in California, Poona and Rajneeshpuram.

Frederick B. Bird is Professor of Religion at Concordia University, Montreal. He received his B.D. at Harvard and his Ph.D. from the Graduate Theological Union, San Francisco. He is the author of *The Pursuit of the Therapeutic* (Montreal: Concordia University, 1983) and numerous articles on new religious movements.

Peter Brent was born in 1931 and educated in Wales. He is a full time writer, specialising in travel books on the Middle and Far East, and the biographies of such figures as Charles Darwin, Lord Byron and T.E. Lawrence.

Lewis F. Carter is Professor of Sociology and Associate Dean of Liberal Arts, Washington State University, Pullman. He is the author of *Charisma and Control at Rajneeshpuram: The Role of Shared Values in Creating a Community* (London: Cambridge University Press, 1990).

Ranald O. Clarke is Emeritus Professor of Religious Studies at Oregon State University, Corvellis. His report on *Rajneeshism and Its Principles* was presented to the Oregon Committee for the Humanities, Oregon State University, in 1983.

William T. Drennen received his doctorate in clinical psychology from Florida State University in 1962. He has been on the staff of Augusta V. A. Hospital and the Medical College of Georgia, and is currently Associate Professor in the Department of Psychology, University of Southern Carolina, Columbia. He has published widely in the fields of verbal behaviour, depression and meditation.

Robert E. Gussner (Swami Anand Jina) is Associate Professor of Comparative Religion at the University of Vermont, Burlington. He wrote his Ph.D. at Harvard on "A Stylometric Study of the Authorship of Seventeen Hymns Attributed to Śaṅkara." He has published textual and sociological studies in the *Journal of Oriental Studies* and *Sociological Analysis.*

Bert Hardin, born in 1939, obtained his M.A. in 1969 with a thesis on "Community Development and Sociology" and his Ph.D. in 1975. He is a member of the Department of Sociology of the University of Tübingen and has published extensively, both in German and in English, on new religious movements in Germany.

Reinhart Hummel was born in 1930 and worked as a pastor in Schleswig-Holstein after gaining his degree in New Testament Studies. He was principal of a theological college at Kotapad, India, from 1966 to 1973. In 1979 he gained his doctorate at Heidelberg in the field of Religion and Missiology. His major publications relate to the influence of Indian religious movements on German youth.

Carl A. Latkin is a graduate of Wesleyan and Oregon Universities, and currently serves as a post-doctoral fellow at the School of Public Health, Johns Hopkins University. He has published widely on the application of social psychological theory to new religious movements.

Aubrey Menen has written satires, including *Shela: A Satire* (1963) and *Rama Retold* (1954); travel books, including *London* (1976) and *Venice* (1976); essays; and a spiritual autobiography, *The Space Within the Heart* (New York: McGraw Hill, 1970).

Charles Newman (Swami Devageet) was for many Osho's personal dental surgeon. He is author of the forthcoming *Bhagwan: Messiah of Life, Love and Laughter* (Georgetown, Maryland: North Star Publishers) and a number of other books published by Rebel Publishers, Germany.

Susan Jean Palmer holds a Ph.D. from Concordia University, and currently teaches in the Departments of Religion at Concordia and at Dawson College, Westmount, Province of Quebec. She is editor, with Arvind Sharma, of *The Rajneesh Papers* (Delhi: Motilal Banarsidass 1993), and author of *Moon Sisters, Krishna Mothers, Rajneesh Lovers* (Syracuse University Press, 1994).

William Pennell Rock (Swami Anand Veereshwar) has studied behavioural science and comparative religions and philosophies at Yale, Harvard, The Sorbonne, the Jung Institute in Zurich, and King's College, Cambridge. As Senior Research Fellow at Banaras Hindu University, he co-ordinated a new translation of the *Upanishads*. He has taught at several universities, including the University of California, Santa Barbara, and been a resident and group leader at Esalen and many other growth centres. Dr Rock is author of two books on therapy, *Performing Inside Out* and *Secrets of the Love Story*.

Roy Wallis was formerly Professor of Sociology and Dean of the Faculty of Economics and Social Sciences at the Queen's University of Belfast. He is the author of a large number of studies of new religious movements, including *The Elementary Forms of the New Religious Life* (London: Routledge and Kegan Paul, 1984), and with Steve Bruce, *Sociological Theory, Religion and Collective Action* (Belfast: The Queen's University, 1986).

The editor of this volume, Harry Aveling, is a Senior Lecturer in Asian Studies at La Trobe University (Melbourne, Australia). He was initiated into Sannyas in 1977 by Bhagwan Shree Rajneesh and received the title Yoga Acharya in 1988 from Swami Vishnu Devananda, a direct disciple of Swami Shivananda of Rishikesh. Beside his extensive writings on Indonesian and Malay literature, he is author of *The Laughing Swamis* (1994) and translator, with Mrs. Sudha Joshi, of Osho's discourses on the poet Dayabai.

References

Abbott, C., 1990: "Utopia and bureaucracy: the fall of Rajneeshpuram," *Pacific Historical Review*, 59, 77-103.

Academy of Rajneeshism (eds.), 1983: *Rajneeshism: An Introduction to Bhagwan Shree Rajneesh and His Religion*, 2nd. ed. rev., Rajneesh Foundation, Rajneeshpuram Oregon.

Adler, P. and P. Adler, 1989: "Intense Loyalty in Organisations: A Case Study of College Athletics," *Administrative Science Quarterly*, 33, 401-410.

Allport, Gordon, 1954: *The Nature of Prejudice*, Addison-Wesley, Cambridge Mass.

American Psychiatric Association, 1980: *Diagnostic and Statistical Mental Disorders*, American Psychiatric Association, Washington D. C.

Amitabh, Swami Prem, 1982: "Shree Rajneesh Ashram: A Provocative Community," *Journal of Humanistic Psychology*, 22: 1, 19-42.

Androes, L., 1987: "Cultures in Collision: The Rajneesh Search for a Community," *Communities*, 71-72, 49-54.

Anthony, Dick and Thomas Robbins, 1982: "Spiritual Innovation and the Crisis of American Civil Religion," *Daedalus*, 111, 215-234.

Appleton, Sue, 1987: *Bhagwan Shree Rajneesh: The Most Dangerous Man Since Jesus Christ*, Rebel Publishers, Zurich.

Asia Week, 1983: "Guru in Cowboy Country," July 29, 26-36.

Assagioli, R., 1971: *Psychosynthesis*, Viking, New York.

Aveling, Harry, 1994: *The Laughing Swamis: Australian Sannyasin Disciples of Swami Satyananda Saraswati and Osho Rajneesh*, Motilal Banarsidass, Delhi.

Barker, E., 1985: *The Making of a Moonie*, Blackwell, Oxford.

Beckford, J. A., 1985: *Cult Controversies*, Tavistock, New York.

Beckford, J. A., 1986: *New Religious Movements and Rapid Social Change*, Sage, London.

Belfrage, Sally, 1981: *Flowers of Emptiness: Reflections on an Ashram*, The Women's Press, London.

Bennet J. G., 1973: *Gurdjieff: Making A New World*, Turnstone Books, London.

Berkowitz, L., 1972: "Social Norms, Feelings, and Other Factors affecting Helping and Altruism," *Advances in Experimental Social Psychology*, 6, 63-108.

Berkowitz, L., 1978: "Whatever Happened to the Frustration-aggression Hypothesis?", *American Behavioural Scientist*, 21, 691-708.

Berne, E., 1961: *Transactional Analysis in Psychotherapy*, Grove Books, New York.

Bharti, Ma Satya, 1980: *The Ultimate Risk: Encountering Bhagwan Shree Rajneesh*, Wildwood House, London.

Bharti Franklin, Satya, 1992: *The Promise of Paradise*, Station Hill Press, New York.

Bird, Frederick, 1978: "Charisma and Ritual in New Religious Movements", *Understanding the New Religions*, Seabury, New York, 173-189.

Bird, F. and B. Reimer, 1983: "Participation Rates in New Religious Movements and Parareligious Movements", in *Of Gods and Men, New Religious Movements in the West*, (ed.) E. Barker, Mercer University Press, Macon GA, 215-238.

Blake R. R. and J. S. Mouton, 1979: "Intergroup Problem Solving in Organisations: from Theory to Practice", in *The Social Psychology of Intergroup Relations*, Brooks/ Cole, Monteray, California.

Bouvard, Marguerite, 1975: *The Intentional Community Movement*, Kennikat Press, Port Washington, New York.

Braun, Kirk, 1984: *The Unwelcome Society*, Scouts Creek Press, Scouts Creek, Oregon.

Breche, Max, 1993: *A Passage to America*, Book Quest, Bombay.

Bucke, M. R., 1923: *Cosmic Consciousness*, Dutton, New York.

Callister, Scota, James Long and Leslie L. Zeitz, 1985: "For Love and Money: The Rajneeshee from India to Oregon", *The Oregonian*, Portland, Oregon, June 30 to July 19.

Calverton, Victor Francis, 1941: *Where Angels Dared to Tread*, Books for Libraries Press, Freeport, New York.

Carter, Holly, 1981: "Incorporated City Dream of Rajneesh Disciples", *The Madras Pioneer*, Madras, Oregon, October 22.

Carter Lewis F., 1990: *Charisma and Control in Rajneeshpuram*, Cambridge University, London.

Chitrabhanu, G. S,. 1979: *The Psychology of Enlightenment: Meditations on the Seven Energy Centres*, Dodd, Mead, New York.

Cialdini, R. B., 1980: "Full Cycle in Social Psychology", *Applied Social Psychology Annual*, 1, 21-47.

Clark, J., M. Langone, R. Shecter and R. Daly, 1981: *Destructive Cult Conversion*, American Family Foundation, Weston, Maryland.

Clarke, R. O., 1983 "The teachings of Bhagwan Shree Rajneesh and their social ethical and environmental implictions", *Report to the Oregon Committee for the*

Humanities, Oregon State University, Corvallis, Oregon.

Cohen, S., 1980: "The After-effects of stress on human performance and social behaviour: a review of research and theory", *Psychological Bulletin*, 88, 82-108.

Cohen, S., and H. M. Hoberman, 1983: "Positive Events and Social Supports as Buffers of Life Change", *Journal of Applied Social Psychology*, 13, 99-125.

Cohene, S., T. Kamart and R. Mermelstein (in press): "A Global Measure of Perceived Stress", *Journal of Health and Social Behaviour*.

Denzin, N. K., 1978: *The Research Act: A Theoretical Introduction to Sociological Methods*, 2nd ed., McGraw-Hill, New York.

Dietrich, Bill, 1984: "Bhagwan's Precinct Leading in Poll", *Seattle Times-Post Intelligencer*, October 7.

Drennen, W. T., 1978: "Relaxation and placebo-suggestion as uncontrolled variables in TM Research", *Journal of Humanistic Psychology*, 18: 4, 89-93.

Du Pertuis, Lucy, 1986: "How people recognise charisma: the use of Darshan in Radhasoami and Divine Light Mission", *Sociological Analysis*, 47, 111-124.

Eisenstadt, S. N., 1968: *Max Weber on Charisma and Institution Building*, University of Chicago Press, Chicago.

Ellwood, R. S., 1973: *Religious and Spiritual Groups in Modern America*, Prentice Hall, New Jersey.

Festinger, Leon, 1950: "Informal Social Communication", *Psychological Review*, 57, 271-282.

Festinger, L., 1957: *A Theory of Cognitive Dissonance*, Row Peterson, Evanston, Illinois.

First Annual World Celebration, 1982: *Music Group Songs*, Rajneesh Foundation, Rajneeshpuram Oregon.

Fisher, R. J., 1983: "Third party consultation as a method of conflict resolution", *Journal of Conflict Resolution*, 27, 301-334.

Fiske, S. T. and S. E. Taylor, 1984: *Social Cognition*, Addison-Wesley, Reading, Maryland.

Fitzgerald, Frances, 1986: "A reporter at large: Rajneeshpuram 1", *New Yorker*, September 22, 47-96.

Fitzgerald, Frances, 1986: *Cities on a Hill: A Journey Through Contemporary American Culture*, Simon and Schuster, New York.

Floether, Eckart, with Eric Perment, 1983: *Bhagwan Shree Rajneesh and His New Religious Movement in America*, Intervarsity Press, Downers Grove, Illinois.

Folkman, S. and R. Lazarus, 1980: "An analysis of coping in a middle-aged community sample", *Journal of Health and Social Behaviour*, 21, 219-239.

Foster, Laurence, 1981: *Religion and Sexuality*, Oxford University Press, New York.

Galanter, M, 1989: *Cults: Faith, Healing and Coercion*, Oxford University Press, New York.

Galanter, M., R. Rabkin, J. Rabkin and A. Deutsch 1979: "The 'Moonies': A Psychological Study of Conversion and Membership in a Contemporary Religious Sect", *American Journal of Psychiatry*, 136, 165-170.

Gans, H. J., 1979: *Deciding What's News: A Study of CBS Evening News, NBC Nightly Newsweek and Time*, Vintage Press, New York.

Geertz, C., 1973: *The Interpretation of Culture*, Basic Books, New York.

Gergen, K. J., 1978: "Toward a generative theory", *Journal of Personality and Social Psychology*, 36, 1344-1360.

Glaser, B., and A. L. Strauss, 1967: *The Discovery of Grounded Theory*, Aldine, Chicago.

Goffman, E., 1963: *Behaviour in Public Places*, Free Press, New York.

Gordon, James, 1988: *The Golden Guru*, Stephen Greene Press, New York.

Green E. E., A. M. Green and E. D. Walters 1979: "Biofeedback for mind/body self regulation: healing and creativity", in *Mind/Body Integration*, (ed.) E. Peper, S. Ancoli and M. Quinn, Plenum, New York.

Greenfield, Robert, 1975: *The Spiritual Supermarket: An Account of Gurus Gone Public in America*, Saturday Review Press, E. P. Dutton and Co., New York.

Gunther, Bernard, 1979: *Dying for Enlightment: Living With Bhagwan Shree Rajneesh*, Harper and Row, San Francisco.

Harter, S., 1983: *The Perceived Competence and Social Acceptance Scale for Children*, University of Denver, Denver.

Hasya, Ma Vedanta, 1985: "Meet the New Religions: The Rajneesh", Presentation and Discussion at Meetings of the Society for Scientific Study of Religion, October 26.

Hegel, G., 1949: *The Phenomenology of Mind*, (trans.) J. Baille, Harper and Row, New York.

Heider, F., 1980: *The Psychology of Interpersonal Relations*, Wiley, New York.

Hummel, R., 1981: *Indische Mission Unde neue Frömmigkeit im Westen*, Stuttgart.

Hunt, J. G., 1991: *Leadership*, Sage, Newbury, California.

Jaini, Padmanabh S., 1980: "Karma and the Problem of Rebirth in Jainism", in *Karma and Rebirth in Classical Indian Traditions*, (ed.) W. Doniger O'Flaherty, University of California Press, Berkeley.

Janis, I. L., 1972: *Victims of Groupthink*, Houghton Mifflin, New York.

Johnson, B., 1992: "On founders and followers: some factors in the development of new religious movements", *Sociological Analysis*, 53, S1-13.

Johnson, D. L., 1985: *A Reasoned Look at Asian Religions*, Bethany House, Minneapolis.

Johnson, Doyle Paul, 1979: "Dilemmas of Charismatic

Leadership: The Case of the People's Temple", *Sociological Analysis*, 40: 4.

Joshi, Vasant, 1982: *The Awakened One: The Life and Work of Bhagwan Shree Rajneesh*, Harper and Row, San Francisco.

Jung, Carl Gustav, 1968: *Analytical Psychology: Its Theory and Practice*, Vintage, New York.

Kanter, Rosabeth Moss, 1972: *Commitment and Community: Communes and Utopias in a Sociological Perspective*, Harvard University Press, Cambridge, Massachusetts.

Kanter, Rosabeth Moss (ed.) 1973: *Communes: Creating and Managing the Collective Life*, Harper and Row, New York.

Karlen, Neal and Pamela Abramson 1984: "Bhagwan's Realm", *Newsweek*, December 3.

Katsikis, M. G. and C. A. Latkin, 1988: "Prejudice: A field study", Paper Presented at the Annual Meeting of the Western Psychological Association.

Kernberg, Otto F., 1986: "Factors in Psychoanalytic Treatment of Narcissism", in *Essential Papers on Narcissism*, (ed.) Andrew P. Morrison, New York University Press, New York.

Kilbourne, B. K. and J. T. Richardson, 1984: "Psychotherapy and new religions in a pluralistic society", *American Psychologist*, 39, 1-13.

Kohler, W., 1947: *Gestalt Psychology*, Liveright, New York.

Kout, Heinz and Ernest S. Wolf, 1986: "The Disorders of the Self and Their Treatment: An Outline", in *Essential Papers on Narcissism*, (ed.) Andrew P. Morrison, New York University Press, New York.

Kopp, Sheldon B., 1976: *If You Meet the Buddha on the Road, Kill Him*, Bantam, New York.

Krishna, Gopi 1972: *The Biological Basis of Religion and Genius*, Harper and Row, New York.

Langer, E., 1989: "Minding matters: The consequences of mindlessness-mindfulness", in *Advances in Experimental Social Psychology*, 22, The Academic Press, New York.

Latkin, C. A., 1987: "Rajneeshpuram, Oregon: An Exploration of Gender and Work Roles, Self-concept, and Psychological Well-being in an Experimental Community". Unpublished doctoral dissertation, University of Oregon, Eugene.

Latkin, C. A., 1989: "Gender Roles in an experimental community", *Sex Roles*, 1, 629-52.

Latkin, C. A., 1991: "From device to vice: Social control and intergroup conflict at Rajneeshpuram", *Sociological Analysis*, 52, 363-378.

Latkin, C. A., R. Hagan, R. Littman and N. Sundberg, 1987: "Who lives in utopia: a brief research report on the Rajneeshee project", *Sociological Analysis*, 48, 73-81.

Lattin, Don, 1985: "'Rich man's guru' continues acerbic attack on religions", *Rocky Mountain News*, July 22.

Lazarus, R. S., 1966: *Psychological Stress and Coping Processes*, McGraw-Hill, New York.

Levine, Saul V., 1984: "Radical Departures", *Psychology Today*, August, 20-27.

Lewinsohn, P. M., W. Mischel, W. Chapline and R. Barton, 1980: "Social competence and depression: the role of illusory self-perceptions", *Journal of Abnormal Psychology*, 89, 203-212.

Lewiston Tribune, 1984a: "Guardian Angels Protest Street People Treatment", November 4.

Lewiston Tribune, 1984b: "AIDS Fear: Rajneeshees told to stop kissing", November 18.

Long, James and Leslie I. Zaitz, 1985: "Network of corporations fueled reign of Rajneesh", *The Oregonian*, November 25.

Long, J. Bruce, 1980: "Human Action and Rebirth in the Mahabharata", in *Karma and Rebirth in Classical Indian Traditions*, (ed.) Wendy Doniger O'Flaherty, University of California Press, Berkeley.

Lowen, Alexander, 1983: *Narcissism: The Denial of the True Self*, McMillan, New York.

Mann, W. E., 1991: *The Quest for Total Bliss*, Canadian Scholars' Press, Toronto.

Manuto, R., 1987: "The life and death of Rajneeshpuram and the still lingering dilemma of the religion clause of the first amendment". Paper presented at the annual meeting of the Western Speech Communication Authority.

McCarthy, John 1985: "Allegations against sect leaders may tarnish 'city without crime'", *Lewiston Tribune*, September 17.

McCoy, John, 1985: "Bhagwan urges Sheela to repent", *Seattle Post-Intelligencer*, September 19.

McDermott, James P., 1980: "Karma and Rebirth in Early Buddhism", in *Karma and Rebirth in Classical Indian Traditions*, (ed.) Wendy Doniger O'Flaherty, University of Califoria Press, Berkeley.

Medina Rajneesh Neo-Sannyas Commune, 1982: Programme Brochure, Suffolk, England.

Meher Baba, 1958: *Beams from Meher Baba on the Spiritual Panorama*, Sufism Reoriented, Walnut Creek, California.

Mehta, Gita, 1979: *Karma Cola: Marketing the Mystic East*, Simon and Schuster, New York.

Mehta, Manik, 1984: "West Germany, Disco Divinity", *India Today*, April 15.

Melton, G. J. and R. L. Moore, 1982: *The Cult Experience*, Pilgrim Press, New York.

Menen, Aubrey, 1974: *The New Mystics*, Thames and Hudson, London.

Milgram, S, 1974: *Obedience to Authority*, Harper and Row, New York.

Millon, Theodore 1969: *Modern Psychopathology*, W. B. Sanders Co., Philadelphia.

Milne, Hugh 1986: *Bhagwan: The God That Failed*, Caliban Books, London.

Mitra, Sumit, Richard Draper and Raj Chengrappa, 1985: "Rajneesh: Paradise Lost", *India Today*, December 15.

Moss, C. T., 1974: *The Probability of the Impossible*, New American Library, New York.

Motoyama, H., 1981: *Theories of the Chakras: Bridge to Higher Consciousness*, Quest, Wheaton Illinois.

Muktananda, Swami, 1974: *American Tour, 1970*, Shree Gurudev Siddha Yoga Ashram, Piedmont, California.

Mullan Bob, 1983: *Life as Laughter: Following Bhagwan Shree Rajneesh*, Routledge and Kegan Paul, London.

Murphy, Dell, 1986: *The Rajneesh Story*, Linwood Press, West Linn.

Myers, P. R., 1986: "A Study of Attitudes Toward the Rajneeshees Through Content Analysis of Newspapers." Honours College Thesis, University of Oregon.

Nemeth, C. J. and B. M. Staw 1989: "The tradeoffs of social control and innvovation in groups and organisations", in *Advances in Experimental Social Psychology*, 22, Academic Press, New York, 175-210.

Nesbitt, R. E. and D. Wilson, 1977: "Telling more than we know: verbal reports on the mental process", *Psychological Review*, 84, 251-9.

Nicholas, Jay, 1982: *Undercurrents*, 53, 11.

Nietzsche, Friedrich, 1954a: Beyond Good and Evil, in *The Philosophy of Nietzsche*, (trans.) Thomas Common, Random House, New York.

Nietzsche, Friedrich, 1954b: Thus Spake Zarathustra, in *The Philosophy of Nietzsche*, (trans.) Thomas Common,

Random House, New York.

Nilekani, Rohini, 1983: "Rajneesh Foundation: The Oregon Odyssey", *India Today*, April 30.

Nordhoff, Charles, 1965: *The Communistic Societies of the United States*, Schocken, New York.

Ofshe, Richard, 1980: "The Social Development of the Synanon Cult: The Managerial Strategy of Organisational Transformation", *Sociological Analysis*, 41: 2.

Opotow, S., 1990: "Moral exclusion and injustice", *Journal of Social Issues*, 46, 1-20.

The Oregonian 1985: "On the Road Again", Portland Oregon, December 30.

O'Sullivan, Michael A., 1983: "Sharing the Joke: The Building of Rajneeshpuram". Unpublished manuscript based on March interview with Bhagwan Shree Rajneesh.

Pannikar, R., 1972: "The Law of Karma and the Historical Dimension of Man", *Philosophy East and West*, XXII: 1.

Patterson, T. E., 1980: *The Mass Media Election*, Praeger, New York.

Palmer, Susan J., 1986: "Community and Commitment in the Rajneesh Foundation", *Update*, Aarhus, Denmark.

Palmer, Susan, 1988: "Charisma and abdication: a study in the leadership of Bhagwan Shree Rajneesh", *Sociological Analysis*, 49, 119-135.

Palmer, Susan J. and Arvind Sharma, 1993: *The Rajneesh Papers*, Motilal Banarsidass, Delhi.

Palmer, Susan J., 1994: *Moon Sisters, Krishna Mothers, Rajneesh Lovers: Women' Roles in New Religions*, Syracuse University Press, Syracuse.

Pelletier, K. R. and C. Garfield, 1976: *Consciousness: East and West*, Harper and Row, New York.

Perls, Fritz, 1971: *Gestalt Therapy Verbatim*, Bantam, New York.

Piaget, Jean, 1963: *The Psychology of Intelligence,* Littlefield Adams, Patterson N. J.

Plotkin, W. B. and K. M. Rice, 1981: "Biofeedback as a placebo: Anxiety reduction facilitated by training in either suppression or enhancement of alpha brain waves", *Journal of Counselling and Clinical Psychology,* 49: 4, 590-596.

Prasad, R. C., 1978: *Rajneesh: The Mystic of Feeling,* Motilal Banarsidass, 2nd. rev. ed., Delhi.

Prasad, Swami Prem, 1985: "Meet the New Religions: The Rajneesh" Presentation and discussion at meetings of Society for Scientific Study of Religion, October 26.

Pruitt, D. G. and J. Z. Rubin, 1986: *Social Conflict,* Random House, New York.

Puttick, Elizabeth, 1995: "Sexuality, Gender and the Abuse of Power in the Master Disciple Relationship: the case of the Rajneesh movement", *Journal of Contemporary Religion,* 10: 1, 29-40.

Radloff, L. S., 1977: "The CES-D Scale: A Self-Report Depression Scale of Research in the General Population", *Applied Psychological Measurement,* Vol. 1, 385-401.

Rajneesh, 1986: Ed. Friends of Rajneesh International, Boulder, Colorado.

Rajneesh, Bhagwan Shree, 1970: *Paths of Self-Realization,* Motilal Banarsidass, Delhi.

Rajneesh, Bhagwan Shree, 1973: *The Silent Explosion,* Anand Shila Publications, Bombay.

Rajneesh, Bhagwan Shree, 1974: *When the Shoe Fits,* Rajneesh Foundation, Poona, Cassette recording, No. 3.

Rajneesh, Bhagwan Shree, 1975a: *The Book of Secrets,* Harper Colophon Books, New York, Vol. 2.

Rajneesh Bhagwan Shree, 1975b: *Dimensions Beyond the Known,* Wisdom Garden Books, Los Angeles.

Rajneesh, Bhagwan Shree, 1975c: *The Mustard Seed*, Harper and Row, San Francisco.

Rajneesh Bhagwan Shree, 1975d: *My Way: The Way of the White Clouds*, Grove Press, New York. German translation: *Mein Weg: Der Weg der Weissen Wolke*, Berlin, n. d.

Rajneesh Bhagwan Shree, 1975e: *Neither This Nor That: Discourses on Sosan*, Rajneesh Foundation, Poona.

Rajneesh, Bhagwan Shree, 1976a: *Above All Don't Wobble*, Rajneesh Foundation, Poona.

Rajneesh Bhagwan Shree, 1976b: *The Book of Secrets*, Harper Colophon Books, New York, Vol. 3.

Rajneesh Bhagwan Shree, 1976c: *The Grass Grows by Itself*, Rajneesh Foundation, Poona.

Rajneesh Bhagwan Shree, 1976d: *Hammer on the Rock: A Darshan Diary*, Grove Press, New York.

Rajneesh Bhagwan Shree, 1976e: *Meditation: The Art of Ecstasy*, Harper and Row, New York.

Rajneesh Bhagwan Shree, 1976f: *Only One Sky*, E. P. Dutton and Co., New York.

Rajneesh Bhagwan Shree, 1976g: *Tao: The Three Treasures*, Rajneesh Foundation, Poona, Vol. 2.

Rajneesh Bhagwan Shree, 1976h: *Yoga: The Alpha and the Omega*, Rajneesh Foundation, Poona, Vol. 1.

Rajneesh Bhagwan Shree, 1977a: *I am the Gate: The Meaning of Initiation and Discipleship*, Harper and Row, New York.

Rajneesh Bhagwan Shree, 1977b: *Meditation: The Art of Inner Ecstasy*, Rajneesh Foundation, Poona.

Rajneesh, Bhagwan Shree, 1977c: *The Supreme Doctrine*, Rajneesh Foundation, Poona.

Rajneesh Bhagwan Shree, 1977d: *Yoga: The Alpha and the Omega*, Rajneesh Foundation, Poona, Vol. 4.

Rajneesh Bhagwan Shree, 1977e: *Yoga: The Alpha and the Omega*, Rajneesh Foundation, Poona, Vol. 8.

Rajneesh Bhagwan Shree, 1978a: *And the Flowers Showered,* DeVorss and Co., Marina Del Rey, California.

Rajneesh Bhagwan Shree, 1978b: *Beloved of My Heart,* Rajneesh Foundation, Poona.

Rajneesh Bhagwan Shree, 1978c: *Yoga: The Alpha and the Omega,* Rajneesh Foundation, Poona, Vol. 10.

Rajneesh Bhagwan Shree, 1979a: *The Diamond Sutra,* Rajneesh Foundation, Poona.

Rajneesh Bhagwan Shree, 1979b: *The Perfect Way,* Motilal Banarsidass, Delhi.

Rajneesh Bhagwan Shree, 1979c: *Pointing the Way,* Motilal Banarsidass, Delhi.

Rajneesh Bhagwan Shree, 1979d: *The Psychology of the Esoteric,* Harper and Row, New York.

Rajneesh Bhagwan Shree, 1979e: *Roots and Wings: Talks on Zen,* Routledge and Kegan Paul, London.

Rajneesh Bhagwan Shree, 1979f: *Tao: The Pathless Path,* Rajneesh Foundation, Poona.

Rajneesh Bhagwan Shree, 1979g: *This is It: A Darshan Diary,* Rajneesh Foundation, Poona.

Rajneesh Bhagwan Shree, 1980a: *The Book of Books,* Rajneesh Foundation, Poona, Vols. 1-3.

Rajneesh Bhagwan Shree, 1980b: *The Secret,* Rajneesh Foundation, Poona.

Rajneesh Bhagwan Shree, 1980c: *The Book of Books,* Rajneesh Foundation, Poona, Cassette recording, No. 18.

Rajneesh Bhagwan Shree, 1981a: *The Orange Book,* Rajneesh Foundation, Antelope Oregon.

Rajneesh Bhagwan Shree, 1981b: *Philosophia Perennis,* Rajneesh Foundation Antelope, Vol. 2.

Rajneesh Bhagwan Shree, 1981c: *The White Lotus,* Rajneesh Foundation, Poona.

Rajneesh Bhagwan Shree, 1982a: *The Book of Wisdom*, Rajneesh Foundation, Rajneeshpuram, Oregon, Cassette recording, No. 18.

Rajneesh, Bhagwan Shree, 1982b: *The Goose is Out*, Rajneesh Foundation, Antelope, Oregon.

Rajneesh Bhagwan Shree, 1982c: *The Great Challenge: A Rajneesh Reader*, Grove Press, New York.

Rajneesh Bhagwan Shree, 1983a: *Don't Look Before You Leap*, Rajneesh Foundation, Rajneeshpuram, Oregon.

Rajneesh Bhagwan Shree, 1983b: *God's Got A Thing About You*, Rajneesh Foundation, Rajneeshpuram, Oregon.

Rajneesh Bhagwan Shree, 1984: *The Book: An Introduction to the Teachings of Bhagwan Shree Rajneesh*, Rajneesh Foundation, Rajneeshpuram, Oregon, Vols. 1-3.

Rajneesh Bhagwan Shree, 1985a: *Glimpses of a Golden Childhood*, Rajneesh Foundation, Rajneeshpuram, Oregon.

Rajneesh, Bhagwan Shree, 1985b: *The Rajneesh Bible*, Rajneesh Foundation, Rajneeshpuram, Oregon, Vols. 1-3.

Rajneesh Bhagwan Shree, 1985c: "The Scientific Study of Religion". Videotape discourse prepared for session of meetings of the Society for the Scientific Study of Religion, Savannah Georgia, October 26.

Rajneesh, Bhagwan Shree, n. d. : *Be Still and Know*, Rajneesh Foundation, Poona, Cassette recording, No. 4.

Rajneesh, Bhagwan Shree, forthcoming: *The Rainbow Bridge*, Rajneesh Foundation, Poona.

Rajneesh Meditation and Growth Institute at Geetam, 1982: Programme Brochure, Lucerne Valley California.

Rajneesh: The Newspaper, 1: 1-10, New Day Enterprises, Boulder Colorado, 1986.

Rajneesh Times, 1984a: "Medical Column—AIDS: Questions and Answers", March 30.

Rajneesh Times, 1984b: "The Centre of the Cyclone", August 10.

Rajneesh Times, 1985a: "Sheela Flees—Crimes Revealed", September 20.

Rajneesh Times, 1985b: "Ready for innocence now, kids", September 27.

Rajneesh Times, 1985c: "Out of the inner chaos", October 18.

Rajneesh Times, 1986: "The therapists controversy", July 16.

Reich, Wilhelm, 1973: *Selected Writings*, Farrar, Strauss and Giroux, New York.

Richardson, J. T., 1985: "Methodological Considerations in the study of new religions", in *Divergent Perspectives on the New Religions*, (ed.) B. Kilbourene, American Association for the Advancement of Science, San Francisco, 130-137.

Richardson. J. T., 1986: "Consumer protection and deviant religion", *Review of Religious Research*, 28, 168-79.

Richardson. J. T., J. Lans and F. Derks, 1986: "Leaving and Labelling", in *Research in Social Movements, Conflicts and Change*, JAI Press, Greenwich, Conn.

Ritter, Frank, 1983: "Who are these Rajneeshees?", *The Tennessean*, October 6.

Robbins, T., 1988: *Cults, Converts and Charisma*, Sage, Beverly Hills, California.

Robbins, Thomas, Dick Anthony and James Richardson, 1978: "Theory and Research on Today's 'New Religion'", *Sociological Analysis*, 39.

Rogers, Carl, 1961: *On Becoming A Person*, Houghton Mifflin, Boston.

Rogers, Carl R., 1980: *A Way of Being*, Houghton Mifflin, Boston.

Rosenberg, M., 1965: *Social and Adolescent Self-Image*,

Princeton University Press, Princeton N. J.

Rothbaum S., 1988: "Issues of separation and identity after leaving a religious community", in *Falling from the Faith*, (ed.) D. G. Bromley, Sage, Newbury Park, California, 205-228.

Ray, Roddy, 1984: "Inside Rajneeshpuram: Hello to paradise, Goodbye to privacy", *Spokesman Review*, October 21.

Rubin, J. Z., 1980: "Experimental research on third-party intervention in conflict: towards some generalisations", *Psychological Bulletin*, 87, 379-39.

Satyananda, Swami, 1981: *Im Grunde ist alles ganz einfach*, Frankfurt.

Sagar, H. A. and J. W. Schofield, 1980: "Racial and behaviour cues in black and white children's perceptions of ambiguously aggressive acts", *Journal of Personality and Social Psychology*, 39, 590-598.

Schachter, S. and J. E. Singer, 1962: "Cognitive, social and physiological determinants of emotional states", *Psychological Review*, 69, 379-399.

Schien, E. H., 1985: *Organisational Culture and Leadership*, Josey-Bass, San Francisco.

Senior, Jeanie, 1984a: "Busloads of homeless arrive in Rajneeshpuram", *The Oregonian*, September 7.

Senior, Jeanie, 1984b: "Sheela: It was all just a joke", *The Oregonian*, October 30.

Shapiro, D. H., 1980: *Meditation: Self-regulation strategy and altered states of consciousness*, Aldine, Chicago.

Shay, T. L., 1985: *Rajneeshpuram and the Abuse of Power*, Scout Creek Press, West Linn, Oregon.

Sherif, M., 1966: *In Common Predicament: Social Psychology of Intergroup Conflict and Cooperation*, Houghton Mifflin, Boston.

Shunyo, Ma Prem, n. d. : *Diamond Days with Osho*, Rebel Publishing House, Poona.

Simkins, L., 1982: "Biofeedback: Clinically valid or oversold?", *Psychological Record*, 32, 3-17.

Smith, J. D., 1976: "Psychotherapeutic effects of transcendental meditation using controls for expectation of relief and daily sitting", *Journal of Consulting and Clinical Psychology*, 44, 630-637.

Smith, R. R., 1979: "Mythical elements in television news", *Journal of Communications*, 4, 75-82.

Snell, John, 1984: "Rajneeshee religion: mixture of beliefs", *The Oregonian*, December 9.

Somendra, Swami Anand, 1980: *Energy and Transformation*, Alchemy International, London.

Spokesman-Review, 1984: "Antelope man says Rajneeshee police violated his rights", June 21.

Spokesman-Review, 1985a: "Rajneeshism books make a big bonfire", June 21.

Spokesman-Review, 1985b: "Bhagwan's W. German communes thrive", December 2, 1985.

Spradley, J. P., 1979: *The Ethnographic Interview*, Holt Rinehart and Winston, New York.

Stark, Rodney and William Sims Bainbridge, 1985: *The Future of Religion*, University of California Press, Berkeley.

Stone, Donald, 1976: "The human potential movement", in *The New Religious Consciousness*, (ed.) C. Glock and R. Bellah, University of California Press, Berkeley, 93-115.

Strauss, A. L., 1987: *Qualitative Analysis for Social Scientists*, Cambridge University Press, Cambridge.

Strelley, Kate, with Robert D. San Souci, 1987: *The Ultimate Game: The Rise and Fall of Bhagwan Shree Rajneesh*, Harper and Row, San Francisco.

Taijel, H., 1981: *Human Groups and Social Categories*, Cambridge University Press, London.

Tanner, F., 1986: *Bhagwan—Rogue, Charlatan, God?* Panorama Verlag, Altstätten.

Tart, Charles, 1975: *States of Consciousness*, Dutton, New York.

Tittle, C., 1977: "Sanction, fear and maintenance of social order", *Social Forces*, 55, 579-596.

Thompson, Judith and Paul Heelas, 1986: *The Way of the Heart*, Aquarian Press, Wellingborough.

Turner, J. C., 1978: "Social Comparison and Social Identity: some perspectives for intergroup behaviour", *European Journal of Social Psychology*, 5, 5-34.

Ulrich, Roberta, 1984: "Half of Homeless Leave Commune", *Oregonian*, November 15.

Vallacher R. C. and D. M. Wegner, 1987: "What do people think they're doing? Action identification and human behaviour", *Psychological Review*, 94, 3-15.

Van Driel, B. and T. J. Richardson, 1988: "Research note: categorisation of new movements in American print media", *Sociological Analysis*, 49, 171-183.

Van Leen, W. A., 1980: *O is for Orange*, Concerned Christians Growth Ministries, Perth, Western Australia.

Vaughan, F., 1982: "The transpersonal perspective: a personal overview", *Journal of Transpersonal Psychology*, 14: 1, 37-46.

Volinn, E., 1985: "Eastern Meditation Groups: Why Join?", *Sociological Analysis*, 46, 147-156.

Wallis, Roy, 1982: "Charisma, Commitment and Control in a New Religious Movement", in *Millenialism and Charisma*, The Queen's University, Belfast.

Wallis, Roy, 1984: *The Elementary Forms of the New Religious Life*, Routledge and Kegan Paul, London.

Walsh, R. N., 1980: "A model for viewing meditation research", *Journal of Transpersonal Psychology*, 14: 1, 69-84.

Walsh, R. N. and F. Vaughan, 1980: "Beyond the Ego: Toward transpersonal models of the person and psychotherapy", *Journal of Humanistic Psychology*, 20: 1, 5-31.

Wanous, J. P., 1980: *Organisational Entry*, Addison-Wesley, Reading, Maryland.

Webb, James, 1980: *The Harmonious Circle: The Lives and Work of G. I. Gurdjieff, P. D. Ouspensky, and Their Followers*, G. P. Putnam's Sons, New York.

Weber, Max, 1947: *The Theory of Social and Economic Organisation*, Free Press, New York.

Weick, K. E., 1974: *The Social Psychology of Organising*, Addison-Wesley, Reading, Maryland.

Weiss, Mitchell, G., 1980: "Caraka Samhita on the Doctrine of Karma", in *Karma and Rebirth in Classical Indian Traditions*, (ed.) Wendy Doniger O'Flaherty, University of California Press, Berkeley.

Westley, Frances, 1983: *The Complex Forms of Religious Life: A Durkheimian View of New Religious Movements*, Scholars' Press, Chico, California.

Wilber, Ken, 1977: *The Spectrum of Consciousness*, Theosophical Publishing House, Evanston, Illinois.

Wilber, Ken, 1982a: "Odyssey: A personal inquiry into humanistic and transpersonal psychology", *Journal of Humanistic Psychology*, 22: 1, 57-90.

Wilber, Ken, 1982b: "The pre/trans fallacy", *Journal of Humanistic Psychology*, 22: 2, 5-43.

Wilder, D. A. and P. N. Shapiro, 1984: "Role of outgroup cues in determining social identity", *Journal of Personality and Social Psychology*, 48, 342-348.

Wills, T. A., 1981: "Downward comparison principles in social psychology", *Psychological Bulletin*, 90, 245-247.

Wilson, Bryan (ed.), 1981: *The Social Impact of New Religious Movements*, The Rose of Sharon Press, New York.

Worchel, S. and N. Norvell, 1980: "Effect of perceived environmental conditions during cooperation in intergroup attraction", *Journal of Personality and Social Psychology*, 38, 764-772.

Worseley, Peter, 1968: *The Trumpet Shall Sound*, Schocken, New York.

Worthington, Rogers, 1984: "Guru's offer to homeless raises suspicions of neighbours", *Dallas Times Herald*, September 24.

Wright, Charles, 1985: *Oranges and Lemmings*, Greenhouse, Melbourne.

Wright, S. A., 1987: *Leaving Cults*, Society for the Scientific Study of Religion, Washington D. C.

Wuthnow, R., 1976: *The Consciousness Reformation*, University of California Press, Berkeley.

Yancy, W. L., L. Rigsby and J. D. McCarthy, 1972: "Self-Esteem and Social Class", *American Journal of Sociology*, 789, 338-359.

Yatri, Swami Anand (ed.), 1980: *The Sound of Running Water*, Rajneesh Foundation, Poona.

Zimbardo, P. G., 1970: "The human choice: individuation, reason, and order versus deindividuation, impulse and chaos", in *Nebraska Symposium on Motivation*, (ed.) W. J. Arnold and D. Levines, University of Nebraska Press, Lincoln.

Zimbardo, P. G., E. B. Ebbesen and C. Maslach, 1977: *Influencing Attitudes and Changing Behaviour*, Addison-Wesley, Reading, Maryland.

Zucker, L. G., 1977: "The role of institutionalisation in cultural persistence", *American Psychological Review*, 42, 726-743.